CHILTON'S Repair and Tune-Up Guide

Chevrolet
1968–77

ILLUSTRATED

Prepared by the

Automotive Editorial Department

Chilton Book Company

Chilton Way
Radnor, Pa. 19089
215—687-8200

president and chief executive officer **WILLIAM A. BARBOUR;** executive vice president **RICHARD H. GROVES;** vice president and general manager **WILLIAM D. BYRNE;** associate editorial director **GLEN B. RUH;** managing editor **JOHN H. WEISE, S.A.E.;** assistant managing editor **KERRY A. FREEMAN;** technical editors **John G. Mohan, Ronald L. Sessions**

CHILTON BOOK COMPANY   RADNOR, PENNSYLVANIA

Chilton's Repair & Tune-Up Guide: Chevrolet 1968–77
ISBN 0-8019-6615-9 pbk.

Library of Congress Catalog Card No. 76-57317

ACKNOWLEDGMENT

Chilton Book Company expresses appreciation to the following for their generous assistance:

Chevrolet Motor Division
General Motors Corporation
Detroit, Michigan

Information has been selected from Chevrolet shop manuals, owners manuals, service bulletins and technical training manuals.

Contents

Chapter 5   Chassis Electrical 121

Chapter 6   Clutch and Transmission 164

Chapter 7   Drive Train 174

Chapter 8   Suspension and Steering 179

Chapter 9   Brakes 191

Chapter 10   Body 206

Appendix 210

Chapter 1

General Information and Maintenance

How To Use This Book

Chilton's *Repair and Tune-Up Guide for the Chevrolet* is intended to teach you more about the inner workings of your automobile and save you money in its upkeep. The first two chapters will be the most used, since they contain maintenance and tune-up information and procedures. The following seven chapters concern themselves with the systems of the car. Operating systems from engine through brakes are covered to the extent that we feel the average do-it-yourselfer should get involved. Chilton's *Chevrolet* won't explain rebuilding the transmission for the simple reason that the expertise required and the investment in special tools make this task uneconomical. We will tell you how to change your own brake pads and shoes, replace points and plugs, and many more jobs that will save you money, give you personal satisfaction, and help you avoid problems.

Before unloosening any bolts please read through the entire section and the specific procedure. This will give you the overall view of what will be required as far as tools, supplies, and you. There is nothing more frustrating than having to walk to the bus stop on Monday morning because you were short one bolt during your Sunday afternoon repair. So read ahead and plan ahead.

Most sections begin with a brief discussion of the system and what it involves. Adjustments and/or maintenance are then discussed, followed by removal and installation procedures, and then repair or overhaul procedures where they are feasible. When repair is considered to be out of your league, we tell you how to remove the part and then how to install the new or rebuilt replacement. In this way you at least save the labor costs. Backyard repair of such components as the alternator are just not practical.

Two basic mechanic's rules should be mentioned here. One, whenever the left-side of the car is referred to, it is meant to specify the driver's side of the car. Conversely, the right-side of the car means the passenger's side of the car. Second, most screws and bolts are removed by turning counterclockwise and tightened by turning clockwise. Safety is the most important rule. Constantly be aware of the dangers involved in working on an automobile and take the proper precautions. Use jackstands when working under a raised vehicle. Don't smoke or allow an exposed flame to come near the battery or any part of the fuel system. Always use the proper tool and use it correctly, bruised knuckles and skinned fingers aren't a mechanic's standard equipment. Always take your time and have patience, once you have some experience and gain confidence, working on your car will become an enjoyable hobby.

Tools and Equipment

The following list is the basic requirement to perform most of the procedures described in this guide.

1. Sockets, to include a $^{13}/_{16}$ in. or $^5/_8$ in. spark plug socket. If possible, buy various length socket drive extensions.

2. Set of combination (one end open and one box) wrenches.

3. Spark plug wire gauge.

4. Flat feeler gauge for breaker points.

5. Slot and phillips head screwdriver.

6. Timing light, preferably a DC battery hook-up type.

7. Dwell/tachometer.

8. Torque wrench. This assures proper tightening of important fasteners and avoids costly thread stripping (too tight) or leaks (too loose).

9. Oil can filler spout. Much cleaner and neater than the old "punch the can with a screwdriver" trick.

10. Oil filter strap wrench. Makes removal of a tight filter much simpler. Never use to install filter.

11. Pair of channel lock pliers. Always handy to have.

12. Two sturdy jackstands—cinder blocks, bricks, and other makeshift supports are just not safe.

Year Identification

1968

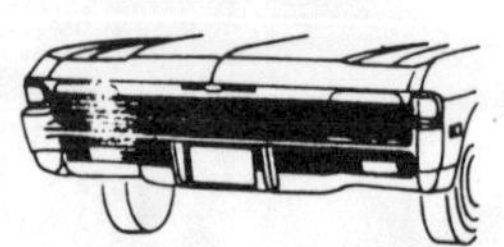

1968 Caprice

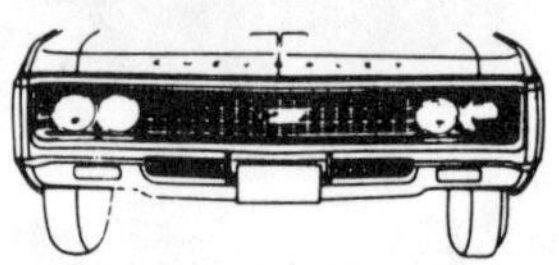

1969

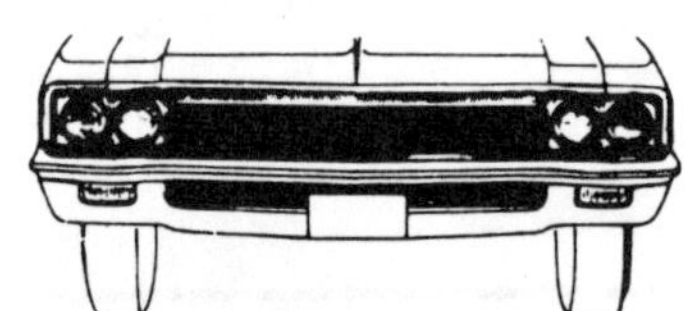

1970

1971

1972 Caprice

1972 Impala

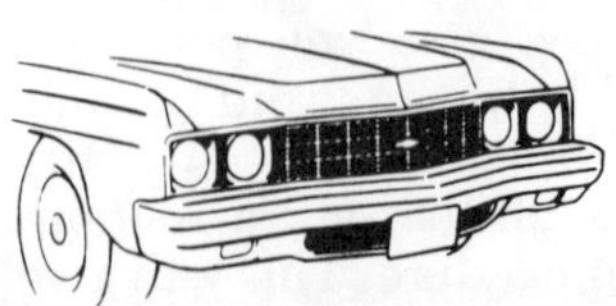

1973 Impala

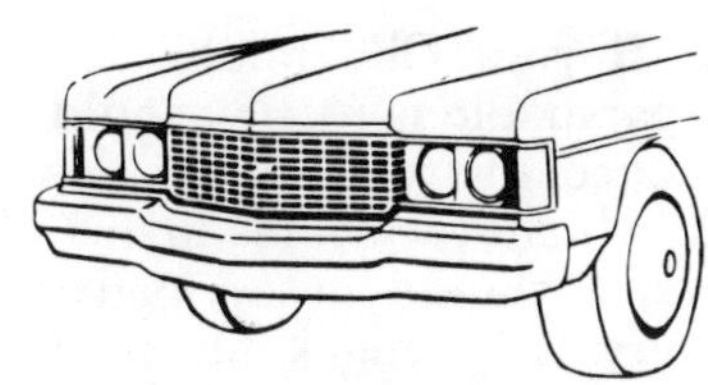

1974 Impala

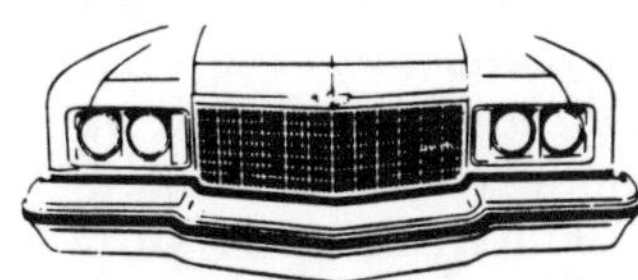

1974 Caprice

1975 Caprice

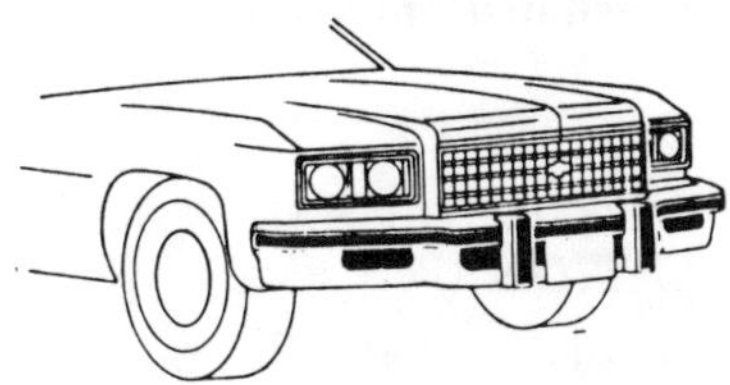

1976 Impala

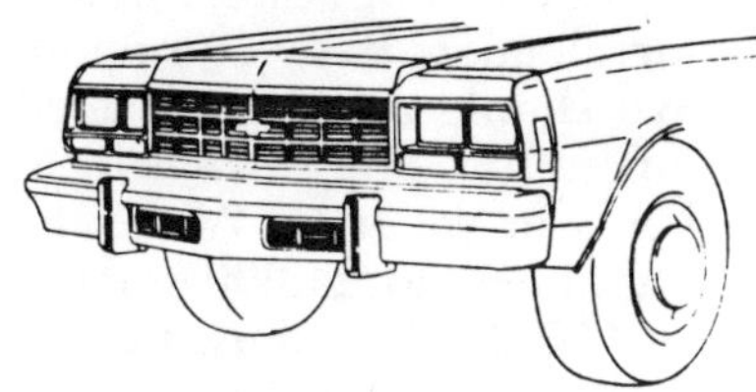

1977 Impala

Serial Number Identification

VEHICLE

The vehicle serial number is located on a plate on the top left-side of the instrument panel and is visible through the windshield.

Interpreting the Serial Number

A typical vehicle serial number tag yields manufacturer's identity, vehicle type, model year, assembly plant and production unit number when broken down as shown in the following charts.

1968–71

Mrf Identity [1]	Body Style [2]	Model Year [3]	Assy Plant [4]	Unit No. [5]
1	5645	8	F	100025

[1] Manufacturer's identity number assigned to all Chevrolet built vehicles
[2] Model identification
[3] Last number of model year (1968)
[4] F-Flint
[5] Unit numbering will start at 100,001 at all plants

1972–77

Mfr Identity [1]	Series Code Letter [2]	Body Style [3]	Engine Model [4]	Model Year [5]	Assembly Plant [6]	Unit Number [7]
1	N	47	R	4	F	100025

[1] Manufacturer's identity number assigned to all Chevrolet built vehicles
[2] Model Identification
[3] Model Identification
[4] Engine code
[5] Last number of model year (1974)
[6] F-Flint
[7] Unit numbering will start at 000001 or 100,001 depending on the model

ENGINE

Six Cylinder Engines

The production code letters immediately follow the engine serial number. The number is found on a pad at the front right-hand side of the cylinder block, just to the rear of the distributor.

V8 Engines

The production code letters immediately follow the engine serial number. The number is found on a pad at the front right-hand side of the cylinder block.

Routine Maintenance

AIR CLEANER

The air cleaner consists of a metal housing for a replaceable paper filter or permanent polyurethane element and the necessary hoses connecting it to the crankcase ventilation system. The air cleaner cover is held by a wing nut on all

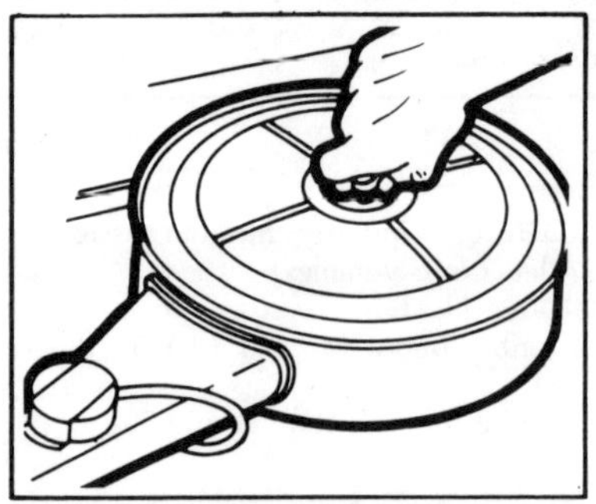

Unscrew the wing nut and remove the cover

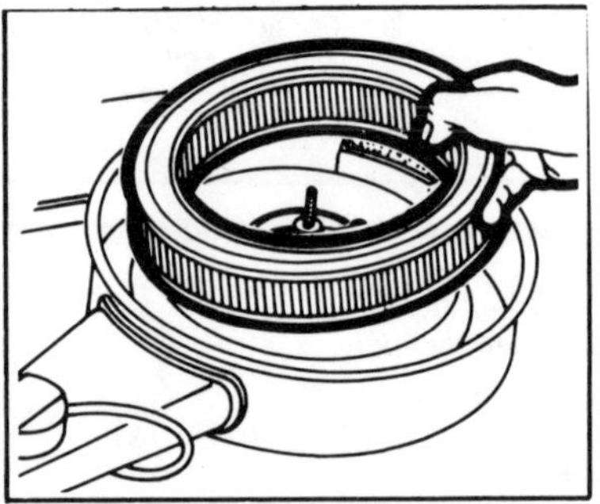

Remove and discard the old filter

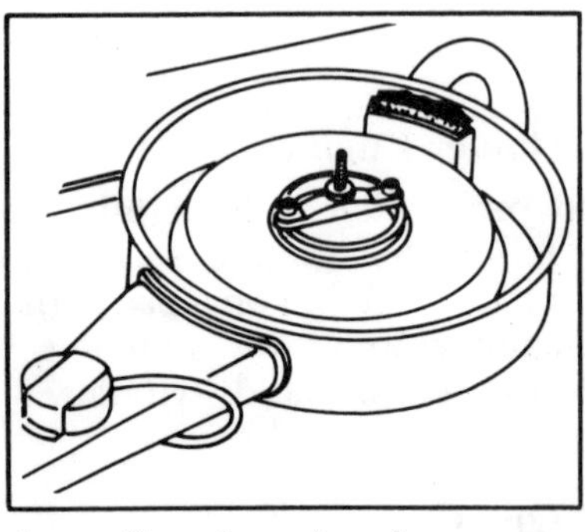

Check the small crankcase breather

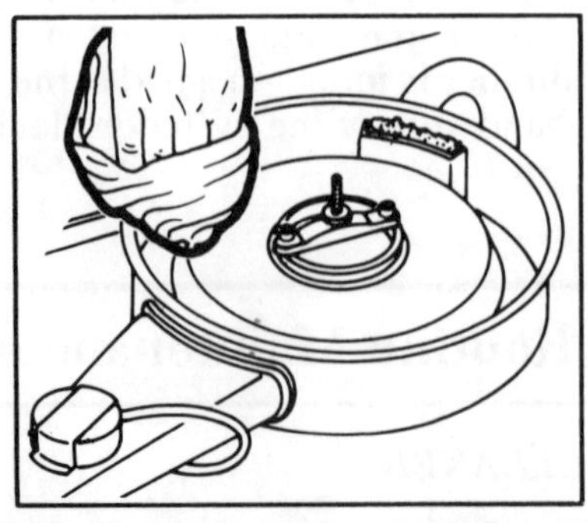

Using a clean rag or paper towel, wipe out the inside of the air cleaner

models. If your Chevrolet is equipped with a paper element, it should be replaced once every 12,000 miles or 12 months, whichever comes first. 1975 and later models should be serviced at 30,000 mile intervals. To check the effectiveness of your paper element, remove the air cleaner assembly and, if the idle speed increases noticeably, the element is restricting airflow and should be replaced. Some models are equipped with air cleaners which use a polyurethane element that must be removed, cleaned, and reoiled at 12,000 mile (15,000 on 1975 and later models), or 12 month intervals. Remove the filter and clean it in kerosene. Squeeze it dry. Allow it to soak in SAE 30 motor oil and then squeeze it dry using a clean cloth to remove excess oil. Clean the inside of the air cleaner housing before reinstalling either type of filter. A clogged air filter will decrease engine efficiency and gas mileage and increase exhaust emissions.

POSITIVE CRANKCASE VENTILATION (PCV)

Once every 12,000 miles or 12 months, check the hoses and clean or replace them as necessary. At the same time, clean and oil the ventilation filter located in the air cleaner, if so equipped. The PCV valve should also be replaced during this operation. The valve is located in the rocker arm cover. PCV service has been lengthened to 24,000 miles or 24 months on 1972–74 models. Replace the PCV valve every 30,000 miles on 1975 through 1976 models, every 15,000 miles for 1977 models.

EVAPORATIVE EMISSIONS CONTROL SYSTEM

This system, standard since 1970, eliminates the release of unburned fuel vapors into the atmosphere. The only periodic maintenance required is an occasional check of the connecting lines of the system for kinks or other damage and deterioration. Lines should only be replaced with quality fuel line or special hose marked "evap." Every 12,000 miles or 12 months, the filter in the bottom of the carbon canister which is located in

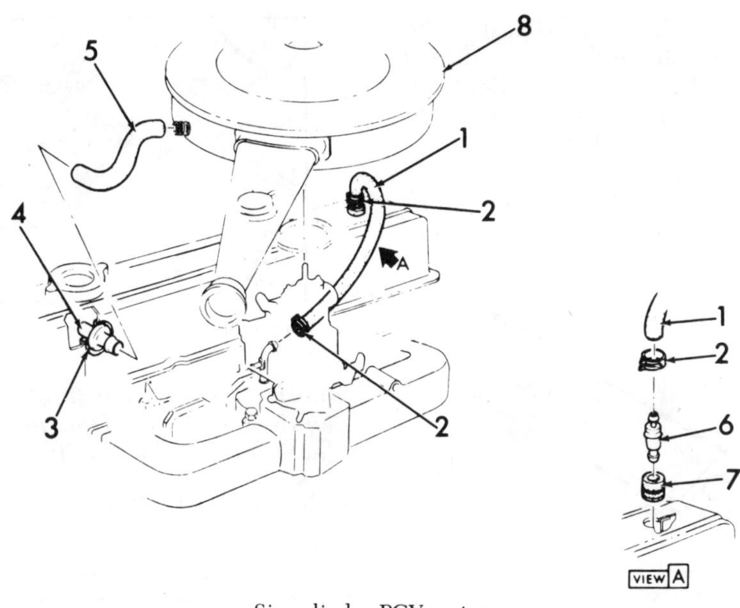

Six-cylinder PCV system

| 1. Hose | 3. Grommet | 5. Hose | 7. Grommet |
| 2. Clamp | 4. Connector | 6. PCV valve | 8. Air cleaner |

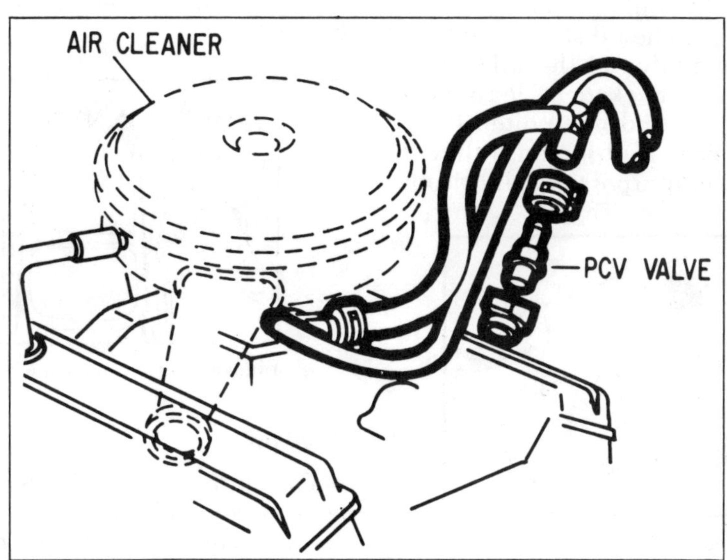

V8 PCV system

the engine compartment should be removed and replaced.

FLUID LEVEL CHECKS

Engine Oil

The engine oil level is checked with the dipstick, which is located at the left-side of the engine block on a V8 and on the right-side of the engine on a 6-cylinder.

NOTE: *The oil should be checked before the engine is started or five minutes after the engine has been shut off. This gives the oil time to drain back to the oil pan and prevents an inaccurate oil level reading.*

Remove the dipstick from its tube,

wipe it clean, and insert it back into the tube. Remove it again and observe the oil level. It should be maintained between the "full" and "add" marks without going above "full" or below "add."

CAUTION: *Do not overfill the crankcase. It may result in oil-fouled spark plugs or oil leaks caused by oil seal failure.*

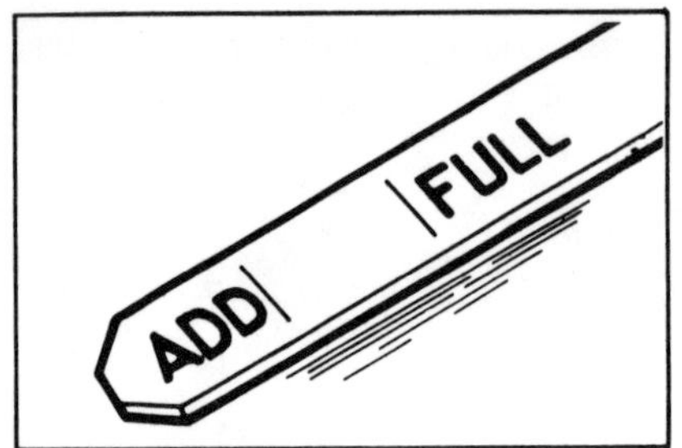

Dipstick marking

Transmission Fluid

MANUAL TRANSMISSION

Remove the filler plug from the side of the transmission. The oil should be level with the bottom edge of the filler hole. This should be checked at least once every 6,000 miles and more often if any leakage or seepage is observed. Fill with SAE 80 or 90 multipurpose gear lubricant.

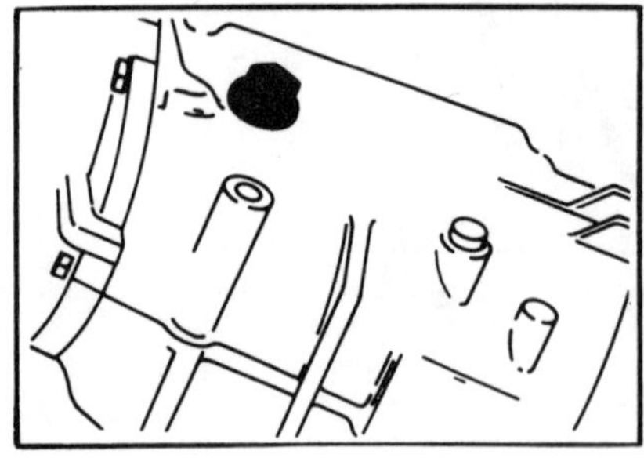

Manual transmission filler plug

AUTOMATIC TRANSMISSION

Run the engine until it reaches normal operating temperature. Park the car on a level surface. With the transmission in Park and the engine idling, the fluid level on the dipstick should be between the "full" mark and 1/4 inch below "full" mark. Replace the dipstick making sure that it is pushed fully into the filler tube.

CAUTION: *Do not overfill the automatic transmission. Use Dexron® auto-*

Adding automatic transmission fluid

matic transmission fluid or any other equivalent fluid. One pint raises the level from "add" to "full."

Brake Master Cylinder

Once every 6,000 miles or four months, check the brake fluid level in the master cylinder. The master cylinder is mounted on the firewall and is divided into two reservoirs and the fluid level in each reservoir must be maintained at 1/4 inch below the top edge. Use only heavy-duty brake fluid which is marked as DOT 3 or 4 grade.

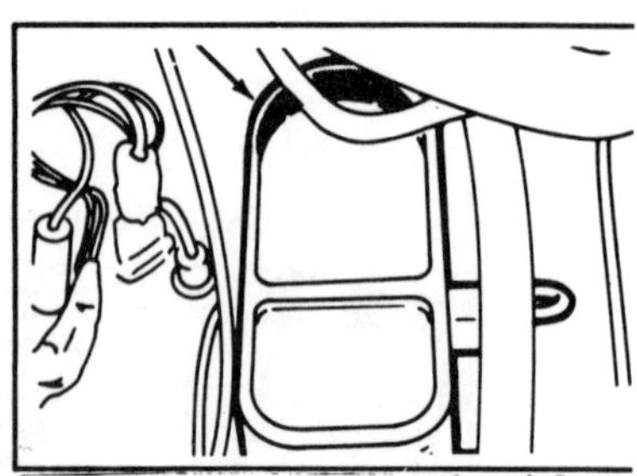

Correct brake fluid level—arrow

Coolant

Check the coolant level when the engine is cold. The level of coolant should be maintained 2 in. below the bottom of the filler neck, or the line on expansion tank-equipped models.

CAUTION: *Allow the engine to cool considerably and then add water while the engine is running.*

Rear Axle

STANDARD DIFFERENTIAL

The rear axle oil level should be checked when the chassis is lubricated. Remove the plug from the side of the housing. The lubricant level should be maintained at the bottom of the filler plug hole. When replacing oil, use SAE 80 or 90 multipurpose hypoid gear lubricant.

POSITRACTION DIFFERENTIAL

Lubricant level should be checked at each chassis lubrication and maintained at the bottom of the filler plug hole. Special Positraction oil must be used in this differential.

CAUTION: *Never use standard differential lubricant in a Positraction differential.*

Steering Gear

Check the lubricant by removing the center bolt on the side cover of the steering gear. Grease must be up to the level of this bolt hole.

Power Steering Reservoir

Maintain the proper fluid level as indicated on the cap of the reservoir. Check this level with the engine off and warm. Use GM power steering fluid or automatic transmission fluid.

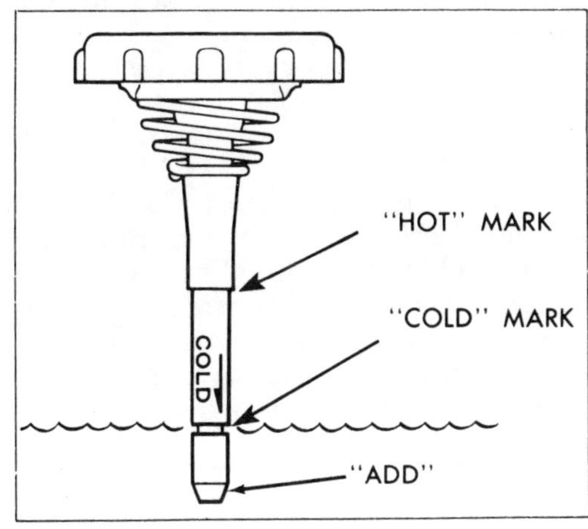

Power steering dipstick

Battery

The electrolyte level in the battery should be checked about once every month and more often during hot weather or long trips. If the level is below the bottom of the split ring, distilled water should be added until the level reaches the ring.

AIR CONDITIONING

This book contains no repair or maintenance procedures for the air conditioning

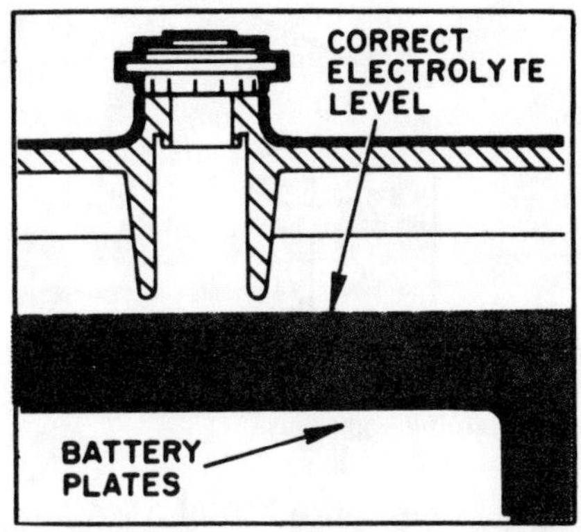

system. It is recommended that any such repairs be left to the experts, whose personnel are well aware of the hazards and who have the proper equipment.

CAUTION: *The compressed refrigerant used in the air conditioning system expands into the atmosphere at a temperature of $-21.7°F$ or lower. This will freeze any surface, including your eyes, that it contacts. In addition, the refrigerant decomposes into a poisonous gas in the presence of flame. Do not open or disconnect any part of the air conditioning system.*

Sight Glass Check

You can safely make a few simple checks to determine if your air conditioning system needs service. The tests work best if the temperature is warm (about 70° F).

1. Place the automatic transmission in Park or the manual transmission in Neutral. Set the parking brake.

2. Run the engine at a fast idle (about 1,500 rpm) either with the help of a friend, or by temporarily readjusting the idle speed screw.

3. Set the controls for maximum cold with the blower on high.

4. Locate the sight glass in one of the system lines. Usually it is on the left alongside the top of the radiator.

5. If you see bubbles, the system must be recharged. Very likely there is a leak at some point.

6. If there are no bubbles, there is either no refrigerant at all or the system is fully charged. Feel the two hoses going to the belt-driven compressor. If they are both at the same temperature, the system is empty and must be recharged.

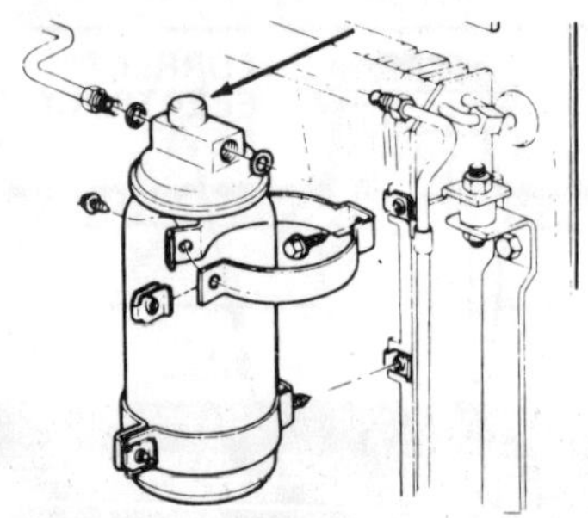

Air conditioning sight glass

7. If one hose (high-pressure) is warm and the other (low-pressure) is cold, the system may be alright. However, you are probably making these tests because you think there is something wrong, so proceed to the next Step.

8. Have an assistant in the car turn the fan control on and off to operate the compressor clutch. Watch the sight glass.

9. If bubbles appear when the clutch is disengaged and disappear when it is engaged, the system is properly charged.

10. If the refrigerant takes more than 45 seconds to bubble when the clutch is disengaged, the system is overcharged. This usually causes poor cooling at low speeds.

CAUTION: *If it is determined that the system has a leak, it should be corrected as soon as possible. Leaks may allow moisture to enter and cause a very expensive rust problem.*

NOTE: *Exercise the air conditioner for a few minutes, every two weeks or so, during the cold months. This avoids the possibility of the compressor seals drying out from lack of lubrication.*

DRIVE BELTS

Check the drive belts every 6,000 miles for evidence of wear such as cracking, fraying, and incorrect tension. Determine the belt tension at a point halfway between the pulleys by pressing on the belt with moderate thumb pressure. The belt should deflect about ¼–½ in. at this point. If the deflection is found to be too much or too little, loosen the mounting bolts and make the adjustments.

TIRES

Check the air pressure in your tires every few weeks. Make sure that the tires are cool, as you will get a false reading when the tires are heated because air pressure increases with temperature. A decal located on your glovebox door will tell you the proper tire pressure for the standard equipment tires. Naturally, when you replace tires you will want to get the correct tire pressures for the new ones from the dealer or manufacturer. It pays to buy a tire pressure gauge to keep in the car, since those at service stations are usually inaccurate or broken.

While you are checking the tire pressure, take a look at the tread. The tread should be wearing evenly across the tire. Excessive wear in the center of the tread indicates overinflation. Excessive wear on the outer edges indicates underinflation. An irregular wear pattern is usually a sign of incorrect front wheel alignment or wheel balance. A front end that is out of alignment will usually pull the car to one side of a flat road when the steering wheel is released. Incorrect wheel balance is usually accompanied by high speed vibration. Front wheels which are out of balance will produce vibration in the steering wheel, while unbalanced rear wheels will result in floor or trunk vibration.

Rotating the tires every 6,000 miles or so will result in increased tread life. Use the correct pattern for your tire switching. Most automotive experts are in agreement that radial tires are better all around performers, giving prolonged wear and better handling. An added benefit which you should consider when purchasing tires is that radials have less rolling resistance and can give up to a 10% increase in fuel economy over a bias-ply tire.

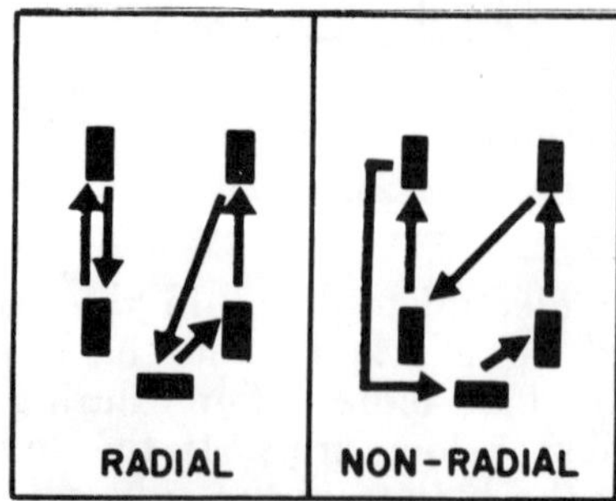

Tire rotation pattern

Tires of different construction should never be mixed. Always replace tires in sets of four or five when switching tire types and never substitute a belted tire for a bias-ply, a radial for a belted tire, etc. An occasional pressure check and periodic rotation could make your tires last much longer than a neglected set and maintain the safety margin which was designed into them.

FUEL FILTER

The filter element should be replaced every 12 months or 12,000 miles (15 months or 15,000 miles on 1975 and later models). To replace, follow these procedures:

1. Using an open-end wrench (preferably a line wrench), disconnect the fuel line connection from the larger fuel filter nut.

2. Remove the larger nut from the carburetor.

3. Remove the filter element and spring from the carburetor.

4. Check the bronze element for dirt blockage by blowing on the cone end. If the element is good, air should pass through easily.

5. If the car has a paper element instead of a bronze element, check by blowing into the fuel inlet end. If air does not pass through easily, replace the element. Do not attempt to clean these elements.

6. Install the spring and then the element into the carburetor, making sure that the small end of the bronze cone is facing outward.

7. Install a new gasket on the large nut and tighten securely.

8. Insert the fuel line and tighten the nut with a line wrench.

NOTE: *Replace the in-line filter, found on some later models, at the same interval as the fuel inlet filter.*

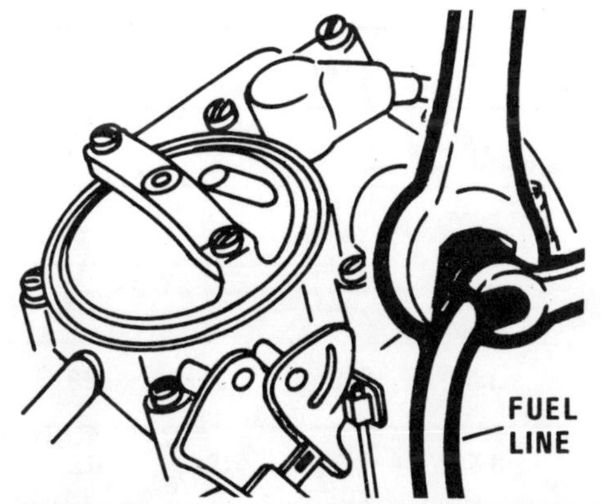

Hold the larger fitting while disconnecting the fuel line

Be careful not to strip the fuel line fitting

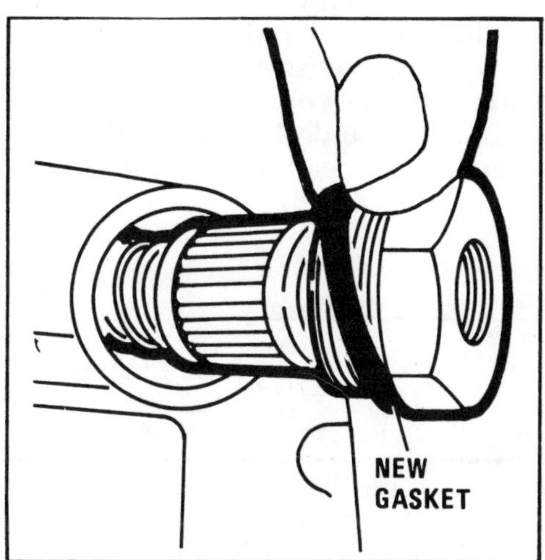

Use a new gasket on the fitting

BATTERY

In addition to routinely checking the electrolyte level of the battery, some other minor maintenance will keep your battery in peak starting condition. Two inexpensive battery tools a hydrometer and a post and cable cleaner, are available in most auto or hardware stores for about a dollar and more than earn back that small outlay. Besides checking the level of electrolyte, you should occasionally take a specific gravity reading to see what's going on inside the battery cells. Using your hydrometer, insert the tip into each cell and withdraw enough electrolyte to make the float ride freely. While holding the hydrometer straight up, take a reading. The specific gravity of a fully charged battery at 80° F) is 1.270.

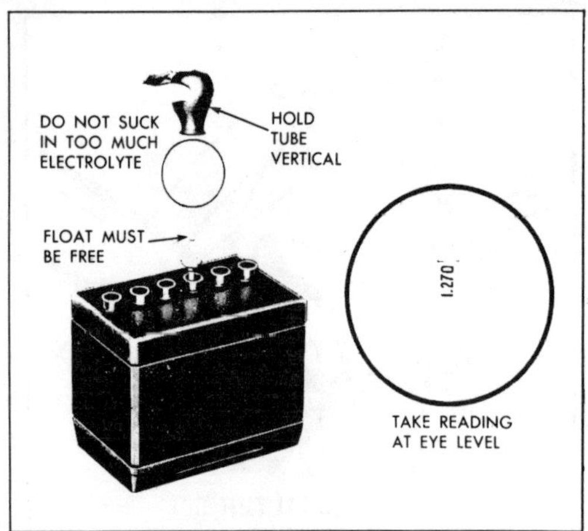

Checking specific gravity of battery electrolyte

Most commercially available hydrometers also have colored sections to save you reading the scale and these will clearly tell you your battery cell is (a) charged, (b) borderline—should be recharged, or (c) dead. Repeat the specific gravity for each cell.

NOTE: *Battery electrolyte or "acid" is very caustic and will dissolve skin and paintwork with equal relish, so be careful. Readings should be taken in as normal a room temperature atmosphere as possible. If the temperature varies from the 80° F standard above, add or subtract four (0.004) points for every 10° above (+) or below (−) the standard.*

The most completely charged battery will do you no good on a cold, rainy evening if the cables and posts are caked with corrosion. This is where your little wire brush cleaner comes in. Loosen and remove the cable clamps from the battery posts. Using the pointed end of the brush, give the inside surface of the clamp a good cleaning until it shines. Next, take the other end and place it over the post. Clean the post with a rotating motion until you achieve a shiny post. This done, install the clamps and retighten.

A slightly different procedure is used

Capacities

Year	ENGINE No. Cyl Displacement (Cu In.)	Engine Crankcase Add 1 Qt For New Filter	TRANSMISSION Pts To Refill After Draining			Drive Axle (pts)	Gasoline Tank (gals) ■	COOLING SYSTEM (qts)	
			Manual		Automatic ●			With Heater	With A/C
			3-Speed	4-Speed					
'68	6-250	4	3	3	6⑦	3.5	24	12	13
	8-307	4	3	3	6	3.5	24	17	18
	8-327	4	3	3	6.5⑥	3.5	24	15	16
	8-396	4	3③	3	6.5⑥	3.5	24	22	22
	8-427	4	3③	3	8	3.5	24	22②	22②
'69	6-250	4	3	3	6⑦	3.5①	24	12	12
	8-327	4	3	3	6.5⑥	3.5①	24	17	17
	8-350	4	3.5	3	6.5⑥	3.5①	24	15	16
	8-396	4	3.5	3	6.5⑥	3.5①	24	23	24
	8-427	4	3.5	3	8	3.5①	24	22②	23
'70	6-250	4	3	—	6	3.5①	25	12	12
	8-350	4	3	—	6.5⑦	3.5①	25	16	16④

Capacities (cont.)

Year	ENGINE No. Cyl Displacement (Cu In.)	Engine Crankcase Add 1 Qt For New Filter	TRANSMISSION Pts To Refill After Draining Manual 3-Speed	4-Speed	Automatic ●	Drive Axle (pts)	Gasoline Tank (gals) ■	COOLING SYSTEM (qts) With Heater	With A/C
'70	8-400	4	—	—	5⑥	3.5①	25	16	17
	8-454	4	—	—	8	3.5①	25	22	22
'71	6-250	4	3	—	6	3.5①	24	12	—
	8-350	4	3	—	6.5⑦	3.5①	24	16	17
	8-400	4	3	—	5⑥	3.5①	24	16	17
	8-402	4	—	—	8	3.5①	24	23	24
	8-454	4	—	—	8	3.5①	24	22	23
'72	6-250	4	3	—	6	4.25⑤	23	12	—
	8-350	4	—	—	5	4.25⑤	23	16	17
	8-400	4	—	—	5	4.25⑤	23	16	17
	8-402	4	—	—	8	4.25⑤	23	23	24
	8-454	4	—	—	8	4.25⑤	23	22	23
'73	6-250	4	3	—	5	4.25⑤	26	12	12
	8-350	4	—	—	5	4.25⑤	26	16	17
	8-400	4	—	—	5	4.25⑤	26	16.5	17.5
	8-454	4	—	—	8	4.25⑤	26	23	24
'74	8-350	4	—	—	8	4.25⑤	26	16	16
	8-400	4	—	—	8⑧	4.25⑤	26	16	16
	8-454	4	—	—	9	4.25⑤	26	22	23
'75	8-350	4	—	—	8	4.25⑤	26	16	16
	8-400	4	—	—	9	4.25⑤	26	16	16
	8-454	4	—	—	9	4.25⑤	26	22	23
'76–'77	6-250	4	—	—	6	4.25	21	14	14
	8-305	4	—	—	8	4.25	21	16	18

Capacities (cont.)

Year	ENGINE No. Cyl Displacement (Cu In.)	Engine Crankcase Add 1 Qt For New Filter	TRANSMISSION Pts To Refill After Draining		Automatic •	Drive Axle (pts)	Gasoline Tank (gals) ■	COOLING SYSTEM (qts)	
			Manual					With Heater	With A/C
			3-Speed	4-Speed					
'76–'77	8-350	4	—	—	8	4.25	21	18⑨	20⑨
	8-400	4	—	—	9	4.25	21	18	20
	8-454	4	—	—	9	4.25	21	23	25

• Specifications do not include torque converter
■ Station wagons: '68–'69—24 gals, '70—22 gals, '71—23 gals, '72–'76—22 gals
① 4 pts with 8.875 diameter ring gear
② 425 hp 427—23 qts
③ 3.5 pts with heavy duty 3-speed
④ 17 qts with 300 hp engine
⑤ 4.9 pts with 8.875 ring gear
⑥ 8 pts with 3-speed Turbo Hydramatic 400
⑦ 5 pts with 3-speed Turbo Hydramatic 350
⑧ 9 with 400 4 bbl
—— Not applicable
⑨ 1977: 16 w/heater; 18 w/A/C

for 1972 and later Chevrolets which are equipped with Delco side terminal batteries. The cable is cleaned in the same manner, but the internal threads in the battery can be cleaned with a special tool now available for that purpose. Exercise care when removing the cable retaining bolts on side terminal batteries, as it is easy to strip them.

All 1977 Chevrolets are equipped with a new type of no maintenance battery. This battery requires no maintenance other than occasionally checking its state of charge by looking at the indicator on the top. If the indicator is dark with a green dot showing in the center, the battery if fully charged. If the indicator is dark but there is no green dot showing, the battery should be charged. If the indicator is light, the battery should be replaced.

Keep the top of the battery clean, as a film of dirt can sometimes completely discharge a battery. A solution of baking soda and water may be used to clean the top surface, but be careful to flush this off with clear water and that none of the solution enters the filler holes.

Lubrication

OIL AND FUEL

Chevrolet recommends the use of a high quality, heavy-duty detergent oil having the proper viscosity for prevailing temperatures and an SE service rating. The SE rating will be printed on the top of the can. Under the classification system adopted by the American Petroleum Institute (API) in May, 1970, SE is the highest designation given for normal passenger car use. The S stands for passenger car and the second letter denotes a more specific application. SA oil, for instance, contains no additives and is suitable only for very light-duty. Oil designated MS may also be used, since this was the highest classification under the

Oil Viscosity Selection Chart

	Anticipated Temperature Range	SAE Viscosity
Multi-grade	Above 32° F	10W—40 10W—50 20W—40 20W—50 10W—30
	May be used as low as — 10° F	10W—30 10W—40
	Consistently below 10° F	5W—20 5W—30
Single-grade	Above 32° F	30
	Temperature between + 32° F and — 10° F	10W

old API rating system. Pick your oil viscosity with regard to the anticipated temperatures during the period before your next oil change. Using the chart below, choose the oil viscosity for the lowest expected temperature. You will be assured of easy cold starting and sufficient engine protection.

Fuel should be selected for the brand and octane which performs without pinging. Find your exact engine model in the "General Engine Specifications" chart in Chapter 3. If the compression ratio is high than 9.0:1, you will have to use a premium gasoline. If your compression ratio is lower than 9.0:1, you can safely go with regular octane. All 1975 and later Chevrolets must be operated on unleaded fuel. Leaded fuel will ruin the catalytic converter.

OIL CHANGES

The mileage figures given in your owner's manual are the Chevrolet recommended intervals for oil and filter changes assuming average driving. If your Chevrolet is being used under dusty, polluted, or off-road conditions, change the oil and filter sooner than specified. The same thing goes for cars driven in stop-and-go traffic or only for short distances.

Always drain the oil after the engine has been running long enough to bring it to operating temperature. Hot oil will flow easier and more contaminants will be removed along with the oil than if it were drained cold. You will need a large capacity drain pan, which you can purchase at any store which sells automotive parts. Another necessity is containers for the used oil. You will find that plastic bottles, such as those used for bleach or fabric softener, make excellent storage jugs. One ecologically desirable solution to the used oil disposal problem is to find a cooperative gas station owner who will allow you to dump your used oil into his tank. Another is to keep the oil for use around the house as a preservative on fences, railroad tie borders, etc.

Chevrolet recommends changing both the oil and filter during the first oil change and the filter every other oil change thereafter. For the small price of an oil filter, it's cheap insurance to replace the filter at every oil change. One of the larger filter manufacturers points out in its advertisements that not changing the filter leaves one quart of dirty oil in the engine. This claim is true and should be kept in mind when changing your oil.

Changing Your Oil

1. Run the engine until it reaches normal operating temperature.

2. Jack up the front of the car and support it on safety stands.

3. Slide a drain pan of at least 6 quarts capacity under the oil pan.

4. Loosen the drain plug. Turn the plug out by hand. By keeping an inward pressure on the plug as you unscrew it, oil won't escape past the threads and you can remove it without being burned by hot oil.

5. Allow the oil to drain completely and then install the drain plug. Don't overtighten the plug, or you'll be buying a new pan or a trick replacement plug for buggered threads.

6. Using a strap wrench, remove the oil filter. Keep in mind that it's holding about one quart of dirty, hot oil.

NOTE: *You can remove the oil filter on six cylinders from above.*

7. Empty the old filter into the drain pan and dispose of the filter.

8. Using a clean rag, wipe off the filter adapter on the engine block. Be sure that the rag doesn't leave any lint which could clog an oil passage.

9. Coat the rubber gasket on the filter with fresh oil. Spin it onto the engine *by hand*; when the gasket touches the adapter surface give it another $1/2$–$3/4$ turn. No more, or you'll squash the gasket and it will leak.

10. Refill the egine with the correct amount of fresh oil. See the "Capacities" chart.

11. Crank the engine over several times and then start it. If the oil pressure "idiot light" doesn't go out or the pressure gauge shows zero, shut the engine down and find out what's wrong.

12. If the oil pressure is OK and there are no leaks, shut the engine off and lower the car.

13. Wait a few minutes and check the oil level. Add oil, as necessary, to bring the level up to Full.

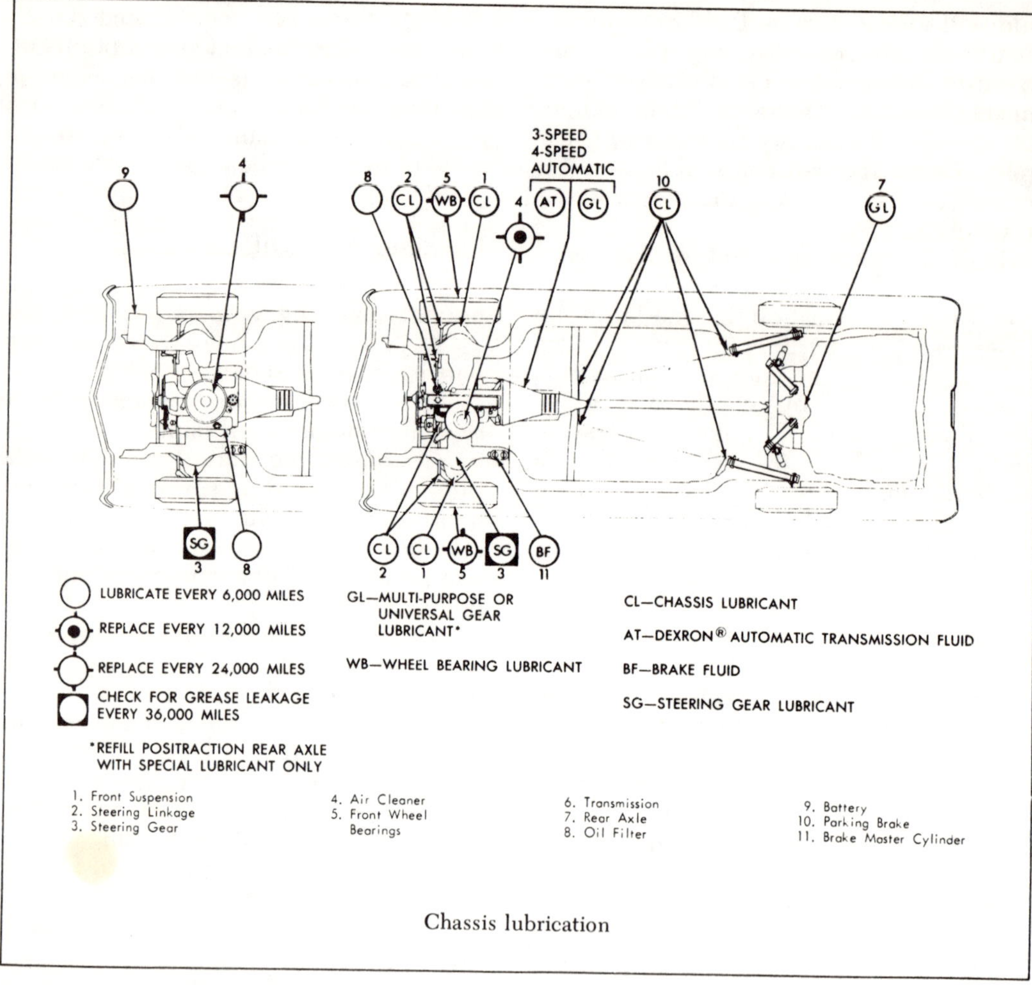

Chassis lubrication

CHASSIS GREASING

Chassis greasing can be performed with a pressurized grease gun or it can be performed at home by using a hand-operated grease gun. Wipe the grease fittings clean before greasing in order to prevent the possibility of forcing any dirt into the component.

WHEEL BEARINGS

Once every 12 months or 12,000 miles, clean and replace wheel bearings with a wheel bearing grease. Use only enough grease to completely coat the rollers. Remove any excess grease from the exposed surface of the hub and seal.

It is important that wheel bearings be properly adjusted after installation. Improperly adjusted wheel beaings can cause steering instability, front-end shimmy and wander, and increased tire wear. For complete adjustment procedures, see the "Wheel Bearing" section in Chapter 9.

Pushing, Towing, Jacking and Jump Starting

PUSH STARTING

This is the least recommended method of starting a car and should be used only in an extreme case. Chances of body damage are high, so be sure that the pushcar's bumper does not override your bumper. If your Chevrolet has an automatic transmission forget any idea of push starting, modern automatics are not designed to be used in this manner. In an emergency, you can start a manual transmission car by pushing. With the bumpers evenly matched, get in your car, switch on the ignition, and place the gearshift in Second or Third gear—do not engage the clutch. Start off slowly. When the speed of the car reaches about 15–20 mph, release the clutch.

JUMP STARTING

When jump starting be sure that the booster cables are properly connected—positive-to-positive and negative-to-negative. Do not use a booster battery with voltage greater than 12 volts. Be careful to avoid causing sparks as there is danger of explosion from the gases given off by the battery.

TOWING

The car can be towed safely (with the transmission in Neutral) from the front at speeds of 35 mph or less. The car must either be towed with the rear wheels off the ground or the driveshaft disconnected if: towing speeds are to be over 35 mph, or towing distance is over 50 miles, or transmission or rear axle problems exist.

When towing the car on its front wheels, the steering wheel must be secured in a straight-ahead position. Tire-to-ground clearance should not exeed 6 in. during towing.

JACKING

The standard jack utilizes slots in the bumper to raise the car. The jack supplied with the car should never be used for any service operation other than tire changing. Never get under the car while it is supported by only a jack. Always block the wheels when changing tires.

The service operations in this book often require that one end or the other, or both, of the car be raised and safely supported. The ideal method, of course, would be a hydraulic hoist. Since this is beyond both the resource and requirement of the do-it-yourselfer, a small hydraulic, screw or scissors jack will suffice for the procedures in this guide. Two sturdy jackstands should be acquired if you intend to work under the car at any time. An alternate method of raising the car would be drive-on ramps. These are available commercially or can be fabricated from heavy boards of steel. Be sure to block the wheels when using ramps.

Chapter 2

Tune-Up and Troubleshooting

Tune-Up Procedures

SPARK PLUGS

In addition to performing their basic function of igniting the air-fuel mixture, spark plugs can also serve as very useful diagnostic tools. Once removed, compare your spark plugs with the samples in the "Troubleshooting" Section at the back of this Chapter. Typical plug conditions are illustrated along with their causes and remedies. Plugs which exhibit only normal wear and deposits can be cleaned, gapped, and reinstalled. Before removing the spark plug leads, number the towers on the distributor cap with tape. Trace the No. 1 lead and then proceed in the firing order. Use the firing order illustrations in Chapter 3 if you get lost. This prevents mix-ups when rein-stalling the leads and also comes in handy when you're replacing wires or the distributor cap. Grasp each spark plug boot and pull it straight out.

Use a $^{13}/_{16}$ in. spark plug socket on all models through 1969, and all V8s through 1971. Six-cylinder models from 1970 and V8s from 1972 are equipped with tapered seat spark plugs which require a $^5/_8$ in. socket. Install the spark plug socket on the plug's hex and remove it. If removal is difficult, loosen the plug only slightly and drip some light oil onto the threads. Allow the oil to penetrate and then un-screw the spark plug. Proceeding this way will prevent damaging the threads in the cylinder head. Be sure to keep the socket straight to avoid breaking the ce-ramic insulator. Inspect the plugs using the "Troubleshooting" Section illustra-tions and then clean or discard them ac-cording to their condition.

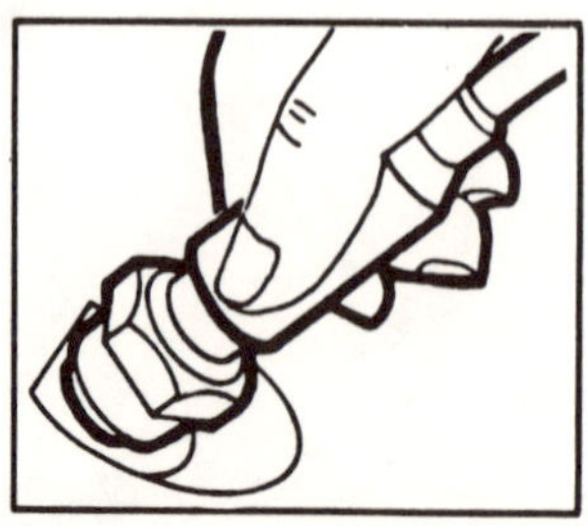

Remove the spark plug wire by pulling off the boot, not the wire itself

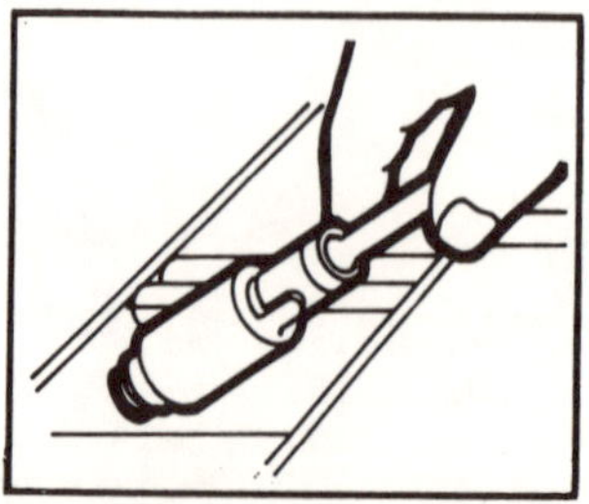

Use a spark plug socket for removing and installing the plugs

Most new spark plugs come pre-gapped, but double check the setting or reset them if you desire a different gap. Recommended spark plug gap is given in the "Tune-Up Specifications" chart. Use a spark plug wire gauge for checking the gap. The wire should pass through the electrodes with just a slight drag. Using the electrode bending tool on the end of the gauge, bend the side electrode to adjust the gap. Never attempt to adjust the center electrode. Lightly oil the threads of the replacement plug and install it. If you have a torque wrench, tighten the plugs to 15 ft lbs on 6 cylinders and all V8s. Be very careful not to overtighten the plug in the cylinder head.

Use a wire gauge to check spark plug gap

NOTE: *Always replace the points and condenser as a unit. Uniset® points are available for V8 engines which combine the point set and condenser, greatly simplifying installation.*

BREAKER POINTS AND CONDENSER

Removal and Replacement

SIX-CYLINDER

1. Remove the distributor cap from the distributor and place it out of the way.
2. Remove the rotor.
3. Make a note of the wire connec-

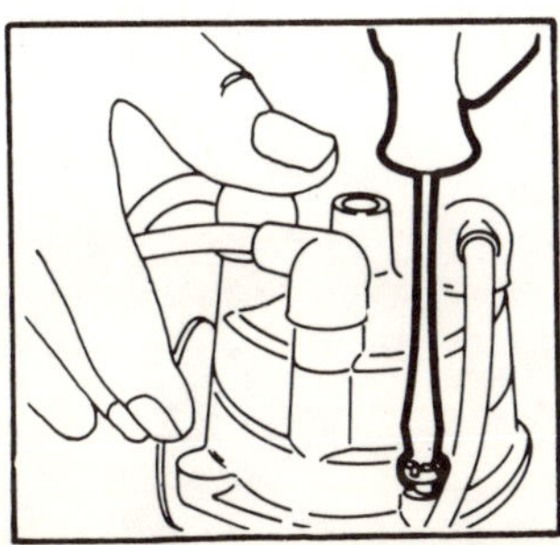

Six-cylinder cap is retained by two captive screws

Remove the six-cylinder rotor by pulling it straight off

tions and then remove the wires from the contact point terminal.

4. Remove the mounting screws and lift the point set condenser from the breaker plate.
5. Clean the braker plate.
6. Install a new point set onto the breaker plate.
7. Install a new condenser and connect the primary and condenser lead wires to the contact point terminal.
8. Check the points for alignment. Contact surfaces must align with each other. If alignment is necessary, bend only the stationary contact support and not the movable one.
9. Using a flat feeler gauge, set the point opening at 0.019 in. for new points, 0.016 in. for used points. Observe the points while an assistant lightly activates the ignition switch. Turning the ignition key to the START position will rotate the distributor shaft and cause the points to open and close. When the points open completely (this occurs when the rubbing block is resting on the high point of the cam lobe), TURN THE IGNITION KEY OFF and check the space between

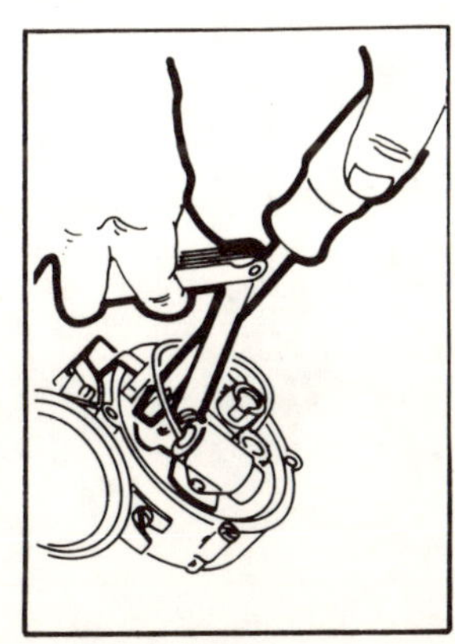

Use a flat feeler gauge to measure point gap

Tune-Up Specifications

When analyzing compression test results, look for uniformity among cylinders rather than specific pressures.

| Year | ENGINE | | SPARK PLUGS | | DISTRIBUTOR | | IGNITION TIMING (deg) ▲ | | VALVES | Fuel Pump Pressure (psi) | IDLE SPEED (rpm) ▲ | |
	No. Cyl Displacement	Hp (cu in.)	Type	Gap (in.)	Point Dwell (deg)	Point Gap (in.)	Man Trans	Auto Trans ●	Intake Opens ■ (deg) ●		Man Trans	Auto Trans
'68	6-250	155	46N	.035	31–34	.019	TDC	4B	16	3½–4½	700②	600②/400③
	8-307	200	45S	.035	28–32	.019	2B	2B	28	5–6½	700	600
	8-327	250	44S	.035	28–32	.019	4B	4B	28	5–6½	700②	600
	8-327	275	44	.035	28–32	.019	TDC	4B	28	5–6½	700②	600②
	8-396	325	43N	.035	28–32	.019	4B	4B	28	5–6½	700	600
	8-427	385	43N	.035	28–32	.019	4B	4B	40	7–8½	700	600
'69	6-250	155	R46N	.035	31–34	.019	TDC	4B	16	4–5	700	550/400③
	8-327	235	R45S	.035	29–31	.019	2A	2B	28	7½–9	700	600
	8-350	255	R44S	.035	29–31	.019	TDC	4B	28	7½–9	700	600
	8-350	300	R44S	.035	29–31	.019	TDC	4B	28	7½–9	700	600
	8-396	265	R44N	.035	29–31	.019	TDC	4B	28	7½–9	700	600
	8-427	335	R44N	.035	29–31	.019	4B	4B	28	7½–9	700	600
	8-427	390	R43N	.035	29–31	.019	4B	4B	56	7½–9	800②	600②

'70	6-250	155	R46T	.035	31–34	.019	TDC	4B	16	4–5	750/400③	600/400②
	8-350	250	R44	.035	29–31	.019	TDC	4B	28	7½–9	700/450③	600/450③
	8-350	300	R44	.035	29–31	.019	TDC	4B	28	7½–9	700	600
	8-400	265	R44	.035	29–31	.019	4B	8B	28	7½–9	700	600/450②
	8-454	345	R44T	.035	28–30	.019	6B	6B	30	7½–9	700	600
	8-454	390	R43T	.035	28–30	.019	6B	6B	56	7½–9	700	600
'71	6-250	145	R46TS	.035	31–34	.019	4B	4B	16	4–5	550	500②
	8-350	245	R44TS	.035	29–31	.019	2B	6B	28	7½–9	600	550②
	8-350	270	R44TS	.035	29–31	.019	4B	8B	28	7½–9	600	550②
	8-400	255	R44TS	.035	29–31	.019	4B	8B	28	7½–9	600	550②
	8-402	300	R44TS	.035	29–31	.019	8B	8B	28	7½–9	600	600②
	8-454	365	R43TS	.035	28–30	.019	8B	8B	56	7½–9	600	600
'72	6-250	110	R46T	.035	31–34	.019	4B	4B	16	4–5	700	600
	8-350	165	R44T	.035	29–31	.019	6B	6B	28(44)	7½–9	900	600
	8-400	170	R44T	.035	29–31	.019	2B	6B	28(44)	7½–9	900	600
	8-402	210	R44T	.035	29–31	.019	8B	8B	30(44)	7½–9	750	600
	8-454	270	R44T	.035	29–31	.019	8B	8B	56	7½–9	750	600

Tune-Up Specifications

When analyzing compression test results, look for uniformity among cylinders rather than specific pressures.

Year	ENGINE No. Cyl Displacement	Hp (cu in.)	SPARK PLUGS Type	Gap (in.)	DISTRIBUTOR Point Dwell (deg)	Point Gap (in.)	IGNITION TIMING (deg) ▲ Man Trans	Auto Trans ●	VALVES Intake Opens ■ (deg) ●	Fuel Pump Pressure (psi)	IDLE SPEED (rpm) ▲ Man Trans	Auto Trans
'73	6-250	100	R46T	.035	31–34	.019	6B	——	16	3½–4½	700/450③	——
	8-350	145	R44T	.035	29–31	.019	——	8B	28	7½–9	——	600/450③
	8-350	175	R44T	.035	29–31	.019	——	12B	28	7½–9	——	600/450③
	8-400	140	R44T	.035	29–31	.019	——	8B	28	7½–9	——	600/450③
	8-454	245⑤	R44T	.035	29–31	.019	——	10B	55	7½–9	——	600/450③
'74	8-350	145	R44T	.035	29–31	.019	——	8B	28(44)	7½–9	——	600
	8-350	160	R44T	.035	29–31	.019	——	12B(8B)	28(44)	7½–9	——	600
	8-400	150	R44T	.035	29–31	.019	——	8B	28(44)	7½–9	——	600
	8-400	180	R44T	.035	29–31	.019	——	8B	28(44)	7½–9	——	600
	8-454	235	R44T	.035	29–31	.019	——	10B	55	7½–9	——	600
'75	8-350	145	R44TX	.060	Electronic		——	6B	28	7½–9	——	600
	8-350	155	R44TX	.060	Electronic		——	6B	28	7½–9	——	600
	8-400	175	R44TX	.060	Electronic		——	8B	28	7½–9	——	600
	8-454	215	R44TX	.060	Electronic		——	16B	55	7½–9	——	650
'76	8-350	145	R45TS	.045	Electronic		——	6B	28	7½–8½	——	600
	8-350	155	R45TS	.045	Electronic		——	⑥	28	7½–8½	——	600

	8 400	175	R45TS	.045	Electronic	—	8B	28	$7\frac{1}{2}$–$8\frac{1}{2}$	—	600
	8-454	215	R45TS	.045	Electronic	—	12B	55	$7\frac{1}{2}$–$8\frac{1}{2}$	—	550
'77	6-250	110	R46TS	.035	Electronic	—	8B(6B)	28	4–5	—	550–600
	8-305	145	R45TS	.045	Electronic	—	8B(6B)	28	$7\frac{1}{2}$–9	—	500–700/650③
	8-350	170	R45TS	.045	Electronic	—	8B	28	$7\frac{1}{2}$–9	—	500–700/650③

▲ See text for procedure
● Figure in parentheses indicates California engine
■ All figures Before Top Dead Center
① Equipped with Air Injection Reactor System
② A/C on

③ Lower figure with Idle Solenoid disconnected
⑤ 215 in wagons
⑥ 8B Federal, 6B California

A After Top Dead Center
B Before Top Dead Center
TDC Top Dead Center
—— Not applicable

the open points. This space or gap should be 0.019 in. for new points. If not, slightly loosen the point set mounting screw and, using a screwdriver to move the point support, adjust the gap until correct. Tighten the mounting screw.

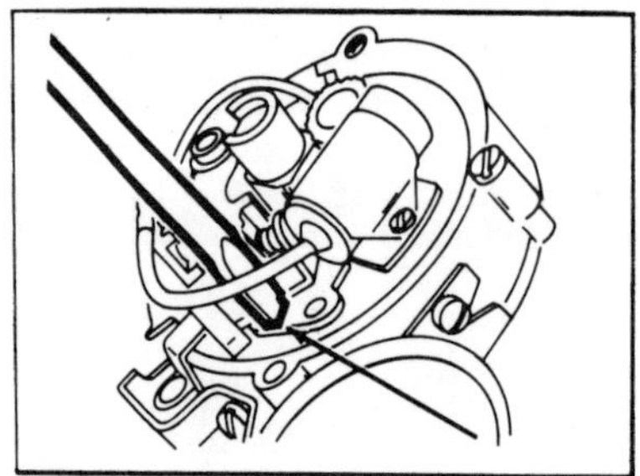

Six-cylinder point gap is adjusted with a screwdriver in the slot—arrow

10. Install the rotor and distributor cap.

11. Start the engine, check the dwell angle and then the ignition timing.

V8

NOTE: *The HEI (High Energy Ignition) system used on some 1974 and all 1975 and later models requires no maintenance other than checking the condition of the cap and wires. There are no points to wear out or adjust.*

Point alignment is preset at the factory and requires no adjustment. Point sets using the push-in type wiring terminal should be used on those distributors equipped with an R.F.I (radio frequency interference) shield (1970–74). Points using a lockscrew type terminal may short out due to the shield contacting the screw.

1. Remove the distributor cap.

Remove the V8 distributor cap by depressing the screw in the cap and rotating the latch off the distributor (there are two latches)

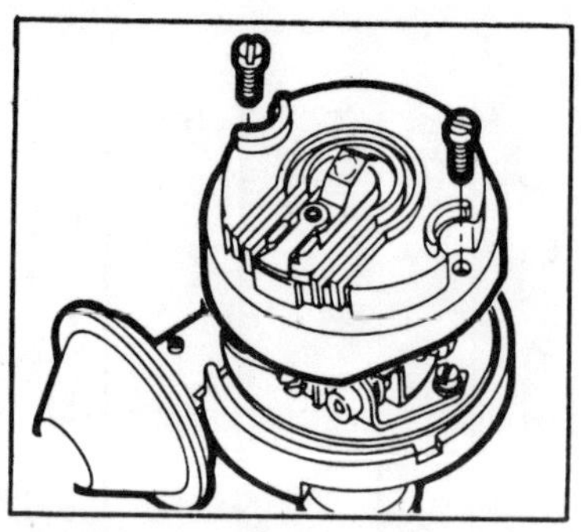

V8 rotor mounting

2. Remove the rotor.

3. If so equipped, remove the two-piece R.F.I shield.

4. Loosen the two mounting screws and slide the contact point set from the breaker plate.

5. Remove the primary and condenser leads from the terminal.

6. Loosen the condenser bracket screw and slide the condenser from the bracket.

7. Install the new point set and condenser and then tighten the mounting screws.

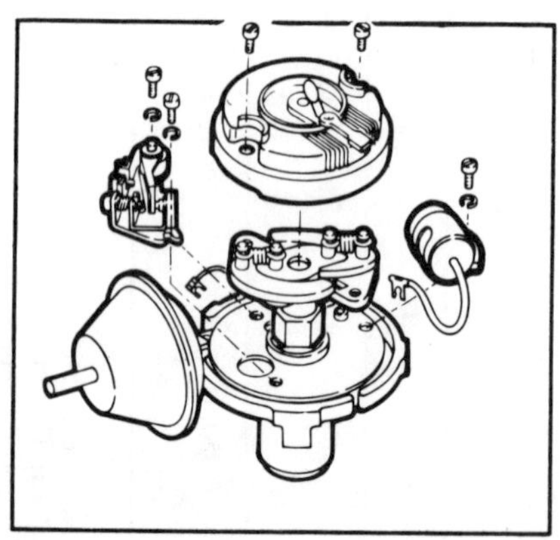

V8 point set and condenser mounting

8. Install the wires to the terminal so that they will not interfere with the cap, weight base, or breaker advance plate. Install the half of the R.F.I. shield which covers the points first.

9. Using a ⅛ in. allen wrench, make an initial point setting of 0.019 in.

10. The cam lubricator (if so equipped) must be replaced after 12 months or 12,000 miles. The end of the lubricator should be adjusted to just touch the cam lobes. Additional grease should not be applied to the lubricator.

11. Install the rotor. The two lugs on

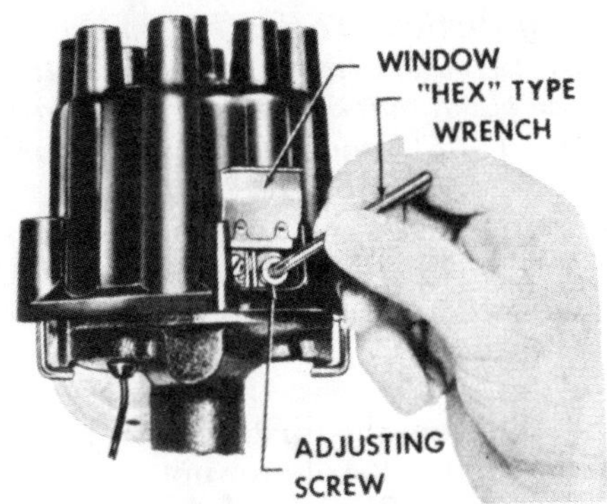

Adjusting V8 point gap (dwell angle)

the bottom of the rotor are shaped differently, so that it can only be installed one way. Tighten the screws. Start the engine and check the point dwell and the ignition timing.

DWELL ANGLE

Dwell angle is the amount of time (measured in degrees of distributor cam rotation) that the contact points remain closed. Initial point gap (0.019 in.) determines dwell angle. If the points are too wide they open gradually and dwell angle (the time they remain closed) is small. This wide gap causes excessive arcing at the points and, because of this, point burning. This small dwell doesn't give the coil sufficient time to build up maximum energy and so coil ouput decreases. If the points are set too close, the dwell is increased but the points may bounce at higher speeds and the idle becomes rough and starting is made harder. The wider the point opening, the smaller the dwell and the smaller the gap, the larger the dwell. Adjusting the dwell by making the initial point gap setting with a feeler gauge is sufficient to get the car started but a finer adjustment should be made. A dwell meter is needed to check the adjustment. Dwell angle cannot be checked on HEI distributors.

SIX-CYLINDER

1. Perform Steps 8 and 9 in the above procedure ("Breaker Points and Condenser Replacement") and then check the dwell angle with a dwell meter. Compare the reading on the meter with that listed in the "Tune-Up Specifications" chart and adjust as necessary. If the dwell angle is less than the specified minimum, check for misaligned points or worn distributor cam lobes. Accelerate the engine to 1,750 rpm and check for dwell variation. If the dwell angle changed more

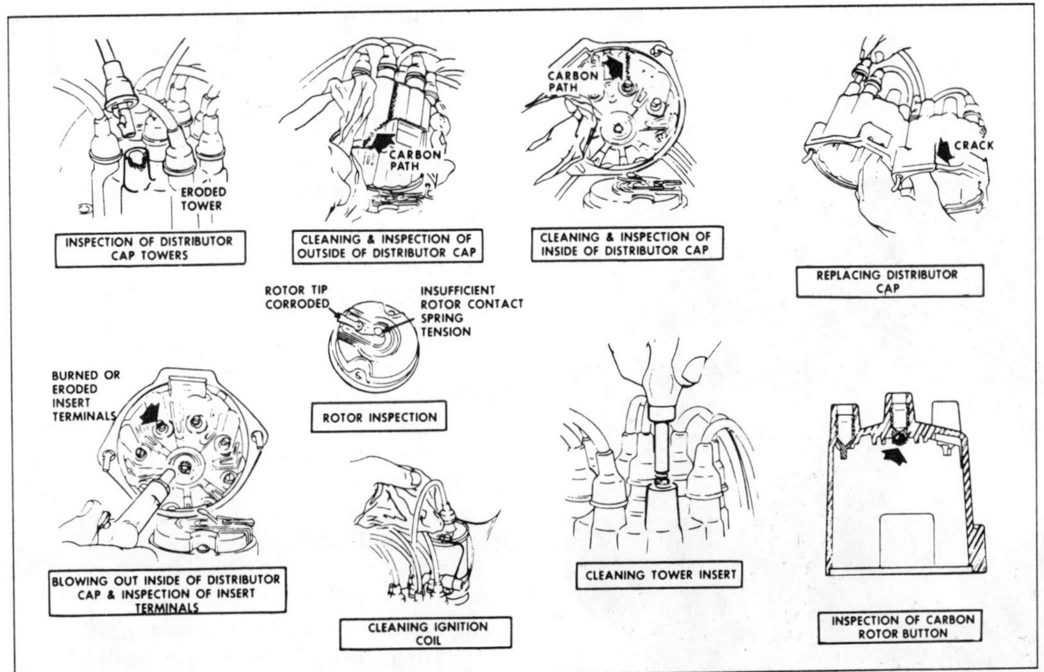

Distributor cap and rotor checkpoints

than three degrees from idle to 1,750 rpm, then check for a worn distributor shaft, shaft bushing, or a loose breaker plate.

IMPORTANT: *After changing the dwell angle, it will be necessary to set the ignition timing. Changing the dwell changes the ignition timing although changing timing does not affect the dwell angle. Therefore, when performing both settings, dwell angle adjustment must be done before timing.*

V8

1. Run the engine to normal operating temperatures and then let it idle.

2. Raise the adjusting window on the distributor cap and insert a ⅛ in. allen wrench into the adjusting screw.

3. Turn the adjusting screw until the specified dwell angle is obtained on the dwell meter.

IGNITION TIMING

Adjustment

1. Disconnect and plug the distributor vacuum advance hose.

2. Start the engine and run it at idle speed.

3. Connect the timing light and, with the engine running at an idle, aim it at the timing tab on the front engine cover.

NOTE: *It may be necessary to clean off the tab and slash mark on the crankshaft pulley before proceeding*

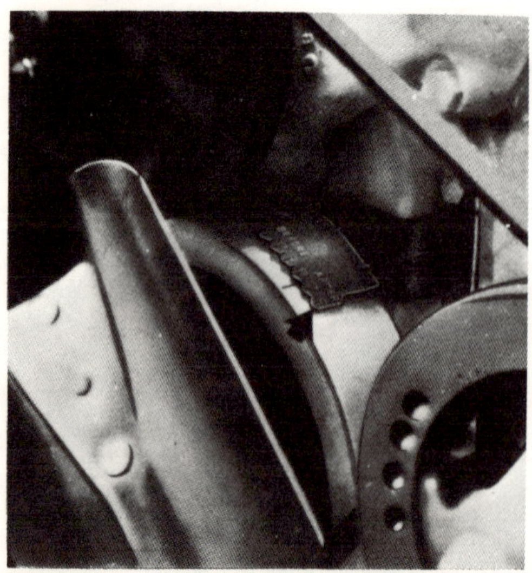

Timing marks (late model V8 shown)

any further. To further improve visibility, take a piece of chalk and fill in the slash mark on the cranskshaft pulley. The "0" marking on the tab is TDC and all the BTDC (before top dead center) settings are on the "before" (advance) side of the "0" or the "A" (advance) side of the "0." Later models are marked to indicate Before and After.

4. Loosen the distributor clamp bolt and turn the distributor until the slash on the crankshaft pulley lines up with the specified timing mark on the tab. Once the timing is correct, tighten the distributor clamp bolt and recheck the timing.

5. Turn off the engine, remove the timing light, and connect the vaccuum advance hose.

CARBURETOR

Idle mixture and speed adjustments are critical aspects of exhaust emission control. It is important that all tune-up instructions be carefully followed to ensure satisfactory engine performance and minimum exhaust pollution. The different combinations of emission systems application on the different engine models have resulted in a great variety of tune-up specifications. See the Tune-Up Specifications at the beginning of this section. Beginning in 1968, all models have a decal conspicuously placed in the engine compartment giving tune-up specifications.

When adjusting a carburetor with two idle mixture screws, adjust them alternately and evenly, unless otherwise stated.

Idle Speed and Mixture Adjustment

See Chapter 4 for illustrations and adjustment specifications of Carter and Rochester carburetors. In the following adjustment procedures the term "lean roll" means turning the mixture adjusting screws in (clockwise) from optimum setting to obtain an obvious drop in engine speed (usually 20 rpm).

ALL 1968–69

Adjust with air cleaner installed.

1. Turn the idle mixture screw/s in until lightly seated, then back out 3 turns.

2. With engine at operating tempera-

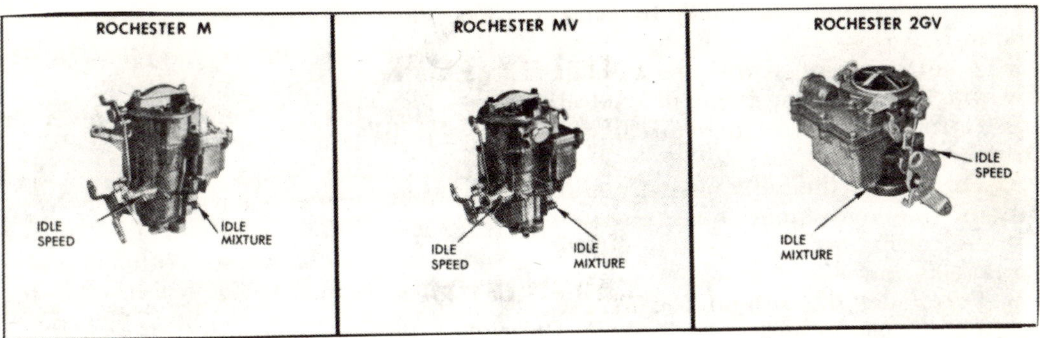

1968–70 one and two-barrel carburetor adjustment screw location

ture, adjust idle speed screw to obtain specified rpm, manual transmission in Neutral and automatic in Drive.

NOTE: *On all 1968 models except L6 with automatic transmission, the air conditioner is turned* off. *On the above-mentioned vehicles the air conditioner is left on. On 1969 models, turn the air conditioner either on or off according to the instructions on the tune-up decal.*

3. Adjust one idle mixture screw to obtain the highest steady idle speed.

4. Adjust the idle speed screw to the speed specified on the tune-up decal.

NOTE: *On models equipped with an idle solenoid, adjust the solenoid plunger hex to obtain 500 rpm on the L6 engine and 600 rpm on V8 engines. Disconnect the wire at the solenoid to de-energize it, allowing the throttle lever to contact the carburetor idle speed screw. Adjust the carburetor idle screw to obtain 400 rpm.*

5. Adjust the mixture screw in to "lean roll" position, then back out (rich) ¼ turn.

6. Repeat Steps 3, 4 and 5 for the other idle mixture screw for 2-bbl. and 4-bbl. engines.

7. Readjust the idle speed screw to obtain final specified rpm, if necessary.

1970

Adjust with air cleaner installed.

If the vehicle is equipped with Evaporative Emission, disconnect the fuel tank line from the vapor canister while making the idle speed and mixture adjustments. Warm up the engine and leave it running with the choke and, if applicable, air cleaner damper door fully open and the air conditioning off.

250 Engine

1. Disconnect and plug the distributor vacuum hose at the distributor end.

2. Turn the idle mixture screw in until it lightly contacts the seat, back it out 4 turns.

3. Adjust the solenoid plunger to obtain 830 rpm (manual transmission in

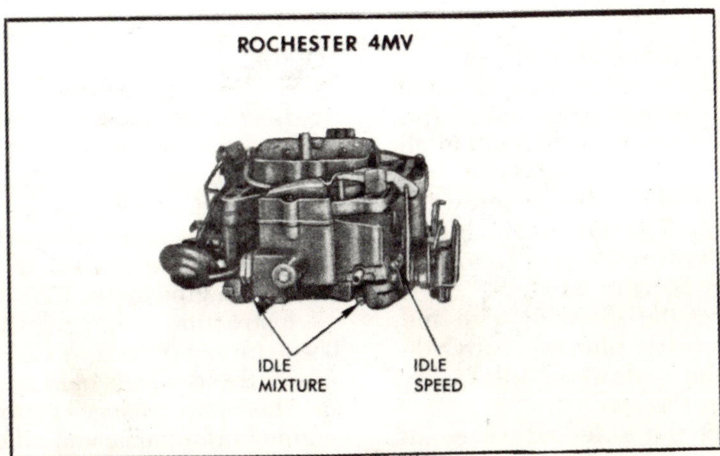

1968–70 four-barrel carburetor adjustment screw location

Neutral) or 630 rpm (automatic transmission in Drive).

4. Adjust mixture screw in to obtain 750 rpm (manual transmission in Neutral) or 600 rpm (automatic transmission in Drive).

5. Disconnect the solenoid wire and, with the solenoid plunger depressed, adjust the carburetor idle speed screw to obtain 400 rpm.

6. Reconnect the solenoid wire and distributor vacuum hose.

400 (265 H.P.) Engine

1. Disconnect and plug the distributor vacuum hose at the distributor end.

2. Turn the idle mixture screws in until they lightly contact the seats, then back them out 4 turns.

3. With manual transmission in Neutral, adjust the carburetor idle speed screw to obtain 800 rpm. With automatic transmission in Drive, adjust the solenoid plunger to obtain 630 rpm.

4. Adjust the idle mixture screws in equally to obtain 700 rpm (manual transmission in Neutral) or 600 rpm (automatic transmission in Drive).

5. If equipped with automatic transmission, disconnect the solenoid wire and, with solenoid plunger depressed, set the carburetor idle speed screw to obtain 450 rpm.

6. Reconnect the solenoid wire and the distributor vacuum hose.

350 (250 H.P.) Engine

1. Disconnect and plug the distributor vacuum hose at the distributor end.

2. Turn the idle mixture screws in until they lightly contact the seats, then back them out 4 turns.

3. With manual transmission in Neutral, adjust the solenoid plunger to obtain 830 rpm. With automatic transmission in Drive, adjust the solenoid plunger to obtain 630 rpm.

4. Adjust the idle mixture screws in equally to obtain 750 rpm (manual transmission in Neutral) or 600 rpm (automatic transmission in Drive).

5. Disconnect the solenoid wire and, with the solenoid plunger fully depressed, set the carburetor idle speed screw to obtain 450 rpm.

6. Reconnect the solenoid wire and distributor vacuum hose.

350 (300 H.P.) Engine

1. Disconnect the vacuum hose at the distributor and plug the hose.

2. Turn the idle mixture screws in until they lightly contact the seats, then back them out 4 turns.

3. With manual transmission in Neutral, adjust the carburetor idle speed screw to obtain 775 rpm. With automatic transmission in Drive, adjust the carburetor idle speed screw to obtain 630 rpm.

4. Adjust the mixture screws in equally to obtain 700 rpm (manual transmission in Neutral) or 600 rpm (automatic transmission in Drive).

5. Reconnect the distributor vacuum hose.

454 (345 H.P.) and
454 (390 H.P.) Engines

1. Disconnect the distributor vacuum hose at the distributor and plug the hose.

2. Turn the idle mixture screws in until they are lightly seated, then back them out 4 turns.

3. With automatic transmission in Drive, adjust the carburetor idle speed screw to obtain 630 rpm. Adjust the idle mixture screws in equally to obtain 600 rpm.

4. With manual transmission in Neutral, adjust the carburetor idle speed screw to obtain 700 rpm. Turn one of the mixture screws in until the engine speed drops to 400 rpm. Readjust the idle speed screw to obtain 700 rpm. Turn in the other mixture screw until the engine speed drops 40 rpm. Readjust the idle speed screw to obtain 700 rpm.

5. Reconnect the distributor vacuum hose.

1971—Initial Adjustments

Adjust with air cleaner installed.

The following initial idle adjustments are part of the normal engine tune-up. There is a tune-up decal placed conspicuously in the engine compartment outlining the specific procedure and settings for each engine application. Follow all of the instructions when adjusting the idle. These tuning procedures are necessary to obtain the delicate balance of variables for the maintenance of both reliable engine performance and efficient exhaust emission control.

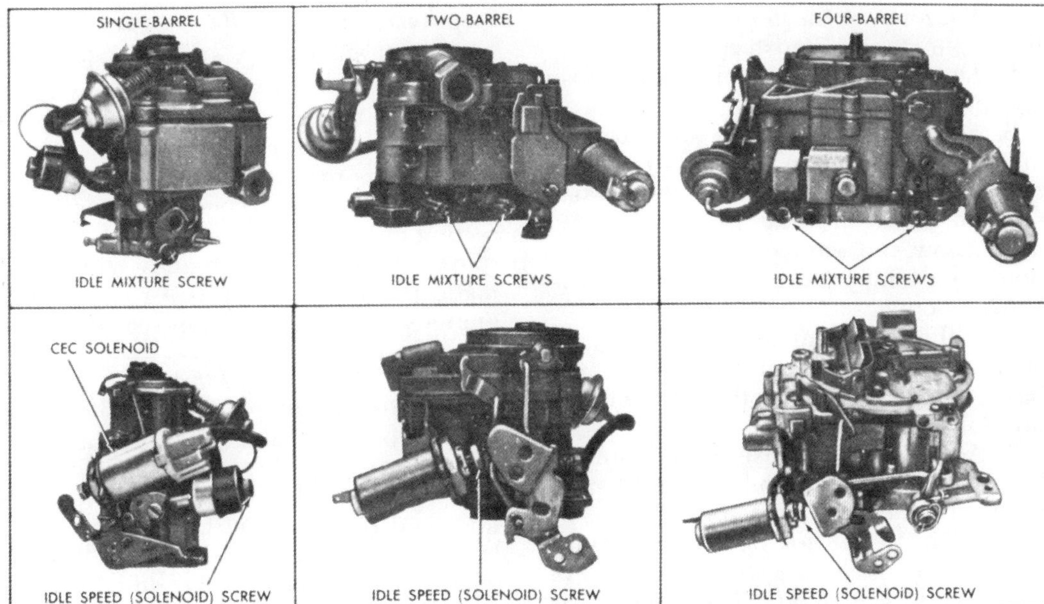

1971–75 carburetor adjustment screw locations

NOTE: *All engines have limiter caps on the mixture adjusting screws. The idle mixture is preset and the limiter caps installed at the factory in order to meet emission control standards. Do not remove these limiter caps unless all other possible causes of poor idle condition have been thoroughly checked out. The solenoid used on 1971 carburetors is different from the one used on earlier models. Combination Emission Control System (C.E.C. solenoid) valve regulates distributor vacuum as a function of transmission gear position.*

CAUTION: *The C.E.C. solenoid is adjusted only after: 1) replacement of the solenoid, 2) major carburetor overhaul, or 3) after the throttle body is removed or replaced.*

All initial adjustments described below are made:

1. With the engine warmed up and running.

2. With the choke fully open.

3. With the fuel tank line disconnected from the Evaporative Emission canister on all models.

4. With the vacuum hose disconnected at the distributor and plugged.

Be sure to reconnect the distributor vacuum hose and to connect the fuel tank to evaporative emission canister line or install the gas cap when idle adjustments are complete.

250 6-Cylinder Engine

Adjust the carburetor idle speed screw (NOT the solenoid plunger) to obtain 550 rpm (manual transmission in Neutral) or 500 rpm (automatic transmission in Drive).

350 and 400 (2-BBL) and 350 (4-BBL Quadrajet) Engines

Adjust the carburetor idle speed screw (NOT the solenoid plunger) to obtain 600 rpm (manual transmission in Neutral with the air conditioner off) or 550 rpm (automatic transmission in Drive with the air conditioner on).

402 and 454 (4-BBL Quadrajet) Engines

Turn the air conditioner off. Adjust the carburetor idle speed screw (NOT the solenoid plunger) to obtain 600 rpm (manual transmission in Neutral or automatic transmission in Drive).

1972

NOTE: *All carburetors are equipped with idle limiter caps and idle mixture is preset at the factory and should not require adjustment:*

1. Disconnect the fuel tank line from the vapor storage canister.

2. Detach the distributor vacuum hose and plug the hose.

3. Set the parking brake and turn the air conditioner (if so equipped) off. On cars equipped with an automatic transmission, chock the wheels.

4. Allow the engine to reach normal operating temperature. Be sure that the choke is open.

5. If the car has an automatic transmission, set the selector in Drive. If the car has a manual transmission keep the transmission in Neutral.

6. Adjust the anti-dieseling solenoid to the *higher* of the two rpm figures given in the specifications.

CAUTION: *Do not turn the solenoid more than one complete turn unless the electrical lead is disconnected (solenoid de-energized).*

7. Disconnect the solenoid lead and set the idle speed to the *lower* of the two figures given in the specifications. Use an allen wrench in the end of the solenoid for this adjustment, on six cylinder engines. On V8's use the normal idle speed adjusting screw.

NOTE: *If no lower figure is given, adjust the idle to 450 rpm.*

8. Reconnect all of the wires and hoses which were disconnected in order to perform these adjustments.

1973

All models are equipped with idle limiter caps and idle solenoids. Disconnect the fuel tank line from the evaporative canister. The engine must be running at operating temperature, choke off, parking brake on, and rear wheels blocked. Disconnect the distributor vacuum hose and plug it. After adjustment, reconnect the vacuum and evaporative hoses.

250 cu in. Six-Cylinder

Adjust the idle stop solenoid for 700 rpm on manual transmission models or 600 rpm on automatics. On manual models, make no attempt to adjust the CEC solenoid (the larger of the two carburetor solenoids) or a decrease in engine braking could result.

Two-barrel 350 and 400 cu in. V8s

1. With air conditioning switched off, adjust the idle stop solenoid screw for a speed of 900 rpm on manual models; 600 rpm on automatics.

2. De-energize the idle stop solenoid and adjust the idle speed screw (screw resting on lower step of the cam) for 400 rpm on 350 and 400 engines with automatic transmission, or 500 rpm on 350 engines with manual transmission.

Four-barrel and 350 and 454 cu in. V8s

1. Adjust the idle stop solenoid screw for 900 rpm on manual, 600 rpm on automatic.

2. Connect the distributor vacuum hose and postition the fast idle cam follower on the top step of the fast idle cam (turn air conditioning off) and adjust the fast idle to 1300 rpm on manual transmission 350 engines; 1600 on manual 454 engines and all automatics (in Park).

1974

The same preconditions as for 1973 apply.

Two-barrel 350 and 400 cu in. V8s

1. Turn the air conditioning off. Adjust the idle stop solenoid screw for 900 rpm on manual; 600 rpm on automatic (in Drive).

2. De-energize the solenoid and adjust the carburetor idle cam screw (on low step of cam) for 400 rpm on automatic models (in Drive); 500 rpm on 350 engines with manual transmission.

Four-barrel 350 and 400 cu in. V8s

1. Turn the air conditioning off. Adjust the idle stop solenoid screw for 900 rpm on manual transmission models; 600 rpm on automatic (in Drive).

2. Connect the distributor vacuum hose. Position the fast idle cam follower on the top step of the fast idle cam and adjust the fast idle speed to 1300 rpm on manual; 1600 on automatic (in Park).

454 cu in. V8

1. Shut off the air conditioning. Adjust the idle stop solenoid screw for 800 rpm on manual; 600 rpm on automatic (in Drive).

2. Connect the distributor vacuum hose and position the fast idle cam follower on the top step of the cam and adjust the fast idle to 1600 rpm on manual; 1500 rpm on automatic (in Park).

1975

Two-barrel Carburetor

1. Idle speed is adjusted with the engine at normal operating temperature, air cleaner on, choke open, and air conditioning off. Hook up a tachometer to the engine.
2. Block the rear wheels and apply the parking brake.
3. Disconnect the fuel tank hose from the evaporative canister.
4. Disconnect and plug the distributor vacuum advance hose.
5. Start the engine and check the ignition timing. Adjust if necessary. Reconnect the vacuum hose.
6. Adjust the idle speed screw to the specified rpm. If the figures given in the "Tune-Up Specifications" chart differ from those on the tune-up decal, those on the decal take precedence. The transmission should be in Drive.
CAUTION: *Make doubly sure that the rear wheels are blocked and the parking brake applied.*
7. Shut off engine, reconnect hose to evaporative canister, and remove blocks from wheels.

Four-barrel Carburetor

Four-barrel carburetors are equipped with idle stop solenoids. There are two idle speeds, one with the solenoid energized and a second with the solenoid de-energized. Both are set with the solenoid. The slower speed (solenoid de-energized) is necessary to prevent dieseling by allowing the throttle plates to close further than at a normal idle speed.

1. Idle speed is set with the engine at normal operating temperature, air cleaner on, choke open, and air conditioning off. Hook up a tachometer to the engine.
2. Block the rear wheels and apply the parking brake.
3. Disconnect the fuel tank hose from the evaporative canister.

4. Disconnect and plug the distributor vacuum advance hose.
5. Start the engine and check the ignition timing. Adjust if necessary. Reconnect the vacuum hose.
6. Disconnect the electrical connector at the idle solenoid.
7. Set the transmission in Drive. Adjust the low idle speed screw for the lower of the two figures given for idle speed.
CAUTION: *Make sure that the drive wheels are blocked and the parking brake is applied.*
8. Reconnect the idle solenoid and open the throttle slightly to extend the solenoid plunger.
9. Turn the solenoid plunger screw in or out to obtain the higher of the two idle speed figures (this is normal curb-idle).
10. Shut off engine, remove blocks from drive wheels, and reconnect hose to evaporative canister.

1976

Adjust the two-barrel carburetor using the same procedure as 1975.

Four-barrel Carburetor

1. Connect a tachometer to the engine. Idle speed is set with the engine at normal operating temperature, air cleaner on, choke open, and air conditioning off.
2. Apply the parking brake and block the rear wheels.
3. Disconnect the fuel tank hose from the vapor canister.
4. Disconnect and plug the vacuum advance hose from the distributor. Check ignition timing and correct if necessary.
5. Remove plug and connect vacuum hose.
6. Adjust the idle speed screw for the correct idle speed. The transmission should be in Drive. Be sure that the brake is on and rear wheels blocked before adjusting.
7. Shut engine off and connect vapor hose.

1976–77

The engine must be at normal operating temperature with the air cleaner on, the choke open, the air conditioner off, and the timing correctly set.

1. Set the brake and block the wheels.

2. Set the automatic transmission in Drive and the manual in neutral. Disconnect the fuel tank hose from the vapor canister in the engine compartment.

3. Use needle nose pliers to break off the mixture screw cap or caps.

1 bbl

4. Adjust the idle speed by turning the solenoid in or out to obtain the higher of the two speeds listed on the sticker. Disconnect the electrical connector from the solenoid and turn the ⅛ in. allen screw in the end of the solenoid body to lower the idle speed to the second figure on the sticker.

2 bbl and 4 bbl

Adjust the idle speed with the idle speed screw to obtain the higher idle speed shown on the sticker. On the 1977 4-bbl, disconnect the electrical connector at the idle solenoid, and adjust the idle speed to the lower of the two figures given on the sticker. Reconnect the electrical connector, open the throttle to extend the solenoid plunger, then turn the solenoid plunger screw to obtain the higher of the two idle speed figures. If the procedure listed here for the 1977 4-bbl differs from the one on the engine tune-up sticker, use the sticker procedure.

5. On all but the 2 bbl, turn out the mixture screws until the highest possible idle speed is reached. If the idle speed becomes excessive (more than that set in Step 4), reset the idle speed to that set in Step 4. On the 2 bbl, turn out the mixture screws to obtain the highest idle and then, turn in the mixture screws to obtain the lower of the two figures listed on the sticker.

6. Turn in the mixture screws equally until the normal idle speed is reached.

7. Replace the vapor canister hose.

Engine tune-up is a procedure performed to restore engine performance, deteriorated due to normal wear and loss of adjustment. The three major areas considered in a routine tune-up are compression, ignition, and carburetion, although valve adjustment may be included.

A tune-up is performed in three steps: *analysis*, in which it is determined whether normal wear is responsible for performance loss, and which parts require replacement or service; *parts replacement or service*; and *adjustment*, in which engine adjustments are returned to original specifications. Since the advent of emission control equipment, precision adjustment has become increasingly critical, in order to maintain pollutant emission levels.

Analysis

The procedures below are used to indicate where adjustments, parts service or replacement are necessary within the realm of a normal tune-up. If, following these tests, all systems appear to be functioning properly, proceed to the Troubleshooting Section for further diagnosis.

—Remove all spark plugs, noting the cylinder in which they were installed. Remove the air cleaner, and position the throttle and choke in the full open position. Disconnect the coil high tension lead from the coil and the distributor cap. Insert a compression gauge into the spark plug port of each cylinder, in succession, and crank the engine with

Maxi. Press. Lbs. Sq. In.	Min. Press. Lbs. Sq. In.	Max. Press. Lbs. Sq. In.	Min. Press. Lbs. Sq. In.
134	101	188	141
136	102	190	142
138	104	192	144
140	105	194	145
142	107	196	147
146	110	198	148
148	111	200	150
150	113	202	151
152	114	204	153
154	115	206	154
156	117	208	156
158	118	210	157
160	120	212	158
162	121	214	160
164	123	216	162
166	124	218	163
168	126	220	165
170	127	222	166
172	129	224	168
174	131	226	169
176	132	228	171
178	133	230	172
180	135	232	174
182	136	234	175
184	138	236	177
186	140	238	178

Compression pressure limits
© Buick Div. G.M. Corp.)

the starter to obtain the highest possible reading. Record the readings, and compare the highest to the lowest on the compression pressure limit chart. If the difference exceeds the limits on the chart, or if all readings are excessively low, proceed to a wet compression check (see Troubleshooting Section).

—Evaluate the spark plugs according to the spark plug chart

in the Troubleshooting Section, and proceed as indicated in the chart.

—Remove the distributor cap, and inspect it inside and out for cracks and/or carbon tracks, and inside for excessive wear or burning of the rotor contacts. If any of these faults are evident, the cap must be replaced.

—Check the breaker points for burning, pitting or wear, and the contact heel resting on the distributor cam for excessive wear. If defects are noted, replace the entire breaker point set.

—Remove and inspect the rotor. If the contacts are burned or worn, or if the rotor is excessively loose on the distributor shaft (where applicable), the rotor must be replaced.

—Inspect the spark plug leads and the coil high tension lead for cracks or brittleness. If any of the wires appear defective, the entire set should be replaced.

—Check the air filter to ensure that it is functioning properly.

Parts Replacement and Service

The determination of whether to replace or service parts is at the mechanic's discretion; however, it is suggested that any parts in questionable condition be replaced rather than reused.

—Clean and regap, or replace, the spark plugs as needed. Lightly coat the threads with engine oil and install the plugs. CAUTION: *Do not over-torque taper-seat spark plugs, or plugs being installed in aluminum cylinder heads.*

—If the distributor cap is to be reused, clean the inside with a dry rag, and remove corrosion from the rotor contact points with fine emery cloth. Remove the spark plug wires one by one, and clean the wire ends and the inside of the towers. If the boots are loose, they should be replaced.

If the cap is to be replaced, transfer the wires one by one, cleaning the wire ends and replacing the boots if necessary.

—If the original points are to remain in service, clean them lightly with emery cloth, lubricate the contact heel with grease specifically designed for this purpose. Rotate the crankshaft until the heel rests on a high point of the distributor cam, and adjust the point gap to specifications.

When replacing the points, remove the original points and condenser, and wipe out the inside of the distributor housing with a clean, dry rag. Lightly lubricate the contact heel and pivot point, and install the points and condenser. Rotate the crankshaft until the heel rests on a high point of the distributor cam, and adjust the point gap to specifications. NOTE: *Always replace the condenser when changing the points.*

—If the rotor is to be reused, clean the contacts with solvent. Do not alter the spring tension of the rotor center contact. Install the rotor and the distributor cap.

—Replace the coil high tension lead and/or the spark plug leads as necessary.

—Clean the carburetor using a spray solvent (e.g., Gumout Spray). Remove the varnish from the throttle bores, and clean the linkage. Disconnect and plug the fuel line, and run the engine until it runs out of fuel. Partially fill the float chamber with solvent, and reconnect the fuel line. In extreme cases, the jets can be pressure flushed by inserting a rubber plug into the float vent, running the spray nozzle through it, and spraying the solvent until it squirts out of the venturi fuel dump.

—Clean and tighten all wiring connections in the primary electrical circuit.

Additional Services

The following services *should* be performed in conjunction with a routine tune-up to ensure efficient performance.

—Inspect the battery and fill to the proper level with distilled water. Remove the cable clamps, clean clamps and posts thoroughly, coat the posts lightly with petroleum jelly, reinstall and tighten.

—Inspect all belts, replace and/or adjust as necessary.

—Test the PCV valve (if so equipped), and clean or replace as indicated. Clean all crankcase ventilation hoses, or replace if cracked or hardened.

—Adjust the valves (if necessary) to manufacturer's specifications.

Adjustments

—Connect a dwell-tachometer between the distributor primary lead and ground. Remove the distributor cap and rotor (unless equipped with Delco externally adjustable distributor). With the ignition off, crank the engine with a remote starter switch and measure the point dwell angle. Adjust the dwell angle to specifications. NOTE: *Increasing the gap decreases the dwell angle and*

vice-versa. Install the rotor and distributor cap.

—Connect a timing light according to the manufacturer's specifications. Identify the proper timing marks with chalk or paint. NOTE: *Luminescent (day-glo) paint is excellent for this purpose.* Start the engine, and run it until it reaches operating temperature. Disconnect and plug any distributor vacuum lines, and adjust idle to the speed required to adjust timing, according to specifications. Loosen the distributor clamp and adjust timing to specifications by rotating the distributor in the engine. NOTE: *To advance timing, rotate distributor opposite normal direction of rotor rotation, and vice-versa.*

—Synchronize the throttles and mixture of multiple carburetors (if so equipped) according to procedures given in the individual car sections.

—Adjust the idle speed, mixture, and idle quality, as specified in the car sections. Final idle adjustments should be made with the air cleaner installed. CAUTION: *Due to strict emission control requirements on 1969 and later models, special test equipment (CO meter, SUN Tester) may be necessary to properly adjust idle mixture to specifications.*

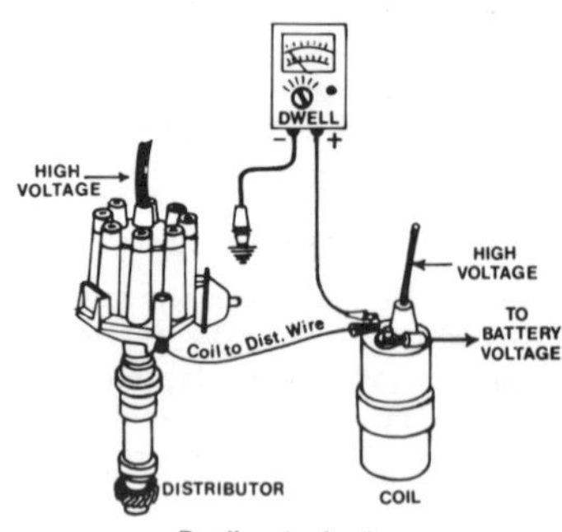

Dwell meter hook-up

The following section is designed to aid in the rapid diagnosis of engine problems. The systematic format is used to diagnose problems ranging from engine starting difficulties to the need for engine overhaul. It is assumed that the user is equipped with basic hand tools and test equipment (tach-dwell meter, timing light, voltmeter, and ohmmeter).

Troubleshooting is divided into two sections. The first, *General Diagnosis*, is used to locate the problem area. In the second, *Specific Diagnosis*, the problem is systematically evaluated.

General Diagnosis

PROBLEM: Symptom	*Begin diagnosis at Section Two, Number* ———
Engine won't start:	
Starter doesn't turn	1.1, 2.1
Starter turns, engine doesn't	2.1
Starter turns engine very slowly	1.1, 2.4
Starter turns engine normally	3.1, 4.1
Starter turns engine very quickly	6.1
Engine fires intermittently	4.1
Engine fires consistently	5.1, 6.1
Engine runs poorly:	
Hard starting	3.1, 4.1, 5.1, 8.1
Rough idle	4.1, 5.1, 8.1
Stalling	3.1, 4.1, 5.1, 8.1
Engine dies at high speeds	4.1, 5.1
Hesitation (on acceleration from standing stop)	5.1, 8.1
Poor pickup	4.1, 5.1, 8.1
Lack of power	3.1, 4.1, 5.1, 8.1
Backfire through the carburetor	4.1, 8.1, 9.1
Backfire through the exhaust	4.1, 8.1, 9.1
Blue exhaust gases	6.1, 7.1
Black exhaust gases	5.1
Running on (after the ignition is shut off)	3.1, 8.1
Susceptible to moisture	4.1
Engine misfires under load	4.1, 7.1, 8.4, 9.1
Engine misfires at speed	4.1, 8.4
Engine misfires at idle	3.1, 4.1, 5.1, 7.1, 8.4

PROBLEM: Symptom	*Probable Cause*
Engine noises: ①	
Metallic grind while starting	Starter drive not engaging completely
Constant grind or rumble	*Starter drive not releasing, worn main bearings
Constant knock	Worn connecting rod bearings
Knock under load	Fuel octane too low, worn connecting rod bearings
Double knock	Loose piston pin
Metallic tap	*Collapsed or sticky valve lifter, excessive valve clearance, excessive end play in a rotating shaft
Scrape	*Fan belt contacting a stationary surface
Tick while starting	S.U. electric fuel pump (normal), starter brushes
Constant tick	*Generator brushes, shreaded fan belt
Squeal	*Improperly tensioned fan belt
Hiss or roar	*Steam escaping through a leak in the cooling system or the radiator overflow vent
Whistle	*Vacuum leak
Wheeze	Loose or cracked spark plug

①—It is extremely difficult to evaluate vehicle noises. While the above are general definitions of engine noises, those starred (*) should be considered as possibly originating elsewhere in the car. To aid diagnosis, the following list considers other potential sources of these sounds.

Metallic grind:
Throwout bearing; transmission gears, bearings, or synchronizers; differential bearings, gears; something metallic in contact with brake drum or disc.

Metallic tap:
U-joints; fan-to-radiator (or shroud) contact.

Scrape:
Brake shoe or pad dragging; tire to body contact; suspension contacting undercarriage or exhaust; something non-metallic contacting brake shoe or drum.

Tick:
Transmission gears; differential gears; lack of radio suppression; resonant vibration of body panels; windshield wiper motor or transmission; heater motor and blower.

Squeal:
Brake shoe or pad not fully releasing; tires (excessive wear, uneven wear, improper inflation); front or rear wheel alignment (most commonly due to improper toe-in).

Hiss or whistle:
Wind leaks (body or window); heater motor and blower fan.

Roar:
Wheel bearings; wind leaks (body and window).

Specific Diagnosis

This section is arranged so that following each test, instructions are given to proceed to another, until a problem is diagnosed.

INDEX

Group		Topic
1	*	Battery
2	*	Cranking system
3	*	Primary electrical system
4	*	Secondary electrical system
5	*	Fuel system
6	*	Engine compression
7	**	Engine vacuum
8	**	Secondary electrical system
9	**	Valve train
10	**	Exhaust system
11	**	Cooling system
12	**	Engine lubrication

*—The engine need not be running.
**—The engine must be running.

SAMPLE SECTION

Test and Procedure	Results and Indications	Proceed to
4.1—Check for spark: Hold each spark plug wire approximately ¼″ from ground with gloves or a heavy, dry rag. Crank the engine and observe the spark.	→ If no spark is evident:	4.2
	→ If spark is good in some cases:	4.3
	→ If spark is good in all cases:	4.6

DIAGNOSIS

1.1—Inspect the battery visually for case condition (corrosion, cracks) and water level.	If case is cracked, replace battery:	1.4
	If the case is intact, remove corrosion with a solution of baking soda and water (CAUTION: *do not get the solution into the battery*), and fill with water:	1.2
1.2—Check the battery cable connections: Insert a screwdriver between the battery post and the cable clamp. Turn the headlights on high beam, and observe them as the screwdriver is gently twisted to ensure good metal to metal contact.	If the lights brighten, remove and clean the clamp and post; coat the post with petroleum jelly, install and tighten the clamp:	1.4
	If no improvement is noted:	1.3

Testing battery cable connections using a screwdriver

1.3—Test the state of charge of the battery using an individual cell tester or hydrometer.		If indicated, charge the battery. NOTE: *If no obvious reason exists for the low state of charge (i.e., battery age, prolonged storage), the charging system should be tested:*	1.4

Spec. Grav. Reading	Charged Condition
1.260-1.280	Fully Charged
1.230-1.250	Three Quarter Charged
1.200-1.220	One Half Charged
1.170-1.190	One Quarter Charged
1.140-1.160	Just About Flat
1.110-1.130	All The Way Down

State of battery charge

The effect of temperature on the specific gravity of battery electrolyte

Test and Procedure	Results and Indications	Proceed to
1.4—Visually inspect battery cables for cracking, bad connection to ground, or bad connection to starter.	If necessary, tighten connections or replace the cables:	2.1

Tests in Group 2 are performed with coil high tension lead disconnected to prevent accidental starting.

Test and Procedure	Results and Indications	Proceed to
2.1—Test the starter motor and solenoid: Connect a jumper from the battery post of the solenoid (or relay) to the starter post of the solenoid (or relay).	If starter turns the engine normally:	2.2
	If the starter buzzes, or turns the engine very slowly:	2.4
	If no response, replace the solenoid (or relay).	3.1
	If the starter turns, but the engine doesn't, ensure that the flywheel ring gear is intact. If the gear is undamaged, replace the starter drive.	3.1
2.2—Determine whether ignition override switches are functioning properly (clutch start switch, neutral safety switch), by connecting a jumper across the switch(es), and turning the ignition switch to "start".	If starter operates, adjust or replace switch:	3.1
	If the starter doesn't operate:	2.3
2.3—Check the ignition switch "start" position: Connect a 12V test lamp between the starter post of the solenoid (or relay) and ground. Turn the ignition switch to the "start" position, and jiggle the key.	If the lamp doesn't light when the switch is turned, check the ignition switch for loose connections, cracked insulation, or broken wires. Repair or replace as necessary:	3.1
	If the lamp flickers when the key is jiggled, replace the ignition switch.	3.3

Checking the ignition switch "start" position

Test and Procedure	Results and Indications	Proceed to
2.4—Remove and bench test the starter, according to specifications in the car section.	If the starter does not meet specifications, repair or replace as needed:	3.1
	If the starter is operating properly:	2.5
2.5—Determine whether the engine can turn freely: Remove the spark plugs, and check for water in the cylinders. Check for water on the dipstick, or oil in the radiator. Attempt to turn the engine using an 18″ flex drive and socket on the crankshaft pulley nut or bolt.	If the engine will turn freely only with the spark plugs out, and hydrostatic lock (water in the cylinders) is ruled out, check valve timing:	9.2
	If engine will not turn freely, and it is known that the clutch and transmission are free, the engine must be disassembled for further evaluation:	Next Chapter

Tests and Procedures	*Results and Indications*	*Proceed to*
3.1—Check the ignition switch "on" position: Connect a jumper wire between the distributor side of the coil and ground, and a 12V test lamp between the switch side of the coil and ground. Remove the high tension lead from the coil. Turn the ignition switch on and jiggle the key.	If the lamp lights:	3.2
	If the lamp flickers when the key is jiggled, replace the ignition switch:	3.3
	If the lamp doesn't light, check for loose or open connections. If none are found, remove the ignition switch and check for continuity. If the switch is faulty, replace it:	3.3

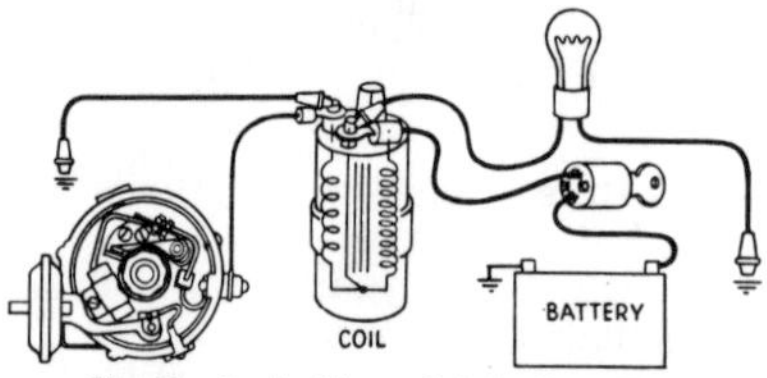

Checking the ignition switch "on" position

3.2—Check the ballast resistor or resistance wire for an open circuit, using an ohmmeter.	Replace the resistor or the resistance wire if the resistance is zero.	3.3
3.3—Visually inspect the breaker points for burning, pitting, or excessive wear. Gray coloring of the point contact surfaces is normal. Rotate the crankshaft until the contact heel rests on a high point of the distributor cam, and adjust the point gap to specifications.	If the breaker points are intact, clean the contact surfaces with fine emery cloth, and adjust the point gap to specifications. If pitted or worn, replace the points and condenser, and adjust the gap to specifications: NOTE: *Always lubricate the distributor cam according to manufacturer's recommendations when servicing the breaker points.*	3.4
3.4—Connect a dwell meter between the distributor primary lead and ground. Crank the engine and observe the point dwell angle.	If necessary, adjust the point dwell angle: NOTE: *Increasing the point gap decreases the dwell angle, and vice-versa.*	3.6
	If dwell meter shows little or no reading:	3.5

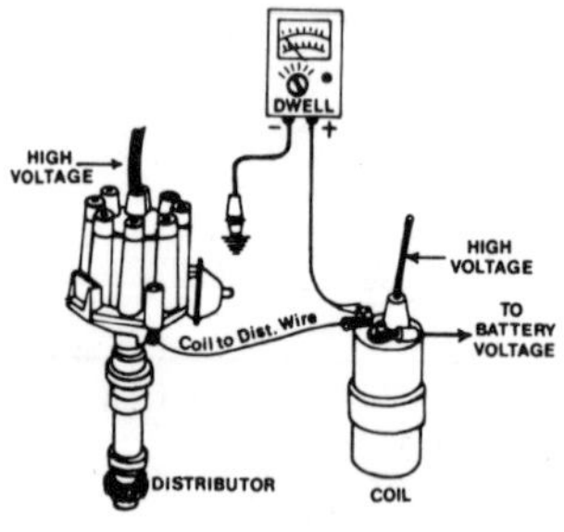

Dwell meter hook-up

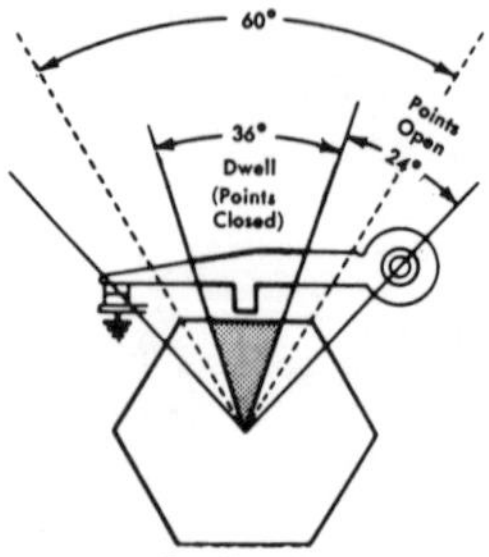

Dwell angle

3.5—Check the condenser for short: Connect an ohmmeter across the condenser body and the pigtail lead.	If any reading other than infinite resistance is noted, replace the condenser:	3.6

Checking the condenser for short

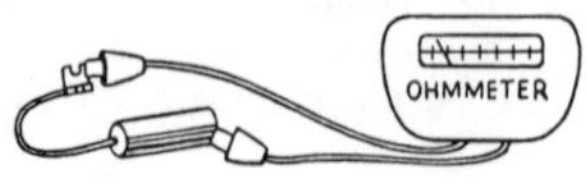

Test and Procedure	*Results and Indications*	*Proceed to*
3.6—Test the coil primary resistance: Connect an ohmmeter across the coil primary terminals, and read the resistance on the low scale. Note whether an external ballast resistor or resistance wire is utilized.	Coils utilizing ballast resistors or resistance wires should have approximately 1.0Ω resistance; coils with internal resistors should have approximately 4.0Ω resistance. If values far from the above are noted, replace the coil:	4.1

Testing the coil primary resistance

Test and Procedure	*Results and Indications*	*Proceed to*
4.1—Check for spark: Hold each spark plug wire approximately $\frac{1}{4}''$ from ground with gloves or a heavy, dry rag. Crank the engine, and observe the spark.	If no spark is evident:	4.2
	If spark is good in some cylinders:	4.3
	If spark is good in all cylinders:	4.6
4.2—Check for spark at the coil high tension lead: Remove the coil high tension lead from the distributor and position it approximately $\frac{1}{4}''$ from ground. Crank the engine and observe spark. CAUTION: *This test should not be performed on cars equipped with transistorized ignition.*	If the spark is good and consistent:	4.3
	If the spark is good but intermittent, test the primary electrical system starting at 3.3:	3.3
	If the spark is weak or non-existent, replace the coil high tension lead, clean and tighten all connections and retest. If no improvement is noted:	4.4
4.3—Visually inspect the distributor cap and rotor for burned or corroded contacts, cracks, carbon tracks, or moisture. Also check the fit of the rotor on the distributor shaft (where applicable).	If moisture is present, dry thoroughly, and retest per 4.1:	4.1
	If burned or excessively corroded contacts, cracks, or carbon tracks are noted, replace the defective part(s) and retest per 4.1:	4.1
	If the rotor and cap appear intact, or are only slightly corroded, clean the contacts thoroughly (including the cap towers and spark plug wire ends) and retest per 4.1:	
	If the spark is good in all cases:	4.6
	If the spark is poor in all cases:	4.5
4.4—Check the coil secondary resistance: Connect an ohmmeter across the distributor side of the coil and the coil tower. Read the resistance on the high scale of the ohmmeter.	The resistance of a satisfactory coil should be between $4K\Omega$ and $10K\Omega$. If the resistance is considerably higher (i.e., $40K\Omega$) replace the coil, and retest per 4.1: NOTE: *This does not apply to high performance coils.*	4.1

Testing the coil secondary resistance

Test and Procedure	Results and Indications	Proceed to
4.5—Visually inspect the spark plug wires for cracking or brittleness. Ensure that no two wires are positioned so as to cause induction firing (adjacent and parallel). Remove each wire, one by one, and check resistance with an ohmmeter.	Replace any cracked or brittle wires. If any of the wires are defective, replace the entire set. Replace any wires with excessive resistance (over 8000Ω per foot for suppression wire), and separate any wires that might cause induction firing.	4.6
4.6—Remove the spark plugs, noting the cylinders from which they were removed, and evaluate according to the chart below.	See below.	See below.

	Condition	Cause	Remedy	Proceed to
	Electrodes eroded, light brown deposits.	Normal wear. Normal wear is indicated by approximately .001″ wear per 1000 miles.	Clean and regap the spark plug if wear is not excessive: Replace the spark plug if excessively worn:	4.7
	Carbon fouling (black, dry, fluffy deposits).	If present on one or two plugs:		
		Faulty high tension lead(s).	Test the high tension leads:	4.5
		Burnt or sticking valve(s).	Check the valve train: (Clean and regap the plugs in either case.)	9.1
		If present on most or all plugs: Overly rich fuel mixture, due to restricted air filter, improper carburetor adjustment, improper choke or heat riser adjustment or operation.	Check the fuel system:	5.1
	Oil fouling (wet black deposits)	Worn engine components. NOTE: *Oil fouling may occur in new or recently rebuilt engines until broken in.*	Check engine vacuum and compression: Replace with new spark plug	6.1
	Lead fouling (gray, black, tan, or yellow deposits, which appear glazed or cinderlike).	Combustion by-products.	Clean and regap the plugs: (Use plugs of a different heat range if the problem recurs.)	4.7

	Condition	Cause	Remedy	Proceed to
	Gap bridging (deposits lodged between the electrodes).	Incomplete combustion, or transfer of deposits from the combustion chamber.	Replace the spark plugs:	4.7
	Overheating (burnt electrodes, and extremely white insulator with small black spots).	Ignition timing advanced too far.	Adjust timing to specifications:	8.2
		Overly lean fuel mixture.	Check the fuel system:	5.1
		Spark plugs not seated properly.	Clean spark plug seat and install a new gasket washer: (Replace the spark plugs in all cases.)	4.7
	Fused spot deposits on the insulator.	Combustion chamber blow-by.	Clean and regap the spark plugs:	4.7
	Pre-ignition (melted or severely burned electrodes, blistered or cracked insulators, or metallic deposits on the insulator).	Incorrect spark plug heat range.	Replace with plugs of the proper heat range:	4.7
		Ignition timing advanced too far.	Adjust timing to specifications:	8.2
		Spark plugs not being cooled efficiently.	Clean the spark plug seat, and check the cooling system:	11.1
		Fuel mixture too lean.	Check the fuel system:	5.1
		Poor compression.	Check compression:	6.1
		Fuel grade too low.	Use higher octane fuel:	4.7

Test and Procedure	Results and Indications	Proceed to
4.7—Determine the static ignition timing: Using the flywheel or crankshaft pulley timing marks as a guide, locate top dead center on the *compression* stroke of the No. 1 cylinder. Remove the distributor cap.	Adjust the distributor so that the rotor points toward the No. 1 tower in the distributor cap, and the points are just opening:	4.8
4.8—Check coil polarity: Connect a voltmeter negative lead to the coil high tension lead, and the positive lead to ground (NOTE: *reverse the hook-up for positive ground cars*). Crank the engine momentarily.	If the voltmeter reads up-scale, the polarity is correct:	5.1
	If the voltmeter reads down-scale, reverse the coil polarity (switch the primary leads):	5.1

Checking coil polarity

Test and Procedure	*Results and Indications*	*Proceed to*
5.1—Determine that the air filter is functioning efficiently: Hold paper elements up to a strong light, and attempt to see light through the filter.	Clean permanent air filters in gasoline (or manufacturer's recommendation), and allow to dry. Replace paper elements through which light cannot be seen:	5.2
5.2—Determine whether a flooding condition exists: Flooding is identified by a strong gasoline odor, and excessive gasoline present in the throttle bore(s) of the carburetor.	If flooding is not evident: If flooding is evident, permit the gasoline to dry for a few moments and restart. If flooding doesn't recur: If flooding is persistant:	5.3 5.6 5.5
5.3—Check that fuel is reaching the carburetor: Detach the fuel line at the carburetor inlet. Hold the end of the line in a cup (not styrofoam), and crank the engine.	If fuel flows smoothly: If fuel doesn't flow (NOTE: *Make sure that there is fuel in the tank*), or flows erratically:	5.6 5.4
5.4—Test the fuel pump: Disconnect all fuel lines from the fuel pump. Hold a finger over the input fitting, crank the engine (with electric pump, turn the ignition or pump on); and feel for suction.	If suction is evident, blow out the fuel line to the tank with low pressure compressed air until bubbling is heard from the fuel filler neck. Also blow out the carburetor fuel line (both ends disconnected): If no suction is evident, replace or repair the fuel pump: NOTE: *Repeated oil fouling of the spark plugs, or a no-start condition, could be the result of a ruptured vacuum booster pump diaphragm, through which oil or gasoline is being drawn into the intake manifold (where applicable).*	5.6 5.6
5.5—Check the needle and seat: Tap the carburetor in the area of the needle and seat.	If flooding stops, a gasoline additive (e.g., Gumout) will often cure the problem: If flooding continues, check the fuel pump for excessive pressure at the carburetor (according to specifications). If the pressure is normal, the needle and seat must be removed and checked, and/or the float level adjusted:	5.6 5.6
5.6—Test the accelerator pump by looking into the throttle bores while operating the throttle.	If the accelerator pump appears to be operating normally: If the accelerator pump is not operating, the pump must be reconditioned. Where possible, service the pump with the carburetor(s) installed on the engine. If necessary, remove the carburetor. Prior to removal:	5.7 5.7
5.7—Determine whether the carburetor main fuel system is functioning: Spray a commercial starting fluid into the carburetor while attempting to start the engine.	If the engine starts, runs for a few seconds, and dies: If the engine doesn't start:	5.8 6.1

Test and Procedures	*Results and Indications*	*Proceed to*
5.8—Uncommon fuel system malfunctions: See below:	If the problem is solved:	6.1
	If the problem remains, remove and recondition the carburetor.	

Condition	*Indication*	*Test*	*Usual Weather Conditions*	*Remedy*
Vapor lock	Car will not restart shortly after running.	Cool the components of the fuel system until the engine starts.	Hot to very hot	Ensure that the exhaust manifold heat control valve is operating. Check with the vehicle manufacturer for the recommended solution to vapor lock on the model in question.
Carburetor icing	Car will not idle, stalls at low speeds.	Visually inspect the throttle plate area of the throttle bores for frost.	High humidity, 32-40° F.	Ensure that the exhaust manifold heat control valve is operating, and that the intake manifold heat riser is not blocked.
Water in the fuel	Engine sputters and stalls; may not start.	Pump a small amount of fuel into a glass jar. Allow to stand, and inspect for droplets or a layer of water.	High humidity, extreme temperature changes.	For droplets, use one or two cans of commercial gas dryer (Dry Gas) For a layer of water, the tank must be drained, and the fuel lines blown out with compressed air.

Test and Procedure	*Results and Indications*	*Proceed to*
6.1—Test engine compression: Remove all spark plugs. Insert a compression gauge into a spark plug port, crank the engine to obtain the maximum reading, and record.	If compression is within limits on all cylinders:	7.1
	If gauge reading is extremely low on all cylinders:	6.2
	If gauge reading is low on one or two cylinders: (If gauge readings are identical and low on two or more adjacent cylinders, the head gasket must be replaced.)	6.2

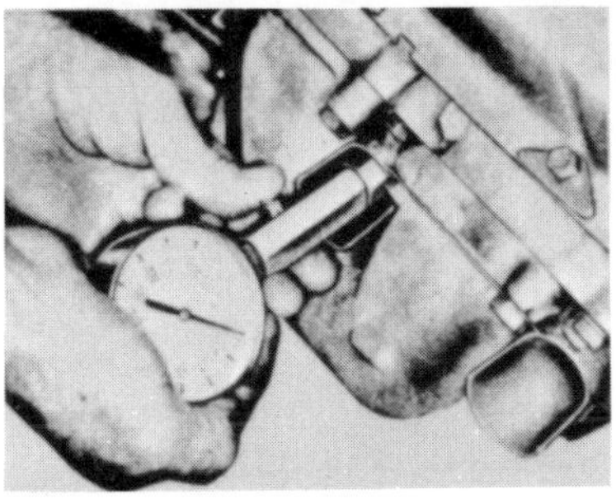

Testing compression
(© Chevrolet Div. G.M. Corp.)

Compression pressure limits
(© Buick Div. G.M. Corp.)

Maxi. Press. Lbs. Sq. In.	Min. Press. Lbs. Sq. In.	Maxi. Press. Lbs. Sq. In.	Min. Press. Lbs. Sq. In.	Max. Press. Lbs. Sq. In.	Min. Press. Lbs. Sq. In.	Max. Press. Lbs. Sq. In.	Min. Press. Lbs. Sq. In.
134	101	162	121	188	141	214	160
136	102	164	123	190	142	216	162
138	104	166	124	192	144	218	163
140	105	168	126	194	145	220	165
142	107	170	127	196	147	222	166
146	110	172	129	198	148	224	168
148	111	174	131	200	150	226	169
150	113	176	132	202	151	228	171
152	114	178	133	204	153	230	172
154	115	180	135	206	154	232	174
156	117	182	136	208	156	234	175
158	118	184	138	210	157	236	177
160	120	186	140	212	158	238	178

Test and Procedure	Results and Indications	Proceed to
6.2—Test engine compression (wet): Squirt approximately 30 cc. of engine oil into each cylinder, and retest per 6.1.	If the readings improve, worn or cracked rings or broken pistons are indicated: If the readings do not improve, burned or excessively carboned valves or a jumped timing chain are indicated: NOTE: *A jumped timing chain is often indicated by difficult cranking.*	Next Chapter 7.1
7.1—Perform a vacuum check of the engine: Attach a vacuum gauge to the intake manifold beyond the throttle plate. Start the engine, and observe the action of the needle over the range of engine speeds.	See below.	See below

	Reading	Indications	Proceed to
	Steady, from 17-22 in. Hg.	Normal.	8.1
	Low and steady.	Late ignition or valve timing, or low compression:	6.1
	Very low	Vacuum leak:	7.2
	Needle fluctuates as engine speed increases.	Ignition miss, blown cylinder head gasket, leaking valve or weak valve spring:	6.1, 8.3
	Gradual drop in reading at idle.	Excessive back pressure in the exhaust system:	10.1
	Intermittent fluctuation at idle.	Ignition miss, sticking valve:	8.3, 9.1
	Drifting needle.	Improper idle mixture adjustment, carburetors not synchronized (where applicable), or minor intake leak. Synchronize the carburetors, adjust the idle, and retest. If the condition persists:	7.2
	High and steady.	Early ignition timing:	8.2

Test and Procedure	Results and Indications	Proceed to
7.2—Attach a vacuum gauge per 7.1, and test for an intake manifold leak. Squirt a small amount of oil around the intake manifold gaskets, carburetor gaskets, plugs and fittings. Observe the action of the vacuum gauge.	If the reading improves, replace the indicated gasket, or seal the indicated fitting or plug: If the reading remains low:	8.1 7.3
7.3—Test all vacuum hoses and accessories for leaks as described in 7.2. Also check the carburetor body (dashpots, automatic choke mechanism, throttle shafts) for leaks in the same manner.	If the reading improves, service or replace the offending part(s): If the reading remains low:	8.1 6.1
8.1—Check the point dwell angle: Connect a dwell meter between the distributor primary wire and ground. Start the engine, and observe the dwell angle from idle to 3000 rpm.	If necessary, adjust the dwell angle. NOTE: *Increasing the point gap reduces the dwell angle and vice-versa.* If the dwell angle moves outside specifications as engine speed increases, the distributor should be removed and checked for cam accuracy, shaft end-play and concentricity, bushing wear, and adequate point arm tension (NOTE: *Most of these items may be checked with the distributor installed in the engine, using an oscilloscope*):	8.2
8.2—Connect a timing light (per manufacturer's recommendation) and check the dynamic ignition timing. Disconnect and plug the vacuum hose(s) to the distributor if specified, start the engine, and observe the timing marks at the specified engine speed.	If the timing is not correct, adjust to specifications by rotating the distributor in the engine: (Advance timing by rotating distributor opposite normal direction of rotor rotation, retard timing by rotating distributor in same direction as rotor rotation.)	8.3
8.3—Check the operation of the distributor advance mechanism(s): To test the mechanical advance, disconnect all but the mechanical advance, and observe the timing marks with a timing light as the engine speed is increased from idle. If the mark moves smoothly, without hesitation, it may be assumed that the mechanical advance is functioning properly. To test vacuum advance and/or retard systems, alternately crimp and release the vacuum line, and observe the timing mark for movement. If movement is noted, the system is operating.	If the systems are functioning: If the systems are not functioning, remove the distributor, and test on a distributor tester:	8.4 8.4
8.4—Locate an ignition miss: With the engine running, remove each spark plug wire, one by one, until one is found that doesn't cause the engine to roughen and slow down.	When the missing cylinder is identified:	4.1

Test and Procedure	*Results and Indications*	*Proceed to*
9.1—Evaluate the valve train: Remove the valve cover, and ensure that the valves are adjusted to specifications. A mechanic's stethoscope may be used to aid in the diagnosis of the valve train. By pushing the probe on or near push rods or rockers, valve noise often can be isolated. A timing light also may be used to diagnose valve problems. Connect the light according to manufacturer's recommendations, and start the engine. Vary the firing moment of the light by increasing the engine speed (and therefore the ignition advance), and moving the trigger from cylinder to cylinder. Observe the movement of each valve.	See below	See below

Observation	*Probable Cause*	*Remedy*	*Proceed to*
Metallic tap heard through the stethoscope.	Sticking hydraulic lifter or excessive valve clearance.	Adjust valve. If tap persists, remove and replace the lifter:	10.1
Metallic tap through the stethoscope, able to push the rocker arm (lifter side) down by hand.	Collapsed valve lifter.	Remove and replace the lifter:	10.1
Erratic, irregular motion of the valve stem.*	Sticking valve, burned valve.	Recondition the valve and/or valve guide:	Next Chapter
Eccentric motion of the pushrod at the rocker arm.*	Bent pushrod.	Replace the pushrod:	10.1
Valve retainer bounces as the valve closes.*	Weak valve spring or damper.	Remove and test the spring and damper. Replace if necessary:	10.1

*—When observed with a timing light.

Test and Procedure	*Results and Indications*	*Proceed to*
9.2—Check the valve timing: Locate top dead center of the No. 1 piston, and install a degree wheel or tape on the crankshaft pulley or damper with zero corresponding to an index mark on the engine. Rotate the crankshaft in its direction of rotation, and observe the opening of the No. 1 cylinder intake valve. The opening should correspond with the correct mark on the degree wheel according to specifications.	If the timing is not correct, the timing cover must be removed for further investigation:	

Test and Procedure	Results and Indications	Proceed to
10.1—Determine whether the exhaust manifold heat control valve is operating: Operate the valve by hand to determine whether it is free to move. If the valve is free, run the engine to operating temperature and observe the action of the valve, to ensure that it is opening.	If the valve sticks, spray it with a suitable solvent, open and close the valve to free it, and retest. If the valve functions properly: If the valve does not free, or does not operate, replace the valve:	 10.2 10.2
10.2—Ensure that there are no exhaust restrictions: Visually inspect the exhaust system for kinks, dents, or crushing. Also note that gasses are flowing freely from the tailpipe at all engine speeds, indicating no restriction in the muffler or resonator.	Replace any damaged portion of the system:	11.1
11.1—Visually inspect the fan belt for glazing, cracks, and fraying, and replace if necessary. Tighten the belt so that the longest span has approximately ½″ play at its midpoint under thumb pressure.	Replace or tighten the fan belt as necessary:	11.2

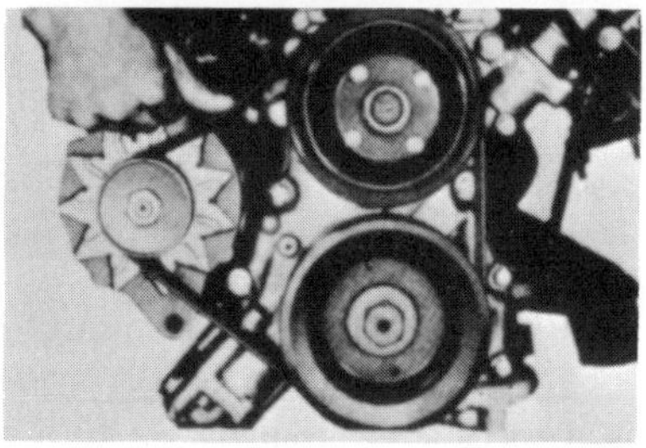

Checking the fan belt tension
(© Nissan Motor Co. Ltd.)

Test and Procedure	Results and Indications	Proceed to
11.2—Check the fluid level of the cooling system.	If full or slightly low, fill as necessary: If extremely low:	11.5 11.3
11.3—Visually inspect the external portions of the cooling system (radiator, radiator hoses, thermostat elbow, water pump seals, heater hoses, etc.) for leaks. If none are found, pressurize the cooling system to 14-15 psi.	If cooling system holds the pressure: If cooling system loses pressure rapidly, re-inspect external parts of the system for leaks under pressure. If none are found, check dipstick for coolant in crankcase. If no coolant is present, but pressure loss continues: If coolant is evident in crankcase, remove cylinder head(s), and check gasket(s). If gaskets are intact, block and cylinder head(s) should be checked for cracks or holes. If the gasket(s) is blown, replace, and purge the crankcase of coolant: NOTE: *Occasionally, due to atmospheric and driving conditions, condensation of water can occur in the crankcase. This causes the oil to appear milky white. To remedy, run the engine until hot, and change the oil and oil filter.*	11.5 11.4 12.6

Test and Procedure	*Results and Indication*	*Proceed to*
11.4—Check for combustion leaks into the cooling system: Pressurize the cooling system as above. Start the engine, and observe the pressure gauge. If the needle fluctuates, remove each spark plug wire, one by one, noting which cylinder(s) reduce or eliminate the fluctuation.  **Radiator pressure tester** (© American Motors Corp.)	Cylinders which reduce or eliminate the fluctuation, when the spark plug wire is removed, are leaking into the cooling system. Replace the head gasket on the affected cylinder bank(s).	
11.5—Check the radiator pressure cap: Attach a radiator pressure tester to the radiator cap (wet the seal prior to installation). Quickly pump up the pressure, noting the point at which the cap releases. **Testing the radiator pressure cap** (© American Motors Corp.)	If the cap releases within ± 1 psi of the specified rating, it is operating properly: If the cap releases at more than ± 1 psi of the specified rating, it should be replaced:	11.6 11.6
11.6—Test the thermostat: Start the engine cold, remove the radiator cap, and insert a thermometer into the radiator. Allow the engine to idle. After a short while, there will be a sudden, rapid increase in coolant temperature. The temperature at which this sharp rise stops is the thermostat opening temperature.	If the thermostat opens at or about the specified temperature: If the temperature doesn't increase: (If the temperature increases slowly and gradually, replace the thermostat.)	11.7 11.7
11.7—Check the water pump: Remove the thermostat elbow and the thermostat, disconnect the coil high tension lead (to prevent starting), and crank the engine momentarily.	If coolant flows, replace the thermostat and retest per 11.6: If coolant doesn't flow, reverse flush the cooling system to alleviate any blockage that might exist. If system is not blocked, and coolant will not flow, recondition the water pump.	11.6 —
12.1—Check the oil pressure gauge or warning light: If the gauge shows low pressure, or the light is on, for no obvious reason, remove the oil pressure sender. Install an accurate oil pressure gauge and run the engine momentarily.	If oil pressure builds normally, run engine for a few moments to determine that it is functioning normally, and replace the sender. If the pressure remains low: If the pressure surges: If the oil pressure is zero:	— 12.2 12.3 12.3

Test and Procedure	Results and Indications	Proceed to
12.2—Visually inspect the oil: If the oil is watery or very thin, milky, or foamy, replace the oil and oil filter.	If the oil is normal:	12.3
	If after replacing oil the pressure remains low:	12.3
	If after replacing oil the pressure becomes normal:	—
12.3—Inspect the oil pressure relief valve and spring, to ensure that it is not sticking or stuck. Remove and thoroughly clean the valve, spring, and the valve body.	If the oil pressure improves:	—
	If no improvement is noted:	12.4

Oil pressure relief valve
(© British Leyland Motors)

Test and Procedure	Results and Indications	Proceed to
12.4—Check to ensure that the oil pump is not cavitating (sucking air instead of oil): See that the crankcase is neither over nor underfull, and that the pickup in the sump is in the proper position and free from sludge.	Fill or drain the crankcase to the proper capacity, and clean the pickup screen in solvent if necessary. If no improvement is noted:	12.5
12.5—Inspect the oil pump drive and the oil pump:	If the pump drive or the oil pump appear to be defective, service as necessary and retest per 12.1:	12.1
	If the pump drive and pump appear to be operating normally, the engine should be disassembled to determine where blockage exists:	Next Chapter
12.6—Purge the engine of ethylene glycol coolant: Completely drain the crankcase and the oil filter. Obtain a commercial butyl cellosolve base solvent, designated for this purpose, and follow the instructions precisely. Following this, install a new oil filter and refill the crankcase with the proper weight oil. The next oil and filter change should follow shortly thereafter (1000 miles).		

Chapter 3

Engine and Engine Rebuilding

Engine Electrical

DISTRIBUTOR

Removal and Installation

1. Remove the distributor cap and position it out of the way. On 1975 and later models, disconnect the electrical plug from the cap.

2. Disconnect the primary coil wire and the vacuum advance hose.

3. Scribe a mark on the distributor body and the engine block showing their relationship. Mark the distributor housing to show the direction in which the rotor is pointing. Note the positioning of the vacuum advance unit.

4. Remove the hold-down bolt and clamp and remove the distributor.

To install the distributor with the engine undisturbed:

5. Reinsert the distributor into its opening, aligning the previously made marks on the housing and the engine block.

6. The rotor may have to be turned either way a slight amount to align the rotor-to-housing marks.

7. Install the retaining clamp and bolt. Install the distributor cap, primary wire or electrical connector, and the vacuum hose.

8. Start the engine and check the ignition timing.

To install the distributor with the engine disturbed:

9. Turn the engine to bring No. 1 piston to the top of its compression stroke. This may be determined by inserting a rag into the No. 1 spark plug hole and slowly turning the engine over. When the timing mark on the crankshaft pulley aligns with the 0 on the timing scale and the rag is blown out by compression, No. 1 piston is at top-dead-center (TDC).

NOTE: *On Mark IV (big block) V8 engines there is a punch mark on the distributor drive gear which indicates the rotor position. Thus, the distributor may be installed with the cap in place. Align the punch mark 2° clockwise from the No. 1 cap terminal, then rotate the distributor body ⅛ turn counterclockwise and push the distributor down into the block.*

10. Install the distributor to the engine block so that the vacuum advance unit points in the correct direction.

11. Turn the rotor so that it will point to No. 1 terminal in the cap.

12. Install the distributor into the engine block. It may be necessary to turn

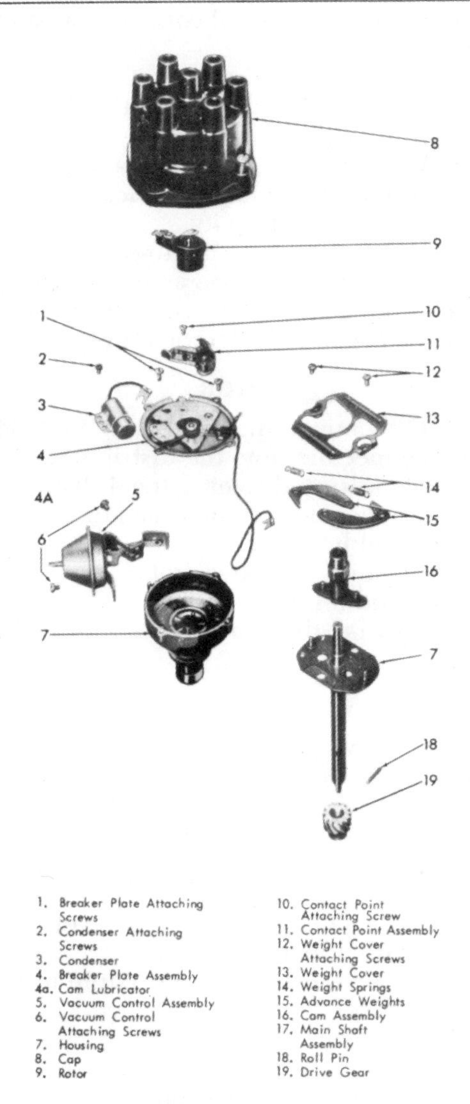

1. Breaker Plate Attaching Screws
2. Condenser Attaching Screws
3. Condenser
4. Breaker Plate Assembly
4a. Cam Lubricator
5. Vacuum Control Assembly
6. Vacuum Control Attaching Screws
7. Housing
8. Cap
9. Rotor
10. Contact Point Attaching Screw
11. Contact Point Assembly
12. Weight Cover Attaching Screws
13. Weight Cover
14. Weight Springs
15. Advance Weights
16. Cam Assembly
17. Main Shaft Assembly
18. Roll Pin
19. Drive Gear

Exploded view of six-cylinder distributor

the rotor a little in either direction in order to engage the gears.

13. Tap the starter a few times to ensure that the oil pump shaft is mated to the distributor shaft.

14. Bring the engine to No. 1 TDC again and check to see that the rotor is indeed pointing toward the No. 1 terminal of the cap.

15. After correct positioning is assured, turn the distributor housing so that the points are just opening. Tighten the retaining clamp.

16. Install the cap and primary wire. Check the ignition timing. Install the vacuum hose.

HIGH ENERGY IGNITION (HEI) DISTRIBUTOR

The Delco-Remy High Energy Ignition (HEI) System is a breakerless, pulse triggered, transistor controlled, inductive discharge ignition system available as an option in 1974 and standard in 1975.

There are only nine external electrical connections; the ignition switch feed wire, and the eight spark plug leads. The ignition coil is located with the distributor cap, connecting directly to the rotor. The major difference between the HEI System and the Unit Ignition System is that the HEI System is a full 12 volt system, while the Unit Ignition System incorporates a resistance wire to limit the voltage to the coil except during periods of starter motor operation.

The magnetic pick-up assembly located inside the distributor contains a permanent magnet, a pole piece with in-

Firing Order

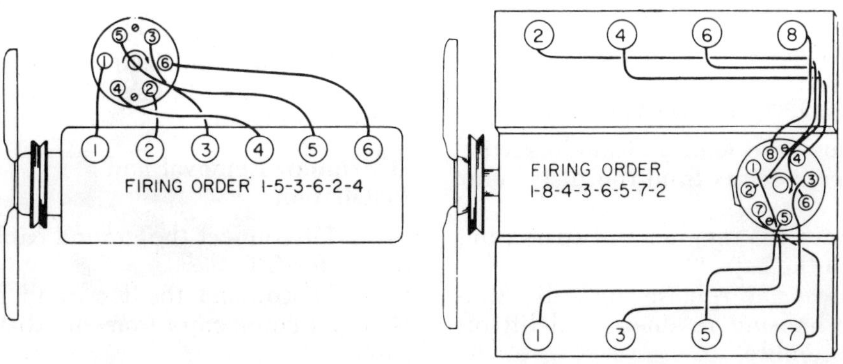

ternal teeth, and a pick-up coil. When the teeth of the rotating timer core and pole piece align, an induced voltage in the pick-up coil signals the electronic module to open the coil primary circuit. As the primary current decreases, a high voltage is induced in the secondary windings of the ignition coil, directing a spark through the rotor and high voltage leads to fire the spark plugs. The dwell period is automatically controlled by the electronic module and is increased with increasing engine rpm. The HEI System features a longer spark duration which is instrumental in firing lean and EGR diluted fuel/air mixtures. The condenser (capacitor) located within the HEI distributor is provided for noise (static) suppression purposes only and is not a regularly replaced ignition system component.

Component Replacement

IGNITION COIL

1. Disconnect the feed and module wire terminal connectors from the distributor cap.
2. Remove the ignition set retainer.
3. Remove the 4 coil cover-to-distributor cap screws and the coil cover.
4. Remove the 4 coil-to-distributor cap screws.
5. Using a blunt drift, press the coil wire spade terminals up out of distributor cap.
6. Lift the coil up out of the distributor cap.
7. Remove and clean the coil spring, rubber seal washer and coil cavity of the distributor cap.
8. Coat the rubber seal with a dielectric lubricant furnished in the replacement ignition coil package.
9. Reverse the above procedures to install.

DISTRIBUTOR CAP

1. Remove the feed and module wire terminal connectors from the distributor cap.
2. Remove the retainer and spark plug wires from the cap.
3. Depress and release the 4 distributor cap-to-housing retainers and lift off the cap assembly.

4. Remove the 4 coil cover screws and cover.
5. Using a finger or a blunt drift, push the spade terminals up out of the distributor cap.
6. Remove all 4 coil screws and lift the coil, coil spring and rubber seal washer out of the cap coil cavity.
7. Using a new distributor cap, reverse the above procedures to assemble being sure to clean and lubricate the rubber seal washer with dielectric lubricant.

ROTOR

1. Disconnect the feed and module wire connectors from the distributor.
2. Depress and release the 4 distributor cap to housing retainers and lift off the cap assembly.
3. Remove the two rotor attaching screws and rotor.
4. Reverse the above procedure to install.

VACUUM ADVANCE

1. Remove the distributor cap and rotor as previously described.
2. Disconnect the vacuum hose from the vacuum advance unit.
3. Remove the two vacuum advance retaining screws, pull the advance unit outward, rotate and disengage the operating rod from its tang.
4. Reverse the above procedure to install.

MODULE

1. Remove the distributor cap and rotor as previously described.
2. Disconnect the harness connector and pick-up coil spade connectors from the module. Be careful not to damage the wires when removing the connector.
3. Remove the two screws and module from the distributor housing.
4. Coat the bottom of the new module with dielectric lubricant supplied with the new module. Reverse the above procedure to install.

Distributor Removal and Installation

1. Disconnect the ground cable from the battery.
2. Disconnect the feed and module terminal connectors from the distributor cap.

3. Disconnect the hose at the vacuum advance.

4. Depress and release the 4 distributor cap-to-housing retainers and lift off the cap assembly.

5. Using crayon or chalk, make locating marks on the rotor and module and on the distributor housing and engine for installation purposes.

6. Loosen and remove the distributor clamp bolt and clamp, and lift distributor out of the engine. Noting the relative position of the rotor and module alignment marks, make a second mark on the rotor to align it with the one mark on the module.

7. With a new O-ring on the distributor housing and the second mark on the rotor aligned with the mark on the module, install the distributor, taking care to align the mark on the housing with the one on the engine. It may be necessary to lift the distributor and turn the rotor slightly to align the gears and the oil pump driveshaft.

8. With the respective marks aligned, install the clamp and bolt finger-tight.

9. Install and secure the distributor cap.

10. Connect the feed and module connectors to the distributor cap.

11. Connect a timing light to the engine and plug the vacuum hose.

12. Connect the ground cable to the battery.

13. Start the engine and set the timing.

14. Turn the engine off and tighten the distributor clamp bolt. Disconnect the timing light and unplug and connect the hose to the vacuum advance.

ALTERNATOR

Alternator Precautions

1. When installing a battery, ensure that the ground polarity of the battery and

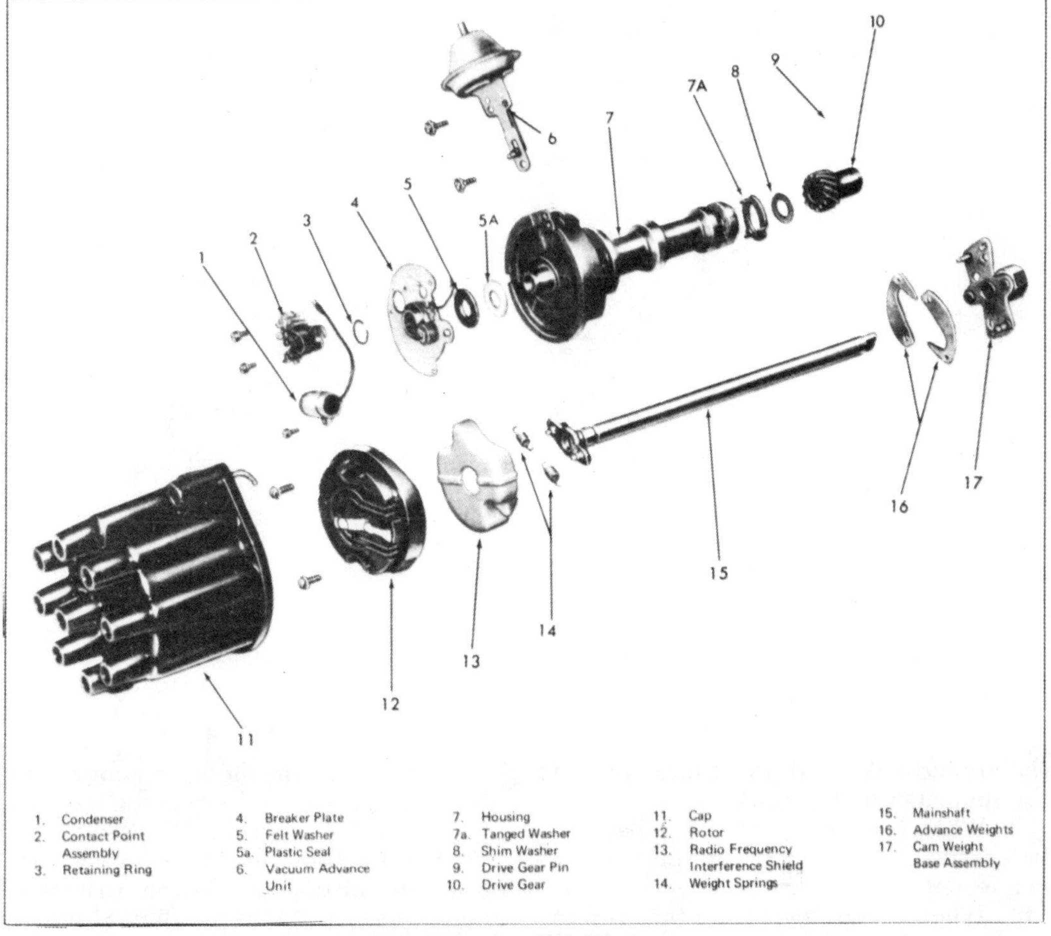

1.	Condenser	4.	Breaker Plate	7.	Housing	11.	Cap	15.	Mainshaft
2.	Contact Point	5.	Felt Washer	7a.	Tanged Washer	12.	Rotor	16.	Advance Weights
	Assembly	5a.	Plastic Seal	8.	Shim Washer	13.	Radio Frequency	17.	Cam Weight
3.	Retaining Ring	6.	Vacuum Advance	9.	Drive Gear Pin		Interference Shield		Base Assembly
			Unit	10.	Drive Gear	14.	Weight Springs		

Exploded view of V8 distributor

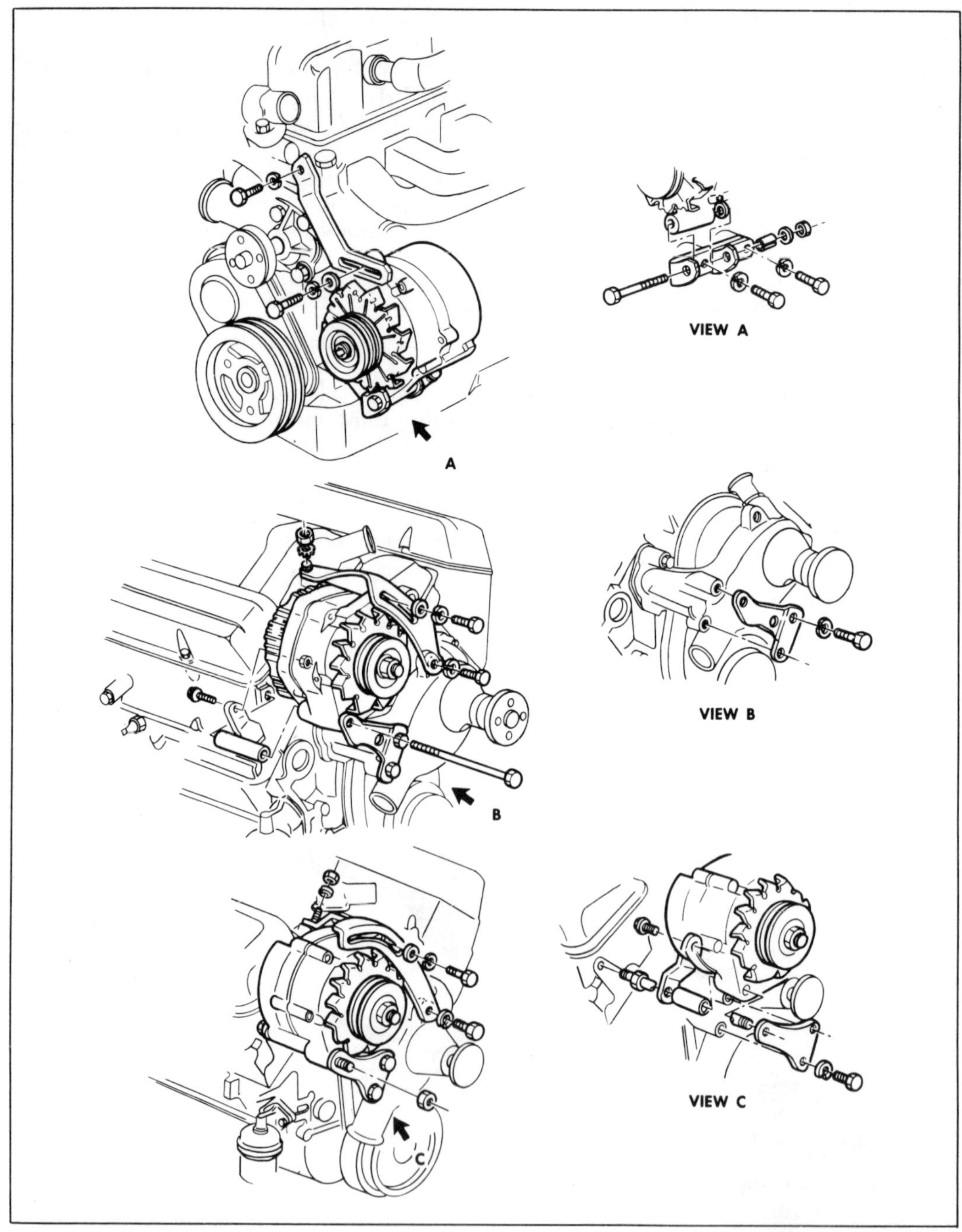

Alternator mounting—six-cylinder (top), small block V8 (center), and big block V8 (bottom)

the ground polarity of the alternator and the regulator are the same.

2. When connecting a jumper battery, be certain that the correct terminals are connected.

3. When charging, connect the correct charger leads to the battery terminals.

4. Never operate the alternator on an open circuit. Be sure that all connections in the charging circuit are tight.

5. Do not short across or ground any of the terminals on the alternator or regulator.

6. Never polarize an AC system.

Removal and Installation

1. Disconnect the battery ground cable to prevent diode damage.

2. Disconnect all wiring to the alternator.

3. Remove the alternator brace bolt. If the car is equipped with power steering, loosen the pump brace and mount nuts.

4. Remove the drive belt(s).

5. Support the alternator and remov the mounting bolts. Remove the altern. tor from the car.

6. Install the unit on the car using the reverse procedure of removal. Adjust the belt to have ¼–½ inch play on its longest run.

REGULATOR

Removal and Installation

1. Disconnect the ground cable from the battery.

2. Disconnect the wiring harness from the regulator.

3. Remove the mounting screws and remove the regulator.

4. Make sure that the regulator base basket is in place before installation.

5. Clean the attaching area for proper grounding.

6. Install the regulator. Do not over-tighten the mounting screws, as this will cancel the cushioning effect of the rubber grommets.

NOTE: *An integral alternator/regulator has been optionally available since 1969 and standard since 1971. Removal or adjustment of the regulator is not possible with this unit.*

Voltage Adjustment

The standard voltage regulator is the conventional double-contact type; however, an optional transistorized regulator was available in 1968. Voltage adjustment procedures are the same for both except for the adjustment points. The double-contact adjusting screw is under the regulator cover; the 1968 transistorized regulator is adjusted externally after removing an allen screw from the adjustment hole.

1. Insert a ¼ ohm–25 watt fixed resistor into the charging circuit at the horn relay junction block, except on 1972 cars, where it is inserted between the positive battery terminal and the starter solenoid.

2. Install a voltmeter as shown in the figure.

3. Warm the engine by running it for about 15 minutes at 1,500 rpm or more.

4. Cycle the voltage regulator by disconnecting and reconnecting the regulator connector.

5. Read the voltage on the voltmeter. If it is between 13.5 and 15.2, the regulator does not need adjustment or replacement. If the voltage is not within these limits, leave the engine running at 1,500 rpm.

6. Disconnect the four-terminal connector and remove the regulator cover (except on 1968 transistorized regulators). Reconnect the four-terminal connector and remove the regulator cover 14.2 and 14.6 volts by turning the adjusting screw while observing the voltmeter.

7. Disconnect the terminal, install the cover, and then reconnect the terminal.

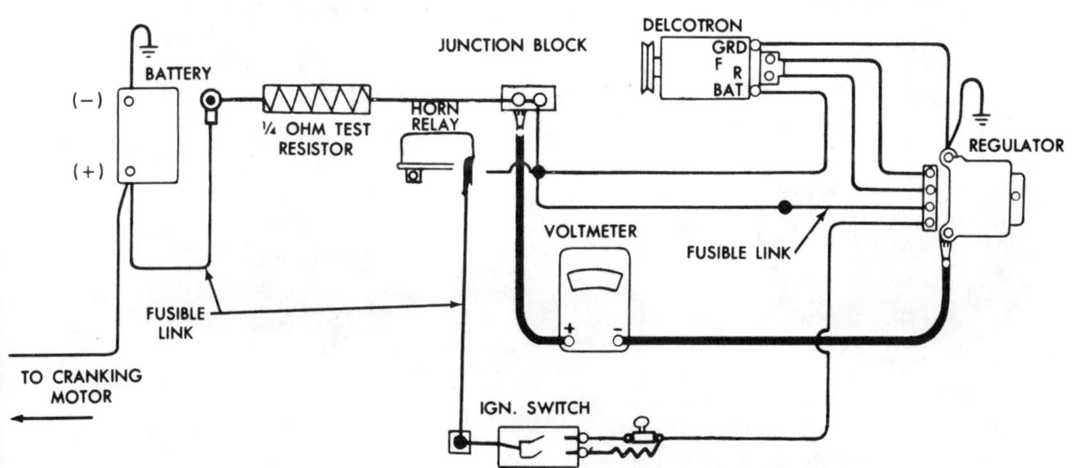

Voltage regulator setting circuit

8. Continue running the engine at 1,500 rpm to re-establish the regulator internal temperature.

9. Cycle the regulator by disconnecting/reconnecting the regulator connector. Check the voltage. If the voltage is between 13.5 and 15.2, the regulator is good.

CAUTION: *Always disconnect the regulator before removing or installing the cover in order to prevent damage by short-circuiting.*

STARTER

Removal and Installation

1. Disconnect the battery ground cable.

2. Raise the car to a convenient working height.

3. Disconnect all wiring from the starter solenoid. Note or tag the wiring positions for installation.

4. Remove the front bracket from the starter and the two mounting bolts. On engines with a solenoid heat shield, remove the front bracket upper bolt and detach the bracket from the starter.

5. Remove the front bracket bolt or nut. Lower the starter front end first, and then remove the unit from the car.

6. Reverse the removal procedures to install the starter. Torque the two mounting bolts to 25–35 ft lbs.

Starter Drive Replacement

1. Disconnect the field straps from the solenoid and remove the starter throughbolts.

2. Remove the commutator end frame, field frame, and armature from the drive housing.

3. To remove the overrunning clutch from the armature shaft:

a. Slide the thrust collar from the end of the armature shaft.

b. Slide a standard ½ in. pipe coupling (or an old pinion of suitable size) onto the armature shaft so that it butts against the snap-ring retainer. Tap the end of the pipe with a hammer, driving the retainer off of the snap-ring.

c. Remove the snap-ring from the groove in the armature shaft.

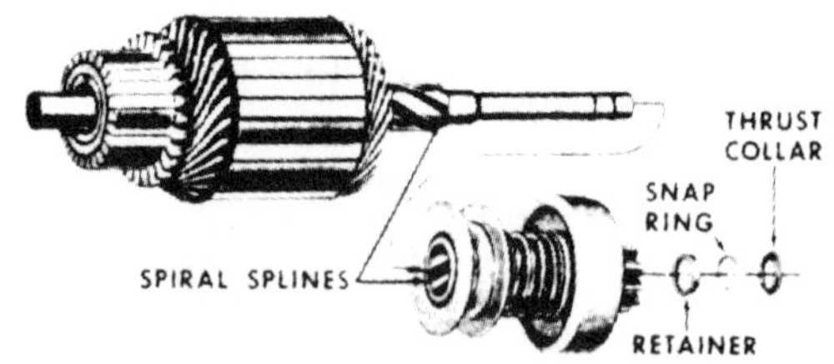

Starter drive assembly

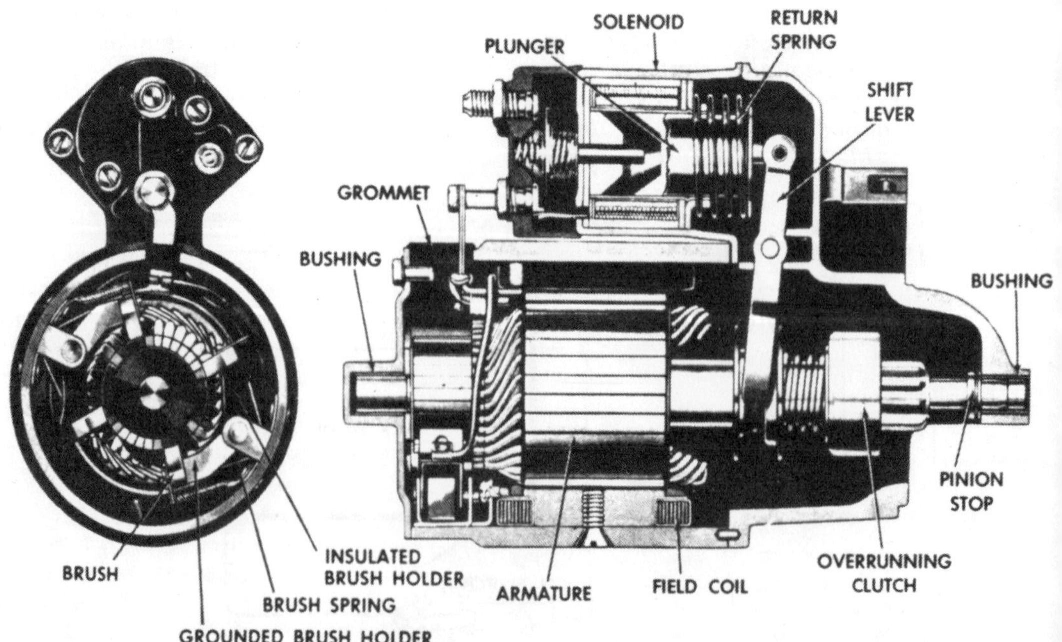

Sectioned view of the starter

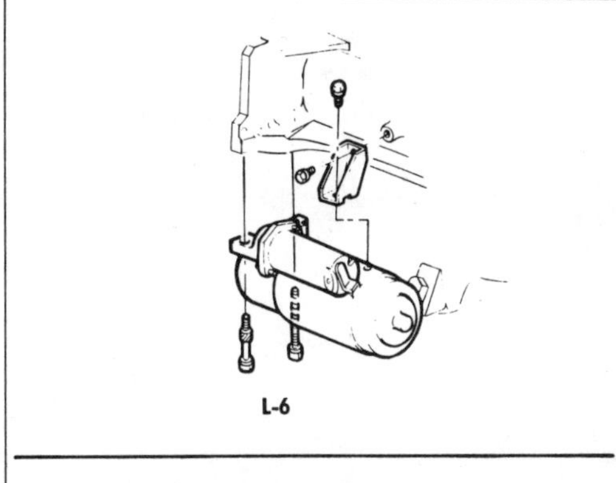

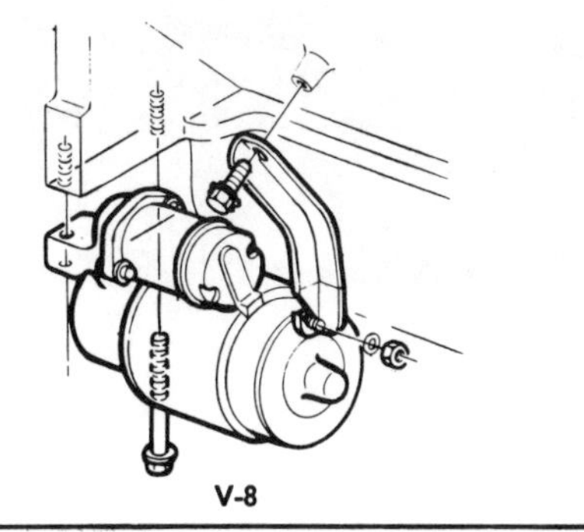

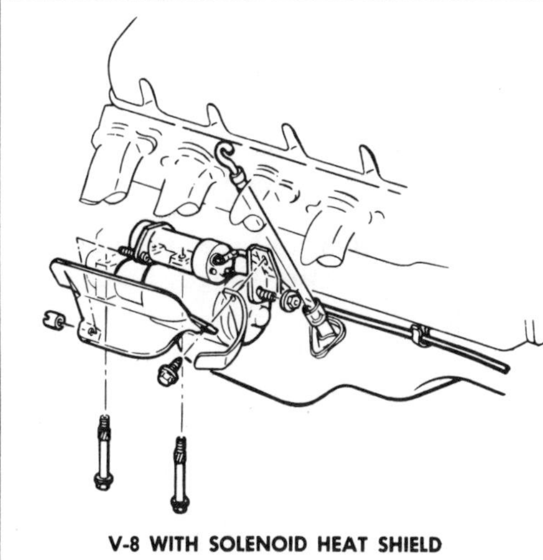

Starter mounting

d. Slide the retainer and clutch from the armature shaft.

4. To reassemble, reverse the above procedure, being sure to:

a. Slide the snap-ring, after it has been forced onto the armature shaft, past the grease groove to the snap-ring groove.

b. Use two pairs of pliers at the same time, on opposite sides of the armature shaft, and grip the retainer and thrust collar and squeeze until the retainer is forced over the snap-ring.

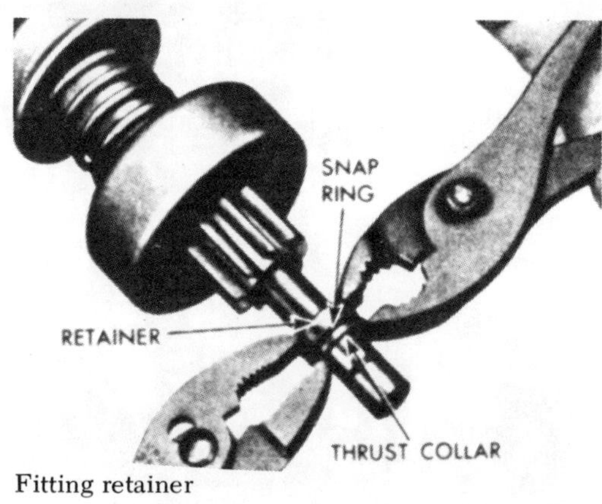

Fitting retainer

Engine Mechanical

DESIGN

All Chevrolet engines, whether L6 or V8, are water-cooled, overhead valve powerplants. All engines use cast iron cylinder blocks and heads.

The 250 cu in. inline six-cylinder crankshaft is supported in seven main bearings, with the thrust taken by No. 7. The camshaft is low in the block and driven by the crankshaft gear, no timing chain is used. Relatively long pushrods actuate the valves through ball-jointed rocker arms.

The small-block family of engines, which includes the 283, 307, 327, 350, and 400 cu in. blocks, have all sprung from the basic design of the 1955, 265 cu in. engine. It was this engine that introduced the ball-joint, rocker arm design which is now used by many car makers. This line of engines features a great deal of interchangeability, and later parts may be utilized on earlier engines for increased reliability and/or performance. In 1968, rod and main bearings were increased in size on the small-block family. The 283 was also dropped in that year and replaced by the 307, which is in effect a 327 crankshaft in a 283 block. The 327 and 350 engines share the same cylinder block, with the difference in displacement being provided by a longer stroke crankshaft. The 400 block was in-

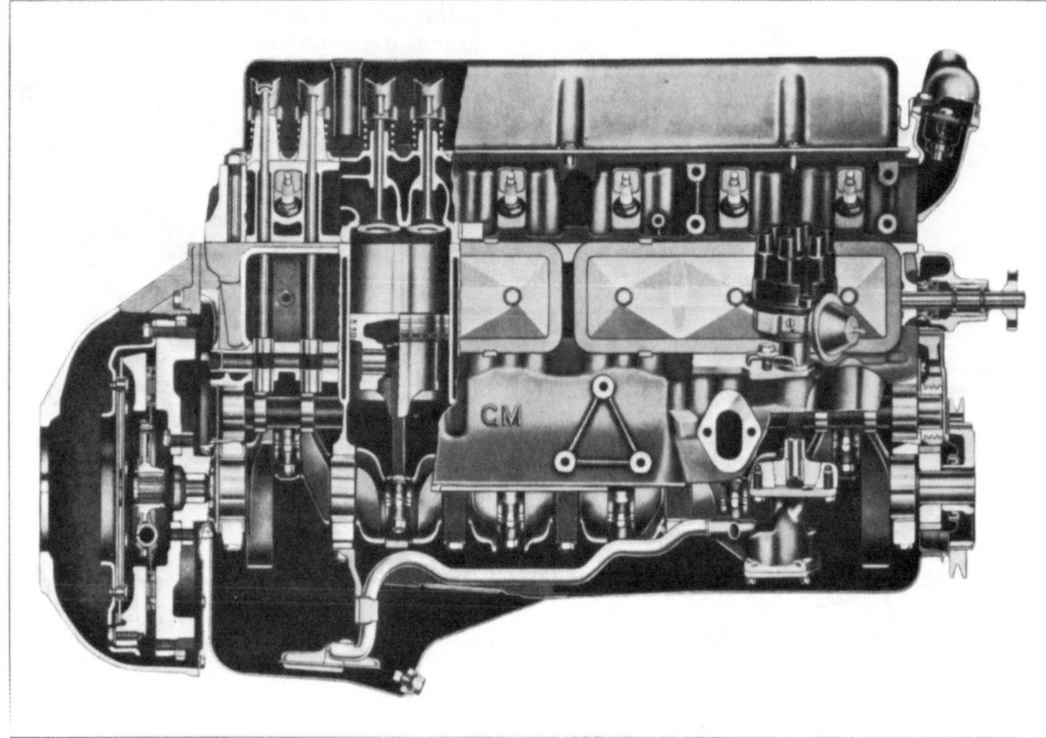

Cutaway of six-cylinder engine

troduced in 1970. The 307 and 350 cu in. engines remain as the most common V8s.

The 396, 402, 427, and 454 cu in. engines are known as the Mark IV engines or big-blocks. These engines feature unusual cylinder heads, in that the intake and exhaust valves are canted at the angle at which their respective port enters the cylinder. The 396 was first used in 1965, and through bore and stroke increases has developed into 454 cu ins. The big-block cylinder heads use ball-joint rockers similar to those on the small block engines.

ENGINE REMOVAL
AND INSTALLATION

1. Remove the hood. Scribe lines around the hinges so that the hood can be installed in its original location.
2. Remove the air cleaner.
3. Disconnect the battery cables at the battery.
4. Remove the radiator and shroud.
5. Remove the fan blade and pulley.
6. Disconnect wires at:
  a. C.E.C. solenoid.
  b. Coil.
  c. Temperature switch.
  d. Delcotron.
  e. Starter solenoid.
  f. Oil pressure sending unit.
7. Disconnect:
  a. Accelerator linkage at the pedal.
  b. Oil pressure gauge line, if so equipped.
  c. Exhaust pipes at the manifold flanges.
  d. Engine cooler lines, if so equipped.
  e. Vacuum line to the power brake unit, if so equipped.
  f. Fuel line (front tank) at the fuel pump.
8. Remove the power steering pump, leaving the hoses attached to the pump.
9. Raise the car on a hoist.
10. Drain the cooling system and the crankcase.
11. Remove the driveshaft.
NOTE: *If a plug for the driveshaft opening in the transmission is not available, drain the transmission.*
12. Disconnect:
  a. Shift linkage at the transmission.
  b. Speedometer cable at the transmission.

Cutaway of V8 engine

c. Transmission cooler lines, if so equipped.

d. TCS switch at the transmission.

13. On vehicles with manual transmissions, disconnect the clutch linkage at the cross-shaft then remove the cross-shaft at the frame bracket.

14. Lower the vehicle and remove the rocker arm covers and install engine lifting adapter on the cylinder heads.

15. Raise the engine enough to take the weight off the front mounts, then remove the front mount through bolts.

16. Remove the rear mount to crossmember bolts.

NOTE: *Make sure, on 1977 models, that the same number of transmission mount shims are reinstalled. These are used to adjust driveshaft angle.*

17. Raise the engine enough to take the weight off the rear mount, then remove the crossmember.

NOTE: *It is necessary to remove the mount from the transmission before the crossmember can be removed.*

18. Remove the engine/transmission assembly as a unit.

19. To remove the clutch and transmission from the engine:

a. Remove the clutch housing cover plate screws.

b. Remove the clutch housing to engine attaching bolts, then, remove the transmission and clutch housing as a unit.

CAUTION: *Do not let the weight of the transmission hang on the spline because the clutch disc may be easily damaged.*

c. Remove the starter and clutch housing rear cover plate.

d. Loosen the clutch mounting bolts one turn at a time (to prevent distortion of the clutch cover) until the spring

General Engine Specifications

Year	Engine No. Cyl Displacement (cu in.)	Carburetor Type	Advertised Horsepower @ rpm ■	Advertised Torque @ rpm (ft lbs) ■	Bore and Stroke (in.)	Advertised Compression Ratio	Oil Pressure @ 2050 rpm
'68	6-250	1 bbl	155 @ 4200	235 @ 1600	3.875 x 3.530	8.5 : 1	58 @ 2000
	8-307	2 bbl	200 @ 4600	300 @ 2400	3.875 x 3.250	9.0 : 1	58 @ 2000
	8-327	4 bbl	250 @ 4800	335 @ 3200	4.001 x 3.250	8.75 : 1	58 @ 2000
	8-327	4 bbl	275 @ 4800	355 @ 3200	4.001 x 3.250	10.00 : 1	58 @ 2000
	8-327	4 bbl	300 @ 5000	360 @ 3400	4.000 x 3.250	10.00 : 1	38 @ 1500
	8-327	4 bbl	350 @ 5800	360 @ 3600	4.000 x 3.250	11.0 : 1	38 @ 1500
	8-396	4 bbl	325 @ 4800	410 @ 3200	4.094 x 3.760	10.25 : 1	62 @ 2000
	8-427	4 bbl	385 @ 5200	460 @ 3400	4.251 x 3.760	10.25 : 1	62 @ 2000
	8-427	4 bbl	390 @ 5400	460 @ 3600	4.250 x 3.760	10.25 : 1	62 @ 2000
'69	6-250	1 bbl	155 @ 4200	235 @ 1600	3.875 x 3.530	8.5 : 1	58 @ 2000
	8-327	2 bbl	235 @ 4800	325 @ 2800	3.875 x 3.530	9.0 : 1	58 @ 2000
	8-350	4 bbl	255 @ 4800	365 @ 3200	4.000 x 3.480	9.0 : 1	58 @ 2000
	8-350	4 bbl	300 @ 4800	380 @ 3200	4.000 x 3.480	10.25 : 1	58 @ 2000
	8-350	4 bbl	350 @ 5600	380 @ 3600	4.000 x 3.480	11.0 : 1	58 @ 2000
	8-396	2 bbl	265 @ 4800	400 @ 2800	4.094 x 3.760	9.0 : 1	62 @ 2000
	8-427	4 bbl	335 @ 4800	460 @ 3200	4.251 x 3.760	10.25 : 1	62 @ 2000
	8-427	4 bbl	390 @ 4800	460 @ 3600	4.251 x 3.760	10.25 : 1	62 @ 2000
'70	6-250	1 bbl	155 @ 4200	235 @ 1600	3.875 x 3.530	8.5 : 1	58 @ 2000
	8-350	2 bbl	250 @ 4800	345 @ 2800	4.000 x 3.480	9.0 : 1	58 @ 2000
	8-350	4 bbl	300 @ 4800	380 @ 3200	4.000 x 3.480	10.25 : 1	58 @ 2000
	8-350	4 bbl	350 @ 5600	380 @ 3600	4.000 x 3.480	11.0 : 1	40 @ 2000
	8-350	4 bbl	370 @ 6000	380 @ 4000	4.000 x 3.480	11.0 : 1	40 @ 2000
	8-400	2 bbl	265 @ 4400	400 @ 2400	4.125 x 3.750	9.0 : 1	58 @ 2000
	8-454	4 bbl	345 @ 4400	500 @ 3000	4.251 x 4.000	10.25 : 1	62 @ 2000

General Engine Specifications (cont.)

Year	Engine No. Cyl Displacement (cu in.)	Carburetor Type	Advertised Horsepower @ rpm ■	Advertised Torque @ rpm (ft lbs) ■	Bore and Stroke (in.)	Advertised Compression Ratio	Oil Pressure @ 2050 rpm
'70	8-454	4 bbl	390 @ 4800	500 @ 3400	4.251 x 4.000	10.25 : 1	62 @ 2000
'71	6-250	1 bbl	145 @ 4200	230 @ 1600	3.875 x 3.530	8.5 : 1	40 @ 2000
	8-350	2 bbl	245 @ 4800	350 @ 2800	4.000 x 3.480	8.5 : 1	40 @ 2000
	8-350	4 bbl	270 @ 4800	360 @ 3200	4.000 x 3.480	8.5 : 1	40 @ 2000
	8-350	4 bbl	330 @ 5600	360 @ 4000	4.000 x 3.480	9.0 : 1	40 @ 2000
	8-400	2 bbl	255 @ 4400	390 @ 2400	4.125 x 3.750	8.5 : 1	40 @ 2000
	8-400 (402 cu in.)	4 bbl	300 @ 4800	400 @ 3200	4.126 x 3.760	8.5 : 1	40 @ 2000
	8-454	4 bbl	365 @ 4800	465 @ 4000	4.251 x 4.000	8.5 : 1	40 @ 2000
'72	6-250	1 bbl	110 @ 3800	185 @ 1600	3.875 x 3.530	8.5 : 1	40 @ 2000
	8-350	2 bbl	165 @ 4000	280 @ 2400	4.000 x 3.480	8.5 : 1	40 @ 2000
	8-350	4 bbl	200 @ 4400	300 @ 2800	4.000 x 3.480	8.5 : 1	40 @ 2000
	8-350	4 bbl	255 @ 5600	280 @ 4000	4.000 x 3.480	9.0 : 1	40 @ 2000
	8-400	2 bbl	170 @ 3400	325 @ 2000	4.126 x 3.750	8.5 : 1	40 @ 2000
	8-402	4 bbl	210 @ 4400	320 @ 2400	4.126 x 3.760	8.5 : 1	40 @ 2000
	8-454	4 bbl	270 @ 4000	390 @ 3200	4.251 x 4.000	8.5 : 1	40 @ 2000
'73	6-250	1 bbl	100 @ 3600	175 @ 1600	3.875 x 3.530	8.25 : 1	40 @ 2000
	8-350	2 bbl	145 @ 4000	255 @ 2400	4.000 x 3.480	8.5 : 1	40 @ 2000
	8-350	4 bbl	175 @ 4000	260 @ 2800	4.000 x 3.480	8.5 : 1	40 @ 2000
	8-400	2 bbl	150 @ 3200	295 @ 2000	4.126 x 3.750	8.5 : 1	40 @ 2000
	8-454	4 bbl	245 @ 4000①	375 @ 2800②	4.251 x 4.000	8.25 : 1	40 @ 2000
'74	8-350	2 bbl	145 @ 3600	250 @ 2200	4.000 x 3.480	8.5 : 1	40 @ 2000
	8-350	4 bbl	160 @ 3800	245 @ 2400	4.000 x 3.480	8.5 : 1	40 @ 2000
	8-400	2 bbl	150 @ 3200	295 @ 2000	4.126 x 3.750	8.5 : 1	40 @ 2000
	8-400	4 bbl	180 @ 3800	290 @ 2400	4.126 x 3.750	8.5 : 1	40 @ 2000

General Engine Specifications (cont.)

Year	Engine No. Cyl Displacement (cu in.)	Carburetor Type	Advertised Horsepower @ rpm ■	Advertised Torque @ rpm (ft lbs) ■	Bore and Stroke (in.)	Advertised Compression Ratio	Oil Pressure @ 2050 rpm
'74	8-454	4 bbl	235 @ 4000	360 @ 2800	4.251 x 4.000	8.25 : 1	40 @ 2000
'75	8-350	2 bbl	145 @ 3600	250 @ 2200	4.000 x 3.480	8.5 : 1	40 @ 2000
	8-350	4 bbl	195 @ 4400	275 @ 2800	4.000 x 3.480	8.5 : 1	40 @ 2000
	8-400	4 bbl	180 @ 3800	290 @ 2400	4.126 x 3.750	8.5 : 1	40 @ 2000
	8-454	4 bbl	215 @ 4000	350 @ 2400	4.251 x 4.000	8.15 : 1	40 @ 2000
'76	8-350	2 bbl	145 @ 3800	250 @ 2200	4.000 x 3.480	8.5 : 1	40 @ 2000
	8-350	4 bbl	165 @ 3800	260 @ 2400	4.000 x 3.480	8.5 : 1	40 @ 2000
	8-400	4 bbl	175 @ 3600	305 @ 2000	4.126 x 3.750	8.5 : 1	40 @ 2000
	8-454	4 bbl	235 @ 4000	360 @ 2800	4.251 x 4.000	8.25 : 1	46 @ 2000
'77	6-250	1 bbl	110 @ 3800	195 @ 1600	3.875 x 3.530	8.3 : 1	40 @ 2000
	8-305	2 bbl	145 @ 3800	245 @ 2400	3.736 x 3.480	8.5 : 1	40 @ 2000
	8-350	4 bbl	170 @ 3800	270 @ 2400	4.000 x 3.480	8.5 : 1	40 @ 2000

■ Beginning 1972, horsepower and torque are SAE net figures. They are measured at the rear of the transmission with all accessories installed and operating. Since the figures vary when a given engine is installed in different models, some are representative rather than exact.

① 215 in wagon

② 345 in wagon

Valve Specifications

Year	Engine No. Cyl Displacement (cu in.)	Seat Angle (deg)	Face Angle (deg)	Spring Test Pressure (lbs @ in.)	Spring Installed Height (in.)	STEM TO GUIDE Clearance (in.) Intake	STEM TO GUIDE Clearance (in.) Exhaust	STEM Diameter (in.) Intake	STEM Diameter (in.) Exhaust
'68	6-250	46	45	60 @ 1.66	1²¹⁄₃₂	.0010–.0037	.0010–.0047	.3414	.3414
	8-307	46	45	80 @ 1.70	1⁵⁄₃₂	.0010–.0037	.0010–.0047	.3414	.3414
	8-327	46	45	80 @ 1.70	1⁵⁄₃₂	.0010–.0037	.0010–.0047	.3414	.3414
	8-396	46	45	90 @ 1.88	1⅞	.0010–.0037	.0015–.0052	.3719	.3717
	8-396①	46	45	100 @ 1.88	1⅞	.0010–.0037	.0015–.0052	.3719	.3717
	8-427	46	45	100 @ 1.88	1⅞	.0010–.0037	.0015–.0052	.3719	.3717

Valve Specifications (cont.)

Year	Engine No. Cyl Displacement (cu in.)	Seat Angle (deg)	Face Angle (deg)	Spring Test Pressure (lbs @ in.)	Spring Installed Height (in.)	STEM TO GUIDE Clearance (in.)		STEM Diameter (in.)	
						Intake	Exhaust	Intake	Exhaust
'69	6-250	46	45	60 @ 1.66	$1\frac{21}{32}$	.0010–.0037	.0010–.0047	.3414	.3414
	8-327	46	45	80 @ 1.70	$1\frac{5}{32}$	.0010–.0037	.0010–.0047	.3414	.3414
	8-350	46	45	80 @ 1.70	$1\frac{5}{32}$	.0010–.0037	.0010–.0047	.3414	.3414
	8-396	46	45	90 @ 1.88	$1\frac{7}{8}$	.0010–.0037	.0010–.0037	.3719	.3719
	8-427	46	45	90 @ 1.88	$1\frac{7}{8}$	.0010–.0037	.0010–.0037	.3719	.3719
'70	6-250	46	45	60 @ 1.66	$1\frac{21}{32}$	.0010–.0037	.0010–.0047	.3414	.3414
	8-350	46	45	80 @ 1.70	$1\frac{23}{32}$	.0010–.0037	.0010–.0047	.3414	.3414
	8-400	46	45	80 @ 1.70	$1\frac{7}{8}$	.0010–.0037	.0010–.0047	.3414	.3414
	8-454	46	45	75 @ 1.88②	$1\frac{7}{8}$	.0010–.0037	.0010–.0047	.3718	.3718
'71	6-250	46	45	60 @ 1.66	$1\frac{21}{32}$	.0010–.0037	.0010–.0047	.3414	.3714
	8-350	46	45	80 @ 1.70	$1\frac{23}{32}$	.0010–.0037	.0010–.0047	.3414	.3714
	8-400	46	45	80 @ 1.70	$1\frac{23}{32}$	.0010–.0037	.0010–.0047	.3414	.3714
	8-400③	46	45	75 @ 1.88②	$1\frac{7}{8}$	.0010–.0037	.0010–.0047	.3719	.3717
	8-454	46	45	75 @ 1.88②	$1\frac{7}{8}$	.0010–.0037	.0010–.0047	.3719	.3717
'72	6-250	46	45	60 @ 1.66	$1\frac{21}{32}$	.0010–.0037	.0010–.0047	.3414	.3414
	8-350	46	45	80 @ 1.70	$1\frac{23}{32}$	.0010–.0037	.0010–.0047	.3414	.3414
	8-400	46	45	80 @ 1.70	$1\frac{23}{32}$	.0010–.0037	.0010–.0047	.3414	.3414
	8-402	46	45	90 @ 1.88	$1\frac{7}{8}$	.0010–.0037	.0010–.0047	.3719	.3717
	8-454	46	45	75 @ 1.88②	$1\frac{7}{8}$	.0010–.0037	.0010–.0047	.3719	.3717
'73	6-250	46	45	60 @ 1.66	$1\frac{21}{32}$	.0010–.0027	.0010–.0027	.3414	.3414
	8-350	46	45	80 @ 1.70	$1\frac{23}{32}$	.0010–.0027	.0010–.0027	.3414	.3414
	8-400	46	45	80 @ 1.70	$1\frac{23}{32}$	.0010–.0027	.0010–.0027	.3414	.3414
	8-454	46	45	80 @ 1.88	$1\frac{7}{8}$	.0010–.0027	.0010–.0027	.3719	.3717
'74	8-350	46	45	80 @ 1.70	$1\frac{23}{32}$	.0010–.0027	.0010–.0027	.3414	.3414

Valve Specifications (cont.)

Year	Engine No. Cyl Displacement (cu in.)	Seat Angle (deg)	Face Angle (deg)	Spring Test Pressure (lbs @ in.)	Spring Installed Height (in.)	STEM TO GUIDE Clearance (in.) Intake	STEM TO GUIDE Clearance (in.) Exhaust	STEM Diameter (in.) Intake	STEM Diameter (in.) Exhaust
'74	8-400	46	45	80 @ 1.70	$1\frac{23}{32}$	.0010–.0027	.0010–.0027	.3414	.3414
	8-454	46	45	80 @ 1.88	$1\frac{7}{8}$	.0010–.0027	.0010–.0027	.3719	.3717
'75–'76	8-350	46	45	80 @ 1.70	$1\frac{23}{32}$	.0010–.0027	.0010–.0027	.3414	.3414
	8-400	46	45	80 @ 1.70	$1\frac{23}{32}$	.0010–.0027	.0010–.0027	.3414	.3414
	8-454	46	45	90 @ 1.80	$1\frac{7}{8}$	.0010–.0027	.0010–.0027	.3719	.3717
'77	6-250	46	45	60 @ 1.66	$1\frac{21}{32}$	.0010–.0027	.0015–.0032	.3414	.3414
	8-305	46	45	80 @ 1.70	$1\frac{23}{32}$	.0010–.0027	.0010–.0027	.3414	.3414
	8-350	46	45	80 @ 1.70④	$1\frac{23}{32}$	.0010–.0027	.0010–.0027	.3414	.3414

① 350 hp
② Inner spring 30 @ 1.78
③ 300 hp
④ '77:80 @ 1.61, exhaust

Crankshaft and Connecting Rod Specifications

All measurements are given in in.

Year	Engine No. Cyl Displacement (cu in.)	CRANKSHAFT Main Brg Journal Dia	CRANKSHAFT Main Brg Oil Clearance	CRANKSHAFT Shaft End-Play	CRANKSHAFT Thrust on No.	CONNECTING ROD Journal Diameter	CONNECTING ROD Oil Clearance	CONNECTING ROD Side Clearance
'68–'69	6-250	2.2983–2.2993	.0003–.0029	.002–.006	7	1.9990–2.0000	.0007–.0027	.009–.013
	8-307, 327	2.4484–2.4493①	.0008–.0020②	.003–.011	5	2.0990–2.1000	.0007–.0028	.009–.013
	8-350**	2.4484–2.4493①	.0008–.0020②	.003–.011	5	2.0990–2.1000	.0007–.0028	.009–.013
	8-396	2.7484–2.7493③	.0010–.0022④	.006–.010	5	2.1990–2.2000	.0009–.0025	.015–.021
	8-427	2.7481–2.7490⑤	.0013–.0025⑥	.006–.010	5	2.1990–2.2000	.0009–.0025	.015–.021
'70	6-250	2.2983–2.2993	.0003–.0029	.002–.006	7	1.9990–2.0000	.0007–.0027	.009–.014
	8-350	2.4484–2.4493⑦	.0003–.0015⑧	.002–.006	5	2.0990–2.1000	.0007–.0028	.008–.014
	8-400 (265 HP)	2.6509	.0008–.0020⑨	.002–.006	5	2.0990–2.1000	.0009–.0030	.008–.014
	8-454	2.7485–2.7494③	.0013–.0025⑩	.006–.010	5	2.1990–2.2000	.0009–.0025	.015–.021

Crankshaft and Connecting Rod Specifications (cont.)

All measurements are given in in.

Year	Engine No. Cyl Displacement (cu in.)	CRANKSHAFT				CONNECTING ROD		
		Main Brg Journal Dia	Main Brg Oil Clearance	Shaft End-Play	Thrust on No.	Journal Diameter	Oil Clearance	Side Clearance
'71	6-250	2.2983–2.2993	.0003–.0029	.002–.006	7	1.9990–2.0000	.0007–.0027	.009–.014
	8-350	2.4484–2.4493⑦	.0008–.0020⑨	.002–.006	5	2.0990–2.1000	.0013–.0035	.008–.014
	8-350 (330 HP)	2.4484–2.4493⑦	.0013–.0025⑬	.002–.006	5	2.0990–2.1000	.0013–.0035	.008–.014
	8-400 (255 HP)	2.6484–2.6493⑭	.0008–.0020⑨	.002–.006	5	2.0990–2.1000	.0013–.0035	.008–.014
	8-402 (300 HP) (Mk IV)	2.7487–2.7496⑮	.0007–.0019⑯	.006–.010	5	2.1990–2.2000	.0009–.0025	.013–.023
	8-454 (365 HP)	2.7485–2.7494⑰	.0013–.0025⑩	.006–.010	5	2.1990–2.2000	.0009–.0025	.015–.021
'72	6-250	2.2983–2.2993	.0003–.0029	.002–.006	7	1.9990–2.0000	.0007–.0027	.009–.014
	8-350	2.4484–2.4493⑫	.0008–.0020⑨	.002–.006	5	2.0990–2.1000	.0013–.0035	.008–.014
	8-350 (255 HP)	2.4484–2.4493⑫	.0013–.0025⑬	.002–.006	5	2.0990–2.1000	.0013–.0035	.008–.014
	8-400 (170 HP)	2.6484–2.6493⑭	.0008–.0020⑨	.002–.006	5	2.0990–2.1000	.0013–.0035	.008–.014
	8-402 (210 HP)	2.7487–2.7496⑮	.0007–.0019⑯	.006–.010	5	2.1990–2.2000	.0009–.0025	.013–.023
	8-454 (270 HP)	2.7485–2.7494⑰	.0013–.0025⑩	.006–.010	5	2.1990–2.2000	.0009–.0025	.015–.021
'73–'77	6-250 All	2.2983–2.2993	.0003–.0029	.002–.006	7	1.9990–2.000	.0007–.0027	.009–.014
	8-305, 350, 145–190 HP	2.4484–2.4493⑱	.0008–.0020⑨	.002–.006	5	2.0990–2.1000	.0013–.0035	.008–.014
	8-400	2.6484–2.6493⑲	.0008–.0020⑨	.002–.006	5	2.0990–2.1000	.0013–.0035	.008–.014
	8-454	2.7485–2.7494⑰	.0013–.0025⑩	.006–.010	5	2.1990–2.2000	.0009–.0025	.015–.021

① No. 5—2.4470–2.4488
② No. 5—.0018–.0034
③ No.'s 3, 4—2.7481–2.7490; No. 5—2.7478–2.7488
④ No.'s 3, 4—.0013–.0025; No. 5—.0015–.0031
⑤ No. 5—2.7478–2.7488
⑥ No. 5—.0015–.0031
⑦ No. 5—2.4479–2.4488
⑧ No.'s 2, 3, 4—.0006–.0018; No. 5—.0008–.0023
⑨ No.'s 2, 3, 4—.011–.0023; No. 5—.0017–.0033
⑩ No. 5—.0024–.0040
⑫ No.'s 2, 3, 4—2.4481–2.4490; No. 5—2.4479–2.4488
⑬ No. 5—.0023–.0033; with auto. trans. No. 1—.0019–.0031
⑭ No. 5—2.6479–2.6488
⑮ No.'s 3, 4—2.7481–2.7490; No. 5—2.7473–2.7483
⑯ No.'s 2, 3, 4—.0013–.0025; No. 5—.0019–.0035
⑰ No.'s 2, 3, 4—2.7481–2.7490; No. 5—2.7478–2.7488
⑱ No. 5—2.4508
⑲ No. 5—2.6509
⑳ No.'s 1, 5—2.7499
㉑ No. 1—2.7499; No. 5—2.7505
°° Not available in 1968

Ring Gap
All measurements are given in in.

Year	Engine No. Cyl	Top Compression	Bottom Compression
'68–'77	6-250, 8-307	.010–.020	.010–.020
'77	8-305	.010–.020	.010–.025
'68–'69	8-327	.013–.023	.013–.025
'69–'71	8-350	.010–.020①	.013–.025①
'68–'76	8-396, 400, 402 427, 454	.010–.020	.010–.020
	All except 8-350	.010–.020	.010–.020
'73–'77	8-350	.010–.020	.013–.025②

Year	Engine No. Cyl	Oil Control
'68–'77	All engines except 8-396, 427	.015–.055
'68–'77	8-396, 427	.010–.030
'75–'76	8-350	.015–.055
	8-400	.010–.035
	8-454	.010–.025

① 250, 300 hp 350 cu in. Top .013–.023
                        2nd .013–.025
② 250, 255 hp 350 cu in. .013–.023

Torque Specifications
All readings in ft lbs

Year	Engine No. Cyl Displacement (cu in.)	Cylinder Head Bolts	Rod Bearing Bolts	Main Bearing Bolts	Crankshaft Pulley Bolt	Flywheel to Crankshaft Bolts	MANIFOLD Intake	Exhaust
'68–'73	6	95	35	65	——	60	30⑥	25⑤
'77	6-250	95	35	65	——	60	——	③
'68–'77	8-302, 305, 307, 350, 400	60–70	45	75①	60④	60	30	③
'68–'77	8-396, 402 (Big Block)	80	50	105②	85④	65	30	30
	8-427, 454	80	50	105②	85	65	30	30

① Engines with 4-bolt mains—Outer bolts 65
② 1968 2-bolt mains 95
③ Center bolts—25–30, end bolts 15–20
④ Where applicable
⑤ Exhaust-to-intake
⑥ Manifold-to-head

pressure is released. Remove all the bolts, clutch disc and pressure plate assembly.

20. To remove the automatic transmission:

    a. Remove the starter and the converter housing underpan.

    b. Remove the flywheel to converter attaching bolts.

    c. Supporting both the engine and transmission, remove the transmission to engine mounting bolts.

    d. Slowly guide the engine from the transmission.

CYLINDER HEAD

Removal and Installation

L6

1. Drain cooling system and remove air cleaner. Disconnect P.C.V. hose.

2. Disconnect the accelerator pedal rod at bell crank on manifold, and fuel and vacuum lines at carburetor.

3. Disconnect exhaust pipe at manifold flange, then remove manifold bolts and clamps and remove manifolds and carburetor as an assembly.

4. Remove fuel and vacuum line re-

taining clip from water outlet. Then disconnect wire harness from heat sending unit and coil, leaving harness clear of clips on rocker arm cover.

5. Disconnect radiator hose at water outlet housing and battery ground strap at cylinder head.

6. Disconnect wires and remove spark plugs. Disconnect coil to distributor primary wire lead at coil and remove the coil.

7. Remove rocker arm cover. Back off rocker arm nuts, pivot rocker arms to clear push rods and remove pushrods.

NOTE: *1977 model sixes do not use a rocker arm cover gasket. RTV sealer is used in its place.*

8. Remove cylinder-head bolts, cylinder head and gasket.

To install:

1. Place a new cylinder-head gasket over dowel pins in cylinder block.

2. Guide and lower cylinder head into place over dowels and gasket.

3. Oil cylinder-head bolts, install and run them down snug.

4. Tighten the cylinder-head bolts a little at a time with a torque wrench in the correct sequence. Final torque should be 90 to 95 ft lbs.

5. Install valve pushrods down through the cylinder-head openings and seat them in their lifter sockets.

6. Install rocker arms, balls and nuts and tighten rocker arm nuts until all push-rod play is taken up.

7. Install thermostat, thermostat housing and water outlet using new gaskets. Then connect radiator hose.

8. Install heat sending switch and torque to 15–20 ft lbs.

9. Clean spark plugs or install new ones. Set gaps to 0.035 in.

10. Use new plug gaskets and torque to 20–25 ft lbs (15 ft lbs 1970–76).

11. Install coil then connect heat sending unit and coil primary wires, and connect battery ground cable at the cylinder head.

12. Clean surfaces and install new gasket over manifold studs. Install manifold. Install bolts and clamps and torque as specified.

13. Connect throttle linkage.

14. Connect P.C.V., fuel and vacuum lines and secure lines in clip at water outlet.

15. Fill cooling system and check for leaks.

16. Adjust the valve lash.

17. Install the rocker arm cover and position the wiring harness in the clips.

18. Clean and install air cleaner.

V8

1. Remove the intake manifold as previously outlined.

2. Remove the exhaust manifolds as previously outlined and tie out of the way.

3. Back off the rocker arm nuts and pivot the rocker arms out of the way so that the pushrods can be removed. Identify the pushrods so that they can be installed in their original positions.

4. Remove the cylinder head bolts and remove the heads.

5. Install the cylinder heads using new gaskets. Install the gaskets with the head up.

NOTE: *Coat a steel gasket on both sides with sealer. If a composition gasket is used, do not use sealer.*

6. Clean the bolts, apply sealer to the threads and install them hand tight.

7. Tighten the head bolts a little at a time in the sequence shown. Head bolt torque is listed in the specifications.

8. Install the intake and exhaust manifolds.

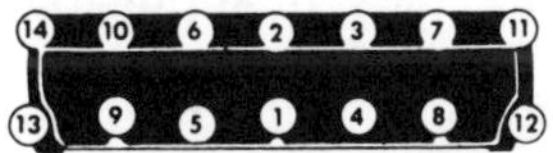

Six-cylinder head tightening sequence

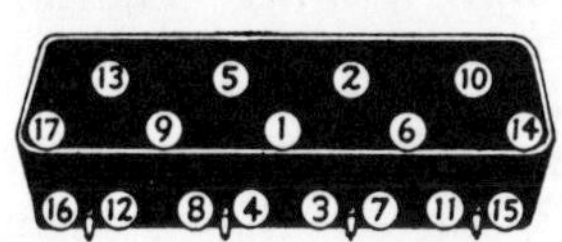

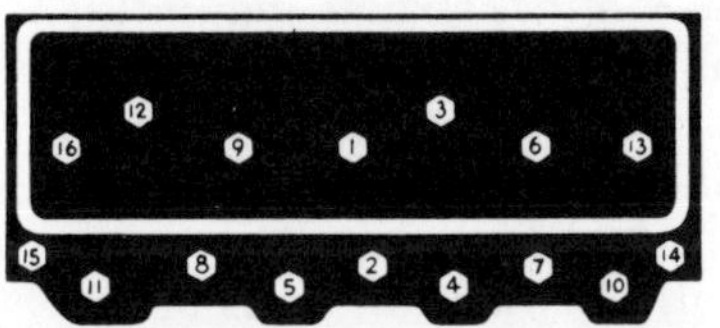

V8 cylinder head tightening sequence (small block on left, big block on right)

9. Adjust the valves as previously described.

Valve Guides

Valve guides are integral with the cylinder head on all engines. Valve guide bores may be reamed to accommodate oversize valves. If wear permits, valve guides can be knurled to allow the retention of standard valves. Maximum allowable valve stem-to-guide bore clearances are listed under valve specifications.

Rocker Arm Removal and Installation

Rocker arms are removed by removing the adjusting nut. Be sure to adjust the valve lash after replacing rocker arms. Coat the replacement rocker arm and ball with SAE 90 gear oil before installation.

NOTE: *When replacing an exhaust rocker, move an old intake rocker to the exhaust rocker arm stud and install the new rocker arm on the intake stud. This will prevent burning of the new rocker arm on the exhaust position.*

Rocker arms studs that have damaged threads or are loose in the cylinder heads may be replaced by reaming the bore and installing oversize studs. Oversizes available are .003 and .013 in. The bore may also be tapped and screw-in studs installed. Several aftermarket companies produce complete rocker arm stud kits with installation tools. Mark IV and late high performance small-block engines use screw-in studs and pushrod guide plates.

Overhaul

See the Engine Rebuilding Section.

INTAKE MANIFOLD

Removal and Installation

L6

NOTE: *1977 six intake manifold is integral with the cylinder head.*

The L6 intake and exhaust manifolds are removed as a unit.

1. Disconnect the exhaust pipe flange and remove all connections to the carburetor.
2. Take off all the vacuum lines at the manifold and carburetor.

3. Remove the carburetor.
4. Remove the retaining bolts from the side of the cylinder head.
5. To separate the intake and exhaust manifold, remove the one retaining bolt and two nuts at the center.
6. Install the manifold in the reverse of the removal procedure.

V8

1. Remove the air cleaner.
2. Drain the radiator.
3. Disconnect:
   a. Battery cables at the battery.
   b. Upper radiator and heater hoses at the manifold.
   c. Crankcase ventilation hoses as required.
   d. Fuel line at the carburetor.
   e. Accelerator linkage at the pedal lever.
   f. Vacuum hose at the distributor.
   g. Power brake hose at the carburetor base or manifold, if applicable.
   h. Ignition coil and temperature sending switch wires.
4. Remove the distributor cap and scribe the rotor position relative to distributor body.
5. Remove the distributor.
6. If applicable, remove the Delcotron upper bracket.
7. Remove the manifold to head attaching bolts, then remove the manifold and carburetor as an assembly.
8. If the manifold is to be replaced, transfer the carburetor (and mounting studs), water outlet and thermostat (use a new gasket), heater hose adapter and, if applicable, the choke coil.
9. Before installing the manifold, thoroughly clean the gasket and seal surfaces of the cylinder heads and manifold.
10. Install the manifold end seals, folding the tabs if applicable, and the manifold/head gaskets, using a sealing compound around the water passages.
11. When installing the manifold, care should be taken not to dislocate the end seals. It is helpful to use a pilot in the distributor opening. Tighten the manifold bolts to 30 ft lbs in the sequence illustrated.
12. Install the ignition coil.
13. Install the distributor with the rotor in its original location as indicated by the scribe line. If the engine has been

1. Valve cover
2. Screw reinforcements
3. Gasket
4. Adjusting nut
5. Rocker arm
6. Valve spring retainer
7. Valve spring
8. Exhaust valve
9. Intake valve
10. Gasket
11. Exhaust manifold
12. Spark plug shield
13. Bolt
14. Washer
15. Head gasket
16. Spark plug
17. Cylinder head
18. Pushrod
19. Spring shield
20. Rocker arm stud
21. Rocker arm ball

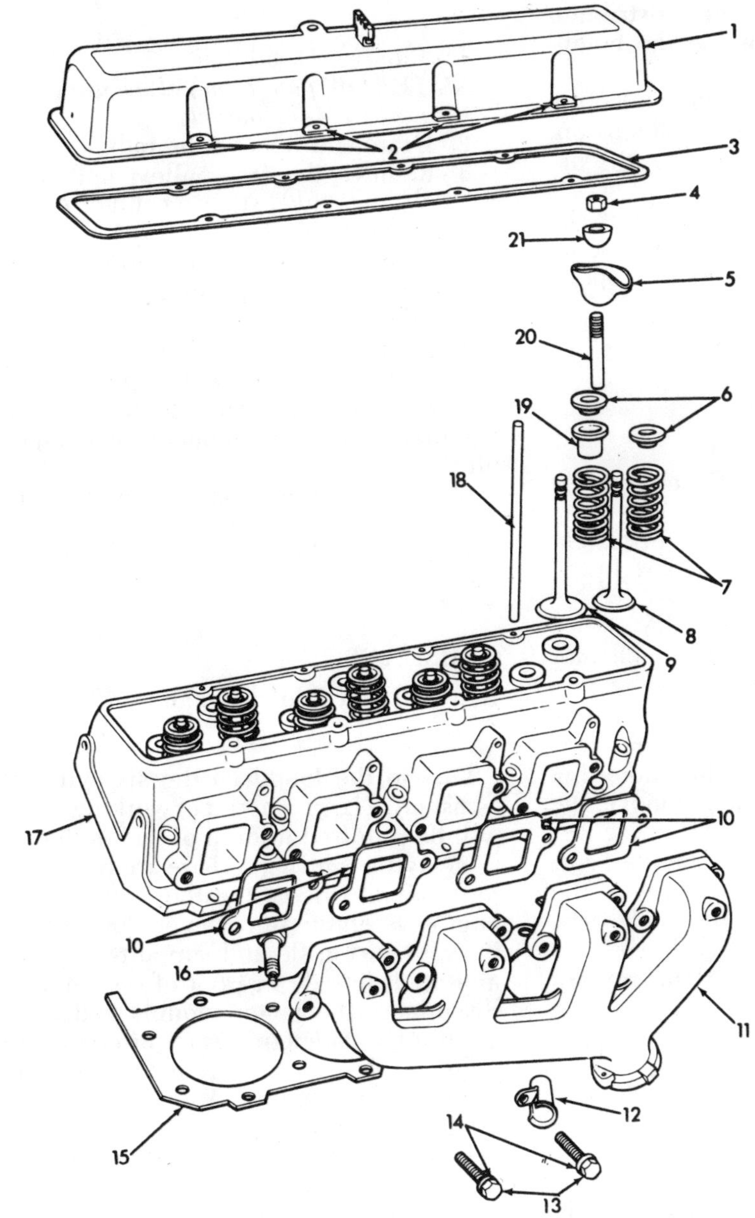

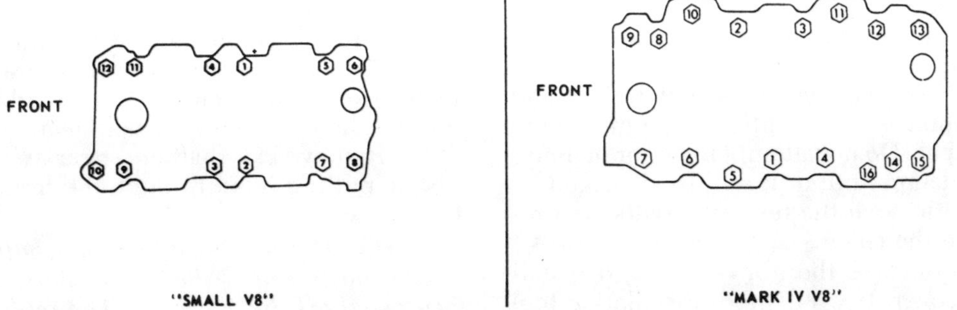

Big block cylinder head components (small block V8 similar)

Intake manifold tightening sequences

disturbed, refer to Step 9 of "Distributor Removal and Installation" at the beginning of this chapter.

14. If applicable, install the Delcotron upper bracket and adjust the belt tension.

15. Connect all components disconnected in Step 3 above.

16. Fill the cooling system, start the engine, check for leaks and adjust the ignition timing and carburetor idle speed and mixture.

EXHAUST MANIFOLD

Removal and Installation

V8

1. If equipped with AIR, remove the air injector manifold assembly. The ¼ in. pipe threads in the manifold are straight threads. Do not use a ¼ in. tapered pipe tap.

2. Disconnect the battery.

3. If applicable, remove the air cleaner pre-heater shroud.

4. Remove the exhaust pipe flange nuts, then hang the pipe with wire.

5. Remove the manifold mounting bolts (end bolts first), then remove the manifold.

6. To install, clean the mating surfaces, then install the manifold with the center bolts first. Install the end bolts, then tighten all bolts to 20 ft lbs.

7. To complete installation, reverse Steps 1 through 3.

TIMING GEAR COVER

Removal and Installation

L6

1. Remove the oil pan.

2. Remove the radiator after draining it.

3. Remove the fan, pulley, and belt. Remove any power steering and/or AIR pump drive belt. Remove any braces for the above pumps which will interfere with cover removal and position the pumps out of the way.

4. Remove the crankshaft pulley and damper. Use a puller to remove the damper. Do not attempt to pry or hammer the damper off, or it will be damaged.

5. Remove the retaining bolts, and remove the cover.

6. Reverse the above steps to install the cover. Use a damper installation tool to pull the damper on.

V8

1. Remove the oil pan.
NOTE: *Oil pan removal is unnecessary on 1974–77 models.*

2. Drain and remove the radiator.

3. Remove the fan, pulley, and belt. Remove any power steering and/or A.I.R. pump drive belts. Remove any braces for these pumps which will interfere with cover removal and position the pumps out of the way.

4. Remove the water pump.

5. Remove the crankshaft pulley and damper. Use a puller on the damper. Do not attempt to pry or hammer the damper off.

6. Remove the retaining bolts, and remove the timing cover.

7. Reverse the above steps to install the cover.

CAMSHAFT

Removal and Replacement

L6

Due to the length of the six cylinder camshaft, a large amount of working room will be required in front of the engine to remove the camshaft. There are two ways to go about this task: either remove the engine assembly from the car, or remove the radiator, grille and supports that are mounted directly in front of the engine, disconnect the motor mounts and raise the front of the engine as required to gain enough clearance to remove the cam from the engine.

1. In addition to removing the timing gear cover, remove the grille and radiator.

2. Remove the valve cover and gasket, loosen all the valve rocker arm nuts and pivot the arms clear of the pushrods.

3. Remove distributor and fuel pump.

4. Remove coil, side cover and gasket. Remove pushrods and valve lifters.

5. Remove the two camshaft thrust plate retaining screws by working through holes in the camshaft gear.

6. Remove camshaft and gear assembly by pulling it out through the front of the block.

NOTE: *If renewing either camshaft or camshaft gear, the gear must be pressed off the camshaft. The replacement parts must be assembled in the same manner (under pressure). In placing the gear on the camshaft, press the gear onto the shaft until it bottoms against the gear spacer ring. The end clearance of the thrust plate should be .001 to .005 in.*

7. Install camshaft assembly in the engine.

NOTE: *Pre-lube the cam lobes with E.O.S. or SAE 90 gear lubricant. Do not dislodge the cam bearings when inserting the camshaft.*

8. Turn crankshaft and camshaft to align and bring the timing marks together. Push the camshaft into this aligned position. Install camshaft thrust plate-to-block screws and torque them to 6–7¼ ft lbs.

9. Runout on either crankshaft or camshaft gear should not exceed .003 in.

10. Backlash between the two gears should be between .004 and .006 in.

11. Install timing gear cover and gasket.

12. Install oil pan and gaskets.

13. Install harmonic balancer.

14. Line up keyway in balancer with key on crankshaft and drive balancer onto shaft until it bottoms against crankshaft gear.

15. Install valve lifters and pushrods. Install side cover with new gasket. Attach coil wires; install fuel pump.

16. Install distributor and set timing as described under distributor at the beginning of the section.

17. Pivot rocker arms over pushrods and adjust the valves.

18. Add oil to the engine. Install and adjust fan felt.

19. Install radiator or shroud.

20. Install grille assembly.

21. Fill cooling system, start engine and check for leaks.

22. Check and adjust timing.

V8

1. Remove intake manifold, valve lifters and timing chain cover (requires oil pan removal) as described in this section.

2. Remove the grille and radiator.

3. Remove fuel pump and pump pushrod.

4. Remove camshaft sprocket bolts, sprocket and timing chain. A light blow to the lower edge of a tight sprocket should free it (use a plastic mallet).

5. Install two 5/16–18 x 4 in. bolts in cam bolt holes and pull cam from block.

6. To install, reverse removal procedure, aligning the timing marks.

NOTE: *Pre-lube the cam lobes with E.O.S. or SAE 90 gear lubricant. Do not dislodge the cam bearings when installing the camshaft.*

PISTONS AND CONNECTING RODS

Removal and Installation

Piston and connecting rod removal/installation and piston ring removal/installation are detailed in the Engine Rebuilding section at the end of this chapter. Removal and installation is outlined with the engine out of the car, but the same procedures may be used with block in the chassis. Remove the cylinder heads and oil pan for piston and connect-

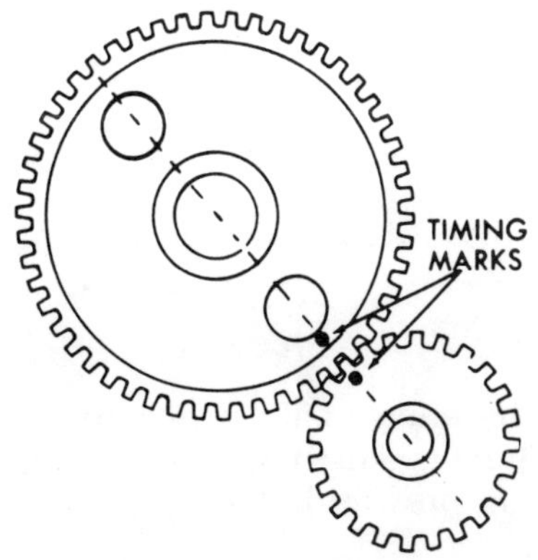

Timing mark alignment for six-cylinder

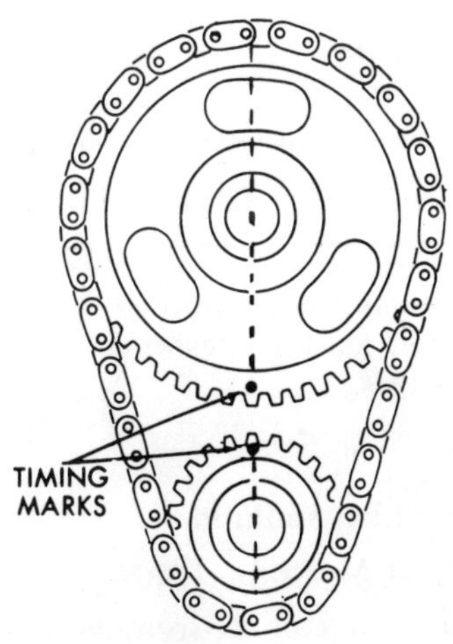

Timing mark alignment for all V8s

ing rod removal. Piston and connecting rod positioning is illustrated in the accompanying figures.

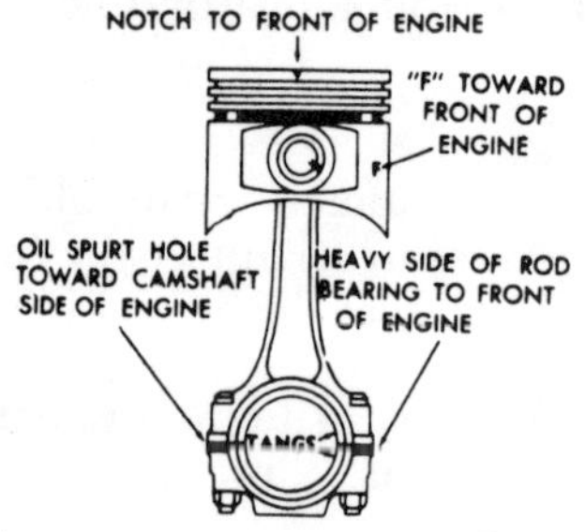

Six-cylinder piston-to-connecting rod relationship

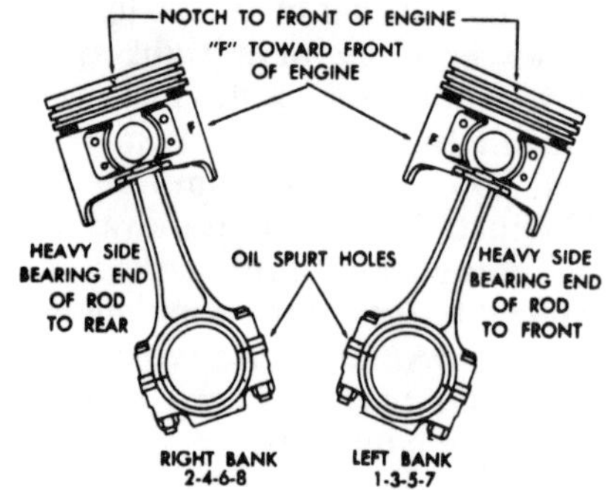

Small block V8 piston-to-connecting rod relationship

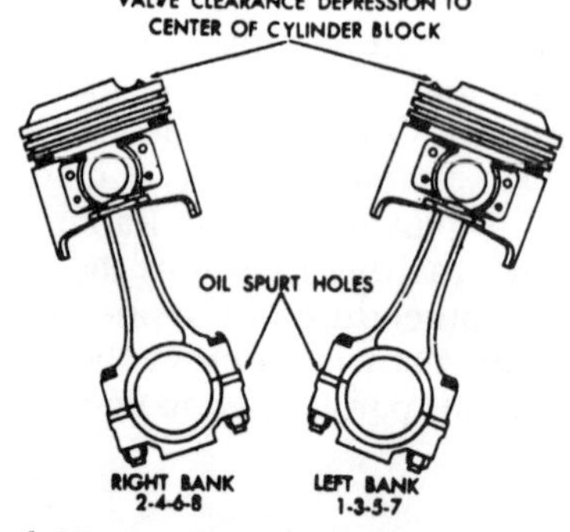

Big block V8 piston-to-connecting rod relationship

Engine Lubrication

Both L6 and V8 engines have pressurized lubrication systems with full-flow oil filters.

OIL PAN

Removal and Installation

L6 WITH MANUAL TRANSMISSION

The oil pan can be removed, either after removing engine, or as folllows:

1. Drain radiator and oil pan.
2. Disconnect gas tank line at fuel pump and upper and lower radiator hoses.
3. Remove clutch housing-to-engine block bolt above dowel on right side.
4. Raise vehicle on hoist or place on jack stands.
5. Rotate engine to align distributor rotor No. 3 and No. 5 plug wire. (This locates No. 6 crank throw part way up.)
6. Remove starter and flywheel front cover plate.
7. Remove front mount through bolts.
8. Jack up front of engine. Raise as far as possible always using care by checking various dash and body tunnel clearances.
9. Remove front engine mount frame bracket on right side and remove oil filter where necessary.
10. Remove oil pan screws and lower pan to frame.
11. Remove oil pump to gain clearance, then remove oil pan by sliding and rotating front to right and then to rear, and down at an angle. (On certain earlier models, these procedures may be varied in some self-evident areas.)
12. Install in reverse of above.
NOTE: *Gasket can be replaced by completely removing pan from vehicle.*

L6 WITH AUTOMATIC TRANSMISSION

1. Drain radiator and crankcase.
2. Disconnect gas tank line at fuel pump, and radiator hoses at radiator.
3. Remove clutch housing-to-engine block bolt above dowel pin on each side.
4. Rotate engine to align distributor between No. 3 and No. 5 plug wires. (This locates No. 6 crank throw part way up.)
5. Raise vehicle on hoist or on jack stands.
6. Remove converter cover pan, and starter assembly.
7. Follow Steps 7 through 12, listed above.

V8

1. Disconnect battery negative cable.
2. Remove distributor cap from distributor to prevent breakage against firewall.
3. Drain cooling system. Remove ra-

diator hoses, and remove oil dipstick and tube, where necessary.

4. Remove fan blade assembly.

5. Raise car, and drain engine oil.

6. Remove bolts from engine front mounts. Disconnect and remove starter.

7. On cars with automatic transmissions, remove converter housing underpan.

8. Disconnect the exhaust Y pipe from the manifolds.

9. Rotate crankshaft until timing mark on the damper is at six o'clock position.

10. Using a block of wood and a suitable jack, raise engine enough to insert 2 x 4 in. wood block under engine mounts then lower engine onto blocks.

11. Remove engine oil pan.

V8 raised and blocked for oil pan removal

12. Install by reversing removal procedures.

NOTE: *The 396, 402, 427, and 454 cu. in. engines use three ¼ in. attaching bolts at crankcase front cover; one at each corner, and one at the lower center.*

Rear Main Oil Seal Replacement

The rear main bearing seal may be replaced without removing the crankshaft. Both upper and lower seals must be replaced at the same time.

1. Remove the oil pan and oil pump.

2. Remove the rear main bearing cap, and pry the seal out from the bottom with a small screwdriver.

3. Remove the upper seal with a small hammer and a brass pin punch. Tap on one end of the seal until the opposite end can be gripped with pliers.

4. Clean the bearing cap and crankshaft.

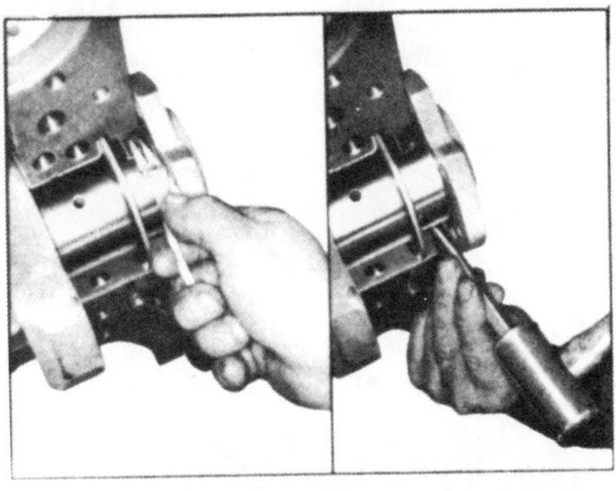

Rear main oil seal replacement

5. Coat the lips and bead of the seal with a light engine oil. Do not get oil on the seal ends.

6. Insert the new seal into the bearing cap, rolling it into place with your finger and thumb. Press lightly on the seal, so that the seal tangs on the cap don't cut the bead on the back of the seal.

7. Lubricate the lip of the new oil seal and slowly push it into place while turning the crankshaft. Make sure that the seal tangs don't cut the bead on the back of the seal.

8. Install the main bearing cap and torque to specifications.

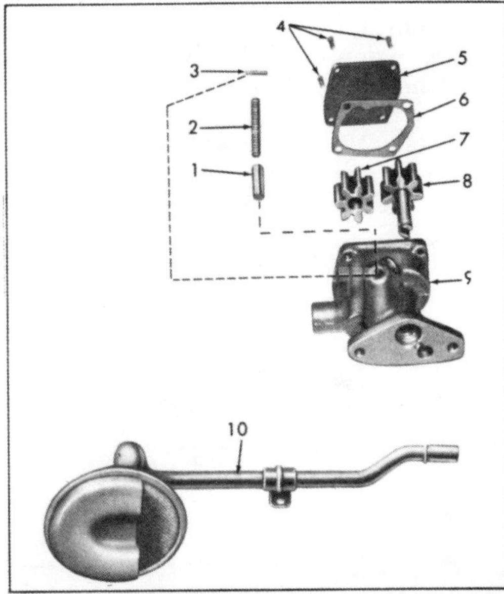

Exploded view of six-cylinder oil pump

1. Pressure regulator valve	6. Cover gasket
2. Pressure regulator spring	7. Idler gear
3. Retaining pin	8. Drive gear and shaft
4. Screws	9. Pump body
5. Pump cover	10. Pickup screen and pipe

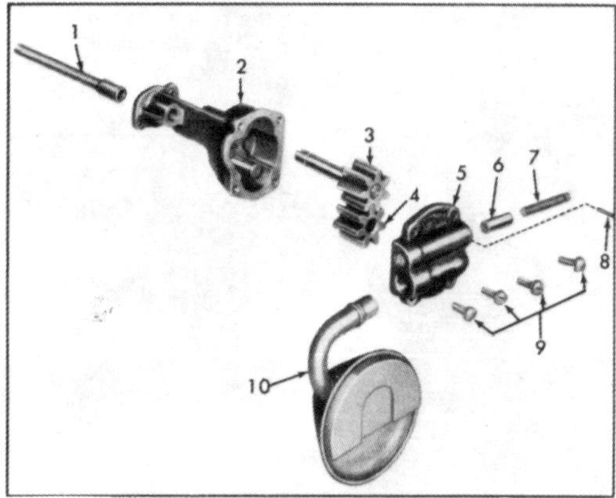

Exploded view of small block V8 oil pump

1. Shaft
2. Pump body
3. Drive gear and shaft
4. Idler gear
5. Pump cover
6. Pressure regulator
7. Pressure regulator spring
8. Retaining pin
9. Screws
10. Pickup screen and pipe

OIL PUMP

The oil pump is a two-piece housing containing a pressure regulator valve and two pump gears. It is driven by the camshaft and the distributor shaft.

Removal and Installation

1. Remove the oil pan as previously described.

2. On L6 engines, remove the two flange mounting bolts, pickup pipe bolt, and then remove the pump and screen as an assembly.

3. On V8 engines, remove the oil pump-to-rear main bearing cap bolt. Remove the pump and the extension shaft.

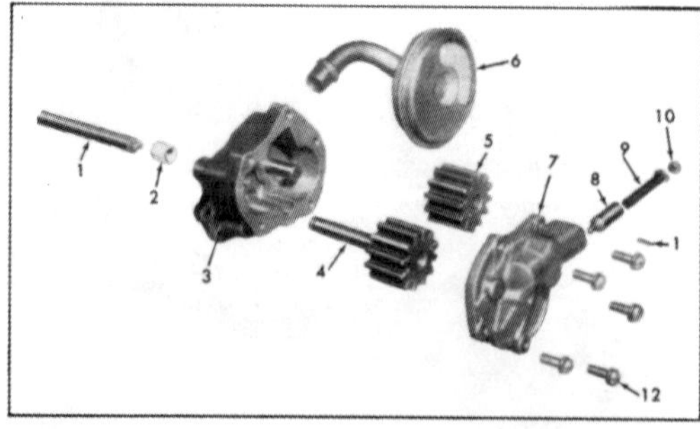

Exploded view of big block V8 oil pump

1. Shaft extension
2. Shaft coupling
3. Pump body
4. Drive gear and shaft
5. Idler gear
6. Pickup screen and pipe
7. Pump cover
8. Pressure regulator valve
9. Pressure regulator spring
10. Washer
11. Retaining pin
12. Screws

Engine Cooling

The cooling system consists of a radiator, belt-driven fan, thermostat, and a mechanical water pump. Air conditioned and high-performance engines are equipped with a viscous drive fan. This fan restricts operation at 1500 rpm in cold weather and 3500 rpm during warmer temperatures. This fan requires less horsepower to drive during high rpm operation and reduces under-hood noise. 1977 models are equipped with a special pressure relief radiator cap. Be sure any replacement cap used is the same.

RADIATOR

Removal and Installation

1. Drain the cooling system.

2. Disconnect the radiator upper and lower hoses and, if applicable, transmission coolant lines. Remove the coolant recovery system line, if so equipped.

3. Remove the radiator upper panel if so equipped.

4. If there is a radiator shroud in front of the radiator, the radiator and shroud are removed as an assembly.

5. If there is a fan shroud, remove the shroud attaching screws and let the shroud hang on the fan.

6. Remove the radiator attaching bolts and remove the radiator.

7. Installation is the reverse of the removal procedure.

WATER PUMP

Removal and Installation

1. Drain the radiator.

2. Loosen the fan pulley bolts.

3. Disconnect the heater hoses, lower radiator hose, and the by-pass hose (if so equipped) at the water pump.

4. Loosen the alternator swivel bolt (remove the upper brace on V8s) and remove the fan belt.

5. Disconnect the power steering and air conditioning belts and swivel the power steering pump to one side (on Mark IV engines).

6. Remove the fan and pulley.

NOTE: *Viscous drive fans should not be stored horizontally. The silicone fluid can leak out of the fan assembly if it is not kept upright.*

7. Remove the water pump-to-cylinder block bolts and the power steering-to-pump bolts. Remove the water pump. On L6 engines, remove the pump by pulling it straight out of the block.

8. Install the pump on the block with a new gasket.

9. Install the pump pulley and the fan onto the pump.

10. Connect the hoses and refill the cooling system. Install the remaining components, bolts, and belts.

11. Start the engine and check for leaks.

THERMOSTAT

Removal and Installation

1. It is not necessary to remove the radiator hose from the thermostat housing.

2. Remove the two retaining bolts from the thermostat housing (located on the front top of the intake manifold on V8s, and directly in front of the valve cover on L6s), and remove the thermostat.

3. Use a new gasket when replacing the thermostat.

Installing thermostat

Engine Rebuilding

This section describes, in detail, the procedures involved in rebuilding a typical engine. The procedures specifically refer to an inline engine, however, they are basically identical to those used in rebuilding engines of nearly all design and configurations. Procedures for servicing atypical engines (i.e., horizontally opposed) are described in the appropriate section, although in most cases, cylinder head reconditioning procedures described in this chapter will apply.

The section is divided into two sections. The first, Cylinder Head Reconditioning, assumes that the cylinder head is removed from the engine, all manifolds are removed, and the cylinder head is on a workbench. The camshaft should be removed from overhead cam cylinder heads. The second section, Cylinder Block Reconditioning, covers the block, pistons, connecting rods and crankshaft. It is assumed that the engine is mounted on a work stand, and the cylinder head and all accessories are removed.

Procedures are identified as follows:

Unmarked—Basic procedures that must be performed in order to successfully complete the rebuilding process.

Starred (*)—Procedures that should be performed to ensure maximum performance and engine life.

Double starred (**)—Procedures that may be performed to increase engine performance and reliability. These procedures are usually reserved for extremely heavy-duty or competition usage.

In many cases, a choice of methods is also provided. Methods are identified in the same manner as procedures. The choice of method for a procedure is at the discretion of the user.

The tools required for the basic rebuilding procedure should, with minor exceptions, be those

TORQUE (ft. lbs.) *

U.S.

Bolt Diameter (inches)	Bolt Grade (SAE)				Wrench Size (inches)	
	1 and 2	5	6	8	Bolt	Nut
1/4	5	7	10	10.5	3/8	7/16
5/16	9	14	19	22	1/2	9/16
3/8	15	25	34	37	9/16	5/8
7/16	24	40	55	60	5/8	3/4
1/2	37	60	85	92	3/4	13/16
9/16	53	88	120	132	7/8	7/8
5/8	74	120	167	180	15/16	1
3/4	120	200	280	296	1-1/8	1-1/8
7/8	190	302	440	473	1-5/16	1-5/16
1	282	466	660	714	1-1/2	1-1/2

Metric

Bolt Diameter (mm)	Bolt Grade				Wrench Size (mm)
	5D	8G	10K	12K	Bolt and Nut
6	5	6	8	10	10
8	10	16	22	27	14
10	19	31	40	49	17
12	34	54	70	86	19
14	55	89	117	137	22
16	83	132	175	208	24
18	111	182	236	283	27
22	182	284	394	464	32
24	261	419	570	689	36

*—Torque values are for lightly oiled bolts. CAUTION: Bolts threaded into aluminum require much less torque.

General Torque Specifications

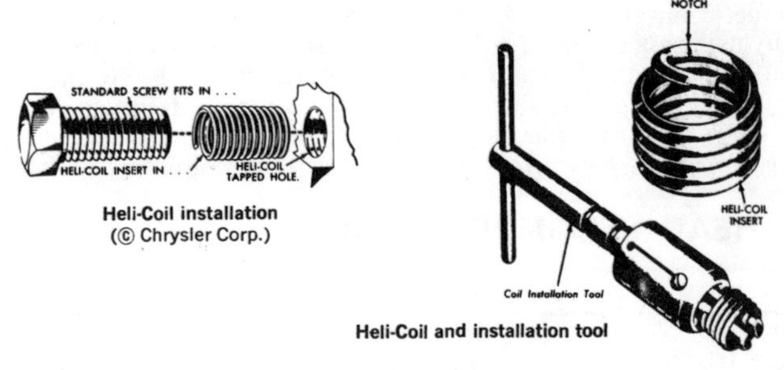

Heli-Coil installation
(© Chrysler Corp.)

Heli-Coil and installation tool

Heli-Coil Insert			Drill	Tap	Insert. Tool	Extract- ing Tool
Thread Size	Part No.	Insert Length (In.)	Size	Part No.	Part No.	Part No.
1/2 -20	1185-4	3/8	17/64(.266)	4 CPB	528-4N	1227-6
5/16-18	1185-5	15/32	Q(.332)	5 CPB	528-5N	1227-6
3/8 -16	1185-6	9/16	X(.397)	6 CPB	528-6N	1227-6
7/16-14	1185-7	21/32	29/64(.453)	7 CPB	528-7N	1227-16
1/2 -13	1185-8	3/4	33/64(.516)	8 CPB	528-8N	1227-16

Heli-Coil Specifications

included in a mechanic's tool kit. An accurate torque wrench, and a dial indicator (reading in thousandths) mounted on a universal base should be available. Bolts and nuts with no torque specification should be tightened according to size (see chart). Special tools, where required, all are readily available from the major tool suppliers (i.e., Craftsman, Snap-On, K-D). The services of a competent automotive machine shop must also be readily available.

When assembling the engine, any parts that will be in frictional contact must be pre-lubricated, to provide protection on initial start-up. Vortex Pre-Lube, STP, or any product specifically formulated for this purpose may be used. NOTE: *Do not use engine oil.* Where semi-permanent (locked but removable) installation of bolts or nuts is desired, threads should be cleaned and coated with Loctite. Studs may be permanently installed using Loctite Stud and Bearing Mount.

Aluminum has become increasingly popular for use in engines, due to its low weight and excellent heat transfer characteristics. The following precautions must be observed when handling aluminum engine parts:

—Never hot-tank aluminum parts.

—Remove all aluminum parts (identification tags, etc.) from engine parts before hot-tanking (otherwise they will be removed during the process).

—Always coat threads lightly with engine oil or anti-seize compounds before installation, to prevent seizure.

—Never over-torque bolts or spark plugs in aluminum threads. Should stripping occur, threads can be restored according to the following procedure, using Heli-Coil thread inserts:

Tap drill the hole with the stripped threads to the specified size (see chart). Using the specified tap (NOTE: *Heli-Coil tap sizes refer to the size thread being replaced, rather than the actual tap size*), tap the hole for the Heli-Coil. Place the insert on the proper installation tool (see chart). Apply pressure on the insert while winding it clockwise into the hole, until the top of the insert is one turn below the surface. Remove the installation tool, and break the installation tang from the bottom of the in-

sert by moving it up and down. If the Heli-Coil must be removed, tap the removal tool firmly into the hole, so that it engages the top thread, and turn the tool counter-clockwise to extract the insert.

Snapped bolts or studs may be removed, using a stud extractor (unthreaded) or Vise-Grip pliers (threaded). Penetrating oil (e.g., Liquid Wrench) will often aid in breaking frozen threads. In cases where the stud or bolt is flush with, or below the surface, proceed as follows:

Drill a hole in the broken stud or bolt, approximately ½ its diameter. Select a screw extractor (e.g., Easy-Out) of the proper size, and tap it into the stud or bolt. Turn the extractor counter-clockwise to remove the stud or bolt.

Magnaflux and Zyglo are inspection techniques used to locate material flaws, such as stress cracks. Magnafluxing coats the part with fine magnetic particles, and subjects the part to a magnetic field. Cracks cause breaks

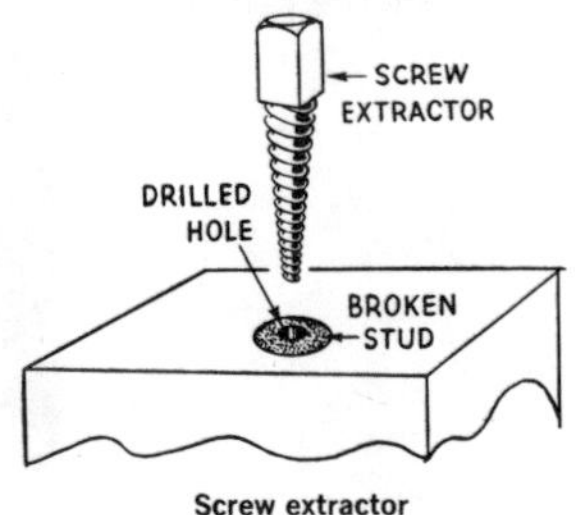

Screw extractor

in the magnetic field, which are outlined by the particles. Since Magnaflux is a magnetic process, it is applicable only to ferrous materials. The Zyglo process coats the material with a fluorescent dye penetrant, and then subjects it to blacklight inspection, under which cracks glow bright-

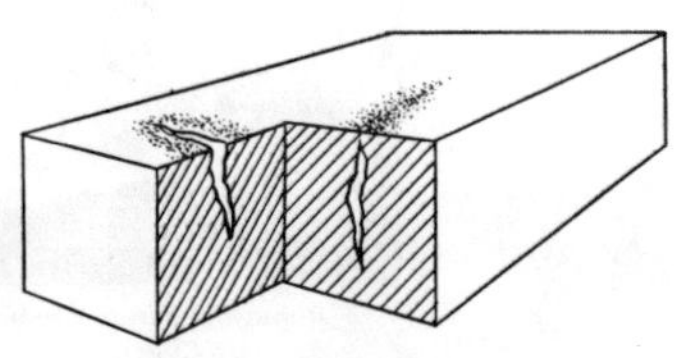

Magnaflux indication of cracks

ly. Parts made of any material may be tested using Zyglo. While Magnaflux and Zyglo are excellent for general inspection, and locating hidden defects, specific checks of suspected cracks may be made at lower cost and more readily using spot check dye. The dye is sprayed onto the suspected area, wiped off, and the area is then sprayed with a developer. Cracks then will show up bright-ly. Spot check dyes will only indicate surface cracks; therefore, structural cracks below the surface may escape detection. When questionable, the part should be tested using Magnaflux or Zyglo.

CYLINDER HEAD RECONDITIONING

Procedure	*Method*
Identify the valves:  **Valve identification** (© SAAB)	Invert the cylinder head, and number the valve faces front to rear, using a permanent felt-tip marker.
Remove the rocker arms:	Remove the rocker arms with shaft(s) or balls and nuts. Wire the sets of rockers, balls and nuts together, and identify according to the corresponding valve.
Remove the valves and springs:	Using an appropriate valve spring compressor (depending on the configuration of the cylinder head), compress the valve springs. Lift out the keepers with needlenose pliers, release the compressor, and remove the valve, spring, and spring retainer.
Check the valve stem-to-guide clearance:  **Checking the valve stem-to-guide clearance** (© American Motors Corp.)	Clean the valve stem with lacquer thinner or a similar solvent to remove all gum and varnish. Clean the valve guides using solvent and an expanding wire-type valve guide cleaner. Mount a dial indicator so that the stem is at 90° to the valve stem, as close to the valve guide as possible. Move the valve off its seat, and measure the valve guide-to-stem clearance by moving the stem back and forth to actuate the dial indicator. Measure the valve stems using a micrometer, and compare to specifications, to determine whether stem or guide wear is responsible for excessive clearance.
De-carbon the cylinder head and valves: 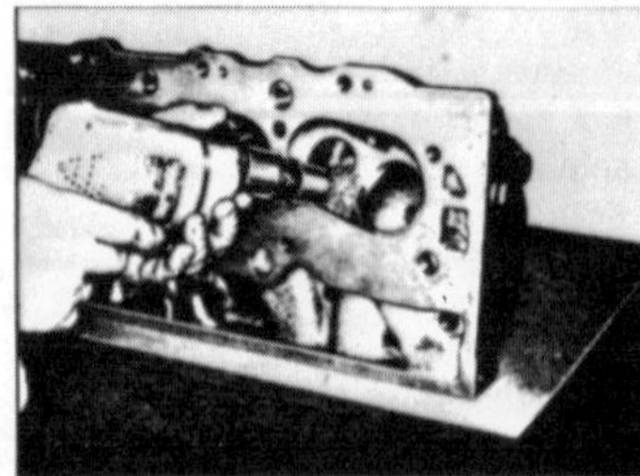 **Removing carbon from the cylinder head** (© Chevrolet Div. G.M. Corp.)	Chip carbon away from the valve heads, combustion chambers, and ports, using a chisel made of hardwood. Remove the remaining deposits with a stiff wire brush. NOTE: *Ensure that the deposits are actually removed, rather than burnished.*

Procedure	*Method*
Hot-tank the cylinder head:	Have the cylinder head hot-tanked to remove grease, corrosion, and scale from the water passages. NOTE: *In the case of overhead cam cylinder heads, consult the operator to determine whether the camshaft bearings will be damaged by the caustic solution.*
Degrease the remaining cylinder head parts:	Using solvent (i.e., Gunk), clean the rockers, rocker shaft(s) (where applicable), rocker balls and nuts, springs, spring retainers, and keepers. Do not remove the protective coating from the springs.
Check the cylinder head for warpage: 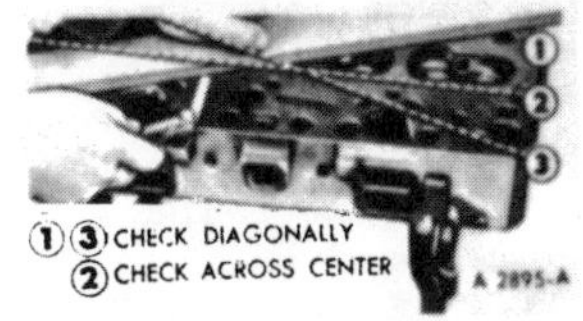 **Checking the cylinder head for warpage** (© Ford Motor Co.)	Place a straight-edge across the gasket surface of the cylinder head. Using feeler gauges, determine the clearance at the center of the straight-edge. Measure across both diagonals, along the longitudinal centerline, and across the cylinder head at several points. If warpage exceeds .003″ in a 6″ span, or .006″ over the total length, the cylinder head must be resurfaced. NOTE: *If warpage exceeds the manufacturers maximum tolerance for material removal, the cylinder head must be replaced.* When milling the cylinder heads of V-type engines, the intake manifold mounting position is altered, and must be corrected by milling the manifold flange a proportionate amount.
** Porting and gasket matching: **Marking the cylinder head for gasket matching** (© Petersen Publishing Co.)**Port configuration before and after gasket matching** (© Petersen Publishing Co.)	** Coat the manifold flanges of the cylinder head with Prussian blue dye. Glue intake and exhaust gaskets to the cylinder head in their installed position using rubber cement and scribe the outline of the ports on the manifold flanges. Remove the gaskets. Using a small cutter in a hand-held power tool (i.e., Dremel Moto-Tool), gradually taper the walls of the port out to the scribed outline of the gasket. Further enlargement of the ports should include the removal of sharp edges and radiusing of sharp corners. Do not alter the valve guides. NOTE: *The most efficient port configuration is determined only by extensive testing. Therefore, it is best to consult someone experienced with the head in question to determine the optimum alterations.*

Procedure	*Method*

** Polish the ports:

Relieved and polished ports
(© Petersen Publishing Co.)

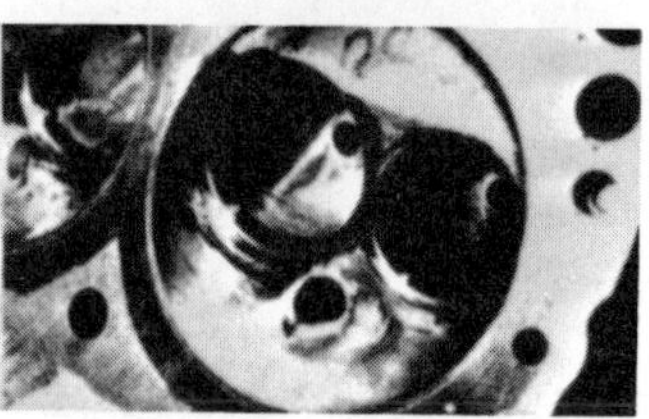

Polished combustion chamber
(© Petersen Publishing Co.)

** Using a grinding stone with the above mentioned tool, polish the walls of the intake and exhaust ports, and combustion chamber. Use progressively finer stones until all surface imperfections are removed. NOTE: *Through testing, it has been determined that a smooth surface is more effective than a mirror polished surface in intake ports, and vice-versa in exhaust ports.*

---

* Knurling the valve guides:

Cut-away view of a knurled valve guide
(© Petersen Publishing Co.)

* Valve guides which are not excessively worn or distorted may, in some cases, be knurled rather than replaced. Knurling is a process in which metal is displaced and raised, thereby reducing clearance. Knurling also provides excellent oil control. The possibility of knurling rather than replacing valve guides should be discussed with a machinist.

Replacing the valve guides: NOTE: *Valve guides should only be replaced if damaged or if an oversize valve stem is not available.*

Valve guide removal tool

Valve guide installation tool (with washers used during installation)

Depending on the type of cylinder head, valve guides may be pressed, hammered, or shrunk in. In cases where the guides are shrunk into the head, replacement should be left to an equipped machine shop. In other cases, the guides are replaced as follows: Press or tap the valve guides out of the head using a stepped drift (see illustration). Determine the height above the boss that the guide must extend, and obtain a stack of washers, their I.D. similar to the guide's O.D., of that height. Place the stack of washers on the guide, and insert the guide into the boss. NOTE: *Valve guides are often tapered or beveled for installation.* Using the stepped installation tool (see illustration), press or tap the guides into position. Ream the guides according to the size of the valve stem.

Procedure	*Method*
Replacing valve seat inserts:	Replacement of valve seat inserts which are worn beyond resurfacing or broken, if feasible, must be done by a machine shop.
Resurfacing (grinding) the valve face:  **Grinding a valve** (© Subaru) 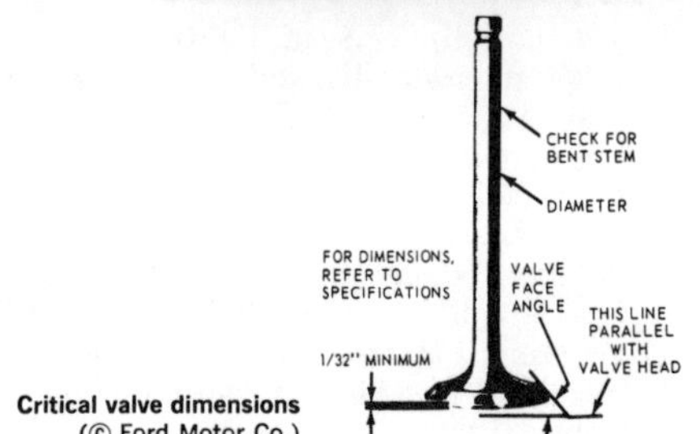 **Critical valve dimensions** (© Ford Motor Co.)	Using a valve grinder, resurface the valves according to specifications. CAUTION: *Valve face angle is not always identical to valve seat angle.* A minimum margin of 1/32″ should remain after grinding the valve. The valve stem tip should also be squared and resurfaced, by placing the stem in the V-block of the grinder, and turning it while pressing lightly against the grinding wheel.
Resurfacing the valve seats using reamers:  **Reaming the valve seat** (© S.p.A. Fiat) 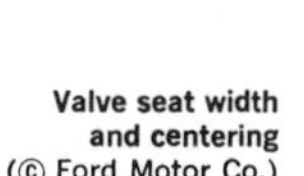 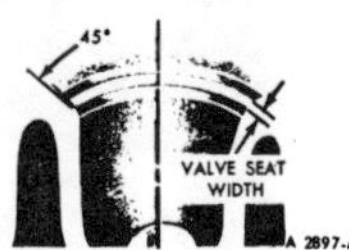 **Valve seat width and centering** (© Ford Motor Co.)	Select a reamer of the correct seat angle, slightly larger than the diameter of the valve seat, and assemble it with a pilot of the correct size. Install the pilot into the valve guide, and using steady pressure, turn the reamer clockwise. CAUTION: *Do not turn the reamer counter-clockwise.* Remove only as much material as necessary to clean the seat. Check the concentricity of the seat (see below). If the dye method is not used, coat the valve face with Prussian blue dye, install and rotate it on the valve seat. Using the dye marked area as a centering guide, center and narrow the valve seat to specifications with correction cutters. NOTE: *When no specifications are available, minimum seat width for exhaust valves should be 5/64″, intake valves 1/16″.* After making correction cuts, check the position of the valve seat on the valve face using Prussian blue dye.
* Resurfacing the valve seats using a grinder:  **Grinding a valve seat** (© Subaru)	Select a pilot of the correct size, and a coarse stone of the correct seat angle. Lubricate the pilot if necessary, and install the tool in the valve guide. Move the stone on and off the seat at approximately two cycles per second, until all flaws are removed from the seat. Install a fine stone, and finish the seat. Center and narrow the seat using correction stones, as described above.

Procedure	*Method*
Checking the valve seat concentricity: 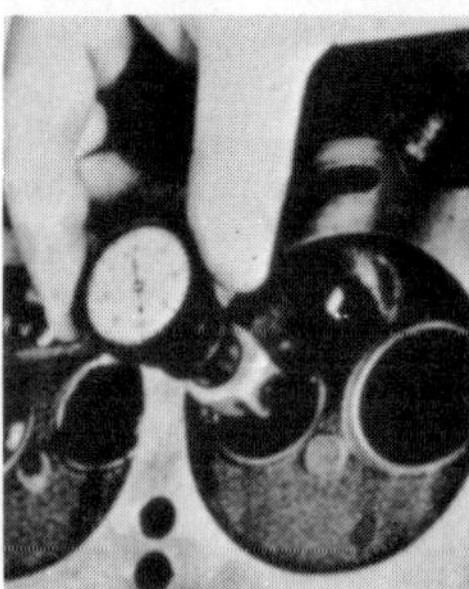 **Checking the valve seat concentricity using a dial gauge** (© American Motors Corp.)	Coat the valve face with Prussian blue dye, install the valve, and rotate it on the valve seat. If the entire seat becomes coated, and the valve is known to be concentric, the seat is concentric.
	* Install the dial gauge pilot into the guide, and rest the arm on the valve seat. Zero the gauge, and rotate the arm around the seat. Run-out should not exceed .002″.
* Lapping the valves: NOTE: *Valve lapping is done to ensure efficient sealing of resurfaced valves and seats. Valve lapping alone is not recommended for use as a resurfacing procedure.*  **Hand lapping the valves** 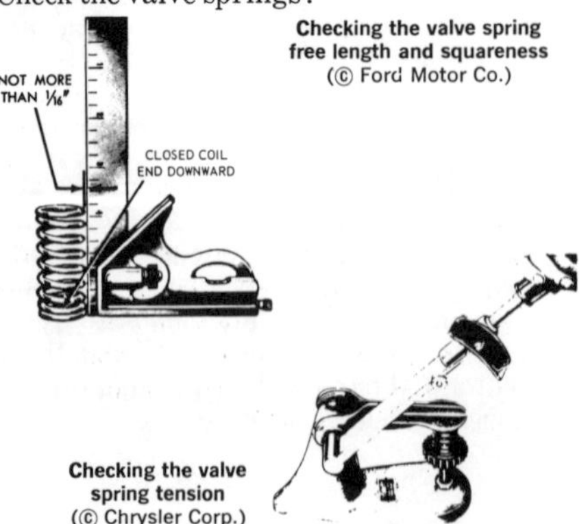 **Home made mechanical valve lapping tool**	* Invert the cylinder head, lightly lubricate the valve stems, and install the valves in the head as numbered. Coat valve seats with fine grinding compound, and attach the lapping tool suction cup to a valve head (NOTE: *Moisten the suction cup*). Rotate the tool between the palms, changing position and lifting the tool often to prevent grooving. Lap the valve until a smooth, polished seat is evident. Remove the valve and tool, and rinse away all traces of grinding compound.
	** Fasten a suction cup to a piece of drill rod, and mount the rod in a hand drill. Proceed as above, using the hand drill as a lapping tool. CAUTION: *Due to the higher speeds involved when using the hand drill, care must be exercised to avoid grooving the seat.* Lift the tool and change direction of rotation often.
Check the valve springs: **Checking the valve spring free length and squareness** (© Ford Motor Co.) **Checking the valve spring tension** (© Chrysler Corp.)	Place the spring on a flat surface next to a square. Measure the height of the spring, and rotate it against the edge of the square to measure distortion. If spring height varies (by comparison) by more than 1/16″ or if distortion exceeds 1/16″, replace the spring.
	** In addition to evaluating the spring as above, test the spring pressure at the installed and compressed (installed height minus valve lift) height using a valve spring tester. Springs used on small displacement engines (up to 3 liters) should be ± 1 lb. of all other springs in either position. A tolerance of ± 5 lbs. is permissible on larger engines.

Procedure	*Method*
* Install valve stem seals:  **Valve stem seal** **installation** (© Ford Motor Co.) SEAL	* Due to the pressure differential that exists at the ends of the intake valve guides (atmospheric pressure above, manifold vacuum below), oil is drawn through the valve guides into the intake port. This has been alleviated somewhat since the addition of positive crankcase ventilation, which lowers the pressure above the guides. Several types of valve stem seals are available to reduce blow-by. Certain seals simply slip over the stem and guide boss, while others require that the boss be machined. Recently, Teflon guide seals have become popular. Consult a parts supplier or machinist concerning availability and suggested usages. NOTE: *When installing seals, ensure that a small amount of oil is able to pass the seal to lubricate the valve guides; otherwise, excessive wear may result.*
Install the valves:	Lubricate the valve stems, and install the valves in the cylinder head as numbered. Lubricate and position the seals (if used, see above) and the valve springs. Install the spring retainers, compress the springs, and insert the keys using needlenose pliers or a tool designed for this purpose. NOTE: *Retain the keys with wheel bearing grease during installation.*
Checking valve spring installed height: 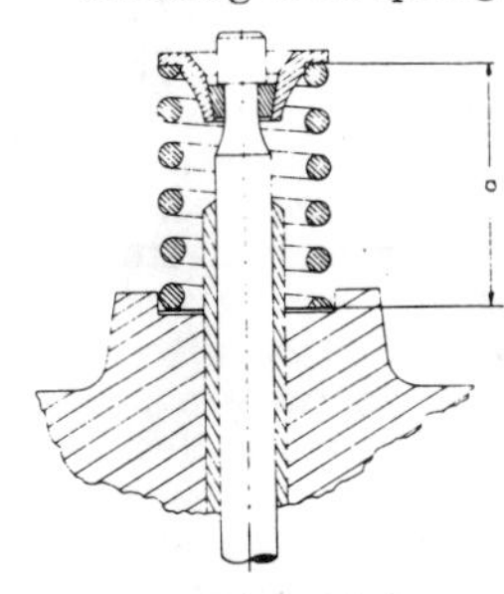 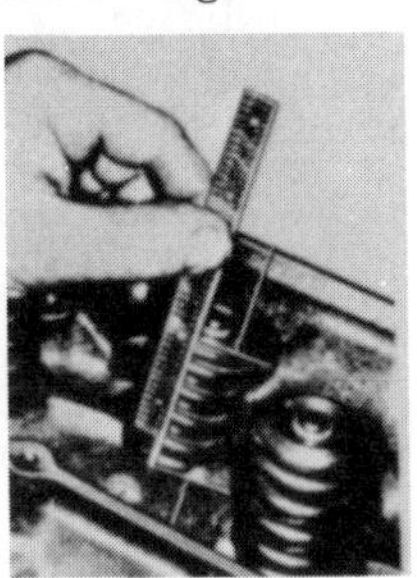 **Valve spring installed** **Measuring valve spring** **height dimension** **installed height** (© Porsche) (© Petersen Publishing Co.)	Measure the distance between the spring pad and the lower edge of the spring retainer, and compare to specifications. If the installed height is incorrect, add shim washers between the spring pad and the spring. CAUTION: *Use only washers designed for this purpose.*
** CC'ing the combustion chambers:	** Invert the cylinder head and place a bead of sealer around a combustion chamber. Install an apparatus designed for this purpose (burette mounted on a clear plate; see illustration) over the combustion chamber, and fill with the specified fluid to an even mark on the burette. Record the burette reading, and fill the combustion chamber with fluid. (NOTE: *A hole drilled in the plate will permit air to escape*). Subtract the burette reading, with the combustion chamber filled, from the previous reading, to determine combustion chamber volume in cc's. Duplicate this procedure in all combustion

Procedure	*Method*

CC'ing the combustion chamber
(© Petersen Publishing Co.)

chambers on the cylinder head, and compare the readings. The volume of all combustion chambers should be made equal to that of the largest. Combustion chamber volume may be increased in two ways. When only a small change is required (usually), a small cutter or coarse stone may be used to remove material from the combustion chamber. NOTE: *Check volume frequently.* Remove material over a wide area, so as not to change the configuration of the combustion chamber. When a larger change is required, the valve seat may be sunk (lowered into the head). NOTE: *When altering valve seat, remember to compensate for the change in spring installed height.*

Inspect the rocker arms, balls, studs, and nuts (where applicable):

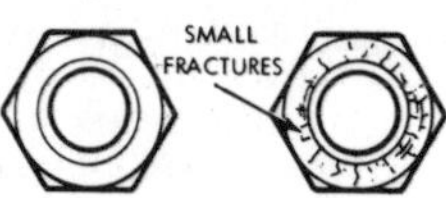

Stress cracks in rocker nuts
(© Ford Motor Co.)

Visually inspect the rocker arms, balls, studs, and nuts for cracks, galling, burning, scoring, or wear. If all parts are intact, liberally lubricate the rocker arms and balls, and install them on the cylinder head. If wear is noted on a rocker arm at the point of valve contact, grind it smooth and square, removing as little material as possible. Replace the rocker arm if excessively worn. If a rocker stud shows signs of wear, it must be replaced (see below). If a rocker nut shows stress cracks, replace it. If an exhaust ball is galled or burned, substitute the intake ball from the same cylinder (if it is intact), and install a new intake ball. NOTE: *Avoid using new rocker balls on exhaust valves.*

Replacing rocker studs:

Reaming the stud bore for oversize rocker studs
(© Buick Div. G.M. Corp.)

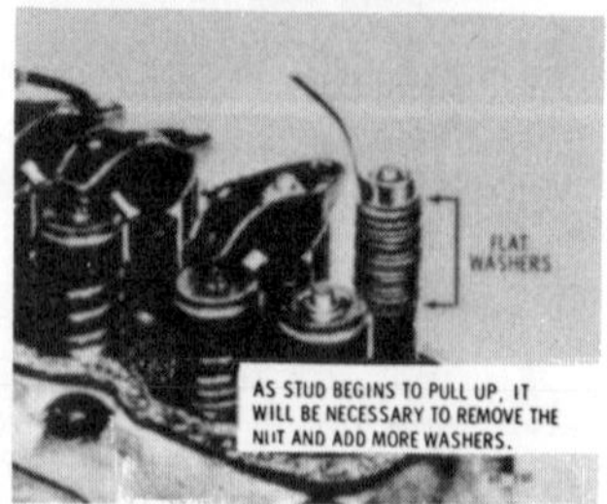

Extracting a pressed in rocker stud
(© Buick Div. G.M. Corp.)

In order to remove a threaded stud, lock two nuts on the stud, and unscrew the stud using the lower nut. Coat the lower threads of the new stud with Loctite, and install.

Two alternative methods are available for replacing pressed in studs. Remove the damaged stud using a stack of washers and a nut (see illustration). In the first, the boss is reamed .005-.006″ oversize, and an oversize stud pressed in. Control the stud extension over the boss using washers, in the same manner as valve guides. Before installing the stud, coat it with white lead and grease. To retain the stud more positively, drill a hole through the stud and boss, and install a roll pin. In the second method, the boss is tapped, and a threaded stud installed. Retain the stud using Loctite Stud and Bearing Mount.

Procedure	*Method*
Inspect the rocker shaft(s) and rocker arms (where applicable):  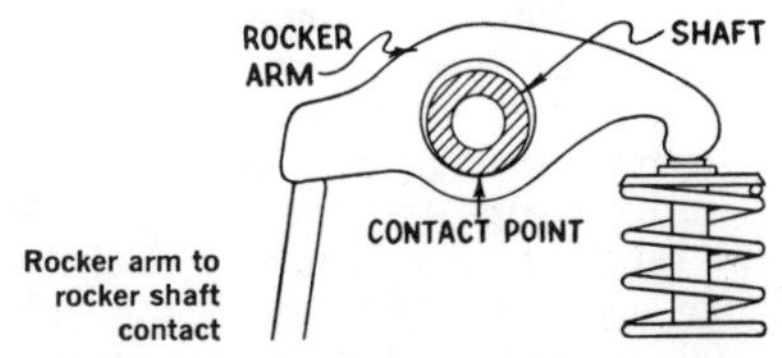 Disassembled rocker shaft parts arranged for inspection (© American Motors Corp.) 	Remove rocker arms, springs and washers from rocker shaft. NOTE: *Lay out parts in the order they are removed.* Inspect rocker arms for pitting or wear on the valve contact point, or excessive bushing wear. Bushings need only be replaced if wear is excessive, because the rocker arm normally contacts the shaft at one point only. Grind the valve contact point of rocker arm smooth if necessary, removing as little material as possible. If excessive material must be removed to smooth and square the arm, it should be replaced. Clean out all oil holes and passages in rocker shaft. If shaft is grooved or worn, replace it. Lubricate and assemble the rocker shaft.
Inspect the camshaft bushings and the camshaft (overhead cam engines):	See next section.
Inspect the pushrods:	Remove the pushrods, and, if hollow, clean out the oil passages using fine wire. Roll each pushrod over a piece of clean glass. If a distinct clicking sound is heard as the pushrod rolls, the rod is bent, and must be replaced.
	* The length of all pushrods must be equal. Measure the length of the pushrods, compare to specifications, and replace as necessary.
Inspect the valve lifters:  Checking the lifter face (© American Motors Corp.)	Remove lifters from their bores, and remove gum and varnish, using solvent. Clean walls of lifter bores. Check lifters for concave wear as illustrated. If face is worn concave, replace lifter, and carefully inspect the camshaft. Lightly lubricate lifter and insert it into its bore. If play is excessive, an oversize lifter must be installed (where possible). Consult a machinist concerning feasibility. If play is satisfactory, remove, lubricate, and reinstall the lifter.
* Testing hydraulic lifter leak down: 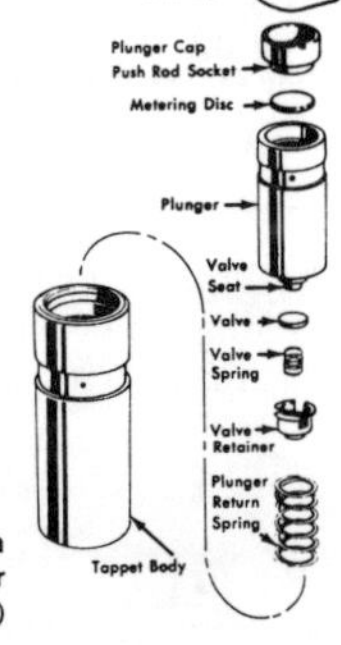 Exploded view of a typical hydraulic lifter (© American Motors Corp.)	Submerge lifter in a container of kerosene. Chuck a used pushrod or its equivalent into a drill press. Position container of kerosene so pushrod acts on the lifter plunger. Pump lifter with the drill press, until resistance increases. Pump several more times to bleed any air out of lifter. Apply very firm, constant pressure to the lifter, and observe rate at which fluid bleeds out of lifter. If the fluid bleeds very quickly (less than 15 seconds), lifter is defective. If the time exceeds 60 seconds, lifter is sticking. In either case, recondition or replace lifter. If lifter is operating properly (leak down time 15-60 seconds), lubricate and install it.

CYLINDER BLOCK RECONDITIONING

Procedure	*Method*

Checking the main bearing clearance:

Plastigage installed on main bearing journal
(© Chevrolet Div. G.M. Corp.)

**Measuring Plastigage to determine
main bearing clearance**
(© Chevrolet Div. G.M. Corp.)

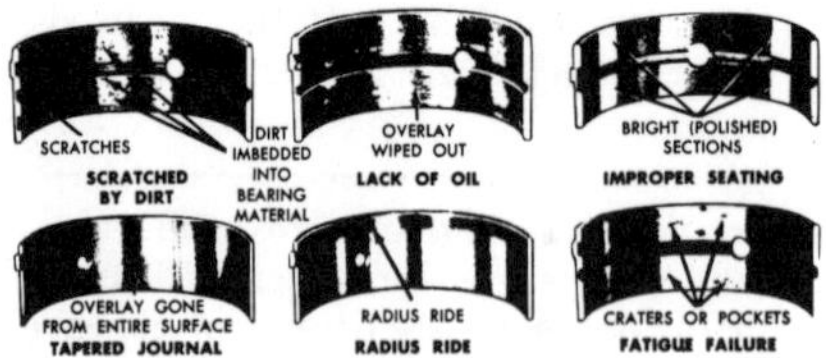

Causes of bearing failure
(© Ford Motor Co.)

Invert engine, and remove cap from the bearing to be checked. Using a clean, dry rag, thoroughly clean all oil from crankshaft journal and bearing insert. NOTE: *Plastigage is soluble in oil; therefore, oil on the journal or bearing could result in erroneous readings.* Place a piece of Plastigage along the full length of journal, reinstall cap, and torque to specifications. Remove bearing cap, and determine bearing clearance by comparing width of Plastigage to the scale on Plastigage envelope. Journal taper is determined by comparing width of the Plastigage strip near its ends. Rotate crankshaft 90° and retest, to determine journal eccentricity. NOTE: *Do not rotate crankshaft with Plastigage installed.* If bearing insert and journal appear intact, and are within tolerances, no further main bearing service is required. If bearing or journal appear defective, cause of failure should be determined before replacement.

* Remove crankshaft from block (see below). Measure the main bearing journals at each end twice (90° apart) using a micrometer, to determine diameter, journal taper and eccentricity. If journals are within tolerances, reinstall bearing caps at their specified torque. Using a telescope gauge and micrometer, measure bearing I.D. parallel to piston axis and at 30° on each side of piston axis. Subtract journal O.D. from bearing I.D. to determine oil clearance. If crankshaft journals appear defective, or do not meet tolerances, there is no need to measure bearings; for the crankshaft will require grinding and/or undersize bearings will be required. If bearing appears defective, cause for failure should be determined prior to replacement.

Checking the connecting rod bearing clearance:

**Plastigage installed on connecting rod
bearing journal**
(© Chevrolet Div. G.M. Corp.)

Connecting rod bearing clearance is checked in the same manner as main bearing clearance, using Plastigage. Before removing the crankshaft, connecting rod side clearance also should be measured and recorded.

* Checking connecting rod bearing clearance, using a micrometer, is identical to checking main bearing clearance. If no other service

Procedure	Method

Measuring Plastigage to determine connecting rod bearing clearance
(© Chevrolet Div. G.M. Corp.)

is required, the piston and rod assemblies need not be removed.

Removing the crankshaft:

Connecting rod matching marks
(© Ford Motor Co.)

Using a punch, mark the corresponding main bearing caps and saddles according to position (i.e., one punch on the front main cap and saddle, two on the second, three on the third, etc.). Using number stamps, identify the corresponding connecting rods and caps, according to cylinder (if no numbers are present). Remove the main and connecting rod caps, and place sleeves of plastic tubing over the connecting rod bolts, to protect the journals as the crankshaft is removed. Lift the crankshaft out of the block.

Remove the ridge from the top of the cylinder:

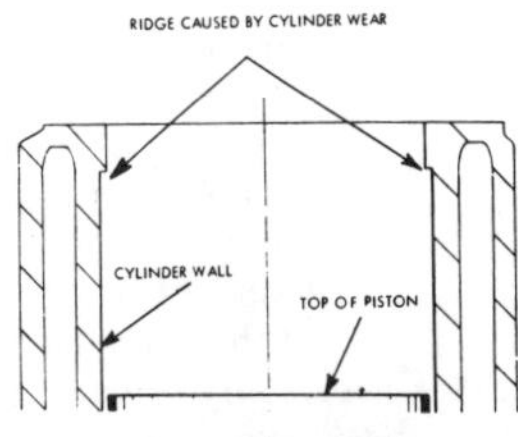

Cylinder bore ridge
(© Pontiac Div. G.M. Corp.)

In order to facilitate removal of the piston and connecting rod, the ridge at the top of the cylinder (unworn area; see illustration) must be removed. Place the piston at the bottom of the bore, and cover it with a rag. Cut the ridge away using a ridge reamer, exercising extreme care to avoid cutting too deeply. Remove the rag, and remove cuttings that remain on the piston. CAUTION: *If the ridge is not removed, and new rings are installed, damage to rings will result.*

Removing the piston and connecting rod:

Removing the piston
(© SAAB)

Invert the engine, and push the pistons and connecting rods out of the cylinders. If necessary, tap the connecting rod boss with a wooden hammer handle, to force the piston out. CAUTION: *Do not attempt to force the piston past the cylinder ridge* (see above).

Procedure	*Method*
Service the crankshaft:	Ensure that all oil holes and passages in the crankshaft are open and free of sludge. If necessary, have the crankshaft ground to the largest possible undersize.
	** Have the crankshaft Magnafluxed, to locate stress cracks. Consult a machinist concerning additional service procedures, such as surface hardening (e.g., nitriding, Tuftriding) to improve wear characteristics, cross drilling and chamfering the oil holes to improve lubrication, and balancing.
Removing freeze plugs:	Drill a hole in the center of the freeze plugs, and pry them out using a screwdriver or drift.
Remove the oil gallery plugs:	Threaded plugs should be removed using an appropriate (usually square) wrench. To remove soft, pressed in plugs, drill a hole in the plug, and thread in a sheet metal screw. Pull the plug out by the screw using pliers.
Hot-tank the block:	Have the block hot-tanked to remove grease, corrosion, and scale from the water jackets. NOTE: *Consult the operator to determine whether the camshaft bearings will be damaged during the hot-tank process.*
Check the block for cracks:	Visually inspect the block for cracks or chips. The most common locations are as follows: Adjacent to freeze plugs. Between the cylinders and water jackets. Adjacent to the main bearing saddles. At the extreme bottom of the cylinders. Check only suspected cracks using spot check dye (see introduction). If a crack is located, consult a machinist concerning possible repairs.
	** Magnaflux the block to locate hidden cracks. If cracks are located, consult a machinist about feasibility of repair.
Install the oil gallery plugs and freeze plugs:	Coat freeze plugs with sealer and tap into position using a piece of pipe, slightly smaller than the plug, as a driver. To ensure retention, stake the edges of the plugs. Coat threaded oil gallery plugs with sealer and install. Drive replacement soft plugs into block using a large drift as a driver.
	* Rather than reinstalling lead plugs, drill and tap the holes, and install threaded plugs.

Procedure	*Method*

Check the bore diameter and surface:

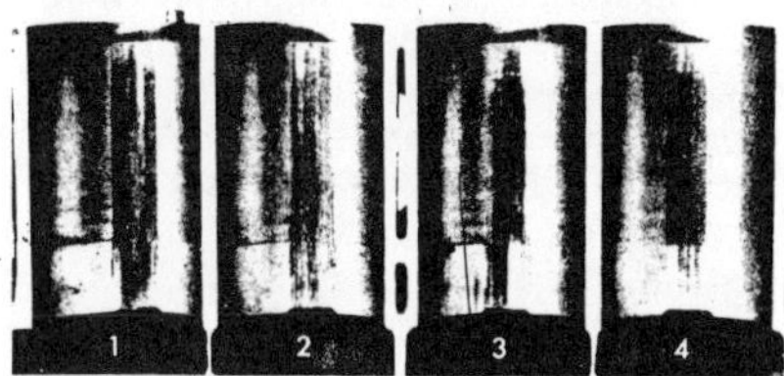

1, 2, 3 Piston skirt seizure resulted in this pattern. Engine
must be rebored

4. Piston skirt and oil ring
seizure caused this damage.
Engine must be rebored

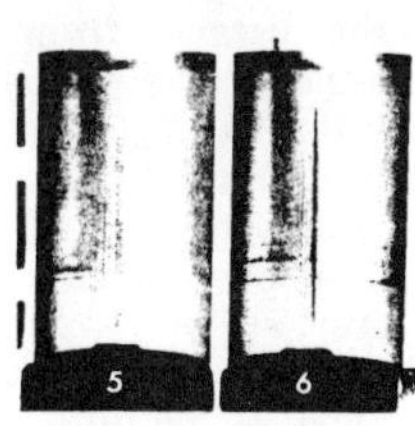

5, 6 Score marks caused by a
split piston skirt. Damage is
not serious enough to warrant
reboring

7. Ring seized longitudinally,
causing a score mark
1 3/16" wide, on the land
side of the piston groove.
The honing pattern is de-
stroyed and the cylinder
must be rebored

8. Result of oil ring seizure.
Engine must be rebored

9. Oil ring seizure here was not
serious enough to warrant
reboring. The honing
marks are still visible

Cylinder wall damage
(© Daimler-Benz A.G.)

Visually inspect the cylinder bores for rough-
ness, scoring, or scuffing. If evident, the cylinder bore must be bored or honed oversize
to eliminate imperfections, and the smallest
possible oversize piston used. The new pistons should be given to the machinist with
the block, so that the cylinders can be bored
or honed exactly to the piston size (plus
clearance). If no flaws are evident, measure
the bore diameter using a telescope gauge
and micrometer, or dial gauge, parallel and
perpendicular to the engine centerline, at
the top (below the ridge) and bottom of the
bore. Subtract the bottom measurements
from the top to determine taper, and the
parallel to the centerline measurements
from the perpendicular measurements to
determine eccentricity. If the measurements
are not within specifications, the cylinder
must be bored or honed, and an oversize piston installed. If the measurements are within specifications the cylinder may be used
as is, with only finish honing (see below).
NOTE: *Prior to submitting the block for
boring, perform the following operation(s).*

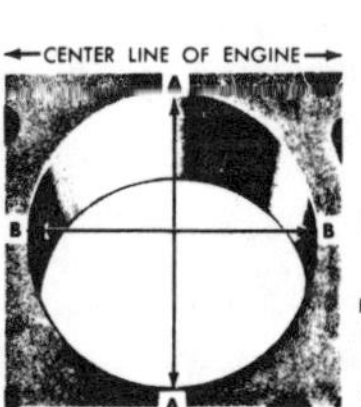

**Cylinder bore measuring
positions**
(© Ford Motor Co.)

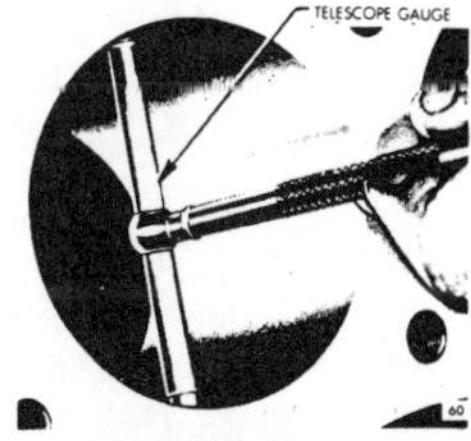

**Measuring the cylinder bore
with a telescope gauge**
(© Buick Div. G.M. Corp.)

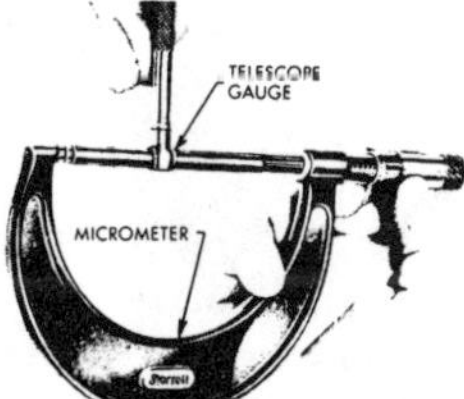

**Determining the cylinder bore
by measuring the telescope
gauge with a micrometer**
(© Buick Div. G.M. Corp.)

**Measuring the cylinder bore
with a dial gauge**
(© Chevrolet Div. G.M. Corp.)

Procedure	*Method*
Check the block deck for warpage:	Using a straightedge and feeler gauges, check the block deck for warpage in the same manner that the cylinder head is checked (see Cylinder Head Reconditioning). If warpage exceeds specifications, have the deck resurfaced. NOTE: *In certain cases a specification for total material removal (Cylinder head and block deck) is provided. This specification must not be exceeded.*
* Check the deck height:	The deck height is the distance from the crankshaft centerline to the block deck. To measure, invert the engine, and install the crankshaft, retaining it with the center main cap. Measure the distance from the crankshaft journal to the block deck, parallel to the cylinder centerline. Measure the diameter of the end (front and rear) main journals, parallel to the centerline of the cylinders, divide the diameter in half, and subtract it from the previous measurement. The results of the front and rear measurements should be identical. If the difference exceeds .005″, the deck height should be corrected. NOTE: *Block deck height and warpage should be corrected concurrently.*
Check the cylinder block bearing alignment:  **Checking main bearing saddle alignment** (ⓒ Petersen Publishing Co.)	Remove the upper bearing inserts. Place a straightedge in the bearing saddles along the centerline of the crankshaft. If clearance exists between the straightedge and the center saddle, the block must be align-bored.
Clean and inspect the pistons and connecting rods: 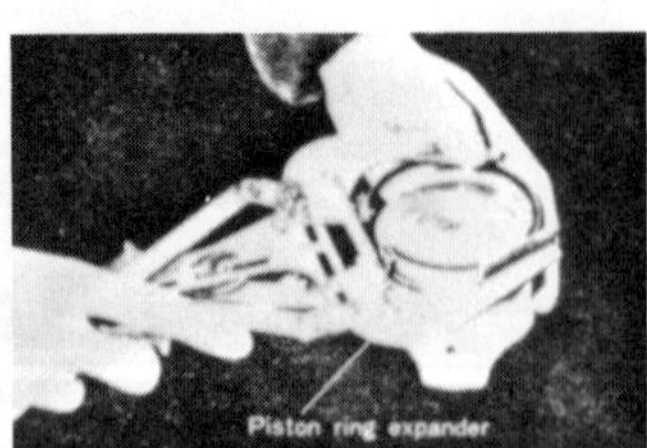 **Removing the piston rings** (ⓒ Subaru)	Using a ring expander, remove the rings from the piston. Remove the retaining rings (if so equipped) and remove piston pin. NOTE: *If the piston pin must be pressed out, determine the proper method and use the proper tools; otherwise the piston will distort.* Clean the ring grooves using an appropriate tool, exercising care to avoid cutting too deeply. Thoroughly clean all carbon and varnish from the piston with solvent. CAUTION: *Do not use a wire brush or caustic solvent on pistons.* Inspect the pistons for scuffing, scoring, cracks, pitting, or excessive ring groove wear. If wear is evident, the piston must be replaced. Check the connecting rod length by measuring the rod from the inside of the large end to the inside of the small end using calipers (see

Procedure	Method

Cleaning the piston ring grooves
(© Ford Motor Co.)

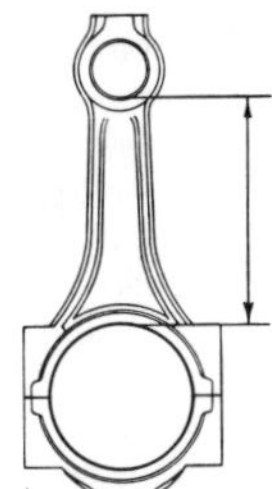

Connecting rod
length checking
dimension

illustration). All connecting rods should be equal length. Replace any rod that differs from the others in the engine.

* Have the connecting rod alignment checked in an alignment fixture by a machinist. Replace any twisted or bent rods.

* Magnaflux the connecting rods to locate stress cracks. If cracks are found, replace the connecting rod.

Fit the pistons to the cylinders:

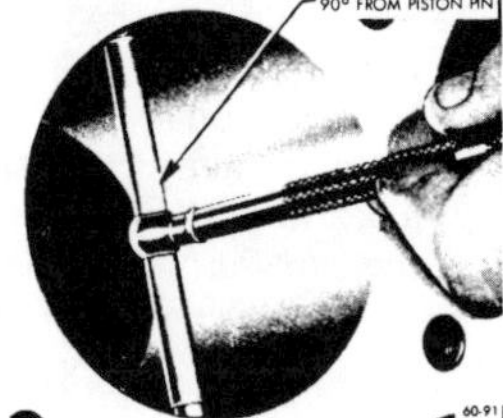

Measuring the cylinder
with a telescope gauge
for piston fitting
(© Buick Div.
G.M. Corp.)

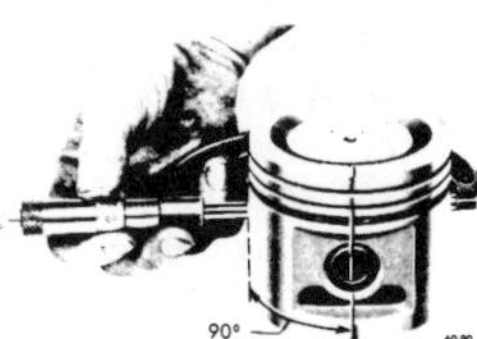

Measuring the piston
for fitting
(© Buick Div.
G.M. Corp.)

Using a telescope gauge and micrometer, or a dial gauge, measure the cylinder bore diameter perpendicular to the piston pin, $2\frac{1}{2}''$ below the deck. Measure the piston perpendicular to its pin on the skirt. The difference between the two measurements is the piston clearance. If the clearance is within specifications or slightly below (after boring or honing), finish honing is all that is required. If the clearance is excessive, try to obtain a slightly larger piston to bring clearance within specifications. Where this is not possible, obtain the first oversize piston, and hone (or if necessary, bore) the cylinder to size.

Assemble the pistons and connecting rods:

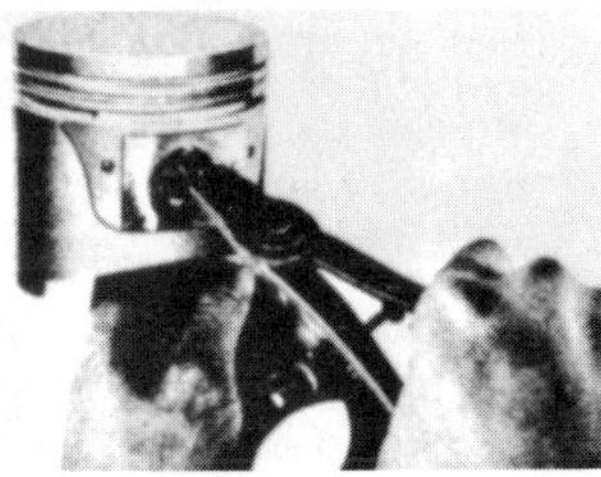

Installing piston pin lock rings
(© Nissan Motor Co., Ltd.)

Inspect piston pin, connecting rod small end bushing, and piston bore for galling, scoring, or excessive wear. If evident, replace defective part(s). Measure the I.D. of the piston boss and connecting rod small end, and the O.D. of the piston pin. If within specifications, assemble piston pin and rod. CAUTION: *If piston pin must be pressed in, determine the proper method and use the proper tools; otherwise the piston will distort.* Install the lock rings; ensure that they seat properly. If the parts are not within specifications, determine the service method for the type of engine. In some cases, piston and pin are serviced as an assembly when either is defective. Others specify reaming the piston and connecting rods for an oversize pin. If the connecting rod bushing is worn, it may in many cases be replaced. Reaming the piston and replacing the rod bushing are machine shop operations.

Procedure	*Method*

Clean and inspect the camshaft:

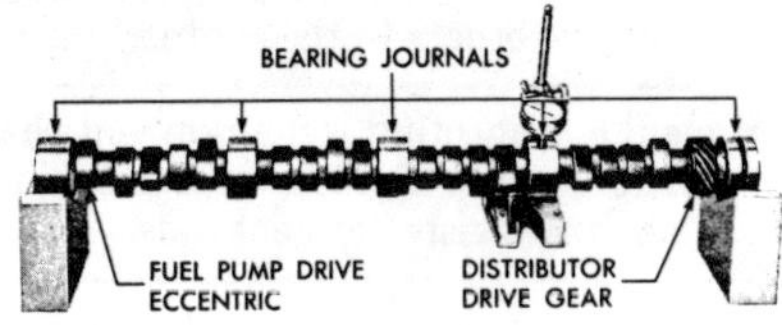

Checking the camshaft for straightness
(© Chevrolet Motor Div. G.M. Corp.)

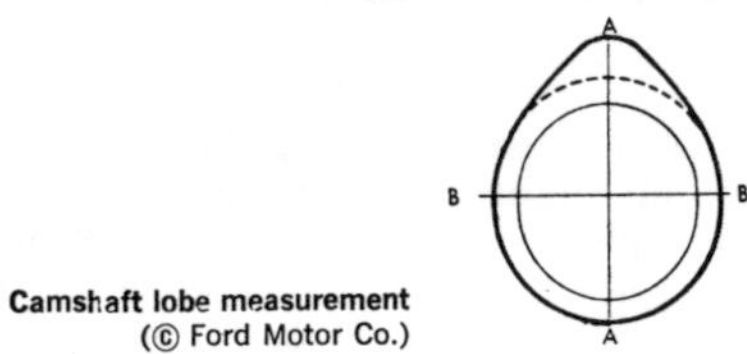

Camshaft lobe measurement
(© Ford Motor Co.)

Degrease the camshaft, using solvent, and clean out all oil holes. Visually inspect cam lobes and bearing journals for excessive wear. If a lobe is questionable, check all lobes as indicated below. If a journal or lobe is worn, the camshaft must be reground or replaced. NOTE: *If a journal is worn, there is a good chance that the bushings are worn.* If lobes and journals appear intact, place the front and rear journals in V-blocks, and rest a dial indicator on the center journal. Rotate the camshaft to check straightness. If deviation exceeds .001″, replace the camshaft.

* Check the camshaft lobes with a micrometer, by measuring the lobes from the nose to base and again at 90° (see illustration). The lift is determined by subtracting the second measurement from the first. If all exhaust lobes and all intake lobes are not identical, the camshaft must be reground or replaced.

Replace the camshaft bearings:

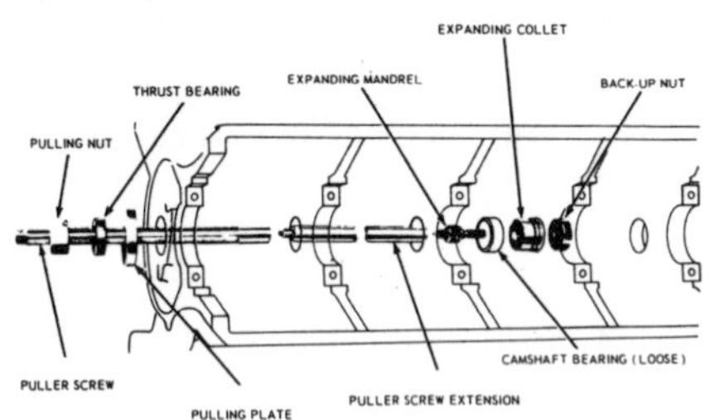

Camshaft removal and installation tool (typical)
(© Ford Motor Co.)

If excessive wear is indicated, or if the engine is being completely rebuilt, camshaft bearings should be replaced as follows: Drive the camshaft rear plug from the block. Assemble the removal puller with its shoulder on the bearing to be removed. Gradually tighten the puller nut until bearing is removed. Remove remaining bearings, leaving the front and rear for last. To remove front and rear bearings, reverse position of the tool, so as to pull the bearings in toward the center of the block. Leave the tool in this position, pilot the new front and rear bearings on the installer, and pull them into position. Return the tool to its original position and pull remaining bearings into position. NOTE: *Ensure that oil holes align when installing bearings.* Replace camshaft rear plug, and stake it into position to aid retention.

Finish hone the cylinders:

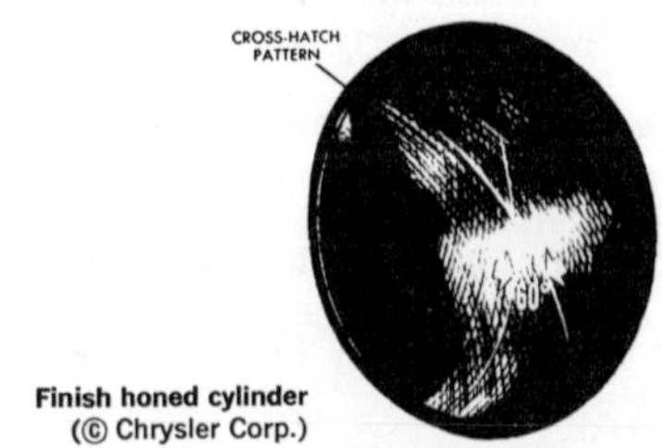

Finish honed cylinder
(© Chrysler Corp.)

Chuck a flexible drive hone into a power drill, and insert it into the cylinder. Start the hone, and move it up and down in the cylinder at a rate which will produce approximately a 60° cross-hatch pattern (see illustration). NOTE: *Do not extend the hone below the cylinder bore.* After developing the pattern, remove the hone and recheck piston fit. Wash the cylinders with a detergent and water solution to remove abrasive dust, dry, and wipe several times with a rag soaked in engine oil.

Procedure	*Method*
Check piston ring end-gap:  **Checking ring end-gap** (© Chevrolet Motor Div. G.M. Corp.)	Compress the piston rings to be used in a cylinder, one at a time, into that cylinder, and press them approximately 1″ below the deck with an inverted piston. Using feeler gauges, measure the ring end-gap, and compare to specifications. Pull the ring out of the cylinder and file the ends with a fine file to obtain proper clearance. CAUTION: *If inadequate ring end-gap is utilized, ring breakage will result.*
Install the piston rings: 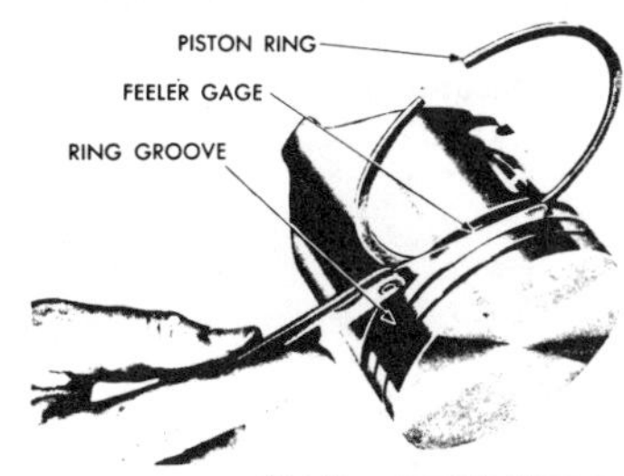 **Checking ring side clearance** (© Chrysler Corp.) 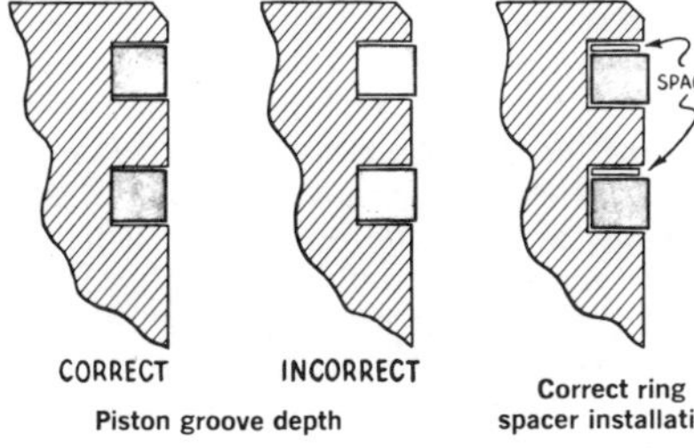 CORRECT INCORRECT **Piston groove depth** **Correct ring spacer installation**	Inspect the ring grooves in the piston for excessive wear or taper. If necessary, recut the groove(s) for use with an overwidth ring or a standard ring and spacer. If the groove is worn uniformly, overwidth rings, or standard rings and spacers may be installed without recutting. Roll the outside of the ring around the groove to check for burrs or deposits. If any are found, remove with a fine file. Hold the ring in the groove, and measure side clearance. If necessary, correct as indicated above. NOTE: *Always install any additional spacers above the piston ring.* The ring groove must be deep enough to allow the ring to seat below the lands (see illustration). In many cases, a "go-no-go" depth gauge will be provided with the piston rings. Shallow grooves may be corrected by recutting, while deep grooves require some type of filler or expander behind the piston. Consult the piston ring supplier concerning the suggested method. Install the rings on the piston, lowest ring first, using a ring expander. NOTE: *Position the ring markings as specified by the manufacturer (see car section).*
Install the camshaft:	Liberally lubricate the camshaft lobes and journals, and slide the camshaft into the block. CAUTION: *Exercise extreme care to avoid damaging the bearings when inserting the camshaft.* Install and tighten the camshaft thrust plate retaining bolts.
Check camshaft end-play: 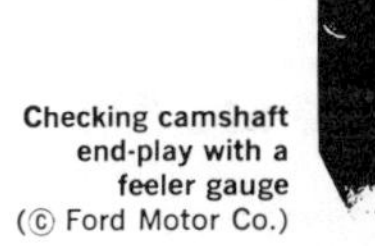 **Checking camshaft end-play with a feeler gauge** (© Ford Motor Co.)	Using feeler gauges, determine whether the clearance between the camshaft boss (or gear) and backing plate is within specifications. Install shims behind the thrust plate, or reposition the camshaft gear and retest end-play.

Procedure	*Method*

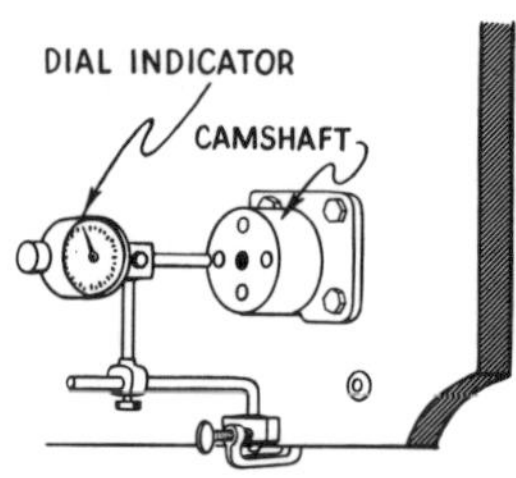

**Checking camshaft end-play with a
dial indicator**

* Mount a dial indicator stand so that the stem of the dial indicator rests on the nose of the camshaft, parallel to the camshaft axis. Push the camshaft as far in as possible and zero the gauge. Move the camshaft outward to determine the amount of camshaft end-play. If the end-play is not within tolerance, install shims behind the thrust plate, or reposition the camshaft gear and retest.

Install the rear main seal (where applicable):

**Seating the rear
main seal**
(© Buick Div. G.M. Corp.)

Position the block with the bearing saddles facing upward. Lay the rear main seal in its groove and press it lightly into its seat. Place a piece of pipe the same diameter as the crankshaft journal into the saddle, and firmly seat the seal. Hold the pipe in position, and trim the ends of the seal flush if required.

Install the crankshaft:

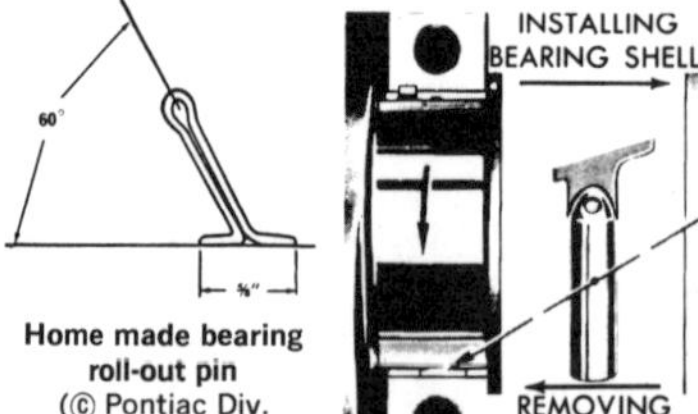

**Home made bearing
roll-out pin**
(© Pontiac Div.
G.M. Corp.)

**Removal and installation of upper
bearing insert using a roll-out pin**
(© Buick Div. G.M. Corp.)

Thoroughly clean the main bearing saddles and caps. Place the upper halves of the bearing inserts on the saddles and press into position. NOTE: *Ensure that the oil holes align.* Press the corresponding bearing inserts into the main bearing caps. Lubricate the upper main bearings, and lay the crankshaft in position. Place a strip of Plastigage on each of the crankshaft journals, install the main caps, and torque to specifications. Remove the main caps, and compare the Plastigage to the scale on the Plastigage envelope. If clearances are within tolerances, remove the Plastigage, turn the crankshaft 90°, wipe off all oil and retest. If all clearances are correct, remove all Plastigage, thoroughly

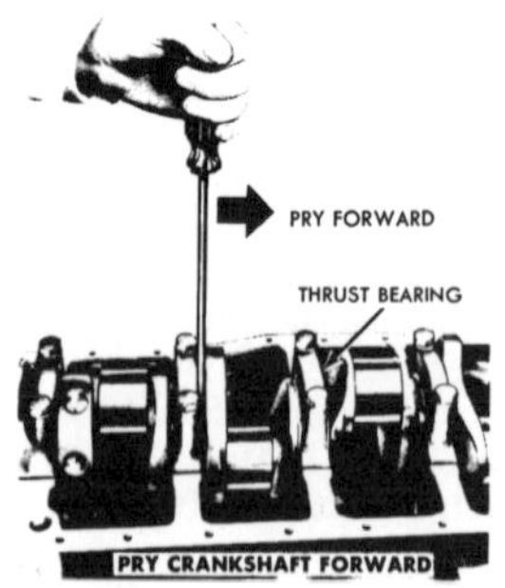

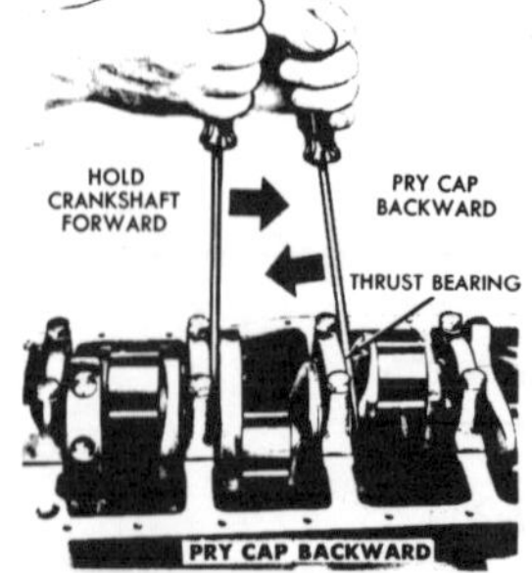

Aligning the thrust bearing
(© Ford Motor Co.)

Procedure	*Method*
	lubricate the main caps and bearing journals, and install the main caps. If clearances are not within tolerance, the upper bearing inserts may be removed, without removing the crankshaft, using a bearing roll out pin (see illustration). Roll in a bearing that will provide proper clearance, and retest. Torque all main caps, excluding the thrust bearing cap, to specifications. Tighten the thrust bearing cap finger tight. To properly align the thrust bearing, pry the crankshaft the extent of its axial travel several times, the last movement held toward the front of the engine, and torque the thrust bearing cap to specifications. Determine the crankshaft end-play (see below), and bring within tolerance with thrust washers.
Measure crankshaft end-play:  **Checking crankshaft end-play with a dial indicator** (© Ford Motor Co.) 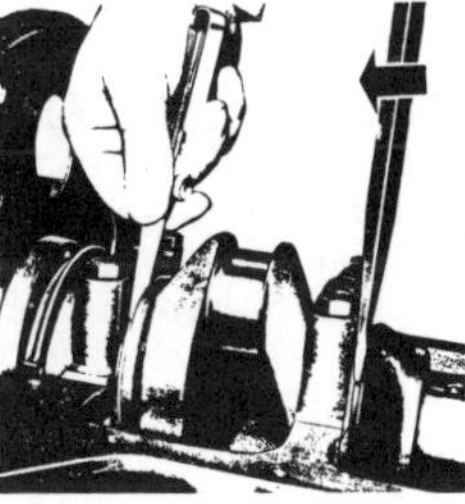 **Checking crankshaft end-play with a feeler gauge** (© Chevrolet Div. (G.M. Corp.)	Mount a dial indicator stand on the front of the block, with the dial indicator stem resting on the nose of the crankshaft, parallel to the crankshaft axis. Pry the crankshaft the extent of its travel rearward, and zero the indicator. Pry the crankshaft forward and record crankshaft end-play. NOTE: *Crankshaft end-play also may be measured at the thrust bearing, using feeler gauges* (see illustration).
Install the pistons:	Press the upper connecting rod bearing halves into the connecting rods, and the lower halves into the connecting rod caps. Position the piston ring gaps according to specifications (see car section), and lubricate the pistons. Install a ring compresser on a piston, and press two long (8″) pieces of plastic tubing over the rod bolts. Using the plastic tubes as a guide, press the pistons into the bores and onto the crankshaft with a wooden hammer handle. After seating the rod on the crankshaft journal, remove the tubes and install the cap finger tight. Install the remaining pistons in the same man-

Procedure	*Method*

**Tubing used as guide when installing
a piston**
(© Oldsmobile Div. G.M. Corp.)

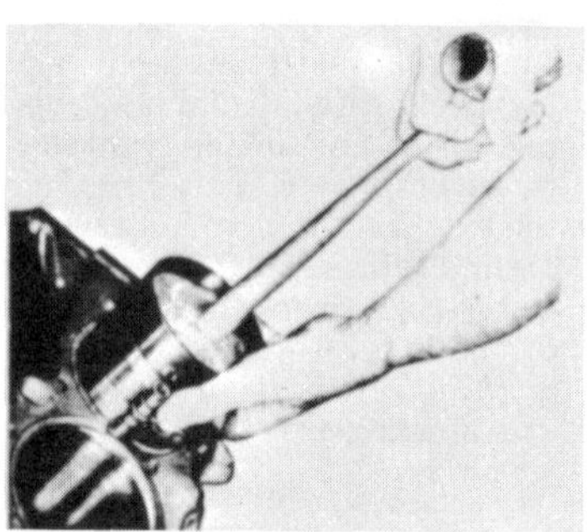

Installing a piston
(© Chevrolet Div. G.M. Corp.)

ner. Invert the engine and check the bearing clearance at two points (90° apart) on each journal with Plastigage. NOTE: *Do not turn the crankshaft with Plastigage installed.* If clearance is within tolerances, remove *all* Plastigage, thoroughly lubricate the journals, and torque the rod caps to specifications. If clearance is not within specifications, install different thickness bearing inserts and recheck. CAUTION: *Never shim or file the connecting rods or caps.* Always install plastic tube sleeves over the rod bolts when the caps are not installed, to protect the crankshaft journals.

Check connecting rod side clearance:

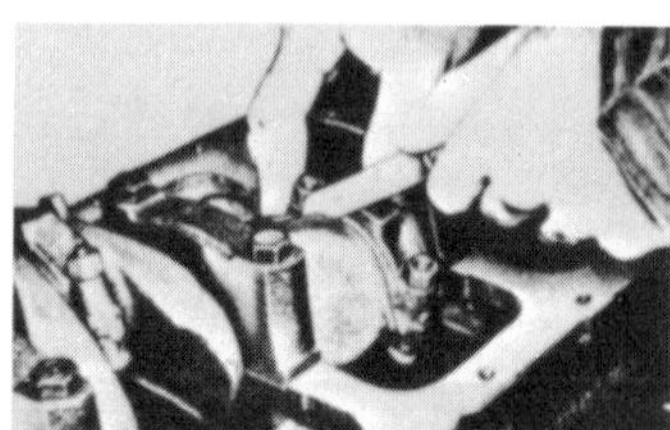

Checking connecting rod side clearance
(© Chevrolet Div. G.M. Corp.)

Determine the clearance between the sides of the connecting rods and the crankshaft, using feeler gauges. If clearance is below the minimum tolerance, the rod may be machined to provide adequate clearance. If clearance is excessive, substitute an unworn rod, and recheck. If clearance is still outside specifications, the crankshaft must be welded and reground, or replaced.

Inspect the timing chain:

Visually inspect the timing chain for broken or loose links, and replace the chain if any are found. If the chain will flex sideways, it must be replaced. Install the timing chain as specified. NOTE: *If the original timing chain is to be reused, install it in its original position.*

Procedure	*Method*
Check timing gear backlash and runout:	Mount a dial indicator with its stem resting on a tooth of the camshaft gear (as illustrated). Rotate the gear until all slack is removed, and zero the indicator. Rotate the gear in the opposite direction until slack is removed, and record gear backlash. Mount the indicator with its stem resting on the edge of the camshaft gear, parallel to the axis of the camshaft. Zero the indicator, and turn the camshaft gear one full turn, recording the runout. If either backlash or runout exceed specifications, replace the worn gear(s).

Checking camshaft gear backlash
(© Chevrolet Div. G.M. Corp.)

Checking camshaft gear runout
(© Chevrolet Div. G.M. Corp.)

Completing the Rebuilding Process

Following the above procedures, complete the rebuilding process as follows:

Fill the oil pump with oil, to prevent cavitating (sucking air) on initial engine start up. Install the oil pump and the pickup tube on the engine. Coat the oil pan gasket as necessary, and install the gasket and the oil pan. Mount the flywheel and the crankshaft vibrational damper or pulley on the crankshaft. NOTE: *Always use new bolts when installing the flywheel.* Inspect the clutch shaft pilot bushing in the crankshaft. If the bushing is excessively worn, remove it with an expanding puller and a slide hammer, and tap a new bushing into place.

Position the engine, cylinder head side up. Lubricate the lifters, and install them into their bores. Install the cylinder head, and torque it as specified in the car section. Insert the pushrods (where applicable), and install the rocker shaft(s) (if so equipped) or position the rocker arms on the pushrods. If solid lifters are utilized, adjust the valves to the "cold" specifications.

Mount the intake and exhaust manifolds, the carburetor(s), the distributor and spark plugs. Adjust the point gap and the static ignition timing. Mount all accessories and install the engine in the car. Fill the radiator with coolant, and the crankcase with high quality engine oil.

Break-in Procedure

Start the engine, and allow it to run at low speed for a few minutes, while checking for leaks. Stop the engine, check the oil level, and fill as necessary. Restart the engine, and fill the cooling system to capacity. Check the point dwell angle and adjust the ignition timing and the valves. Run the engine at low to medium speed (800-2500 rpm) for approximately ½ hour, and retorque the cylinder head bolts. Road test the car, and check again for leaks.

Follow the manufacturer's recommended engine break-in procedure and maintenance schedule for new engines.

Chapter 4

Emission Controls and Fuel System

Systems Description and Service

POSITIVE CRANKCASE VENTILATION

This system draws crankcase vapors that are formed through normal combustion into the intake manifold and subsequently into the combustion chamber to be burned. Fresh air is introduced to the crankcase by way of a hose connected to the carburetor air cleaner. Manifold vacuum is used to draw the vapors from the crankcase through a PCV valve and into the intake manifold.

AIR INJECTION REACTOR

The A.I.R. system injects compressed air into the exhaust system, close enough to the exhaust valves to continue the burning of the normally unburned segment of the exhaust gases. To do this it

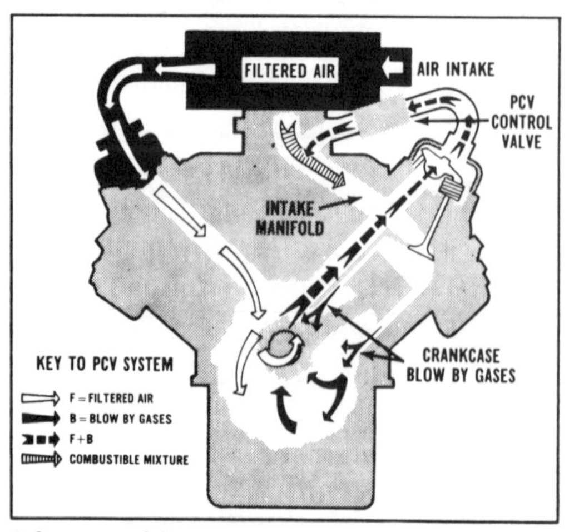

Schematic of PCV system

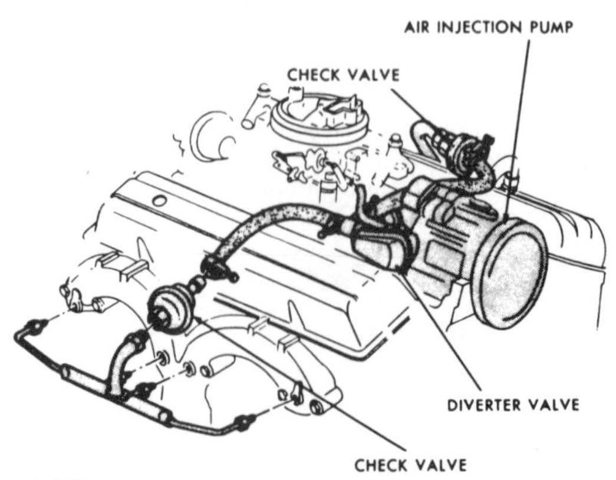

A.I.R. system components

employs an air injection pump and a system of hoses, valves, tubes, etc., necessary to carry the compressed air from the pump to the exhaust manifolds. Carburetors and distributors for A.I.R. engines have specific modifications to adapt them to the air injection system; these components should not be interchanged with those intended for use on engines that do not have the system.

A diverter valve is used to prevent backfiring. The valve senses sudden increases in manifold vacuum and ceases the injection of air during fuel-rich periods. During coasting, this valve diverts the entire air flow through the muffler and during high engine speeds, expels it through a relief valve. Check valves in the system prevent exhaust gases from entering the pump.

Air Pump R & R

1. Disconnect the air hoses at the pump.
2. Hold the pump pulley from turning and loosen the pulley bolts.
3. Loosen the pump mounting bolt and adjustment bracket bolt. Remove the drive belt.
4. Remove the mounting bolts and then remove the pump.
5. Install the pump using a reverse of the removal procedure.

CONTROLLED COMBUSTION SYSTEM

This system increases combustion efficiency by means of leaner carburetor mixtures and revised distributor calibration. On most installations, thermostatically controlled air cleaner intakes draw warm air from an exhaust manifold shroud. This allows leaner carburetor settings and improves engine warm-up. A higher temperature thermostat is employed on C.C.S. cars.

Particular attention must be paid to the tuning of C.C.S. equipped engines to maintain performance and efficient exhaust emission control.

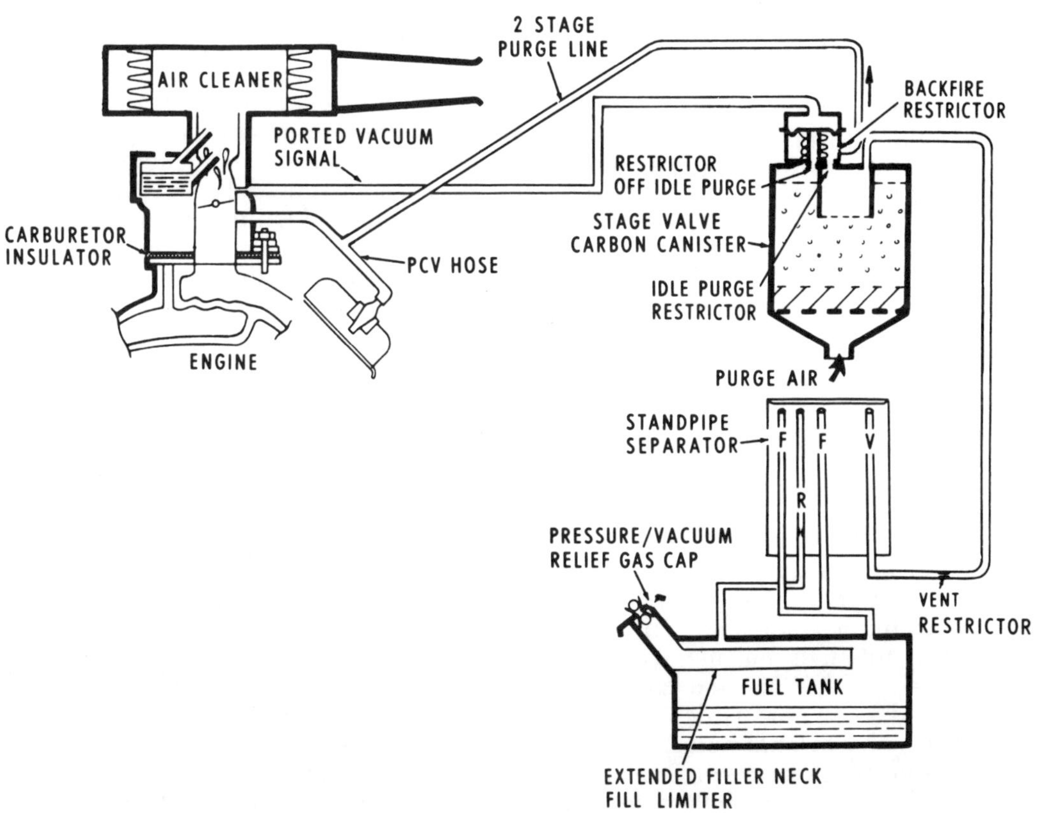

Schematic of evaporative emissions system

EVAPORATIVE EMISSION CONTROL

Introduced on California cars in 1970, and nationwide in 1971, this system reduces the amount of escaping gasoline vapors. Float bowl emissions are controlled by internal carburetor modifications. Redesigned bowl vents, reduced bowl capacity, heat shields, and improved intake manifold-to-carburetor insulation serve to reduce vapor loss into the atmosphere. The venting of fuel tank vapors into the air has been eliminated. Fuel vapors are now directed through lines to a canister containing an activated charcoal filter. Unburned vapors are trapped here until the engine is running, the canister is purged by air drawn in by manifold vacuum. The air and fuel vapors are then directed into the engine to be burned. This system is designed to reduce fuel vapor emission. The canister filter should be replaced every 12 months or 12,000 miles. To remove the canister and replace the filter, proceed as follows:

1. Note the positions of the hoses, then disconnect them from the canister.

2. Loosen the clamps and remove the canister.

3. Remove the bottom of the canister and pull out the filter.

4. Install a new filter and assemble the bottom to the canister.

5. Install the canister and tighten the clamp bolts.

6. Install the hoses in their original positions.

ANTI-DIESELING SOLENOID

Beginning in 1968 some models may have an idle speed solenoid on the carburetor. All 1972–75 models have idle solenoids. Due to the leaner carburetor settings required for emission control, the engine may have a tendency to "diesel" or "run-on" after the ignition is turned off. The carburetor solenoid, energized when the ignition is on, maintains the normal idle speed. When the ignition is turned off, the solenoid is de-energized and permits the throttle valves to fully close, thus preventing run-on. For adjustment of carburetors with idle solenoids see carburetor adjustments

IDLE SPEED SOLENOID

V8 models with air conditioning are equipped with an idle speed solenoid mounted on the carburetor. This solenoid increases the idle speed to prevent stalling when the air conditioning is being used.

TRANSMISSION CONTROLLED SPARK

Introduced in 1970, this system controls exhaust emissions by eliminating vacuum advance in the lower forward gears.

1970

The 1970 system consists of a transmission switch, solenoid vacuum switch, time delay relay, and a thermostatic water temperature switch. The solenoid vacuum switch is energized in the lower gears via the transmission switch and closes off distributor vacuum. The two-way transmission switch is activated by the shifter shaft on manual transmissions, and by oil pressure on automatic transmissions. The switch de-energizes the solenoid in high gear, the plunger extends and uncovers the vacuum port, and the distributor receives full vacuum. The temperature switch overrides the system when engine temperature is below 63° or above 232°. This allows vacuum advance in all gears. A time delay relay opens 15 seconds after the ignition is switched on. Full vacuum advance during this delay eliminates the possibility of stalling.

1971

The 1971 system is similar, except that the vacuum solenoid (now called a Combination Emissions Control solenoid) serves two functions. One function is to control distributor vacuum; the added function is to act as a deceleration throttle stop in high gear. This cuts down on emissions when the vehicle is coming to a stop in high gear. The CEC solenoid is controlled by a temperature switch, a transmission switch, and a 20 second time delay relay. This system also contains a reversing relay, which energizes the solenoid when the transmission switch, temperature switch or time delay completes the CEC circuit to ground. This system is directly opposite the 1970 system in operation. The 1970 vacuum solenoid was normally open to allow vacuum advance and when energized, closed to block vacuum. The 1971 system is normally closed blocking vacuum advance and when energized, opens to allow vacuum advance. The temperature switch completes the CEC circuit to ground when engine temperature is below 82°. The time delay relay allows vacuum advance (and raised idle speed) for 20 seconds after the ignition key is turned to the "on" position. Models with an automatic transmission and air conditioning also have a solid state timing device which engages the air conditioning compressor for three seconds after the ignition key is turned to the "off" position to prevent the engine from running-on. Two throttle settings are necessary; one for curb idle and one for emission control on coast. Both settings are described in the tune-up section.

1972–74

The 1972 L6 system is similar to that used in 1971, except that an idle stop solenoid has been added to the system. In the energized position, the solenoid maintains engine speed at a predetermined fast idle. When de-energized the solenoid allows the throttle plates to close beyond the normal idle position; thus cutting off the air supply and preventing engine run-on. The L6 is the only 1972 engine with a CEC valve, which serves the same deceleration function as in 1971. The 1972 time delay relay delays full vacuum 20 seconds after the transmission is shifted into high gear. This relay is not used on 1973 V8 engines with small blocks. V8 engines use a vacuum advance solenoid similar to that used in 1970. This relay is normally closed to block vacuum and opens when energized to allow vacuum advance. The solenoid controls distributor vacuum advance and performs no throttle positioning function. The idle stop solenoid used operates in the same manner as the one on L6 engines. All air-conditioned cars have an additional anti-diesel (run-on) solenoid which engages the compressor clutch for three seconds after the ignition is switched off. The 1973–74 Chevrolet TCS system differs from the 1972 system in three ways. The 23 second upshift

delay has been replaced by a 20 second starting relay. This relay closes to complete the TCS circuit and open the TCS solenoid, allowing vacuum advance, for 20 seconds after the key is turned to the "on" position. The operating temperature of the temperature override switch has been raised to 93°, and the switch that was used to engage the A/C compressor when the key was turned "off" has been eliminated. All models are equipped with an electric throttle control solenoid to prevent run-on. The 1973 TCS system is used on all full-size station wagons equipped with a 165 hp 350 or a 170 hp 400.

Any of the methods of exhaust emission control requires close and frequent attention to tune-up factors of engine maintenance. TCS is not used on 1975 models.

EXHAUST GAS RECIRCULATION

All 1973–77 engines are equipped with exhaust gas recirculation (EGR). This system consists of a metering valve, a vacuum line to the carburetor, and cast-in exhaust gas passages in the intake manifold. The EGR valve is controlled by carburetor vacuum, and accordingly opens and closes to admit exhaust gases into the fuel/air mixture. The exhaust gases lower the combustion temperature, and reduce the amount of oxides of nitrogen (NO_x) produced. The valve is closed at idle between the two extreme throttle positions.

As the car accelerates, the carburetor throttle plate uncovers the vacuum port for the EGR valve. At 3–5 in. Hg, the

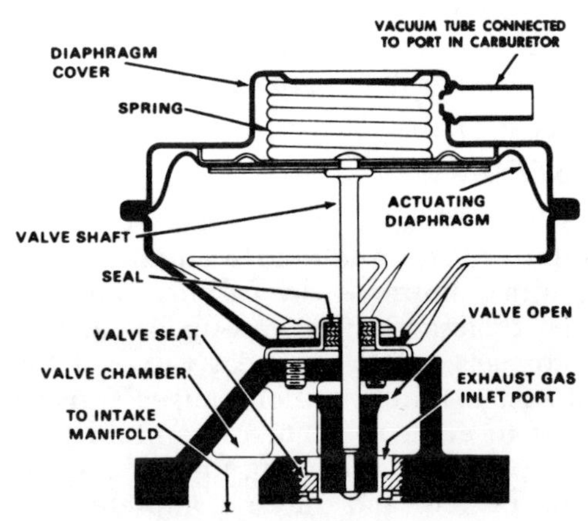

Cutaway view of EGR system

EGR valve opens and then some of the exhaust gases are allowed to flow into the air/fuel mixture to lower the combustion temperature. At full-throttle the valve closes again.

Some California engines are equipped with a dual diaphragm EGR valve. This valve further limits the exhaust gas opening (compared to the single diaphragm EGR valve) during high intake manifold vacuum periods, such as high-speed cruising, and provides more exhaust gas recirculation during acceleration when manifold vacuum is low. In addition to the hose running to the thermal vacuum switch, a second hose is connected directly to the intake manifold.

For 1977, all California models and cars delivered in areas above 4000 ft are equipped with back pressure EGR valves. The EGR valve receives exhaust back pressure through its hollow shaft. This exerts a force on the bottom of the control valve diaphragm, opposed by a light spring. Under low exhaust pressure (low engine load and partial throttle), the EGR signal is reduced by an air bleed. Under conditions of high exhaust pressure (high engine load and large throttle opening), the air bleed is closed and the EGR valve responds to an unmodified vacuum signal. At wide open throttle, the EGR flow is reduced in proportion to the amount of vacuum signal available.

EGR Valve Removal and Installation

1. Detach the vacuum line from the EGR valve.

2. Unfasten the two bolts which attach the valve to the manifold. Withdraw the valve.

3. Installation is the reverse of removal. Always use a new gasket between the valve and the manifold.

EARLY FUEL EVAPORATION SYSTEM

1975 and later models are equipped with this system to reduce engine warm-up time, improve driveability, and reduce emissions. On start-up, a vacuum motor acts to close a heat valve in the exhaust manifold which causes exhaust gases to enter the intake manifold heat riser passages. Incoming fuel mixture is then heated and more complete fuel evaporation is provided during warm-up.

CATALYTIC CONVERTER

All 1975 and later models are equipped with a catalytic converter. The converter is located midway in the exhaust system. Stainless steel exhaust pipes are used ahead of the converter. The converter is stainless steel with an aluminized steel cover and a ceramic felt blanket to insulate the converter from the floor-pan. The catalyst pellet bed inside the converter consists of noble metals which cause a reaction that converts hydrocarbons and carbon monoxide into water and carbon dioxide. 1977 six cylinder engines are equipped with an additional convertor located directly under the exhaust manifold.

Fuel System

FUEL PUMP

The fuel pump is a single action AC diaphragm type. All fuel pumps used on inline and V8 engines are diaphragm type and because of design are serviced by replacement only. No adjustments or repairs are possible.

The pump is operated by an eccentric on the camshaft. On L6 engines, the eccentric acts directly on the pump rocker arm. On V8 engines, a pushrod between the camshaft eccentric and the fuel pump operates the pump rocker arm.

Testing the Fuel Pump

Fuel pumps should always be tested on the vehicle. The larger line between the pump and tank is the suction side of the system and the smaller line, between the pump and carburetor is the pressure side. A leak in the pressure side would be apparent because of dripping fuel. A leak in the suction side is usually only apparent because of a reduced volume of fuel delivered to the pressure side.

1. Tighten any loose line connections and look for any kinks or restrictions.

2. Disconnect the fuel line at the carburetor. Disconnect the distributor-to-coil primary wire. Place a container at the end of the fuel line and crank the engine a few revolutions. If little or no gasoline flows from the line, either the fuel pump

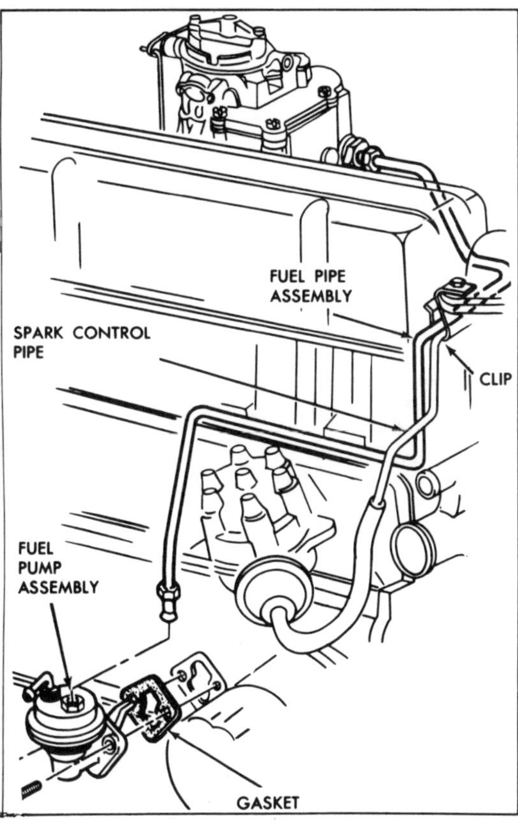

Six-cylinder fuel pump mounting

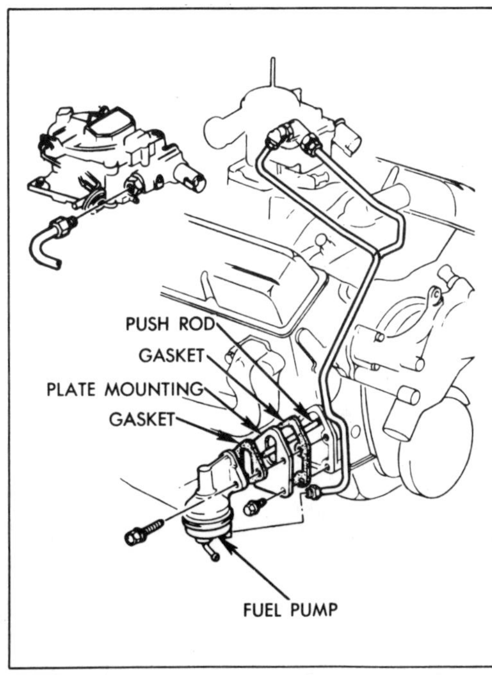

V8 fuel pump mounting

is inoperative or the line is plugged. Blow through the lines with compressed air and try the test again. Reconnect the line.

3. If fuel flows in good volume, check the fuel pump pressure to be sure.

4. Attach a pressure gauge to the pressure side of the fuel line with a "Tee" fitting.

5. Run the engine and note the reading on the gauge. Stop the engine and compare the reading with the specifications listed in the "Tune-Up Specifications" chart. If the pump is operating properly, the pressure will be as specified and will be constant at idle speed. If pressure varies sporadically or is too high or low, the pump should be replaced.

6. Remove the pressure gauge.

Removal and Installation

NOTE: *When you connect the fuel pump outlet fitting, always use 2 wrenches to avoid damaging the pump.*

1. Disconnect the fuel intake and outlet lines at the pump and plug the pump intake line.

2. On small-block V8 engines, remove the upper bolt from the right front mounting boss. Insert a longer bolt (⅜–16 x 2 in.) in this hole to hold the fuel pump pushrod.

3. Remove the two pump mounting bolts and lockwashers; remove the pump and its gasket.

4. If the rocker arm pushrod is to be removed from V8s, remove the two adapter bolts and lockwashers and remove the adapter and its gasket.

5. Install the fuel pump with a new gasket reversing the removal procedure. Coat the mating surfaces with sealer.

6. Connect the fuel lines and check for leaks.

CARBURETOR

Removal and Installation

ALL CARBURETORS

1. Remove the air cleaner and its gasket.

2. Disconnect the fuel and vacuum lines from the carburetor.

3. Disconnect the choke coil rod or heated air line tube.

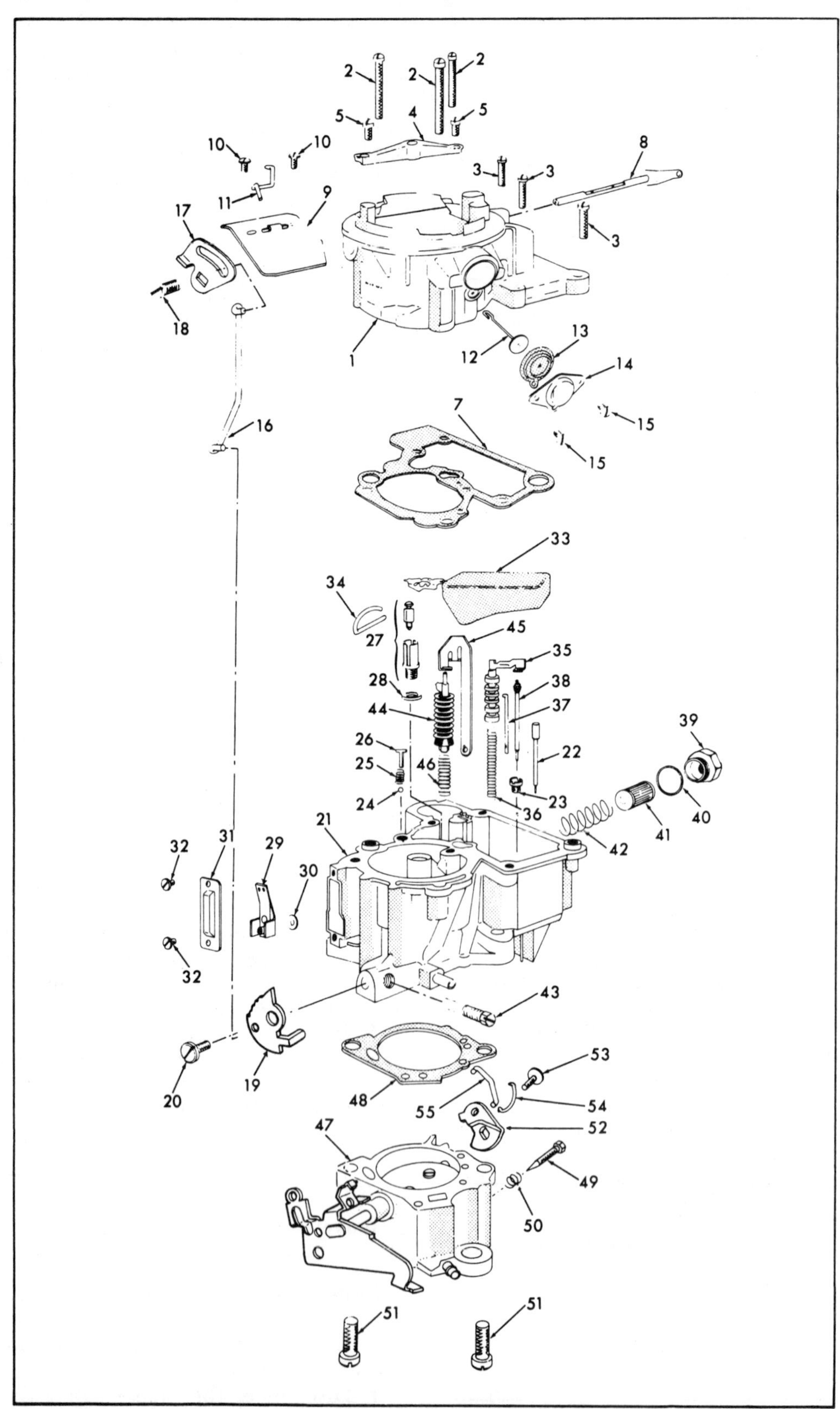

Exploded view of MV carburetor

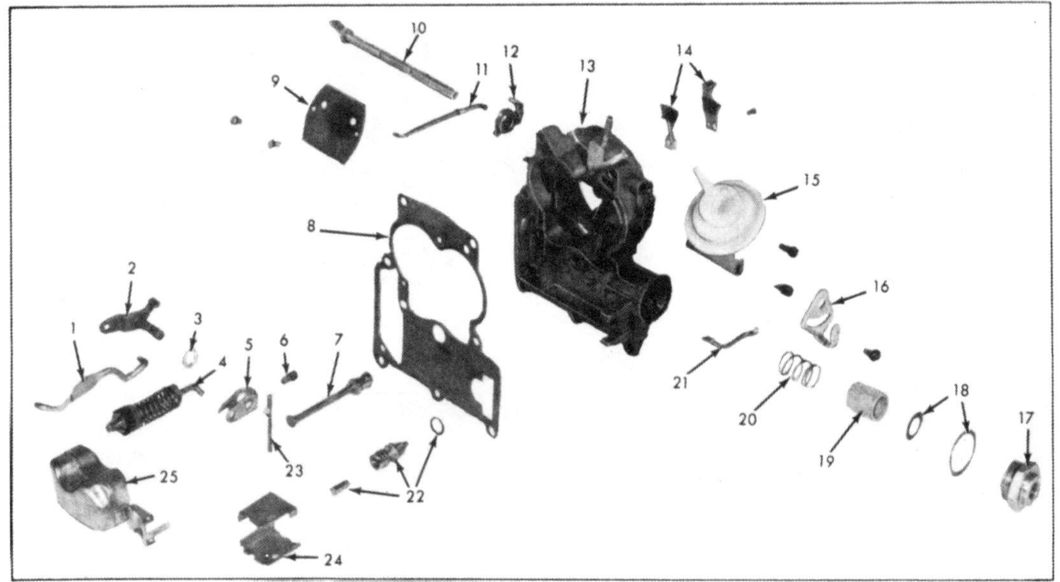

Exploded view of 2GV (1¼) air horn

1. Pump rod	7. Power piston	13. Air horn	20. Filter spring
2. Pump outer lever	8. Air horn-to-bowl	14. Vent valve and shield	21. Diaphragm link
3. Washer	gasket	15. Vacuum diaphragm	22. Float needle and seat
4. Accelerator pump	9. Choke valve	16. Choke lever	23. Float hinge pin
5. Pump inner lever	10. Choke shaft	17. Fuel inlet nut	24. Splash shields
6. Pump inner lever	11. Choke rod	18. Gaskets	25. Float
retainer	12. Choke kick lever	19. Fuel filter	

4. Disconnect the throttle linkage.

5. On automatic transmission cars, disconnect the throttle valve linkage.

6. Remove the CEC valve vacuum hose and electrical connector. Disconnect the EGR line, if so equipped.

7. Remove the idle stop electrical wiring from the idle stop solenoid, if so equipped.

8. Remove the carburetor attaching nuts and/or bolts, gasket or insulator, and remove the carburetor.

9. Install the carburetor using a reverse of the removal procedure. Use a new gasket and fill the float bowl with gasoline to ease starting the engine.

Overhaul

ALL TYPES

Efficient carburetion depends greatly on careful cleaning and inspection during overhaul, since dirt, gum, water, or varnish in or on the carburetor parts are often responsible for poor performance.

Overhaul your carburetor in a clean,

1. Air horn assembly	20. Cam attaching screw	38. Metering rod and spring assembly
2. Long air horn screw	21. Float bowl assembly	39. Fuel inlet filter nut
3. Short air horn screw	22. Idle tube assembly	40. Filter nut gasket
4. Air cleaner stud bracket	23. Main metering jet	41. Fuel inlet filter
5. Bracket attaching screw	24. Pump discharge ball	42. Fuel filter spring
7. Air horn gasket	25. Pump discharge spring	43. Slow idle screw
8. Choke shaft and lever assembly	26. Pump discharge guide	44. Pump assembly
9. Choke plate	27. Needle and seat assembly	45. Pump actuating lever
10. Choke plate screw	28. Needle seat gasket	46. Pump return spring
11. Vacuum break link lever	29. Idle compensator assembly	47. Throttle body assembly
12. Vacuum break link assembly	30. Idle compensator gasket	48. Throttle body gasket
13. Vacuum break diaphragm	31. Idle compensator cover	49. Idle needle
14. Vacuum break cover	32. Cover screw	50. Idle needle spring
15. Cover screw	33. Float assembly	51. Throttle body screw
16. Choke rod	34. Float hinge pin	52. New pump and power rods lever
17. Choke lever	35. Power piston assembly	53. Lever attaching screw
18. Choke lever screw	36. Power piston spring	54. Power piston rod link
19. Fast idle cam	37. Power piston rod	55. Pump lever link

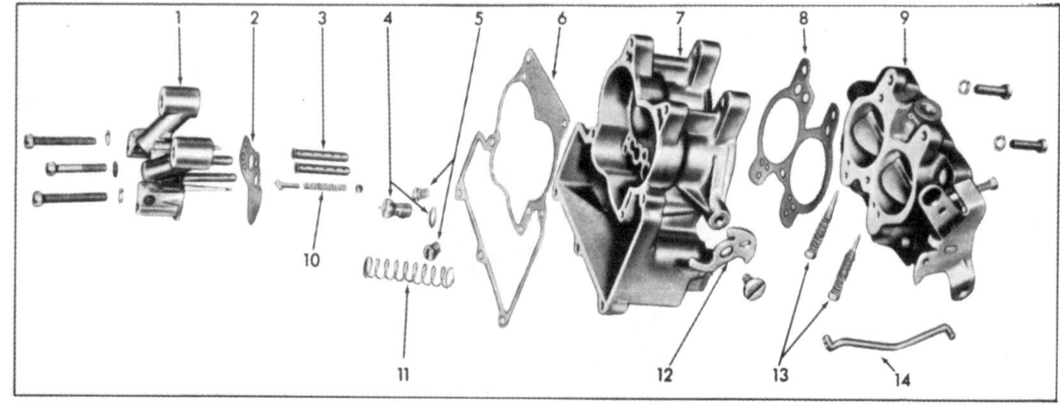

Exploded view of 2GV (1¼) float bowl and throttle body

1. Cluster assembly
2. Gasket
3. Splash shield—main well
4. Power valve assembly
5. Main jets
6. Air horn gasket
7. Bowl assembly
8. Throttle body-to-bowl gasket
9. Throttle body assembly
10. Pump discharge check assembly
11. Accelerator pump spring
12. Fast idle cam
13. Idle mixture screws
14. Choke rod

dust-free area. Carefully disassemble the carburetor, referring often to the exploded views and directions packaged with the rebuilding kit. Keep all similar and look-alike parts segregated during disassembly and cleaning to avoid accidental interchange during assembly. Make a note of all jet sizes.

When the carburetor is disassembled, wash all parts (except diaphragms, electric choke units, pump plunger, and any other plastic, leather, fiber, or rubber

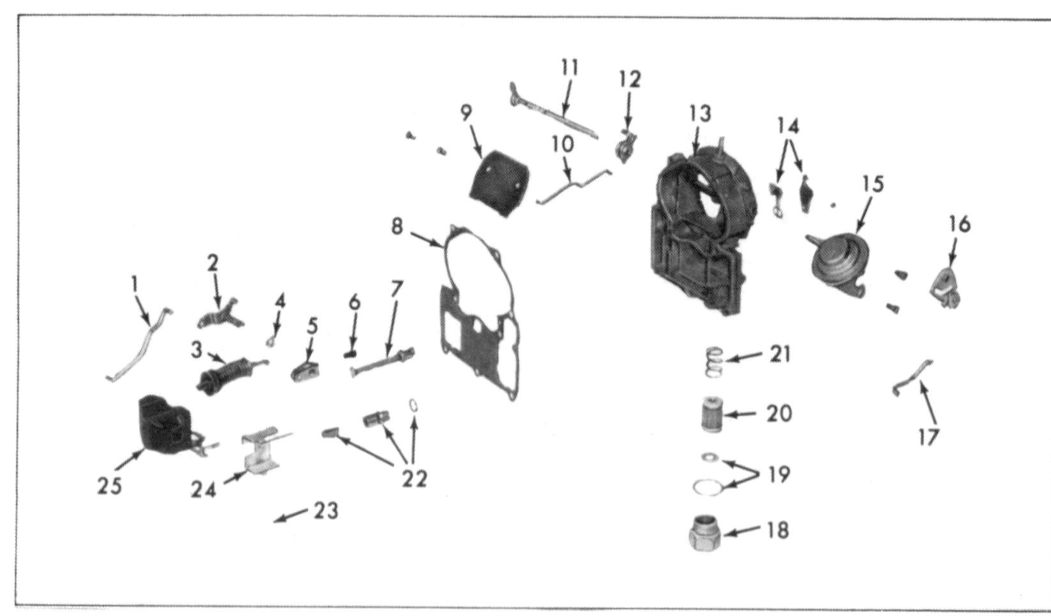

Exploded view of 2GV (1½) air horn

1. Pump rod
2. Pump outlet lever
3. Accelerator pump
4. Washer
5. Pump inner lever
6. Pump inner lever retainer
7. Power piston
8. Air horn-to-bowl gasket
9. Choke valve
10. Choke rod
11. Choke shaft
12. Choke kick lever
13. Air horn
14. Vent valve and shield
15. Vacuum diaphragm
16. Choke lever
17. Diaphragm link
18. Fuel inlet nut
19. Gaskets
20. Fuel filter
21. Filter spring
22. Float needle and seat
23. Float hinge pin
24. Splash shield
25. Float

parts) in clean carburetor solvent. Do not leave parts in the solvent any longer than is necessary to sufficiently loosen the deposits. Excessive cleaning may remove the special finish from the float bowl and choke valve bodies, leaving these parts unfit for service. Rinse all parts in clean solvent and blow them dry with compressed air or allow them to air dry. Wipe clean all cork, plastic, leather, and fiber parts with a clean, lint-free

Blow out all passages and jets with compressed air and be sure that there are no restrictions or blockages. Never use wire or similar tools to clean jets, fuel passages, or air bleeds. Clean all jets and valves separately to avoid accidental interchange.

Check all parts for wear or damage. If wear or damage is found, replace the defective parts. Especially check the following:

1. Check the float needle and seat for wear. If wear is found, replace the complete assembly.

2. Check the float hinge pin for wear and the float(s) for dents or distortion. Replace the float if fuel has leaked into it.

3. Check the throttle and choke shaft bores for wear or an out-of-round condition. Damage or wear to the throttle arm, shaft, or shaft bore will often require replacement of the throttle body. These

parts require a close tolerance of fit; wear may allow air leakage, which could affect starting and idling.

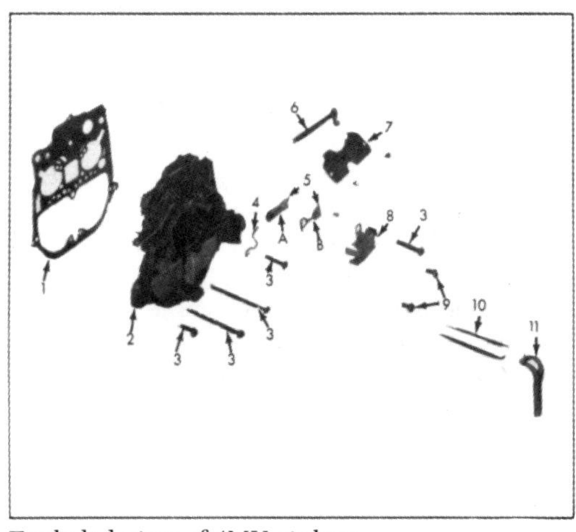

Exploded view of 4MV air horn

1. Air horn-to-bowl gasket
2. Air horn assembly
3. Air horn-to-bowl retaining screws (2 long, 5 short, 2 countersunk—Item No. 9)
4. Idle vent valve lever
5. Idle vent valve
   a. Bimetal
   b. Spring
6. Choke shaft and lever
7. Choke valve
8. Idle vent shield
9. Countersunk air horn retaining screws
10. Secondary metering rods
11. Metering rod hanger

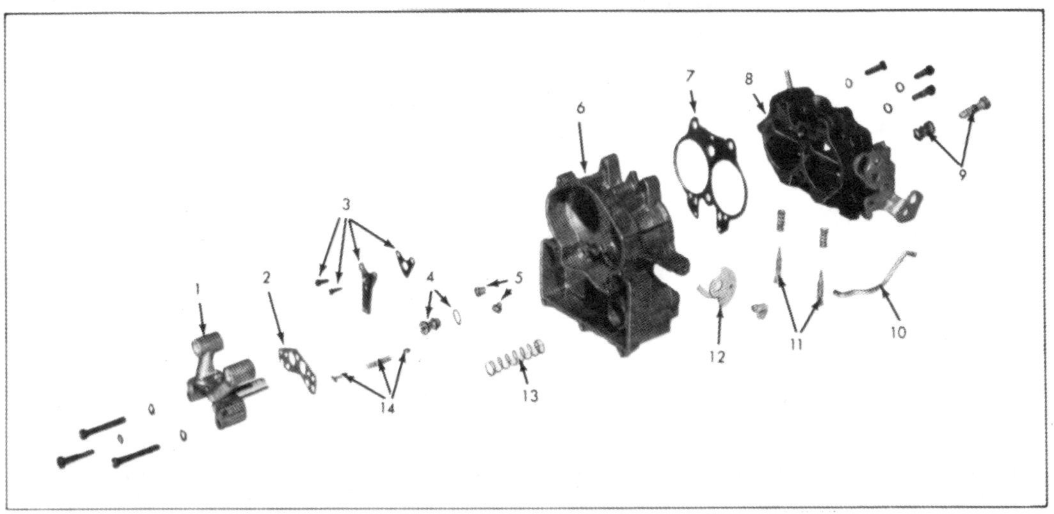

Exploded view of 2GV (1½) float bowl

1. Cluster assembly	6. Bowl assembly	9. Idle speed screw	13. Accelerator pump spring
2. Cluster gasket	7. Throttle body-to-bowl gasket	10. Choke rod	14. Pump discharge check assembly
3. Hot idle compensator	8. Throttle body assembly	11. Idle mixture screws	
4. Power valve assembly		12. Fast idle cam	
5. Main jets			

NOTE: *Throttle shafts and bushings are not included in overhaul kits. They can be purchased separately.*

4. Inspect the idle mixture adjusting needles for burrs or grooves. Any such condition requires replacement of the needle, since you will not be able to obtain a satisfactory idle.

5. Test the accelerator pump check valves. They should pass air one way but not the other. Test for proper seating by blowing and sucking on the valve. Replace the valve as necessary. If the valve is satisfactory, wash the valve again to remove breath moisture.

6. Check the bowl cover for warped surfaces with a straightedge.

7. Closely inspect the valves and seats for wear and damage, replacing as necessary.

8. After the carburetor is assembled, check the choke valve for freedom of operation.

Carburetor overhaul kits are recommended for each overhaul. These kits contain all gaskets and new parts to replace those which deteriorate most rapidly. Failure to replace all parts supplied with the kit (especially gaskets) can result in poor performance later.

Some carburetor manufacturers supply overhaul kits of three basic types: minor repair; major repair; and gasket kits. Basically, they contain the following:

Minor Repair Kits:
   All gaskets
   Float needle valve
   All diaphragms
   Spring for the pump diaphragm

Major Repair Kits:
   All jets and gaskets
   All diaphragms
   Float needle valve
   Pump ball valve
   Float
   Complete intermediate rod
   Intermediate pump lever
   Some cover hold-down screws and washers

Gasket Kits:

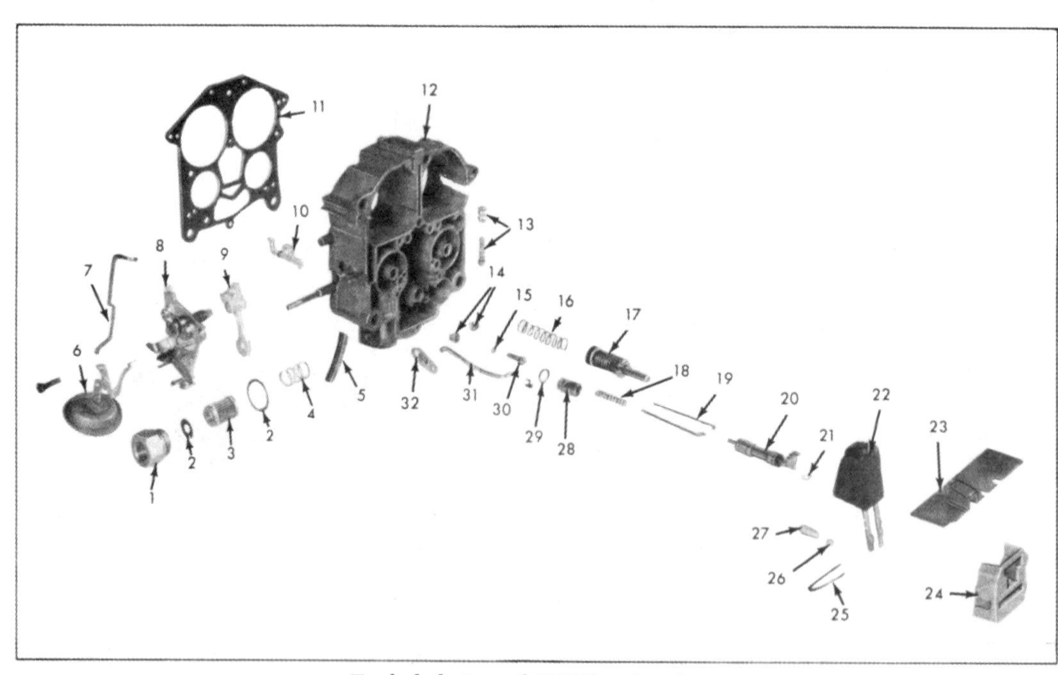

Exploded view of 4MV float bowl

1. Fuel inlet nut	10. Secondary throttle lockout	17. Accelerator pump	26. Float needle pull clip
2. Gasket	11. Throttle body-to-bowl gasket	18. Power piston spring	27. Float needle
3. Fuel filter	12. Float bowl assembly	19. Primary metering rods	28. Float needle seat
4. Fuel filter spring	13. Idle speed screw	20. Power piston	29. Needle seat gasket
5. Vacuum break hose	14. Primary jets	21. Metering rod retainer	30. Discharge ball retainer
6. Vacuum diaphragm	15. Pump discharge ball	22. Float	31. Choke rod
7. Air valve dashpot	16. Pump return spring	23. Secondary air baffle	32. Choke lever
8. Choke control bracket		24. Float bowl insert	
9. Fast idle cam		25. Float hinge pin	

All gaskets

After cleaning and checking all components, reassemble the carburetor, using new parts and referring to the exploded view. When reassembling, make sure that all screws and jets are tight in their seats, but do not overtighten as the tips will be distorted. Tighten all screws gradually, in rotation. Do not tighten needle valves into their seats; uneven jetting will result. Always use new gaskets. Be sure to adjust the float level when reassembling.

Preliminary Checks (All Carburetors)

The following should be observed before attempting any adjustments.

1. Thoroughly warm the engine. If the engine is cold, be sure that it reaches operating temperature.

2. Check the torque of all carburetor mounting nuts. Also check the intake manifold-to-cylinder head bolts. If air is leaking at any of these points, any attempts at adjustment will inevitably lead to frustration.

3. Check the manifold heat control valve (if used) to be sure that it is free.

4. Check and adjust the choke as necessary.

5. Adjust the idle speed and mixture. If any adjustments are performed that might possibly change the idle speed or mixture, adjust the idle and mixture again when you are finished.

ROCHESTER MODEL MV

The model MV carburetor is a single bore, down-draft carburetor with an aluminum throttle body, automatic choke, internally balanced venting, and a hot idle compensating system for cars equipped with automatic transmissions. Newer models are also equipped with Combination Emission Control valves (C.E.C.) and an Exhaust Gas Recirculation (EGR) system. An electrically operated idle stop solenoid replaces the idle stop screw of older models.

The MV carburetor is used on six cylinder cars from 1968 and service procedures apply to all MV carburetors.

Fast Idle Adjustment

NOTE: *The fast idle adjustment must be made with the transmission in Neutral.*

1. Position the fast idle lever on the high step of the fast idle cam.

2. Be sure that the choke is properly adjusted and in the wide open position with the engine warm.

3. Bend the fast idle lever until the specified speed is obtained.

Choke Rod (fast idle cam) Adjustment

NOTE: *Adjust the fast idle before making choke rod adjustments.*

1. Place the fast idle cam follower on the second step of the fast idle cam and hold it firmly against the rise to the high step.

2. Rotate the choke valve in the direction of a closed choke by applying force to the choke coil lever.

3. Bend the choke rod, at the point shown in the illustration, to give the

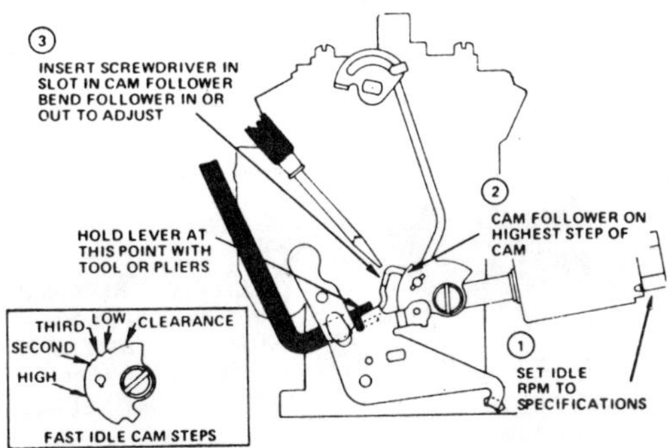

MV fast idle adjustment

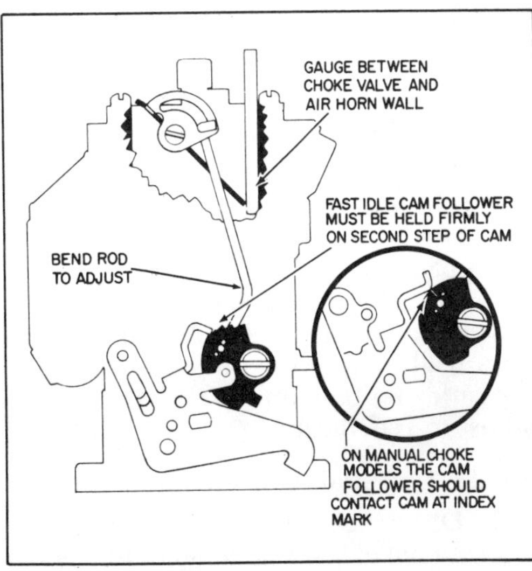

MV choke rod adjustment

specified opening between the lower edge of the choke valve and the inside air horn wall.

NOTE: *Measurement must be made at the center of the choke valve.*

Choke Vacuum Break Adjustments

The adjustment of the vacuum break diaphragm unit insures correct choke valve opening after engine starting.

1. Remove the air cleaner on vehicles with Therm AC air cleaner; plug the sensor's vacuum take off port.

2. Using an external vacuum source, apply vacuum to the vacuum break diaphagm until the plunger is fully seated.

3. When the plunger is seated, push the choke valve toward the closed position.

4. Holding the choke valve in this position, place the specified gauge between the lower edge of the choke valve and the air horn wall.

5. If the measurement is not correct, bend the vacuum break rod at the point shown in the illustration.

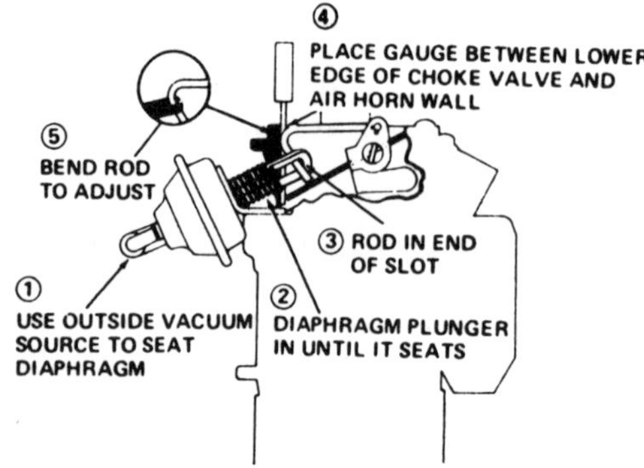

MV vacuum break adjustment

Choke Unloader Adjustment

1. Apply pressure to the choke valve and hold it in the closed position.

2. Open the throttle valve to the wide open position.

3. Check the dimension between the lower edge of the choke plate and the air horn wall; if adjustment is needed, bend the unloader tang on the throttle lever to adjust to specification.

Choke Coil Rod Adjustment

1. Disconnect the coil rod from the upper choke lever and hold the choke valve closed.

2. Push down on the coil rod to the end of its travel.

3. The top of the rod should be even with the bottom hole in the choke lever.

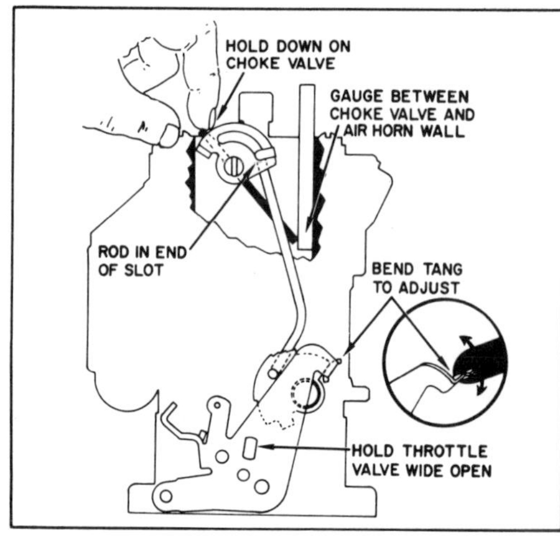

MV choke unloader adjustment

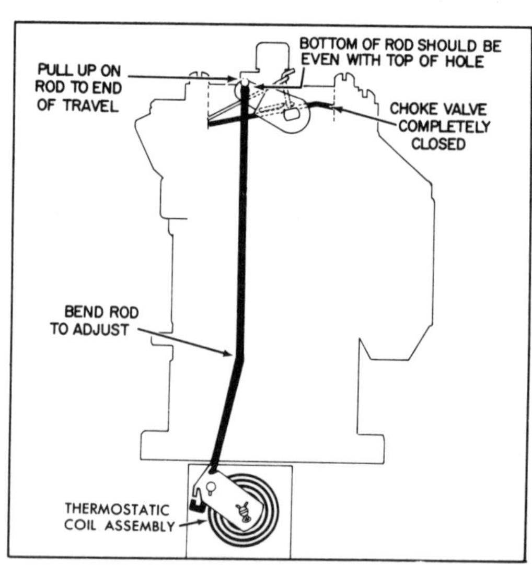

MV choke coil rod adjustment

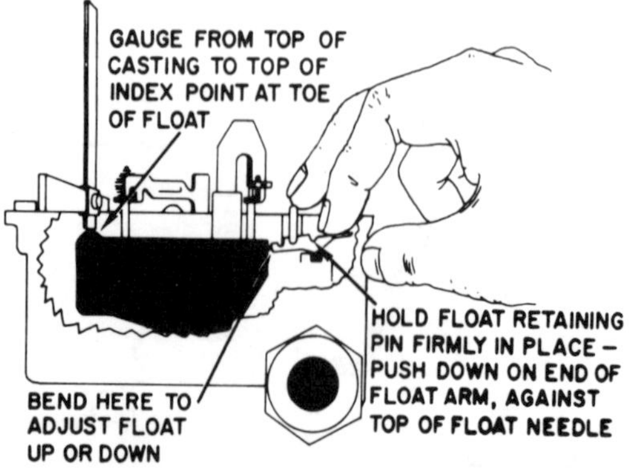

MV float level adjustment

MV Carburetor Specifications

Year	Carburetor Identification[1]	Float Level (in.)	Metering Rod (in.)	Pump Rod	Idle Vent (in.)	Vacuum Break (in.)	Fast Idle Off Car (in.)	Choke Rod (in.)	Choke Unloader (in.)	Fast Idle Speed (rpm)
1968	7028014	$\frac{9}{32}$	0.120	——	0.050	0.245	$1\frac{1}{2}$	0.150	0.350	2400[2]
	7028015	$\frac{9}{32}$	0.130	——	0.050	0.275	$1\frac{1}{2}$	0.150	0.350	2400[2]
	7028017	$\frac{9}{32}$	0.130	——	0.050	0.275	$1\frac{1}{2}$	0.150	0.350	2400[2]
1969	7029014	$\frac{1}{4}$	0.070	——	0.050	0.245	0.100	0.170	0.350	2400[2]
	7029015	$\frac{1}{4}$	0.090	——	0.050	0.275	0.100	0.200	0.350	2400[2]
	7029017	$\frac{1}{4}$	0.090	——	0.050	0.275	0.100	0.200	0.350	2400[2]
1970	7040014	$\frac{1}{4}$	0.070	——	——	0.200	0.110	0.170	0.350	2400[2]
	7040017	$\frac{1}{4}$	0.090	——	——	0.160	0.100	0.190	0.350	2400[2]
1971	7041014	$\frac{1}{4}$	0.080	——	——	0.200	0.100	0.160	0.350	——
	7041017	$\frac{1}{4}$	0.080	——	——	0.230	0.100	0.180	0.350	——
	7041023	$\frac{1}{16}$	——	——	——	0.200	0.110	0.120	0.350	——
1972	7042014	$\frac{1}{4}$	0.080	——	——	0.190	——	0.125	0.500	2400[2]
	7042017	$\frac{1}{4}$	0.078	——	——	0.225	——	0.150	0.500	2400[2]
	7042984	$\frac{1}{4}$	0.078	——	——	0.190	——	0.125	0.500	2400[2]
	7042987	$\frac{1}{4}$	0.076	——	——	0.225	——	0.150	0.500	2400[2]
1973	7043014	$\frac{1}{4}$	0.080	——	——	0.300	——	0.245	0.500	1800[2]
	7043017	$\frac{1}{4}$	0.080	——	——	0.350	——	0.275	0.500	1800[2]

[1] The carburetor identification tag is located at the rear of the carburetor on one of the air horn screws.
[2] High step of cam.

4. To make adjustments, bend the rod at the point shown in the illustration.

Float Adjustment

1. Hold the float retainer in place and the float arm against the top of the float needle by pushing down on the float arm at the outer end toward the float bowl casting.

2. Using an adjustable T scale, measure the distance from the toe of the float to the float bowl gasket surface.

NOTE: *The float bowl gasket should be removed and the gauge held on the index point on the float for accurate measurement.*

3. Adjust the float level by bending the float arm up or down at the float arm junction.

Metering Rod Adjustments

1. Hold the throttle valve wide open and push down on the metering rod

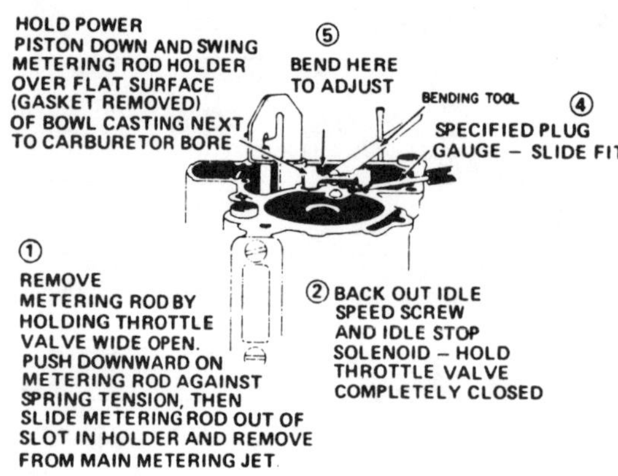

MV metering rod adjustment

against spring tension, then remove the rod from the main metering jet.

2. In order to check adjustment, the slow idle screw must be backed out and the fast idle cam rotated so that the fast idle cam follower does not contact the steps on the cam.

3. With the throttle valve closed, push down on the power piston until it contacts its stop.

4. With the power piston depressed, swing the metering rod holder over the flat surface of the bowl casting next to the carburetor bore.

5. Insert a specified size drill between the bowl casting sealing bead and the lower surface of the metering rod holder. The drill should slide smoothly between both surfaces.

6. If adjustment is needed, carefully bend the metering rod holder up or down at the point shown. After adjustment, reinstall the metering rod.

Idle Vent Adjustment

1. The engine idle must be set at the specified RPM and the choke valve held wide open so that the fast idle cam follower is not contacting the cam.

NOTE: *If the carburetor is off the car, a preliminary idle setting can be made by turning the idle speed screw in 1½ turns from the closed throttle valve position.*

2. With the throttle stop screw held against the idle stop screw, the idle vent valve should be open to specification. To check a drill of specified size may be inserted between the top of the air horn casting and the bottom surface of the valve.

3. If adjustment is necesssary, turn the slotted vent valve head with a screwdriver. Turning the head clockwise *increases* the clearance.

ROCHESTER 2GC, 2GV

1968–74 models are equipped with 2GV (choke coil on manifold); 1975–76 with 2GC (choke on carburetor). 2GC choke is adjusted by loosening three cover screws and rotating the cover to align the index marks while holding the choke closed.

Fast Idle Adjustment

On 2GC and 2GV models the fast idle is set automatically when the curb idle and mixture is set.

Choke Rod (fast idle cam)

1. Turn in the idle cam stop screw until it just contacts the bottom step of the fast idle cam. Then turn the screw one full turn.

2. Place the idle screw on the second step of the fast idle cam against the shoulder of the high step.

3. Hold the choke valve closed and check the clearance between the upper edge of the choke valve and the air horn wall.

4. Adjust the clearance by bending the tang on the choke lever.

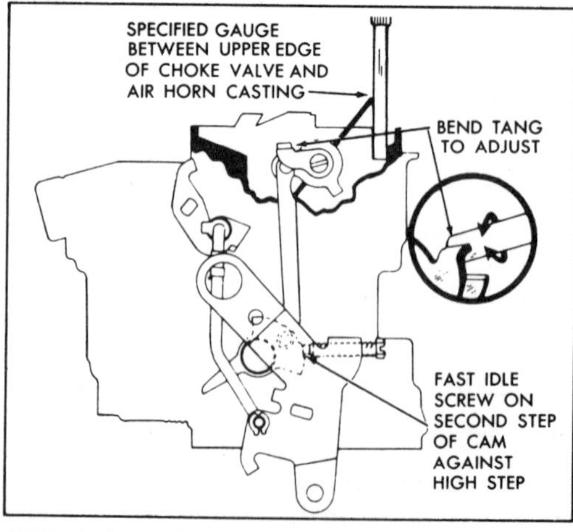

2GV choke rod adjustment (fast idle cam adjustment)

Vacuum Break Adjustment

1. Remove the air cleaner. Vehicles with a Therm AC air cleaner should

have the sensor's vacuum take-off port plugged.

2. Seat the diaphragm plunger, using an outside vacuum source.

3. When the plunger is seated, push the choke valve toward the closed position.

4. Holding the choke valve in this position, place the specified size gauge between the lower edge of the choke valve and the air horn wall.

5. If the measurement is not correct, bend the vacuum break rod at the point shown in the illustration.

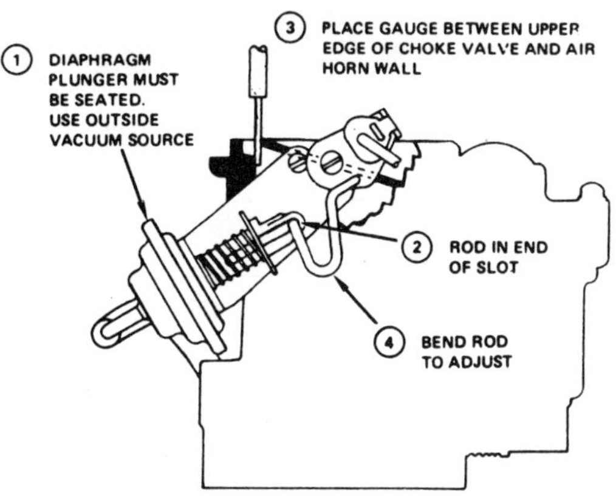

2GV vacuum break adjustment

Choke Unloader Adjustment

1. Hold the throttle valves wide open.
2. Close the choke valve.
3. Bend the unloader tang to obtain the proper clearance between the upper edge of the choke valve and air horn wall.

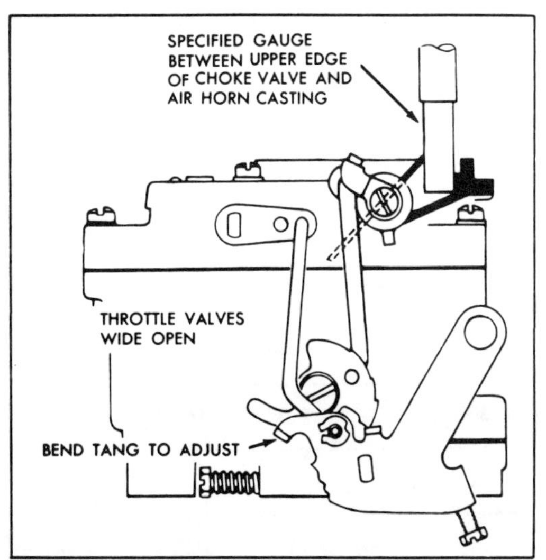

2GV choke unloader adjustment

Choke Coil Rod Adjustment

1. Hold the choke valve completely open.

2. Disconnect the coil rod from the upper lever and push down on the rod to the end of its travel.

3. When the rod is all the way down, it should line up with the bottom of the slotted hole on the choke valve linkage.

4. Adjust by bending the lever at the point shown in illustration.

Float Level

With the air horn assembly upside down, measure the distance from the air horn gasket to the lip at the toe of the float. Bend the float arm to adjust to specifications.

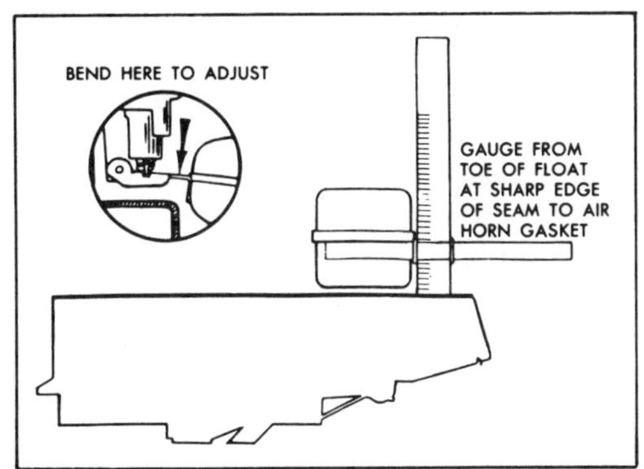

2GV float level adjustment (brass float)

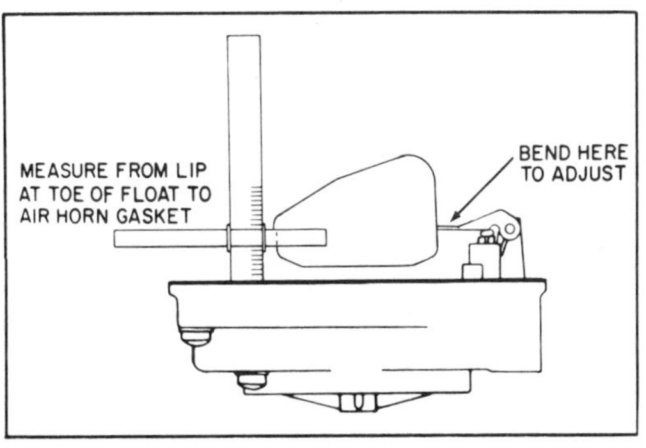

2GV float level adjustment (nitrophyl float)

Float Drop

Holding the air horn assembly upright, measure the distance from the gasket to the lip at the toe of the float. If correction is necessary, bend the float tang at the rear, next to the needle and seat.

Rochester 2GC, 2GV Specifications

Year	Carburetor Identification[1]	Float Level (in.)	Float Drop (in.)	Pump Rod (in.)	Idle Vent (in.)	Vacuum Break (in.)	Automatic Choke	Choke Rod (in.)	Choke Unloader (in.)	Fast Idle Speed
1968	7028110	¾	1¾	1⅛	1.000	0.100	——	0.060	0.200	——
	7028101	¾	1¾	1⅛	1.000	0.100	——	0.060	0.200	——
	7028112	¾	1¾	1⅛	1.000	0.100	——	0.060	0.200	——
	7028103	¾	1¾	1⅛	1.000	0.100	——	0.060	0.200	——
1969	7029101	$^{27}/_{32}$	1¾	1⅛	0.020	0.100	——	0.060	0.215	——
	7029103	$^{27}/_{32}$	1¾	1⅛	0.020	0.100	——	0.060	0.215	——
	7029110	$^{27}/_{32}$	1¾	1⅛	0.020	0.100	——	0.060	0.215	——
	7029112	$^{27}/_{32}$	1¾	1⅛	0.020	0.100	——	0.060	0.215	——
	7029102	¾	1¾	$1^{13}/_{32}$	0.020	0.215	——	0.085	0.275	——
	7029104	¾	1¾	$1^{13}/_{32}$	0.020	0.215	——	0.085	0.275	——
	7029127	¾	1¾	$1^{13}/_{32}$	0.020	0.215	——	0.085	0.275	——
	7029129	¾	1¾	$1^{13}/_{32}$	0.020	0.215	——	0.085	0.275	——
	7029117	¾	1¾	$1^{13}/_{32}$	0.020	0.215	——	0.085	0.275	——
	7029118	¾	1¾	$1^{13}/_{32}$	0.020	0.215	——	0.085	0.275	——
	7029119	⅝	1¾	$1^{13}/_{32}$	0.020	0.215	——	0.085	0.275	——
	7029120	⅝	1¾	$1^{13}/_{32}$	0.020	0.215	——	0.085	0.275	——
1970	7040110	$^{27}/_{32}$	1¾	1⅛	0.020	0.100	——	0.060	0.215	——
	7040112	$^{27}/_{32}$	1¾	1⅛	0.020	0.100	——	0.060	0.215	——
	7040101	$^{27}/_{32}$	1¾	1⅛	0.020	0.125	——	0.060	0.160	——
	7040103	$^{27}/_{32}$	1¾	1⅛	0.020	0.125	——	0.060	0.225	——
	7040114	$^{23}/_{32}$	1⅜	$1^{17}/_{32}$	0.020	0.200	——	0.085	0.325	——
	7040116	$^{23}/_{32}$	1⅜	$1^{17}/_{32}$	0.020	0.200	——	0.085	0.325	——
	7040113	$^{23}/_{32}$	1⅜	$1^{17}/_{32}$	0.020	0.215	——	0.085	0.275	——
	7040115	$^{23}/_{32}$	1⅜	$1^{17}/_{32}$	0.020	0.215	——	0.085	0.275	——

Rochester 2GC, 2GV Specifications (cont.)

Year	Carbu-retor Identifi-cation[1]	Float Level (in.)	Float Drop (in.)	Pump Rod (in.)	Idle Vent (in.)	Vacuum Break (in.)	Auto-matic Choke	Choke Rod (in.)	Choke Unloader (in.)	Fast Idle Speed
1970	7040118	$2\frac{3}{32}$	$1\frac{3}{8}$	$1\frac{17}{32}$	0.020	0.215	——	0.085	0.325	——
	7040120	$2\frac{3}{32}$	$1\frac{3}{8}$	$1\frac{17}{32}$	0.020	0.215	——	0.085	0.325	——
	7040117	$2\frac{3}{32}$	$1\frac{3}{8}$	$1\frac{17}{32}$	0.020	0.215	——	0.085	0.325	——
	7040119	$2\frac{3}{32}$	$1\frac{3}{8}$	$1\frac{17}{32}$	0.020	0.215	——	0.085	0.325	——
1971	7041024	$\frac{1}{16}$	——	——	——	0.140	——	0.080	0.350	——
	7041101	$1\frac{3}{16}$	$1\frac{3}{4}$	$1\frac{3}{64}$	——	0.110	——	0.075	0.215	——
	7041110	$1\frac{3}{16}$	$1\frac{3}{4}$	$1\frac{3}{64}$	——	0.080	——	0.040	0.215	——
	7041102	$2\frac{5}{32}$	$1\frac{3}{8}$	$1\frac{5}{32}$	——	0.170	——	0.100	0.325	——
	7041114	$2\frac{5}{32}$	$1\frac{3}{8}$	$1\frac{5}{32}$	——	0.170	——	0.100	0.325	——
	7041113	$2\frac{3}{32}$	$1\frac{3}{8}$	$1\frac{5}{32}$	——	0.180	——	0.100	0.325	——
	7041127	$2\frac{3}{32}$	$1\frac{3}{8}$	$1\frac{5}{32}$	——	0.180	——	0.100	0.325	——
	7041117	$2\frac{3}{32}$	$1\frac{3}{8}$	$1\frac{5}{32}$	——	0.170	——	0.100	0.325	——
	7041118	$2\frac{3}{32}$	$1\frac{3}{8}$	$1\frac{5}{32}$	——	0.170	——	0.100	0.325	——
	7041181	$\frac{5}{8}$	$1\frac{3}{4}$	$1\frac{3}{8}$	——	0.120	——	0.080	0.180	——
	7041182	$\frac{5}{8}$	$1\frac{3}{4}$	$1\frac{3}{8}$	——	0.120	——	0.080	0.180	——
1972	7042111	$2\frac{3}{32}$	$1\frac{9}{32}$	$1\frac{1}{2}$	——	0.180	——	0.100	0.325	——
	7042113	$2\frac{3}{32}$	$1\frac{9}{32}$	$1\frac{1}{2}$	——	0.180	——	0.100	0.325	——
	7042831	$2\frac{3}{32}$	$1\frac{9}{32}$	$1\frac{1}{2}$	——	0.180	——	0.100	0.325	——
	7042833	$2\frac{3}{32}$	$1\frac{9}{32}$	$1\frac{1}{2}$	——	0.180	——	0.100	0.325	——
	7042112	$2\frac{3}{32}$	$1\frac{9}{32}$	$1\frac{1}{2}$	——	0.170	——	0.100	0.325	——
	7042114	$2\frac{3}{32}$	$1\frac{9}{32}$	$1\frac{1}{2}$	——	0.170	——	0.100	0.325	——
	7042118	$2\frac{3}{32}$	$1\frac{9}{32}$	$1\frac{1}{2}$	——	0.190	Auto-matic	0.100	0.325	——
	7042832	$2\frac{3}{32}$	$1\frac{9}{32}$	$1\frac{1}{2}$	——	0.170	——	0.100	0.325	——
	7042834	$2\frac{3}{32}$	$1\frac{9}{32}$	$1\frac{1}{2}$	——	0.170	——	0.100	0.325	——

Rochester 2GC, 2GV Specifications (cont.)

Year	Carburetor Identification[1]	Float Level (in.)	Float Drop (in.)	Pump Rod (in.)	Idle Vent (in.)	Vacuum Break (in.)	Automatic Choke	Choke Rod (in.)	Choke Unloader (in.)	Fast Idle Speed
1972	7042838	$^{23}\!/_{32}$	$1^9\!/_{32}$	$1\frac{1}{2}$	——	0.190	——	0.100	0.325	——
	7042100	$^{25}\!/_{32}$	$1^{31}\!/_{32}$	$1^5\!/_{16}$	——	0.080	——	0.040	0.215	——
	7042820	$^{25}\!/_{32}$	$1^{31}\!/_{32}$	$1^5\!/_{16}$	——	0.080	——	0.040	0.215	——
	7042101	$^{25}\!/_{32}$	$1^{31}\!/_{32}$	$1^5\!/_{16}$	——	0.110	——	0.075	0.215	——
	7042821	$^{25}\!/_{32}$	$1^{31}\!/_{32}$	$1^5\!/_{16}$	——	0.110	——	0.075	0.215	——
1973	7043100	$^{21}\!/_{32}$	$1^9\!/_{32}$	$1^5\!/_{16}$	——	0.080	——	0.150	0.215	——
	7043101	$^{21}\!/_{32}$	$1^9\!/_{32}$	$1^5\!/_{16}$	——	0.080	——	0.150	0.215	——
	7043120	$^{21}\!/_{32}$	$1^9\!/_{32}$	$1^5\!/_{16}$	——	0.080	——	0.150	0.215	——
	7043105	$^{21}\!/_{32}$	$1^9\!/_{32}$	$1^5\!/_{16}$	——	0.080	——	0.150	0.215	——
	7043114	$1^9\!/_{32}$	$1^9\!/_{32}$	$1^7\!/_{16}$	——	0.130	——	0.245	0.325	——
	7043113	$1^9\!/_{32}$	$1^9\!/_{32}$	$1^7\!/_{16}$	——	0.140	——	0.200	0.250	——
	7043112	$1^9\!/_{32}$	$1^9\!/_{32}$	$1^7\!/_{16}$	——	0.130	——	0.245	0.325	——
	7043111	$1^9\!/_{32}$	$1^9\!/_{32}$	$1^7\!/_{16}$	——	0.140	——	0.200	0.250	——
	7043118	$1^9\!/_{32}$	$1^9\!/_{32}$	$1^7\!/_{16}$	——	0.130	——	0.245	0.325	——
1974–77	7044111	$1^9\!/_{32}$	$1^9\!/_{32}$	$1^9\!/_{32}$	——	0.140	——	——	0.250	1600[2]
	7044112	$1^9\!/_{32}$	$1^9\!/_{32}$	$1^3\!/_{16}$	——	0.130	——	——	0.325	1600[2]
	7044113	$1^9\!/_{32}$	$1^9\!/_{32}$	$1^9\!/_{32}$	——	0.140	——	——	0.250	1600[2]
	7044114	$1^9\!/_{32}$	$1^9\!/_{32}$	$1^3\!/_{16}$	——	0.130	——	——	0.325	1600[2]
	7044115	$1^9\!/_{32}$	$1^9\!/_{32}$	$1^9\!/_{32}$	——	0.140	——	——	0.250	1600[2]
	7044116	$1^9\!/_{32}$	$1^9\!/_{32}$	$1^3\!/_{16}$	——	0.130	——	——	0.325	1600[2]
	7044118	$1^9\!/_{32}$	$1^9\!/_{32}$	$1^3\!/_{16}$	——	0.130	——	——	0.325	1600[2]
	7044123	$1^9\!/_{32}$	$1^9\!/_{32}$	$1^9\!/_{32}$	——	0.140	——	——	0.250	1600[2]
	7044124	$1^9\!/_{32}$	$1^9\!/_{32}$	$1^3\!/_{16}$	——	0.130	——	——	0.320	1600[2]

[1] The carburetor identification tag is located at the rear of the carburetor on one of the air horn screws.

[2] This setting is with the low idle at 500 rpm with the clutch fan disengaged.

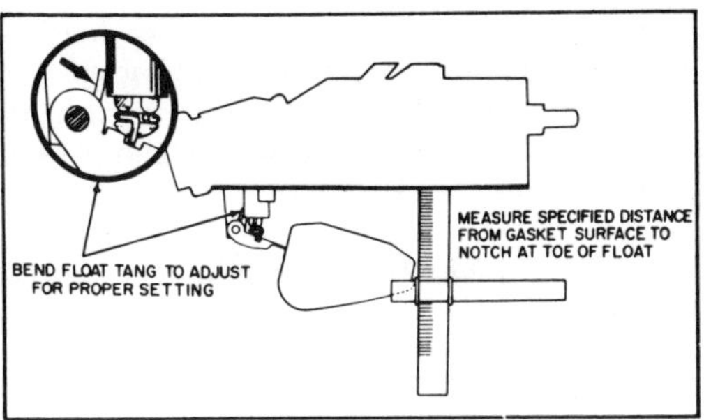

2GV float drop adjustment (nitrophyl float)

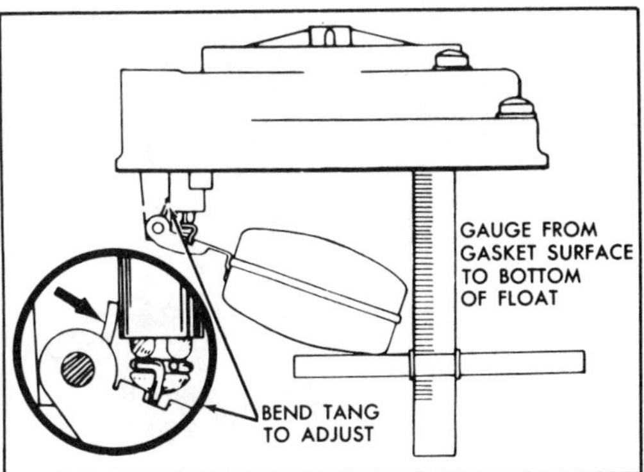

2GV float drop adjustment (brass float)

Accelerator Pump Rod

1. Back out the idle speed screw and completely close the throttle valves.

2. Place the pump gauge across the air cleaner mounting surface.

3. With the T-scale set to the specified height, the lower leg of the gauge should

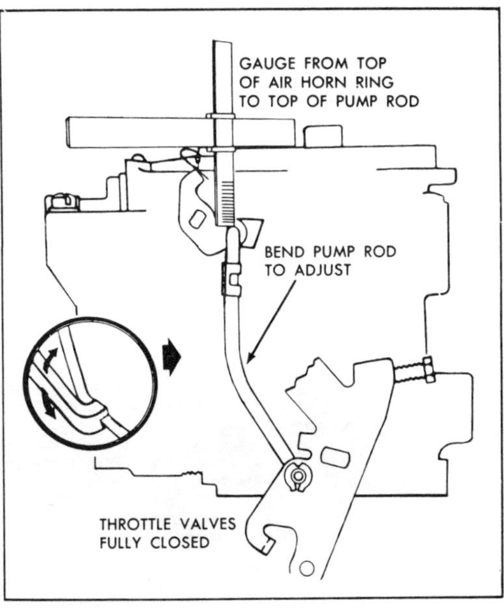

2GV accelerator pump rod adjustment

just touch the top of the accelerator pump rod.

4. Bend the pump rod to adjust.

ROCHESTER 4MC, 4MV

The Rochester Quadrajet carburetor is a two stage, four-barrel downdraft carburetor. The designation MC or MV refers to the type of choke system the carburetor is designed for. The MV model is equipped with a manifold thermostatic choke coil. The MC model has a choke housing and coil mounted on the side of the float bowl.

The primary side of the carburetor is equipped with 1⅜ diameter bores and a triple venturi with plain tube nozzles. During off idle and part throttle operation, the fuel is metered through tapered metering rods operating in specially designed jets positioned by a manifold vacuum responsive piston.

The secondary side of the carburetor contains two 2¼ bores. An air valve is used on the secondary side for metering control and supplements the primary bores.

The secondary air valve operates tapered metering rods which regulate the fuel in constant proportion to the air being supplied.

Fast Idle

1. Position the fast idle lever on the high step of the fast idle cam.

2. Be sure that the choke is wide open and the engine warm.

3. Turn the fast idle screw to gain the proper fast idle rpm.

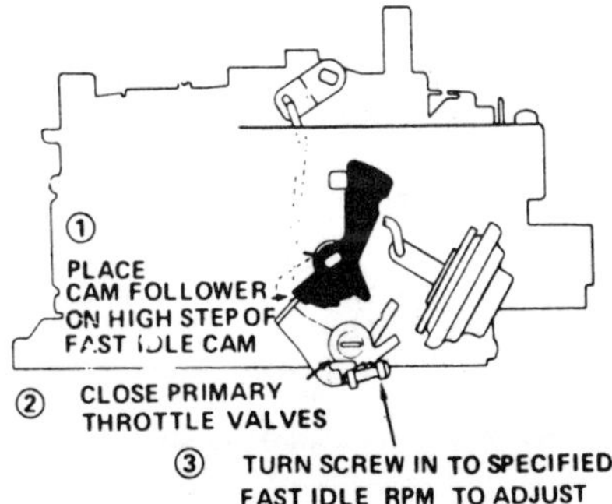

4MV, MC fast idle adjustment

Choke Rod (Fast idle cam)

1. Place the cam follower on the second step of the fast idle cam.

2. Close the choke valve by exerting counterclockwise pressure on the external choke lever.

3. Insert a gauge of the proper size between the lower edge of the choke valve and the inside air horn wall.

4. To adjust, bend the choke rod.

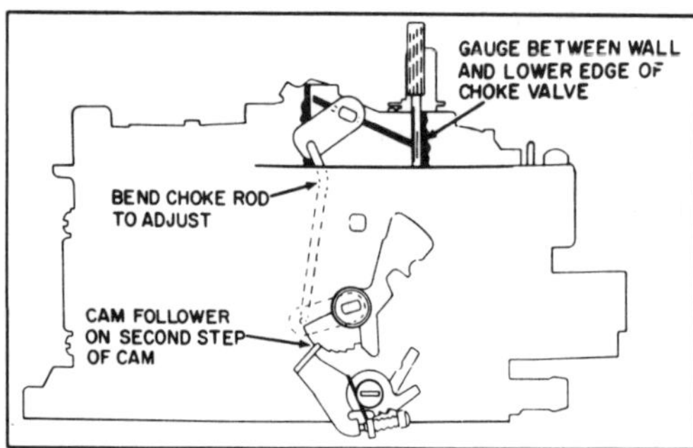

4MV, MC choke rod adjustment

Vacuum Break

1. Fully seat the vacuum break diaphragm using an outside vacuum source.

2. Open the throttle valve enough to allow the fast idle cam follower to clear the fast idle cam.

3. The end of the vacuum break rod should be at the outer end of the slot in the vacuum break diaphragm plunger.

4. The specified clearance should register from the lower end of the choke valve to the inside air horn wall.

5. If the clearance is not correct, bend the vacuum break link at the point shown in the illustration.

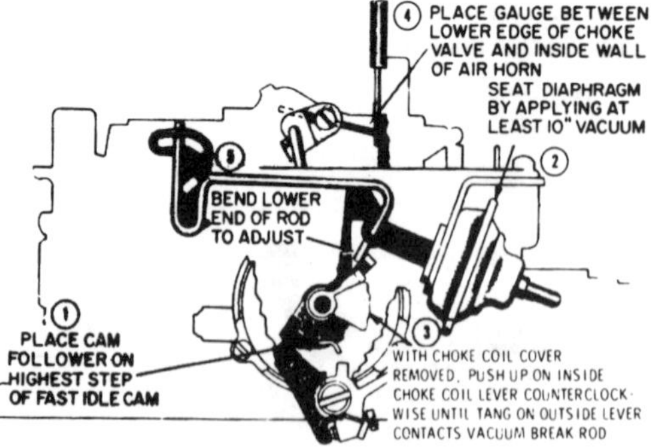

4MV, MC vacuum break adjustment

Secondary Vacuum Break

1. Using an outside vacuum source, seat the auxiliary vacuum break diaphragm plunger.

2. Rotate the choke lever in the closed position until the spring loaded diaphragm plunger is fully extended.

3. Holding the choke valve closed, check the distance between the lower edge of the choke valve and the airhorn wall.

4. To adjust to specifications, bend the vacuum break link.

Choke Unloader

1. Push up on the vacuum break lever and fully open the throttle valves.

2. Measure the distance from the lower edge of the choke valve to the air horn wall. To adjust, bend the tang on the fast idle lever.

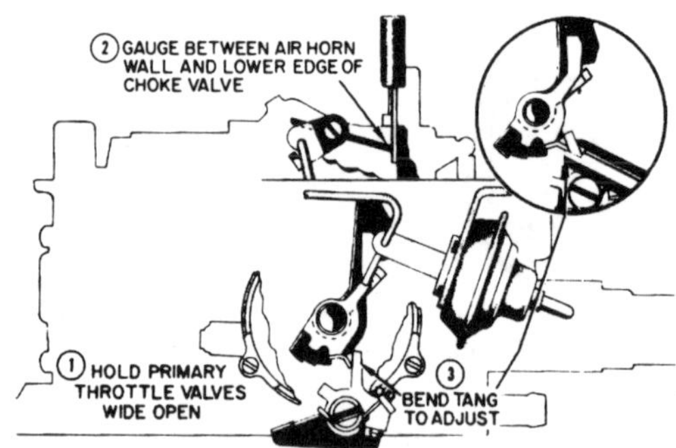

4MV, MC choke unloader adjustment

Choke Coil Rod

1. Close the choke valve by rotating the choke coil lever counterclockwise.

2. Disconnect the thermostatic coil rod from the upper lever.

3. Push down on the rod until it contacts the bracket of the coil.

4. The rod must fit in the notch of the upper lever.

5. If it does not, it must be bent on the curved portion just below the upper lever.

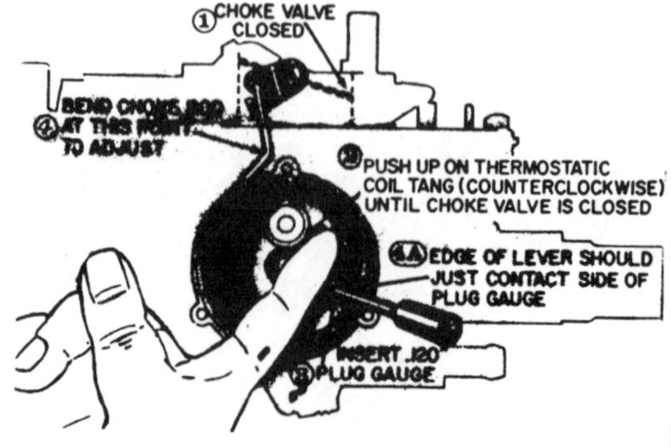

4MV, MC choke coil rod adjustment

Secondary Closing Adjustment

This adjustment assures proper closing of the secondary throttle plates.

1. Set the slow idle as per instructions in the appropriate car section. Make sure that the fast idle cam follower is not resting on the fast idle cam.

2. There should be 0.020 in. clearance between the secondary throttle actuating rod and the front of the slot on the secondary throttle lever with the closing tang on the throttle lever resting against the actuating lever.

3. Bend the tang on the primary throttle actuating rod to adjust.

Secondary Opening Adjustment

1. Open the primary throttle valves until the actuating link contacts the upper tang on the secondary lever.

2. With two point linkage, the bottom of the link should be in the center of the secondary lever slot.

3. With three point linkage, there should be 0.070 in. clearance between the link and the middle tang.

4. Bend the upper tang on the secondary lever to adjust as necessary.

Float Level

With the air horn assembly upside down, measure the distance from the air horn gasket surface (gasket removed) to the top of the float at the toe.

NOTE: *Make sure the retaining pin is*

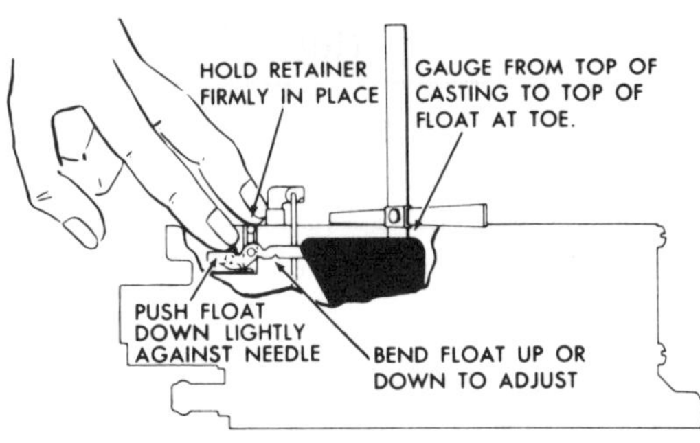

4MV, MC float level adjustment

firmly held in place and that the tang of the float is firmly against the needle and seat assembly.

Secondary Metering Rod Adjustment

1. Measure from the top of each metering rod to the top of the air horn casting.

2. The measurement should be $^{53}/_{64}$ in.; if not, correct by ending the metering rod hanger. Make sure both rods are adjusted correctly.

Accelerator Pump

1. Close the primary throttle valves by backing out the slow idle screw and making sure that the fast idle cam follower is off the steps of the fast idle cam.

2. Bend the secondary throttle closing tang away from the primary throttle lever.

3. With the pump in the appropriate hole in the pump lever, measure from the top of the choke valve wall to the top of the pump stem.

4. To adjust, bend the pump lever.

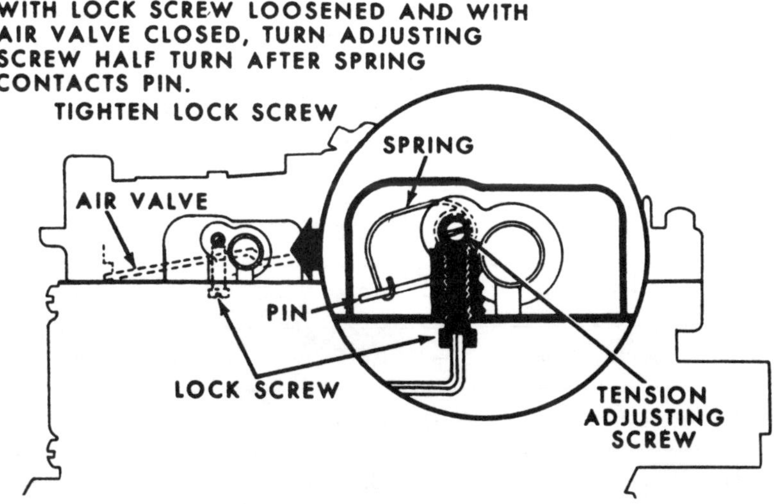

4MV, MC air valve adjustment

Rochester 4MV, 4MC Specifications

Year	Carburetor Identification [1]	Float Level (in.)	Air Valve Spring	Pump Rod (in.)	Idle Vent (in.)	Vacuum Break (in.)	Secondary Opening (in.)	Choke Rod (in.)	Choke Unloader (in.)	Fast Idle Speed (rpm)
1968	7028212	9/32	3/8 turn	9/32	3/8	0.160	0.010	0.100	0.260	——
	7028213	9/32	3/8 turn	9/32	3/8	0.245	0.010	0.100	0.300	——
	7028229	9/32	7/8 turn	9/32	3/8	0.245	0.010	0.100	0.300	——
	7028208	9/32	3/8 turn	9/32	3/8	0.160	0.010	0.100	0.260	——
	7028207	9/32	3/8 turn	9/32	3/8	0.245	0.010	0.100	0.300	——
	7028219	9/32	7/8 turn	9/32	3/8	0.245	0.010	0.100	0.300	——
	7028218	3/16	7/8 turn	9/32	3/8	0.160	0.010	0.100	0.300	——
	7028217	3/16	7/8 turn	9/32	3/8	0.245	0.010	0.100	0.300	——
	7028210	3/16	7/8 turn	9/32	3/8	0.160	0.010	0.100	0.300	——
	7028211	3/16	7/8 turn	9/32	3/8	0.245	0.010	0.100	0.300	——
	7028216	3/16	7/8 turn	9/32	3/8	0.160	0.010	0.100	0.300	——
	7028209	3/16	7/8 turn	9/32	3/8	0.245	0.010	0.100	0.300	——
1969	7029203	7/32	7/16 turn	5/16	3/8	0.245	0.015	0.100	0.450	——
	7029202	7/32	7/16 turn	5/16	3/8	0.180	0.015	0.100	0.450	——
	7029207	3/16	13/16 turn	5/16	3/8	0.245	0.015	0.100	0.450	——
	7029215	1/4	13/16 turn	5/16	3/8	0.245	0.015	0.100	0.450	——
	7029204	1/4	13/16 turn	5/16	3/8	0.180	0.015	0.100	0.450	——
1970	7040202	1/4	7/16 turn	5/16	——	0.245	——	0.100	0.450	——
	7040203	1/4	7/16 turn	5/16	——	0.275	——	0.100	0.450	——
	7040207	1/4	13/16 turn	5/16	——	0.275	——	0.100	0.450	——
	7040200	1/4	13/16 turn	5/16	——	0.245	——	0.100	0.450	——
	7040201	1/4	13/16 turn	5/16	——	0.275	——	0.100	0.450	——
	7040204	1/4	13/16 turn	5/16	——	0.245	——	0.100	0.450	——
	7040205	1/4	13/16 turn	5/16	——	.0275	——	0.100	0.450	——

Rochester 4MV, 4MC Specifications (cont.)

Year	Carbu- retor Identifi- cation[1]	Float Level (in.)	Air Valve Spring	Pump Rod (in.)	Idle Vent (in.)	Vacuum Break (in.)	Secondary Opening (in.)	Choke Rod (in.)	Choke Unloader (in.)	Fast Idle Speed (rpm)
1971	7041200	$\frac{1}{4}$	$\frac{7}{16}$ turn	——	——	0.260	——	0.100	——	——
	7041202	$\frac{1}{4}$	$\frac{7}{16}$ turn	——	——	0.260	——	0.100	——	——
	7041204	$\frac{1}{4}$	$\frac{7}{16}$ turn	——	——	0.260	——	0.100	——	——
	7041212	$\frac{1}{4}$	$\frac{7}{16}$ turn	——	——	0.260	——	0.100	——	——
	7041201	$\frac{1}{4}$	$\frac{7}{16}$ turn	——	——	0.275	——	0.100	——	——
	7041203	$\frac{1}{4}$	$\frac{7}{16}$ turn	——	——	0.275	——	0.100	——	——
	7041205	$\frac{1}{4}$	$\frac{7}{16}$ turn	——	——	0.275	——	0.100	——	——
	7041213	$\frac{1}{4}$	$\frac{7}{16}$ turn	——	——	0.275	——	0.100	——	——
1972	7042220	$\frac{1}{4}$	$\frac{7}{16}$ turn	$\frac{3}{8}$	——	0.250	——	0.100	0.450	——
	7042216	$\frac{1}{4}$	$\frac{7}{16}$ turn	$\frac{3}{8}$	——	0.250	——	0.100	0.450	——
	7042215	$\frac{1}{4}$	$\frac{7}{16}$ turn	$\frac{3}{8}$	——	0.250	——	0.100	0.450	——
	7042217	$\frac{1}{4}$	$\frac{7}{16}$ turn	$\frac{3}{8}$	——	0.250	——	0.100	0.450	——
	7042202	$\frac{1}{4}$	$\frac{1}{2}$ turn	$\frac{3}{8}$	——	0.215	——	0.100	0.450	——
	7042203	$\frac{1}{4}$	$\frac{1}{2}$ turn	$\frac{3}{8}$	——	0.215	——	0.100	0.450	——
	7042902	$\frac{1}{4}$	$\frac{1}{2}$ turn	$\frac{3}{8}$	——	0.215	——	0.100	0.450	——
	7042903	$\frac{1}{4}$	$\frac{1}{2}$ turn	$\frac{3}{8}$	——	0.215	——	0.100	0.450	——
1973	7043202	$\frac{7}{32}$	$\frac{1}{2}$ turn	$\frac{13}{32}$	——	0.250	——	0.430	0.450	——
	7043203	$\frac{7}{32}$	$\frac{1}{2}$ turn	$\frac{13}{32}$	——	0.250	——	0.430	0.450	——
	7043212	$\frac{7}{32}$	1 turn	$\frac{13}{32}$	——	0.250	——	0.430	0.450	——
	7043213	$\frac{7}{32}$	1 turn	$\frac{13}{32}$	——	0.250	——	0.430	0.450	——
	7043200	$\frac{1}{4}$	$\frac{11}{16}$ turn	$\frac{13}{32}$	——	0.250	——	0.430	0.450	——
	7043201	$\frac{1}{4}$	$\frac{11}{16}$ turn	$\frac{13}{32}$	——	0.250	——	0.430	0.450	——
1974– 75	7044202	$\frac{1}{4}$	$\frac{7}{8}$ turn	$\frac{13}{32}$[2]	——	0.230	——	0.430	0.450	1600[3]
	7044203	$\frac{1}{4}$	$\frac{7}{8}$ turn	$\frac{13}{32}$[2]	——	0.230	——	0.430	0.450	1600[3]

Rochester 4MV, 4MC Specifications (cont.)

Year	Carburetor Identification[1]	Float Level (in.)	Air Valve Spring	Pump Rod (in.)	Idle Vent (in.)	Vacuum Break (in.)	Secondary Opening (in.)	Choke Rod (in.)	Choke Unloader (in.)	Fast Idle Speed (rpm)
1974–75	7044206	$\frac{1}{4}$	$\frac{7}{8}$ turn	$\frac{13}{32}$[2]	——	0.230	——	0.430	0.450	1600[3]
	7044207	$\frac{1}{4}$	$\frac{7}{8}$ turn	$\frac{13}{32}$[2]	——	0.230	——	0.430	0.450	1600[3]
	7044223	$\frac{3}{8}$	$\frac{7}{16}$ turn	$\frac{13}{32}$[2]	——	0.220	——	0.430	0.450	1600[3]
	7044201	$\frac{3}{8}$	$\frac{7}{16}$ turn	$\frac{13}{32}$[2]	——	0.250	——	0.430	0.450	1600[3]
	7044500	$\frac{3}{8}$	$\frac{7}{16}$ turn	$\frac{13}{32}$[2]	——	0.250	——	0.430	0.450	1600[3]
	7044208	$\frac{1}{4}$	1 turn	$\frac{13}{32}$[2]	——	0.230	——	0.430	0.450	1600[3]
	7044209	$\frac{1}{4}$	1 turn	$\frac{13}{32}$[2]	——	0.230	——	0.430	0.450	1600[3]
	7044210	$\frac{1}{4}$	1 turn	$\frac{13}{32}$[2]	——	0.230	——	0.430	0.450	1600[3]
	7044211	$\frac{1}{4}$	1 turn	$\frac{13}{32}$[2]	——	0.230	——	0.430	0.450	1600[3]
	7044502	$\frac{1}{4}$	$\frac{7}{8}$ turn	$\frac{13}{32}$[2]	——	0.230	——	0.430	0.450	1600[3]
	7044503	$\frac{1}{4}$	$\frac{7}{8}$ turn	$\frac{13}{32}$[2]	——	0.230	——	0.430	0.450	1600[3]
	7044506	$\frac{1}{4}$	$\frac{7}{8}$ turn	$\frac{13}{32}$[2]	——	0.230	——	0.430	0.450	1600[3]
	7044507	$\frac{1}{4}$	$\frac{7}{8}$ turn	$\frac{13}{32}$[2]	——	0.230	——	0.430	0.450	1600[3]
1977	17056202	$\frac{13}{32}$	$\frac{7}{8}$ turn	$\frac{9}{32}$[2]	——	0.185	——	0.325	0.325	1600[3]
	17056228	$\frac{13}{32}$	$\frac{3}{4}$ turn	$\frac{9}{32}$[2]	——	0.185	——	0.325	0.325	1600[3]
	17056200	$\frac{13}{32}$	$\frac{7}{8}$ turn	$\frac{9}{32}$[2]	——	0.240	——	0.190	[4]	1600[3]

[1] The carburetor identification tag is located at the rear of the carburetor on one of the air horn screws.
[2] Without vacuum advance.
[3] Vacuum advance connected and EGR disconnected and the throttle positioned on the high step of cam.
[4] Electric choke.

5. After adjusting, readjust the secondary throttle tang and the slow idle screw.

Idle Vent Adjustment

After adjusting the accelerator pump rod as specified above, open the primary throttle valve enough to just close the idle vent. Measure from the top of the choke valve wall to the top of the pump plunger stem. If adjustment is necessary, bend the wire tang on the pump lever.

Air Valve Spring Adjustment

To adjust the air valve spring windup, loosen the Allen head lockscrew and turn the adjusting screw counterclockwise to remove all spring tension. With the air valve closed, turn the adjusting screw clockwise the specified number of turns after the torsion spring contacts the pin on the shaft. Hold the adjusting screw in this position and tighten the lockscrew.

Chapter 5

Chassis Electrical

Heater

BLOWER

Removal and Installation

1. Disconnect the battery.
2. Unclip the hoses from fender skirt.
3. Disconnect electrical feed from motor. Disconnect the motor air-cooling hose on air-conditioned cars.
4. Turn the front wheels to the extreme right.
5. Remove the right front fender skirt bolts and allow skirt to drop, resting it on top of tire. It may be wedged away from fender lower flange with block of wood to provide better access to bolts.
6. Remove screws attaching motor mounting plate to air inlet housing.
7. Remove screws attaching motor to mounting plate.
8. Remove clip attaching cage to shaft and remove blower motor.
9. Install in reverse of above.

CORE

Removal and Installation

ALL EXCEPT AIR CONDITIONED CARS

1. Drain the radiator.
2. Remove heater hoses at connections beside air inlet assembly.
3. Remove cable and electrical connectors from heater and defroster assembly.
4. On engine side of dash, remove screws and nuts holding air inlet to dash panel.
5. Inside vehicle, pull entire assembly from firewall and remove assembly from vehicle.
6. Remove core assembly retaining springs and remove core.
7. Install in reverse of above.
NOTE: *This procedure is not applicable to air-conditioned cars, except pre-1970 models with the dealer-installed, under dash unit.*

1968–71 WITH AIR CONDITIONING

1. Remove the battery ground cable.
2. Drain the cooling system. It is not necessary to evacuate the A.C. refrigerant.
3. Remove the heater hoses at the firewall.
4. Remove the nuts from the heater distributor studs protruding through the firewall.
5. Remove the glove compartment.
6. Remove the five center distributor duct hoses, duct cables, center duct-to-selector duct screws, and the center duct.
7. From inside the car, drill out the lower case stud using a $1/4$ in. drill.

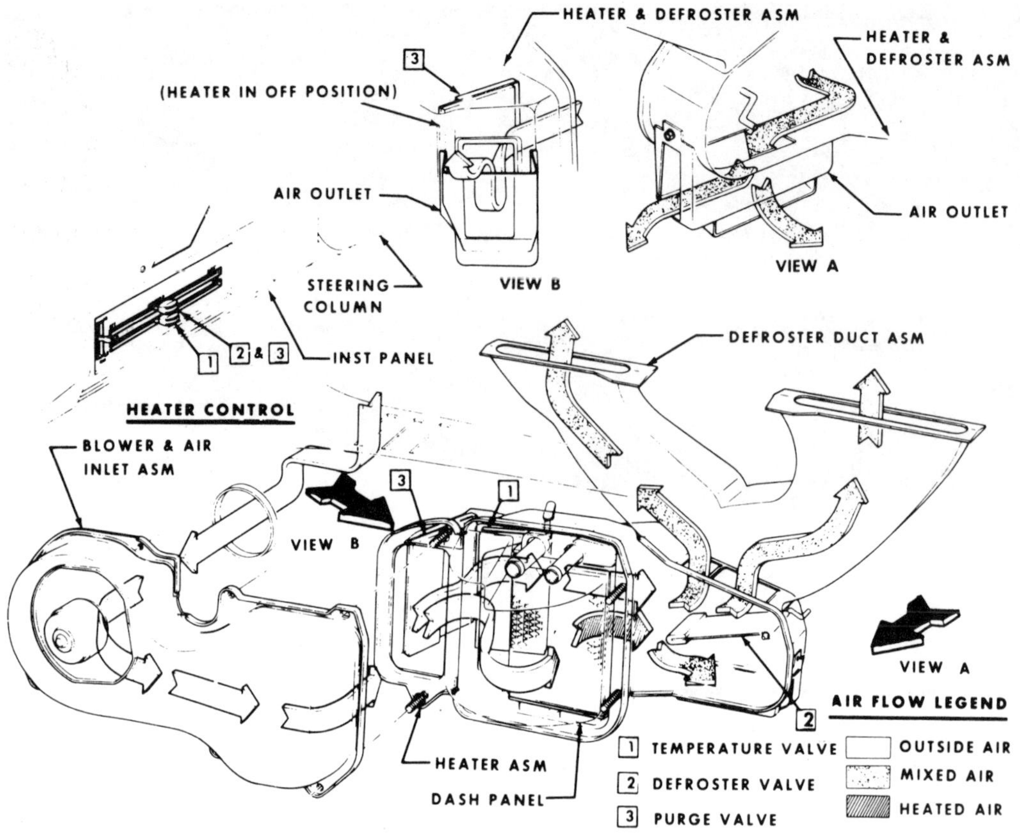

Heater airflow diagram

8. Remove the floor distributor duct.

9. Remove the firewall screws and pull the selector from the firewall.

10. Remove all wires, vacuum lines, and cables attached to the assembly, and remove it from the car.

11. Scribe the temperature door camming plate-to-selector duct relationship and remove the plate.

12. Remove the heater core and core housing from the selector duct.

13. Reverse the removal steps to install.

1972–76 WITH AIR CONDITIONING

1. Drain the cooling system. It is not necessary to evacuate the A.C. refrigerant.

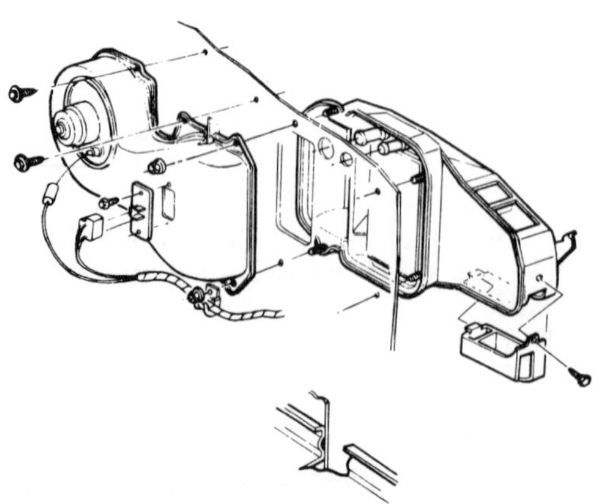

Heater blower mounting

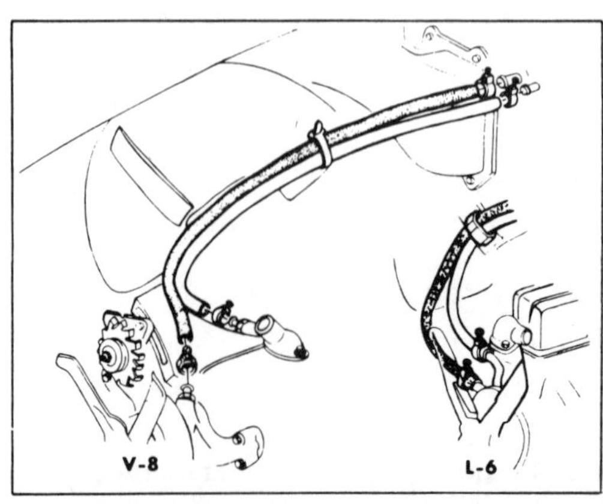

Heater hose routing

2. Disconnect the battery ground cable and compressor clutch connector.

3. Disconnect the vacuum line from the vacuum check valve and push the grommet through the firewall into the passenger compartment.

4. Disconnect the heater hoses at the firewall.

5. Remove the three screws and nuts retaining the heater and selector duct. The inner fender must be pried out from the firewall to gain access to one screw.

6. Remove the lap cooler assembly.

7. Remove the glove compartment.

8. Remove the floor outlet duct and dash panel pad.

9. Disconnect the distributor duct hoses and connector.

10. Remove the duct from the selector.

11. Loosen the defroster duct and move it to provide access to the selector and core assembly.

12. Disconnect the temperature door cable.

13. Separate the inline vacuum connector and the outside air diaphragm line.

14. Lift the heater and air selector duct out as an assembly.

15. Remove the retaining screws and remove the heater core from the selector.

1977

1. Disconnect the battery ground cable then remove and plug the heater hoses at the core.

2. Remove the diagnostic connector plug to heater case screws.

3. Remove the connectors from the blower motor, resistor, blower relay and the thermostatic switch.

4. Remove the air conditioning wiring harness retainer from the blower case shroud.

5. Remove the module screen assembly screws and remove the screen.

6. Remove the upper case half to lower case half cowl attaching screws. Two of these screws are inside the air intake at the case separation point.

7. Remove the thermostatic switch by removing the electrical connector, the switch attaching screws and the small tube running from the switch to the evaporator inlet pipe. To remove the small pipe, remove the insulation at the evaporator inlet pipe and loosen the two clamps. When you reinstall this line make sure the line is replaced in its original position.

8. Remove the evaporator inlet pipe support bracket.

9. Remove the heater-evaporator core case cover, making sure you do not damage the sealer.

10. Remove the heater core to case attaching screw and pull up firmly to release the core from the spring loaded clip.

11. To reinstall the core, line up the core base with the clip at the bottom of the case before you insert the core. The top retaining bracket will line up with the hole at the top of the core when properly seated.

12. Reverse Steps 1–9 to install the remainder of the components.

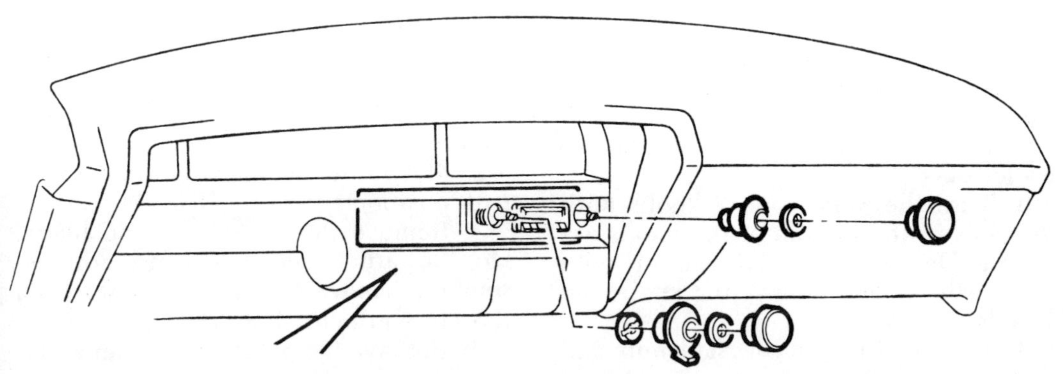

Typical radio mounting

Radio

Removal and Installation

1968–72

1. Disconnect battery.
2. Remove ash tray, retainer attaching screws and retainer.

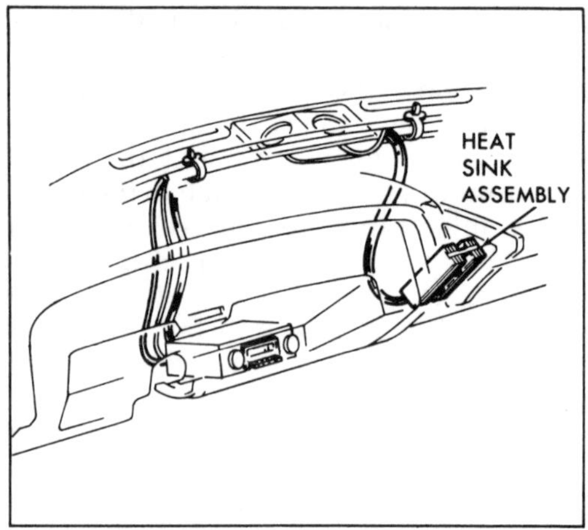

Radio heat sink location

3. Remove heater control panel retaining screws and push panel assembly from console.

NOTE: *If interference between control panel and radio is met, loosen radio retaining nuts.*

4. Remove radio control knobs, bezels and retaining nuts.
5. Disconnect radio wiring harness, and antenna lead-in.
6. Remove radio rear brace attaching screw, and remove radio from the car.
7. Remove speaker retaining bolt and remove speaker.
8. To install, reverse removal procedure.

1973–76

1. Disconnect the negative battery cable.
2. On cars with A/C, remove the lap cooler duct.
3. Turn the radio control knobs until the slots in the bottom of the knobs are visible. Depress the metal retainers with a screwdriver and remove the knobs and bezels.
4. Remove the control shaft nuts and washers.

5. Remove the right side bracket-to-instrument panel bolt and the stud nut on the left side of the radio.
6. Pull the radio forward and disconnect the wiring from the radio and remove the radio from the car.
7. Installation is the reverse of removal.

1977

1. Disconnect the battery negative cable and pull the knobs off their shafts.
2. Remove the three trim plate screws and remove the trim plate.
3. Remove the two screws and bottom mounting nut holding the radio mounting bracket to the instrument panel.
4. Remove the electrical and antenna connectors from the back of the radio.
5. Remove the radio along with its mounting bracket.
6. To install the radio, reverse the previous steps.

Windshield Wipers

MOTOR

Removal and Installation

1. With wiper motor in park position and hood open; disconnect the washer hoses and all wiring from the motor assembly.
2. Remove the access cover.
3. Loosen the nuts which retain the drive link to the crank arm ball stud.
4. Remove the motor mounting screws or nuts and remove the motor.
5. To install, reverse the above procedure.

LINKAGE

Removal and Installation

1. Open the hood and disconnect the battery.
2. Make sure that the wiper motor is in park position.
3. Remove the wiper arm and blade. On the articulated left hand arm assembly, remove the retaining clip from the pin on the drive arm.
4. Remove the plenum chamber air intake grill or screen.

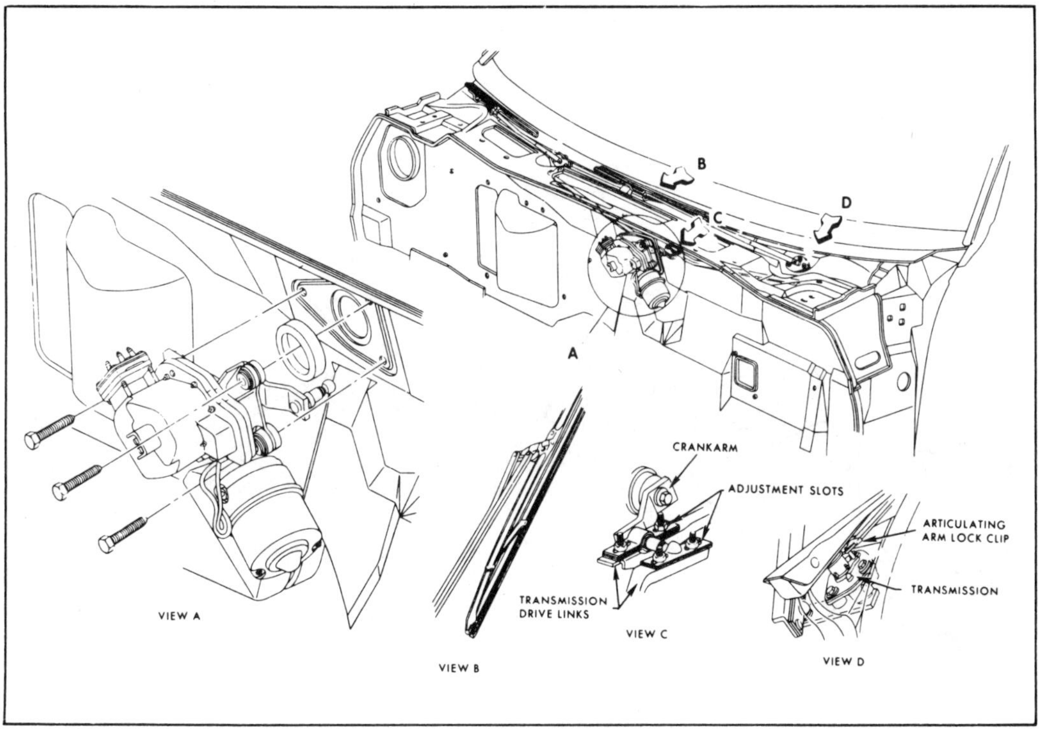

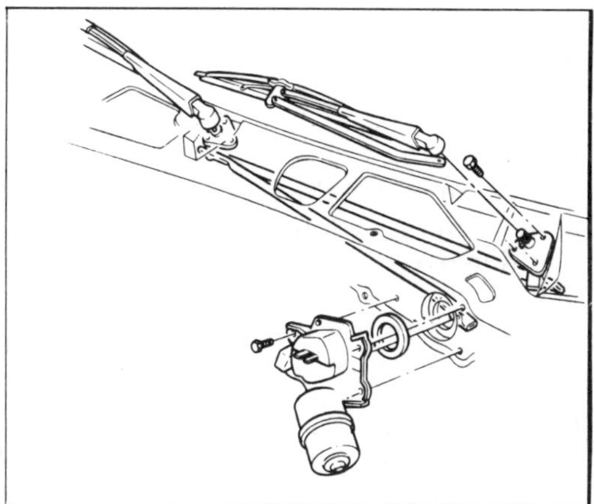

Wiper motor mounting

Wiper motor and linkage

Instrument Cluster

Removal and Installation

1968

1. Disconnect battery.
2. Unplug forward wiring harness

5. Loosen the nuts which retain the drive rod ball stud to the crank arm and detach the drive rod from the crank arm.

6. Remove the transmission retaining screws or nuts, then lower the drive rod assemblies into the plenum chamber.

7. Remove the transmission and linkage from the plenum chamber through the cowl opening.

8. To install, reverse the above procedure.

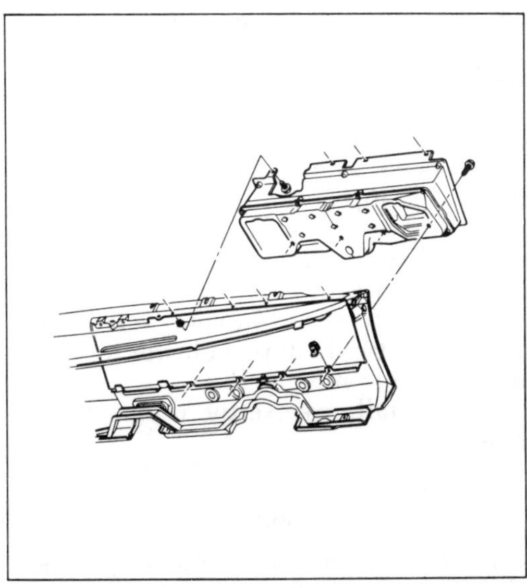

1968 instrument cluster mounting

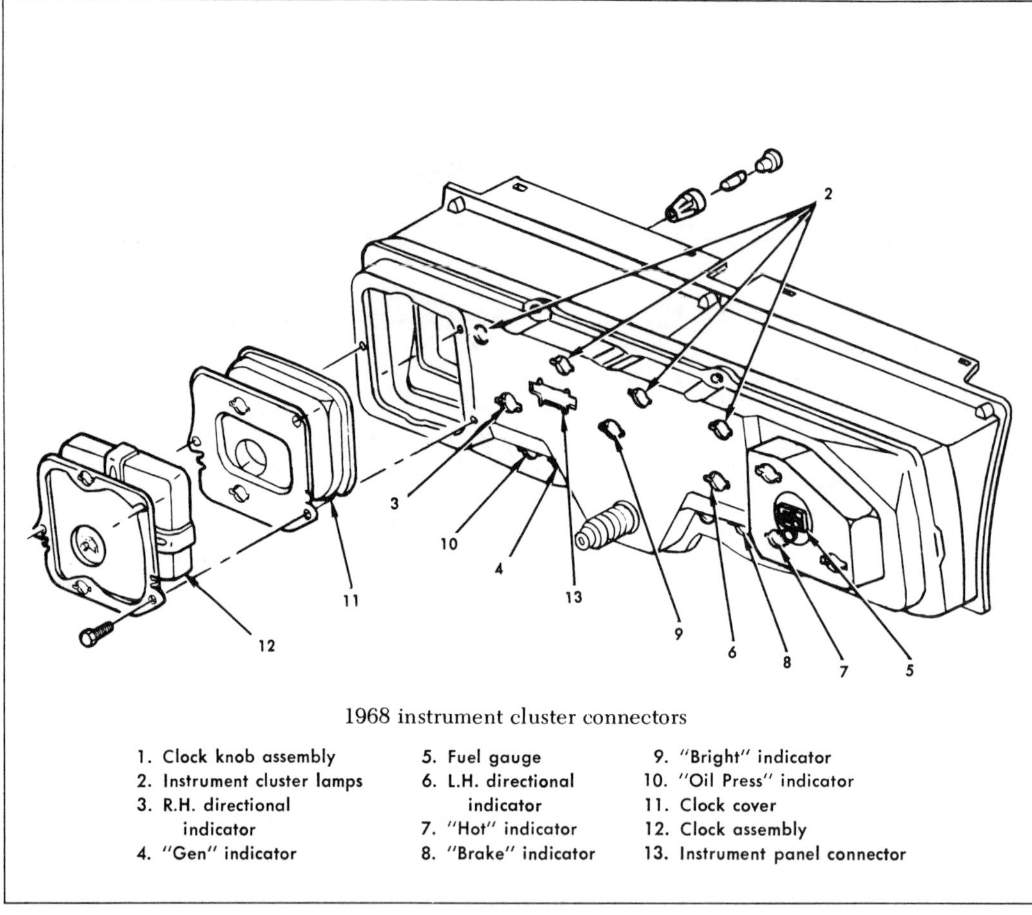

1968 instrument cluster connectors

1. Clock knob assembly
2. Instrument cluster lamps
3. R.H. directional indicator
4. "Gen" indicator
5. Fuel gauge
6. L.H. directional indicator
7. "Hot" indicator
8. "Brake" indicator
9. "Bright" indicator
10. "Oil Press" indicator
11. Clock cover
12. Clock assembly
13. Instrument panel connector

from fuse panel and remove panel from firewall.

3. Remove screws retaining cluster to instrument panel.

4. From mast jacket, remove screws retaining column-mounted automatic transmission pointer cable.

5. From behind cluster, disconnect speedometer cable, harness connector, clock, speed warning device, defogger, convertible top or tail gate switches and vacuum hoses, if so equipped. If equipped with gauge pack, disconnect oil pressure line.

6. Using care to prevent scratching mast jacket, tip the top of cluster forward and remove from vehicle.

7. To install, reverse the removal procedure.

1969

1. Disconnect the battery ground cable.

2. Remove the glove box and air conditioner center dash outlet.

3. Remove the four screws above the instruments and gently pull instrument panel pad loose from dash clips.

4. If so equipped, remove air conditioner lap cooler from under the steering column and stereo tape player.

5. Remove the three bolts from the underside of the dash.

6. Disconnect the shift indicator cable wire on the steering column.

7. Disconnect the radio wiring.

8. Lower the steering column.

9. Remove the instrument panel top attaching screws and gently lift and tilt the panel forward.

10. Disconnect speedometer cable (press snap retainer) and all electrical connections.

11. Remove the six top illumination can attaching screws.

12. Remove the indicator bulb bezel push in on the right-side of each cover to

expose the screws, then remove the bezel retainer screws (4).

13. Remove the rear cluster to carrier attaching screws and remove the cluster.

14. Install by reversing the removal procedure.

1970

1. Disconnect the battery ground cable.

2. If applicable, remove the air conditioning lap cooler from under the steering column.

3. Lower the steering column being sure to support it.

4. Remove the dash pad and, if applicable disconnect the center air conditioning outlet hose.

5. Disconnect the shift indicator cable on the steering column and remove the indicator bulb bezel.

6. Remove shift indicator lamp housing.

7. Remove the radio.

8. Remove the instrument panel trim plate, the plate is held in place with snap-in studs on the left-side, right-side and to the right of the steering column. Use a hooked tool to pull the trim plate free.

9. Remove the air conditioner heater control assembly.

10. Remove the lower instrument cluster-to-bracket and parking brake pedal bracket screws.

11. Remove the ash tray and retaining bracket.

12. Remove the three screws at the top of the instrument cluster and tilt it forward.

13. Disconnect the speedometer cable and instrument wiring harness. The illu-

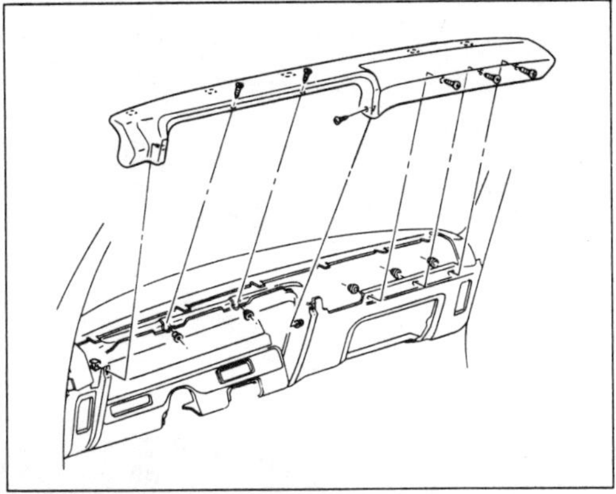

1970 dash pad

mination cover must be removed to get at the wiring.

14. Remove the instrument cluster.

15. Installation is the reverse of the above procedure.

1971–76

1. Disconnect the battery.

2. Remove the cigar lighter knob and the screw beneath it.

3. Pull out the headlight switch and remove screw in middle of shaft.

4. Remove the two screws in the lower corners and remove the shroud.

5. Remove the clock stem set knob.

6. Remove the lens and lens retaining strip. There are three screws holding the lens retaining strip.

7. Tilt the filter housing back and remove.

8. The speedometer, fuel gauge, or clock may be removed.

9. Install in the reverse of the above procedure.

1977

1. Disconnect the battery ground cable and remove the steering column lower cover.

2. Disconnect the shift indicator cable from the steering column.

3. Remove the two screws holding the steering column and lower the steering column. After lowering the steering column, make sure it is adequately supported on the seat.

4. Remove six screws and three snap-in fasteners from around the edge of the instrument cluster lens.

5. Remove two screws from the sheet

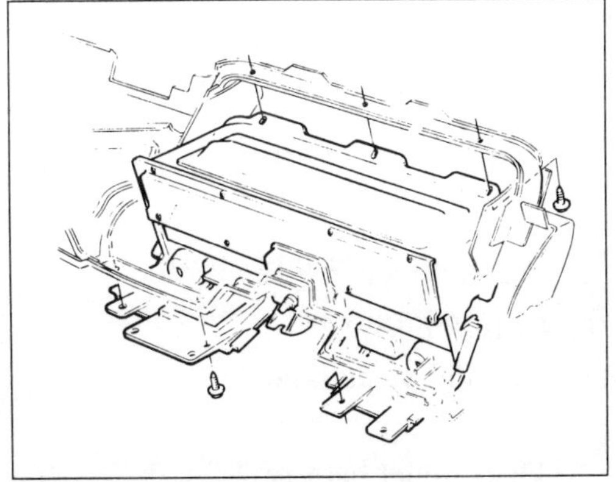

1970 instrument cluster mounting

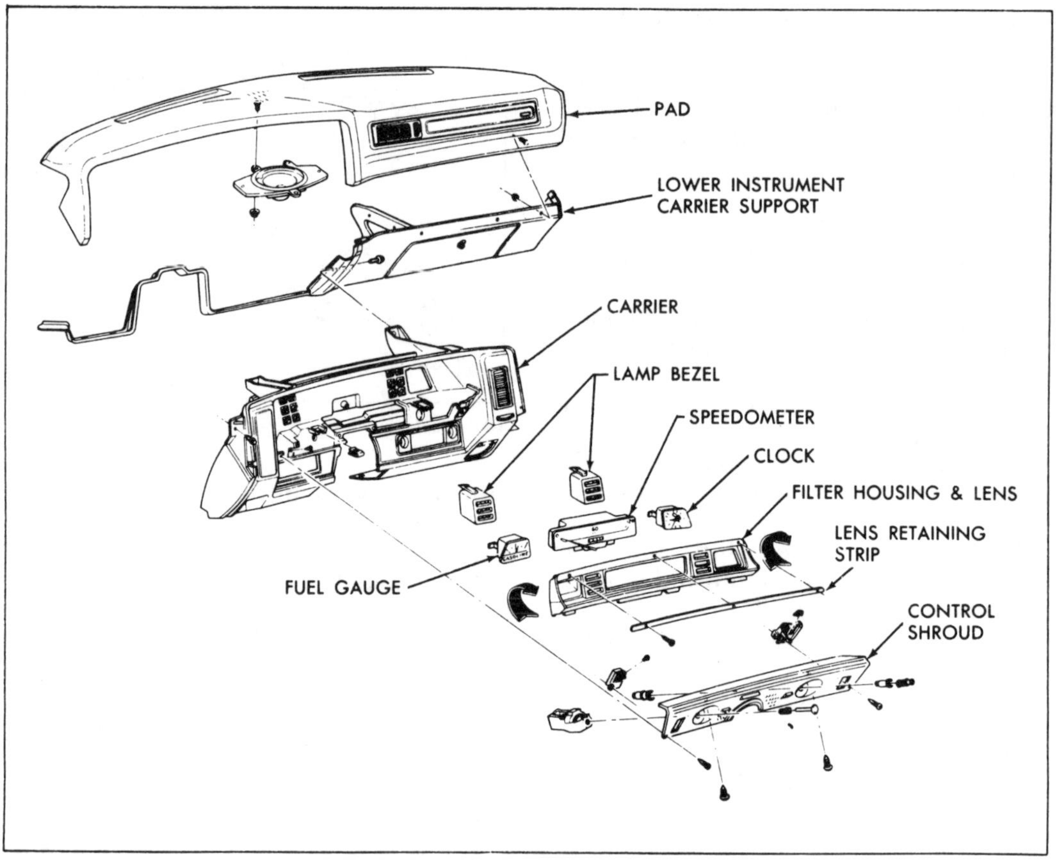

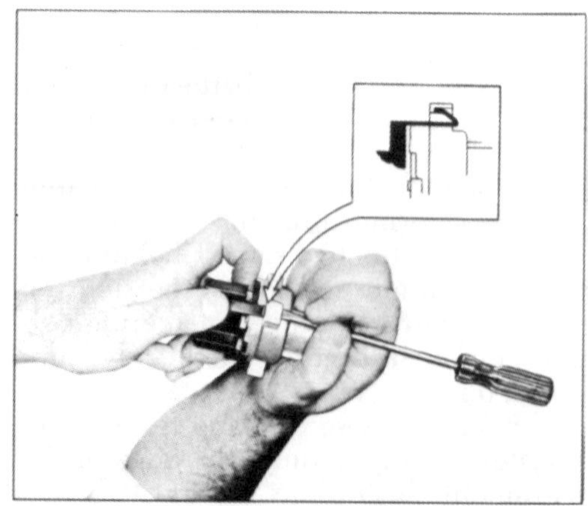

1972 dash components

metal trim plate, then remove two nuts from the studs at the lower corner of the cluster.

6. Reach up behind the cluster and disconnect the speedometer cable, then remove the cluster by pulling out.

7. Reverse Steps 1–6 to install the cluster.

Unlocking ignition switch connector

IGNITION SWITCH (DASH MOUNTED)

Removal and Installation

1968

1. Disconnect battery.

2. Remove cylinder by placing in lock position and insert stiff wire in small hole to depress plunger. Turn cylinder counter-clockwise until cylinder can be removed.

3. Remove holding nut.

4. Pull switch from under dash and remove connectors.

5. Using a screwdriver, unsnap the locking tangs of the "theft resistant" connector.

6. Install in reverse of above.

HEADLIGHT SWITCH

Removal and Installation

1. Disconnect battery.

2. Pull knob out to on position.

3. Reach under instrument panel and depress the switch shaft retainer. Remove knob and shaft assembly.

4. Remove the windshield wiper switch ('77s only), then remove the retaining ferrule nut.

5. Remove switch from instrument panel.

6. Disconnect the multi-plug connector from the switch. A screwdriver inserted in the side of the switch to pry out the connector will help.

7. Replace in reverse of above. (In checking lights before installation, switch must be grounded to test dome light.)

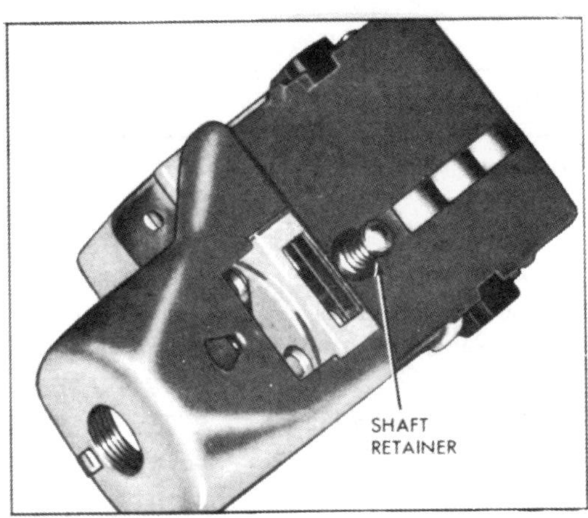

Headlight switch

Seatbelt System

WARNING SYSTEM

1972–73

The seat belt warning system consists of lap belt retractor switches, a pressure-sensitive switch underneath the right-hand front passenger's seat, a warning lamp and a buzzer.

On manual transmission-equipped cars, the circuit is wired through the ignition switch, the parking brake warning light switch, and a relay, which is located between the instrument cluster wiring and the switch on the parking brake. A diode is used to prevent feedback into the parking brake warning circuit.

On cars having automatic transmissions, the seat belt warning circuit is wired through the ignition switch and the combination back-up lamp/neutral safety switch.

With the ignition key in the "RUN" position, a weight of 40–50 lbs on the driver's or passenger's seat (pressure-sensitive switch) energizes the circuit when the gear selector is placed in a forward drive range.

A warning light will glow and a buzzer will sound with the circuit energized, unless the seat belts are withdrawn from the retractors and fastened over the laps of the two outboard front seat occupants.

SEATBELT/STARTER INTERLOCK SYSTEM

1974–75

As required by law, all 1974 and some 1975 Chevrolet passenger cars cannot be started until the front seat occupants are seated and have fastened their seat belts. If the proper sequence is not followed, e.g., the occupants fasten their seat belts and then sit on them, the engine cannot be started.

If, after the car is started, the seat belts are unfastened, a warning buzzer and light will be activated in a similar manner to that described for 1972–73 models.

The shoulder harness and lap belt are permanently fastened together, so that they both must be worn. The shoulder harness uses an inertia-lock reel to allow freedom of movement under normal driving conditions.

NOTE: *This type of reel locks up when the car decelerates rapidly, as during a crash.*

The lap belts use the same ratchet-type retractors that the 1972–73 models use.

The switches for the interlock system have been removed from the lap belt retractors and placed in the belt buckles. The seat sensors remain the same as those used in 1972–73.

For ease of service, the car may be started from outside, by reaching in and turning the key, but without depressing the seat sensors.

In case of system failure or for service, an override switch is located under the hood. This is a "one start" switch and it must be reset each time it is used.

Headlights

Removal and Installation

1. Remove headlight bezel.
2. Unhook the spring from the headlight retaining ring if so equipped.
3. Unscrew the retaining ring and remove it.

NOTE: *Do not disturb the two long aiming screws.*

4. Unplug the old sealed beam.
5. Connect the replacement bulb and install into the receptacle.
6. Install the retaining ring and connect the spring.
7. Install the headlight bezel.

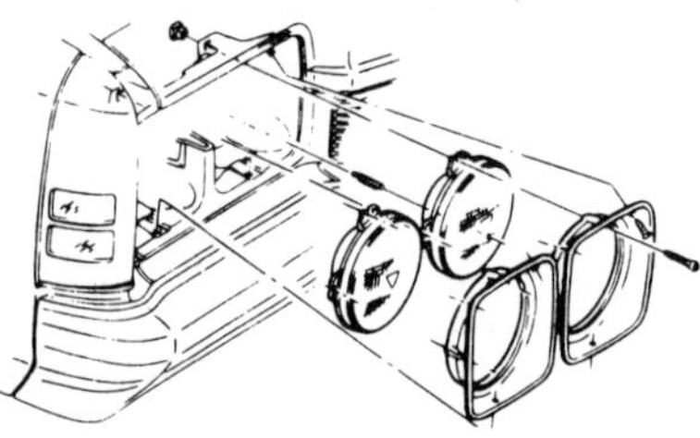

Exploded view of typical headlight assembly (1968–76)

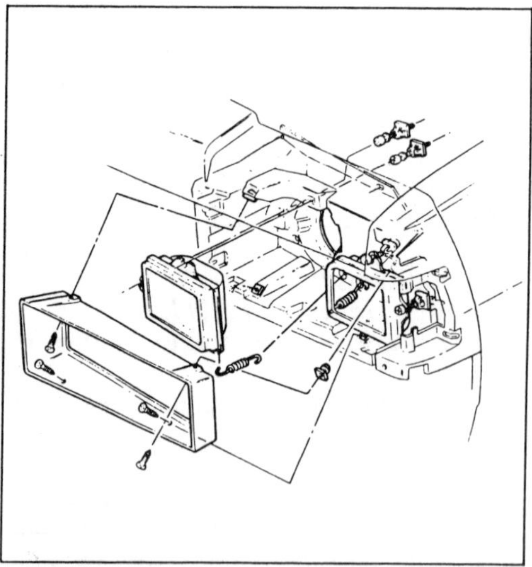

1977 headlight assembly

Light Bulbs

1968

Lamp Usage	Candle Power	Bulb Number
Headlamp (outer)	37½–55 W	4002
Headlamp (inner)	37½ W	4001
Parking and front directional, tail and stop and rear directional	4–32 CP	1157
Tail lamp (belair)	4 CP	1155
Back-up lamp	32 CP	1156
Instrument lamps, panel compartment, temperature, oil pressure, generator, hi-beam indicator, clock lamp	2 CP	1895
A.T. quadrant, directional signal, ignition lock, heater control panel	1 CP	1445
Dome lamp	15 CP	1004
License plate lamp	4 CP	1155
Radio dial lamp	2 CP	1893
Brake alarm lamp	2 CP	257

1969–73

Lamp Usage	Candle Power	Bulb Number
Headlamp unit		
Chevrolet		
Outer—high beam	37½ Watts	4002
Outer—low beam	55 Watts	4002
Inner—high beam only	37½ Watts	4001
Parking lamp and directional signal		
Chevrolet	3–32	1157
Tail, stop and directional signal	3–32	1157
Backing lamp	32	1156
Instrument illumination lamps		
Chevrolet	2	194
Temperature indicator	2	194
Oil pressure indicator	2	194
Generator indicator	2	194
Hi-beam indicator	2	194
Directional indicator	2	194
Warning lamps		
Low fuel	2	194
Check doors	2	194
Seat belt	2	194
Heater or A/C control panel		
Chevrolet	2	1895
Glove box lamps		
Chevrolet, without A/C	2	1895
Chevrolet with A/C	2	1893
Dome and courtesy lamps		
Cartridge type (all)	12	211
Bayonet type (exc. station wagon third seat)	6	631
Station wagon third seat	6	90
Seat separator-courtesy lamp	6	212
Side marker-front	2	194
Side marker-rear	2	194

Light Bulbs (cont.)

1969–73

Lamp Usage	Candle Power	Bulb Number
License plate lamp	4	67
Radio dial lamps		
All AM only radios	2	293
All tape players and FM radios	2	1893
Tape player lens illumination lamp	1	216
Stereo indicator lamp	3	2182D
Automatic transmission control indicator lamp	2	194
Brake alarm lamp	2	194
Luggage compartment lamp	15	1003
Map lamp (mirror)	4	563
Underhood	15	93
Rear window defogger lamp	2	194

1974–77

Lamp Usage	Candle Power	Bulb Number
Headlamp unit	(4652 and 4651 for 1976 Caprice)	
Outer—high beam	37½ W	4000
low beam	55 W	(Sealed beam) 5001
Inner—high beam	37½ W	(Sealed beam)
Parking lamp and front directional signal	24-2.2	1157NA
Tail and stop lamps, rear directional signal	32-3	1157
License plate lamp	3	168
Back-up lamp	32	1156
Glove compartment lamp	2	1891
Indicator lamps Clock lamp Temperature indicator lamp Oil pressure indicator lamp Generator indicator lamp Hi-beam indicator lamp Auto. trans. quadrant lamp Directional signal indicator lamp Brake system warning lamp Seat belt warning lamp Door open warning lamp	2	194
Instrument panel cluster lamps	3	168
Side marker—front	2	194
Side marker—rear	2	194
Heater, A/C control panel lamp	2	1895
Dome lamp	12	211-2 or 211-1
Luggage compartment lamp	15	1003
Underhood lamp	15	93
Courtesy lamp	6	631

1974–77

Lamp Usage	Candle Power	Bulb Number
Radio dial lamp (All exc. stereo and tape player)	3	1816
Radio dial lamp (stereo and tape player)	2	564
Reading lamp	15	1004
Radio indicator	1	66

Fuses and Circuit Breakers

1968–69

A Circuit Breaker in the light control switch protects the headlamp and parking lamp circuits, thus eliminating one fuse. Where current load is too heavy, the circuit breaker intermittently opens and closes, protecting the circuit until the cause is found and eliminated.

Fuses, located in the Junction Block beneath the dash are:

Instrument lights	3AG/AGC-	6 amp
Radio, tape player, accessories	3AG/AGC-	10 amp
Heater and air conditioning	3AG/AGC-	25 amp
Instrument lamps	3AG/AGC-	5 amp
Tail, side marker and fender lamps	3AG/AGC-	20 amp
Stop and hazard warning lamps	3AG/AGC-	20 amp
Courtesy, dome, cig. lighter, clock lamps	3AG/AGC-	20 amp
Backup, turn signal, and cruise control	3AG/AGC-	20 amp
Gauges, and tell-tale lamps	3AG/AGC-	10 amp
Windshield wiper	3AG/AGC-	20 amp

Overdrive Fuse, 3AG/AGC- 15 amp, In-line fuse between horn relay and overdrive relay.

An Air Conditioning high blower speed fuse, SAE-30 amp (Four Season) or SAE-20 amp G.M. Chevrolet), is located in an in-line fuse holder running from horn relay to Air Conditioning relay.

Do not use fuses of higher amperage rating than those recommended above.

Fusible Links are incorporated into the wiring system. These are wires of such a gauge that they will fuse (or melt) before damage occurs to an entire wiring harness in the event of an electrical overload.

1970–71

The headlamp circuit is protected by a circuit breaker in the light switch. An overload on the breaker will cause the lamps to "flicker" on and off. If this condition develops, have your headlamp wiring checked immediately. Also, a circuit breaker, mounted on the firewall, protects the power window, power seat, and power top circuits if vehicle is so equipped. Where current load is too heavy, the circuit breaker intermittently opens and closes, protecting the circuit until the cause is found and eliminated.

Fuses, located in the Junction Block beneath the dash are:

Fuses and Circuit Breakers (cont.)

1970–71

Radio, TCS sol., rear defogger, hydra-matic downshift	10A
W/S wiper	25A
Stop lamps, hazard flasher	20A
Heater, A/C	25A
Dir. sig., B/U lamps, cruise-master, power window relay	20A
Inst. lamps, heater dial	3A
Inst. panel warning lamps, gauges	10A
Clock, courtesy light, lighter, anti-diesel control, deck lid lock, glove box light and light watch	20A
Tail lamps, parking lamps, license, dome lamp, luggage lamp and side marking lamp	20A

An Air Conditioning high blower speed fuse, 30 amp, is located in an in-line fuse holder running from horn relay to Air Conditioning relay.

Do not use fuses of higher amperage rating than those recommended above.

Fusible Links are incorporated into the wiring system. These are wires of such a gauge that they will fuse (or melt) before damage occurs to an entire wiring harness in the event of an electrical overload.

1972

The headlamp circuit is protected by a circuit breaker in the light switch. An electrical overload on the breaker will cause the lamps to go on and off or in some cases remain off. If this condition develops, have your wiring circuits checked immediately. Also, a 30 amp circuit breaker, mounted on the fuse panel, protects the power window and power seat circuits if vehicle is so equipped. Where current load is too heavy, the circuit breaker intermittently opens and closes, protecting the circuit until the cause is found and eliminated.

Fuses, located in the Junction Block beneath the dash on the driver's side are:

Radio, tape player, accessories	10 amp
Dir. sig., backup lamps, cruise master, blocking relay	20 amp
Instrument lamps	3 amp
Tail, parking, side marker lamps, and license	20 amp
Stop and hazard warning lamps	20 amp
Courtesy, dome, cig. lighter, clock lamps, HD lamp	20 amp
Gauges, and tell-tale lamps	10 amp
Wiper	25 amp
Air conditioning, TCS sol., heater	25 amp

An Air Conditioning high blower speed fuse, 30 amp, is located in an in-line fuse holder running from horn relay to Air Conditioning relay.

Do not use fuses of higher amperage rating than those recommended above.

Fusible Links are incorporated into the wiring system. These are wires of such a gauge that they will fuse (or melt) before damage occurs to an entire wiring harness in the event of an electrical overload.

1973

The headlamp circuit is protected by a circuit breaker in the light switch. An electrical overload on the breaker will cause the lamps to go on and off or in some cases to remain off. If this condition develops, have your wiring circuits checked immediately. Also, a circuit breaker, mounted on the firewall, protects the power window, power seat, and power top circuits if vehicle is so equipped. Where current load is too heavy, the circuit breaker intermittently opens and closes, protecting the circuit until the cause is found and eliminated.

Fuses, located in the Junction Block beneath the dash on the driver's side are:

Radio, TCS sol., rear defogger, hydra-matic downshift	10A
W/S wiper	25A
Stop lamps, hazard flasher	20A
Heater, A/C	25A
Dir. sig., B/U lamps, cruise-master, power window relay	20A
Inst. lamps, heater dial	3A
Inst. panel warning lamps, gauges	10A
Clock, courtesy light, lighter, anti-diesel control, glove box light and light watch	20A
Tail lamps, parking lamp, license, dome lamp, luggage lamp, and side marking lamp	20A

An Air Conditioning high blower speed fuse, 30 amp, is located in an in-line fuse holder running from horn relay to Air Conditioning relay.

Do not use fuses of higher amperage rating than those recommended above.

Fusible Links are incorporated into the wiring system. These are wires of such a gauge that they will fuse (or melt) before damage occurs to an entire wiring harness in the event of an electrical overload.

1974–76

The headlamp circuits are protected by a circuit breaker in the light switch. An electrical overload will cause the lamps to go on and off, or in some cases to remain off. If this condition develops, have your wiring circuits checked immediately. In addition to a fuse, the windshield wiper motor is also protected by a circuit breaker. If the motor overheats, due to overloading caused by heavy snow, etc. the wipers will remain stopped until the motor cools. Also, a circuit breaker, mounted on the firewall, protects the power window, power seat, and power top circuits if vehicle is so equipped. Where current load is too heavy, the circuit breaker intermittently opens and closes, protecting the circuit until the cause is found and eliminated.

Fuses, located in the Junction Block beneath the dash on the driver's side are:

Radio, TCS sol., hydra-matic downshift and anti-diesel control, pulse wiper system, choke pull off	10A
W/S wiper	25A
Stop lamps, hazard flasher	20A
Heater A/C	25A
Dir. sig., B/U lamps, Power window relay	20A
Inst. lamps, heater dial	3A
Inst. panel warning lamps, gauges, cruise control, rear defogger override relay, seat belt warning buzzer	10A
Warning buzzer, luggage lamp, clock, courtesy light, lighter, glove box light	20A
Tail lamp, parking lamp, license, and side marking lamp	20A

An Air Conditioning high blower speed fuse, 30 amps, is located in an in-line fuse holder running from junction block to Air Conditioning relay.

Do not use fuses of higher amperage rating than those recommended above.

Fusible Links are incorporated into the wiring system. These are wires of such a gauge that they will fuse (or melt) before damage occurs to an entire wiring harness in the event of an electrical overload.

1977

1977 Chevrolets use a different type of fuse which is easier to remove than previous models. The fuse amperage is marked clearly on the fuse, and there is a terminal located to the left or right of each fuse to let you check fuse continuity with a test light or volt-ohmmeter. Never replace a fuse with one of a higher amperage. The fuse function is marked on the fuse panel.

Wiring Diagrams

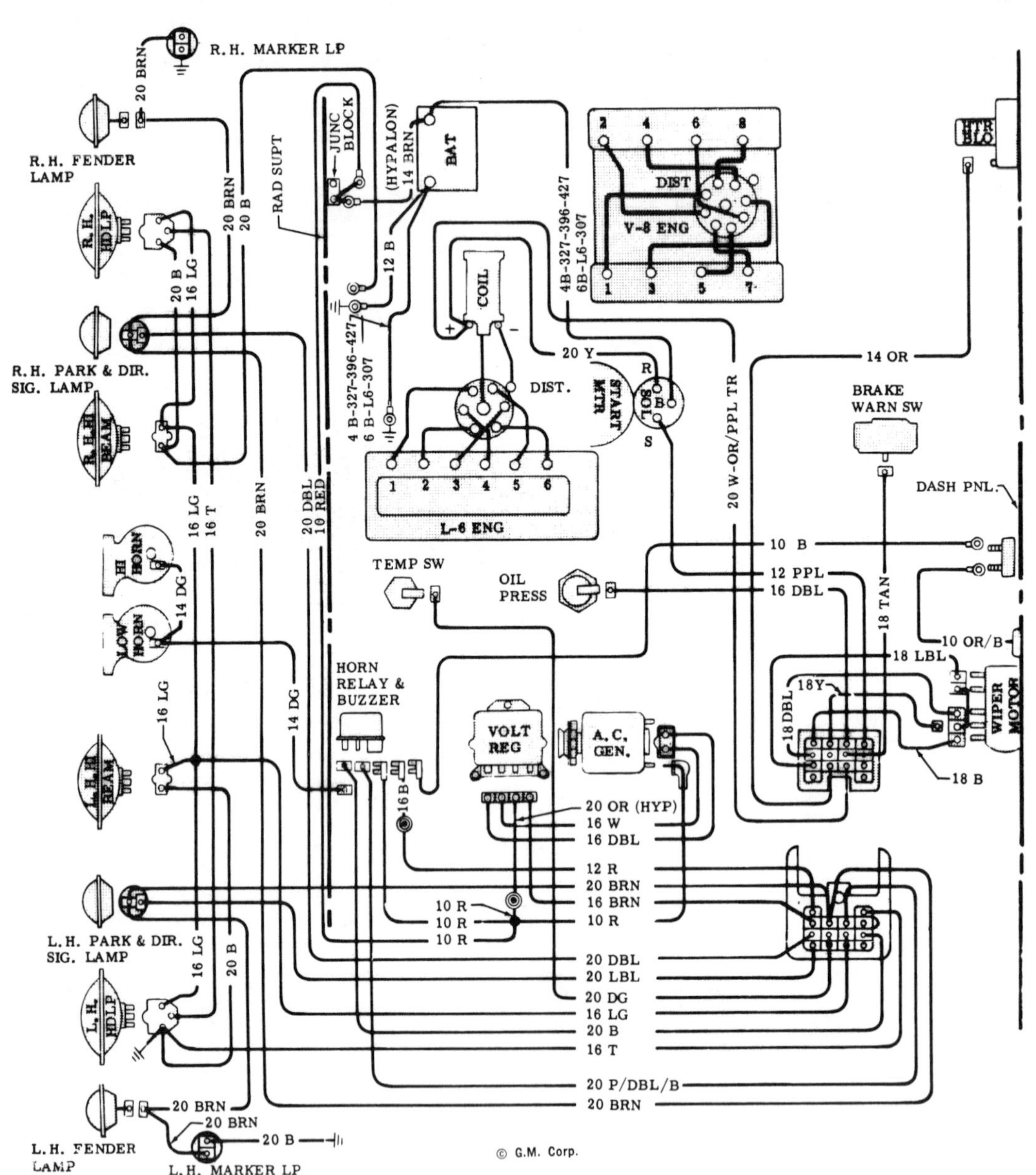

1968 front section

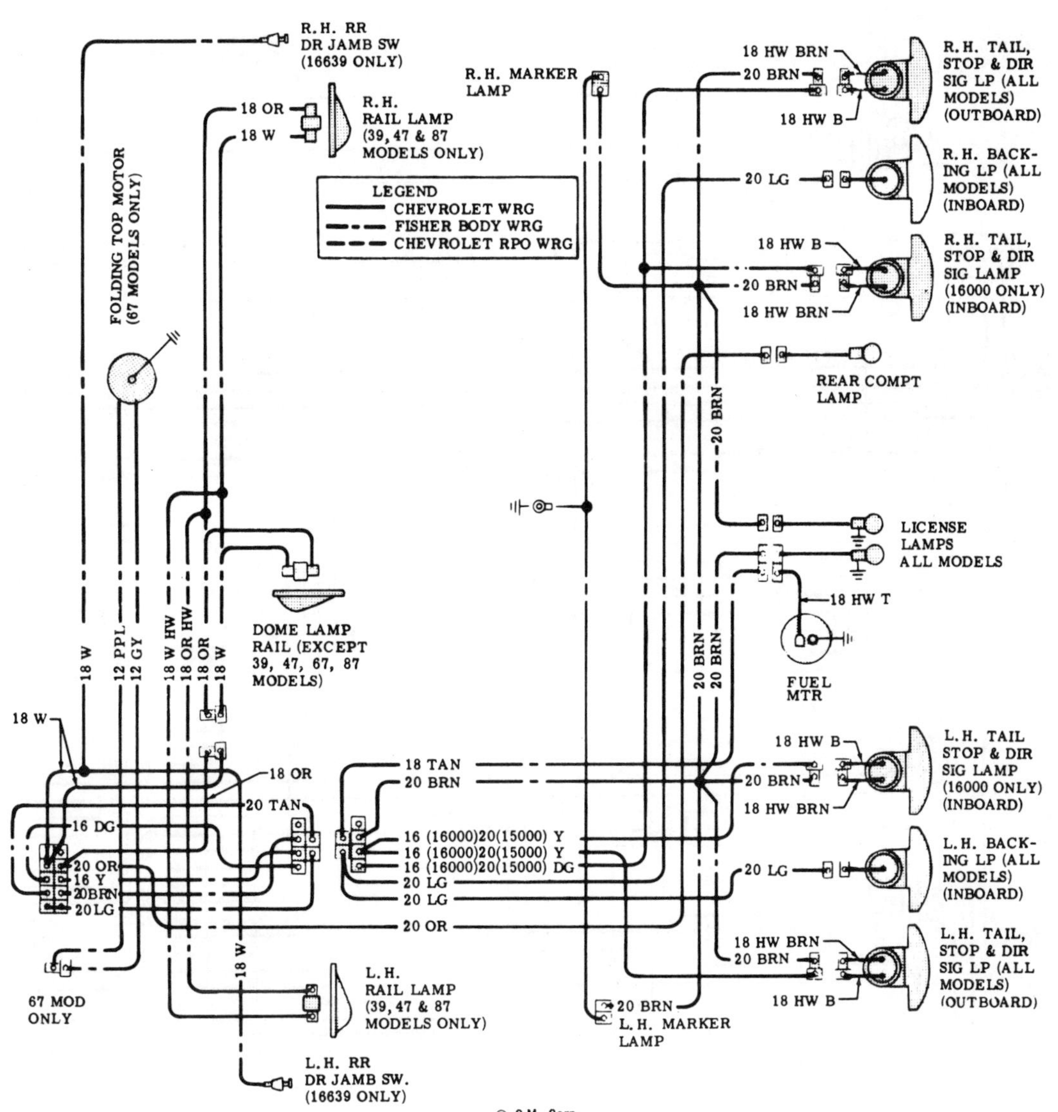

1968 rear section

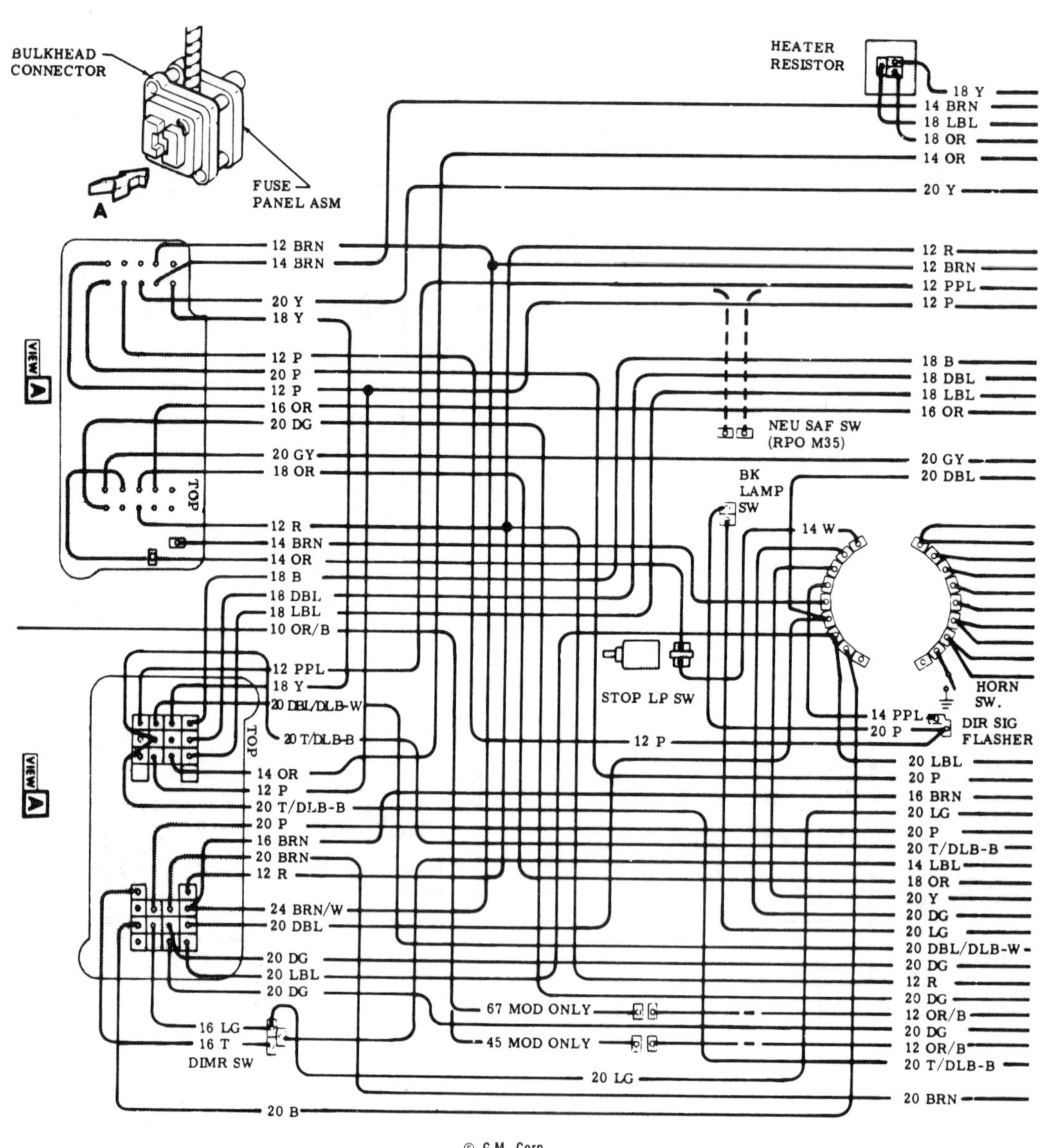

1968 center section

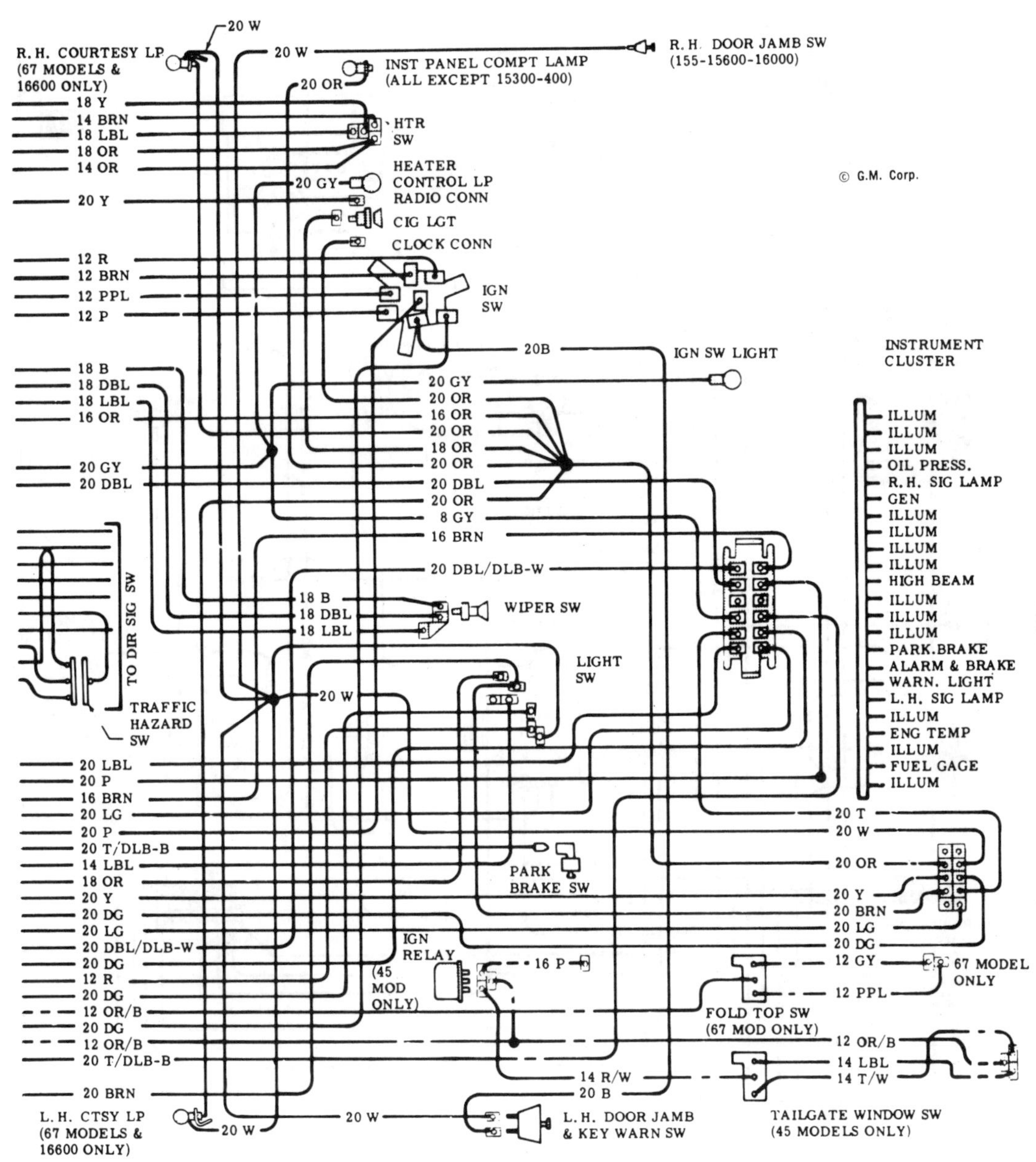

1968 center section

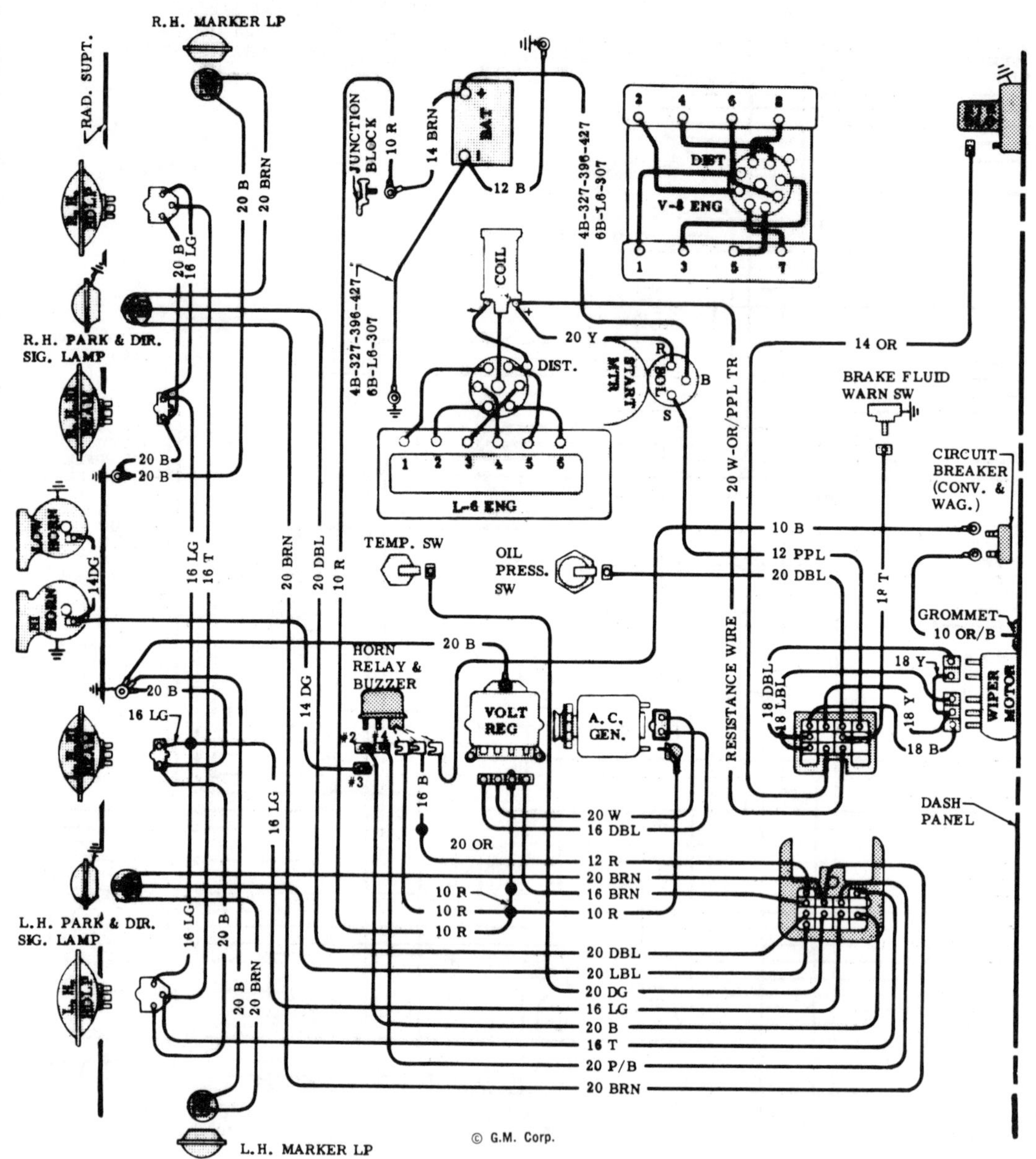

1969 front section

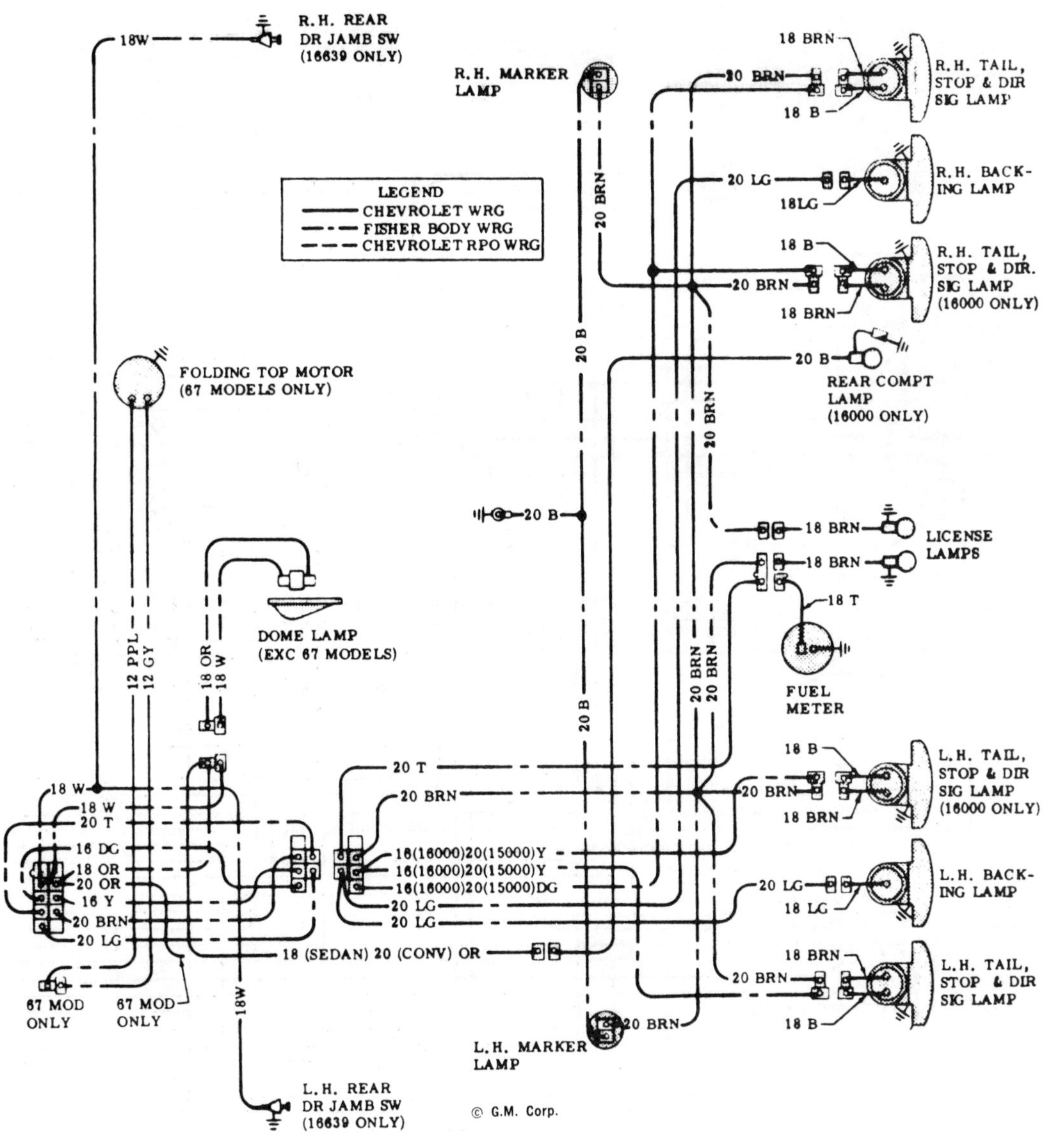

1969 rear section (except station wagon)

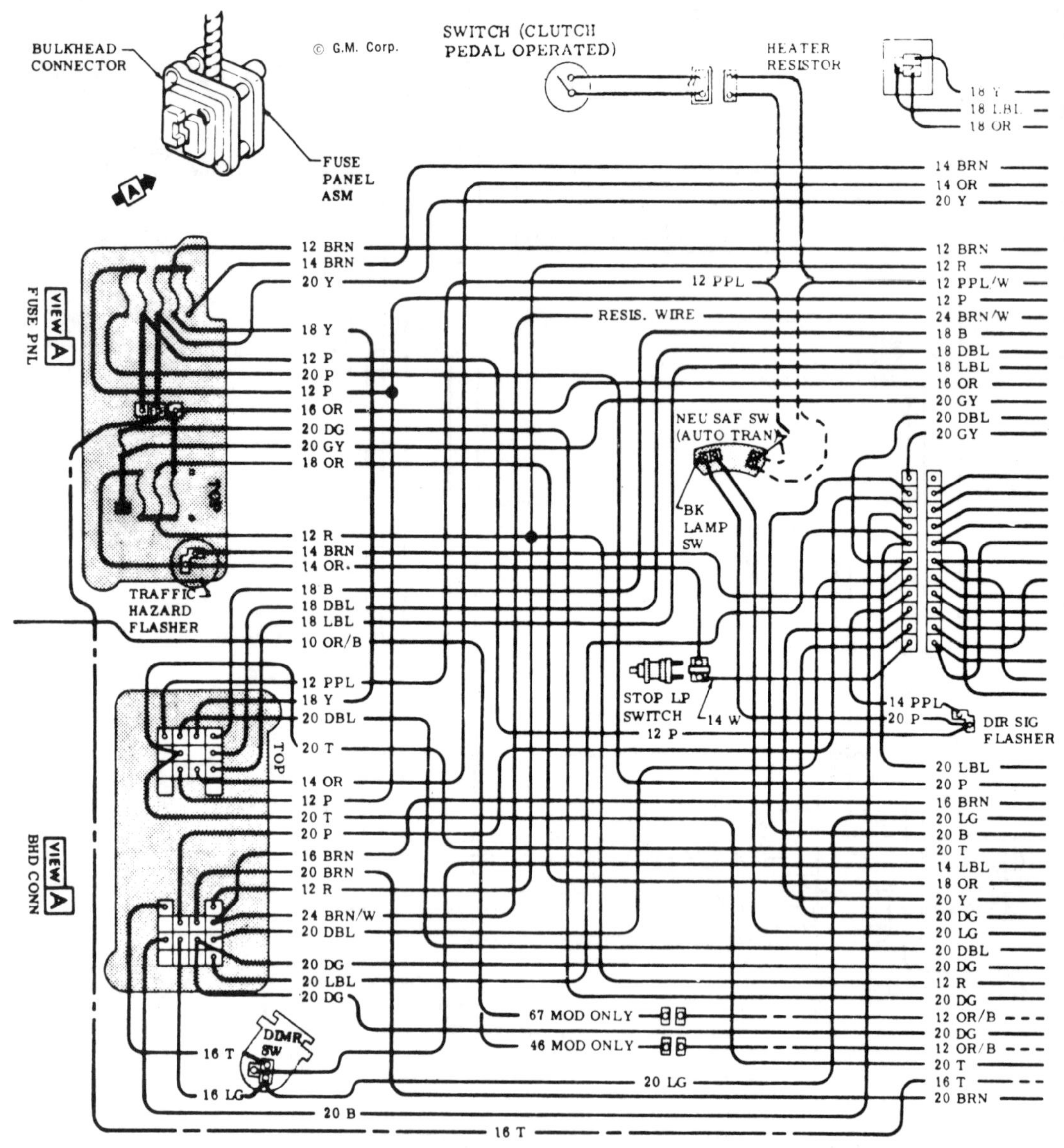

1969 center section

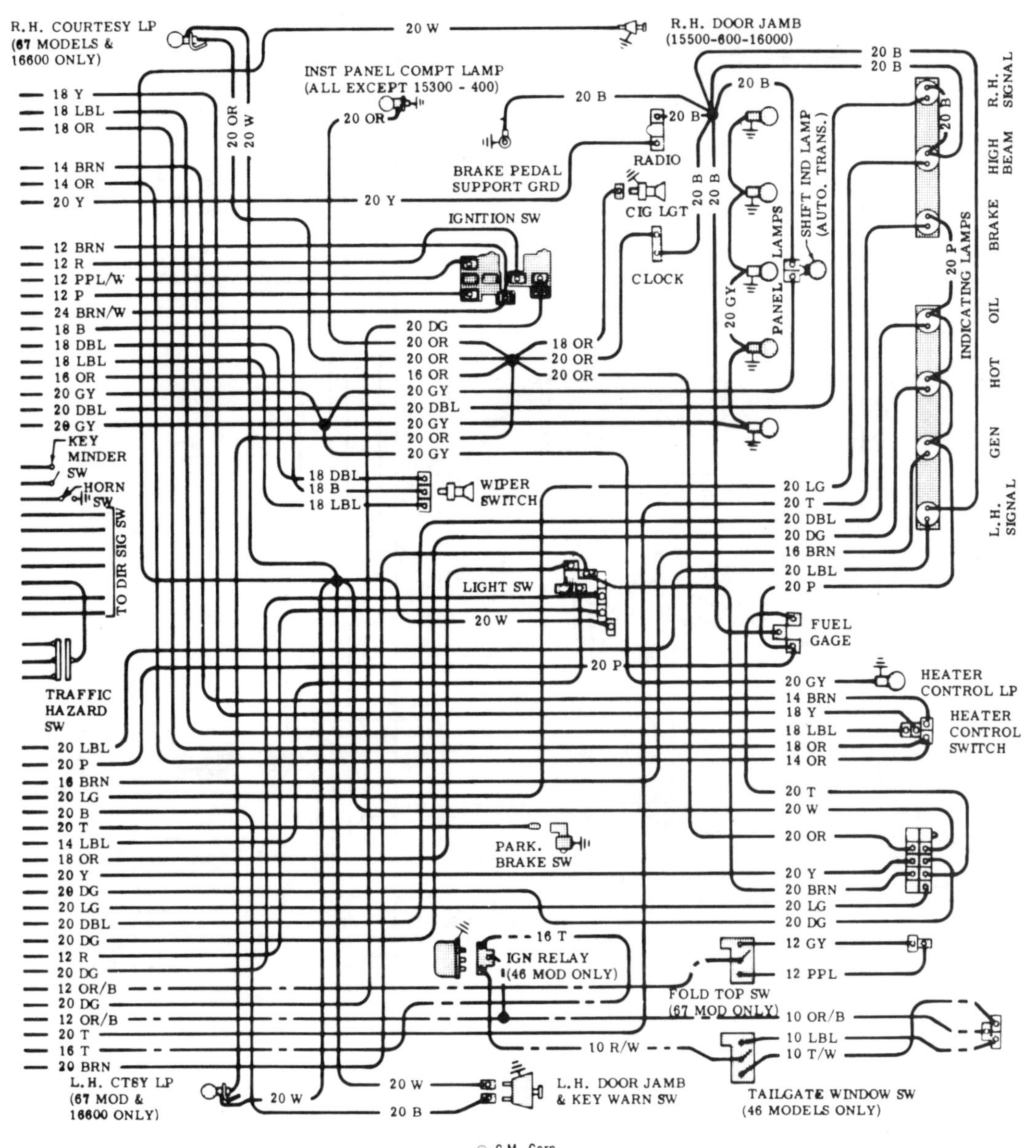

1969 center section

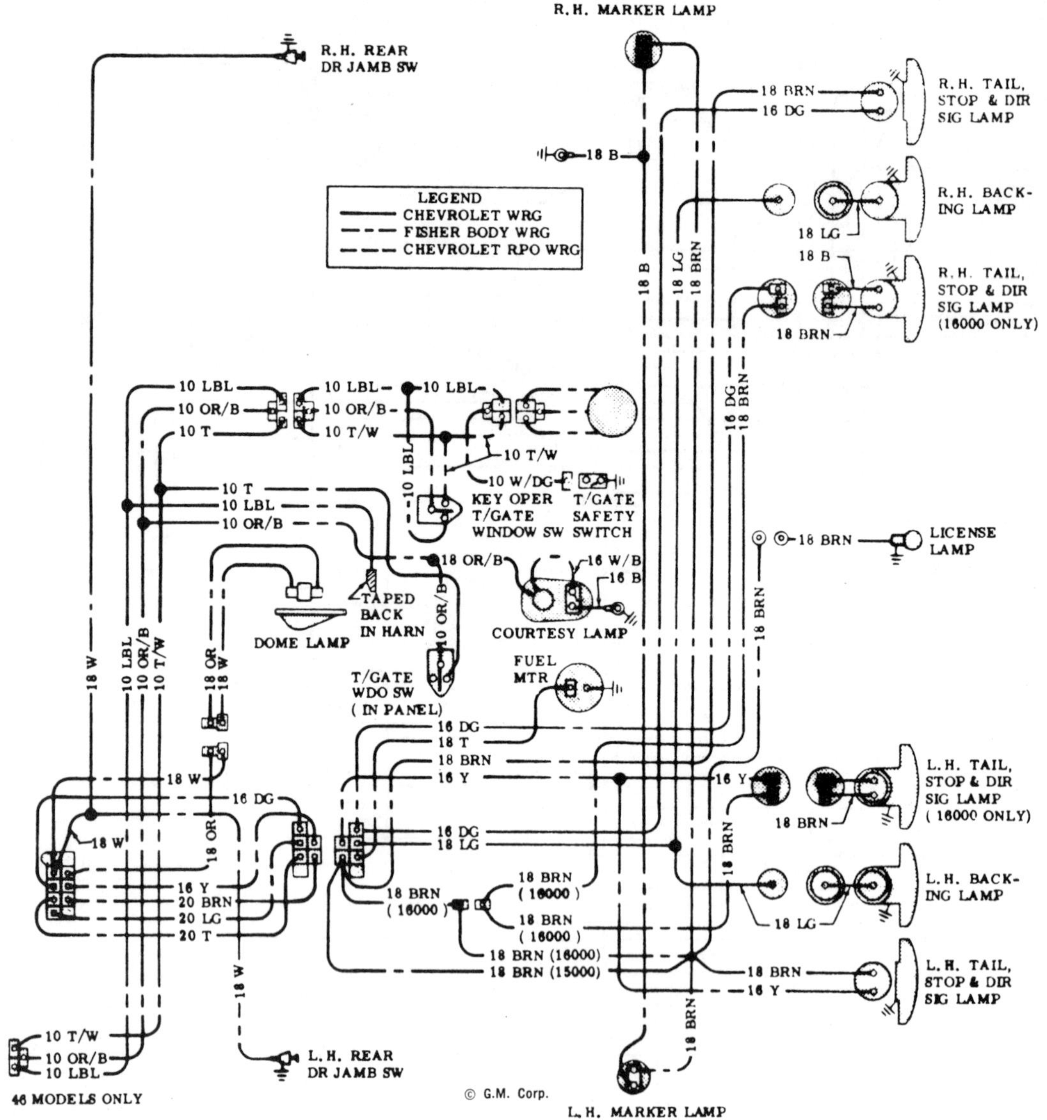

1969 rear section—station wagon

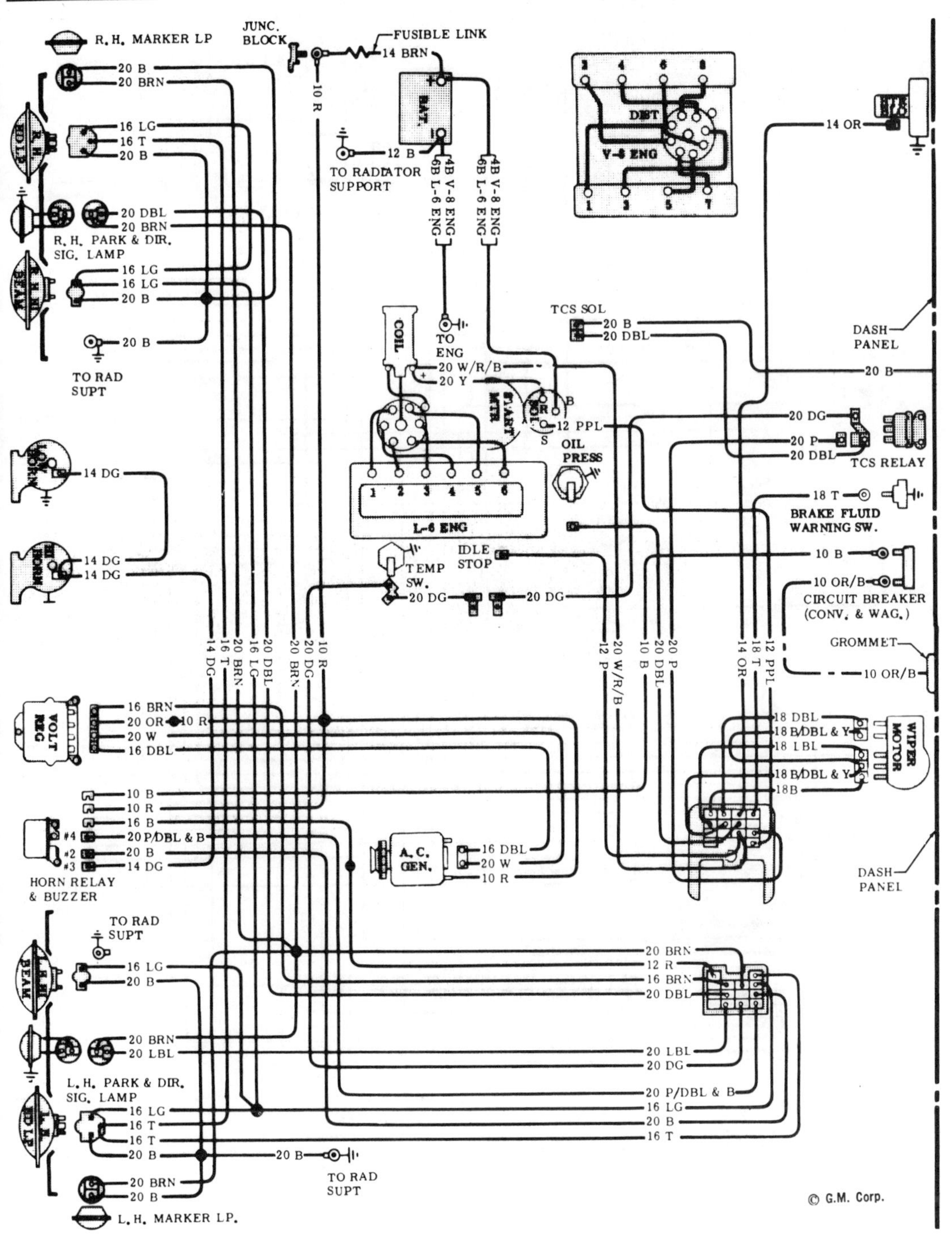

1970 front section

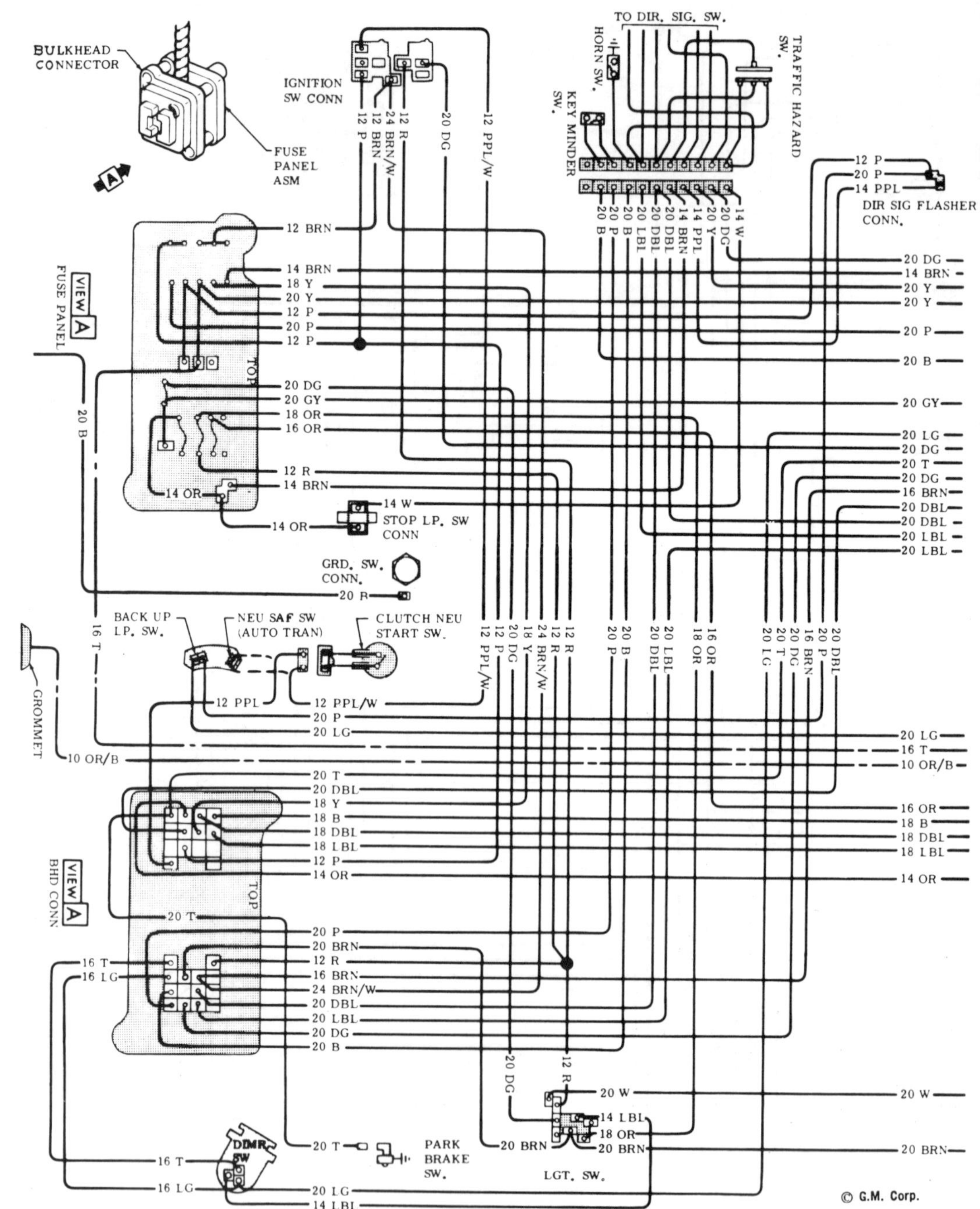

1970 center section

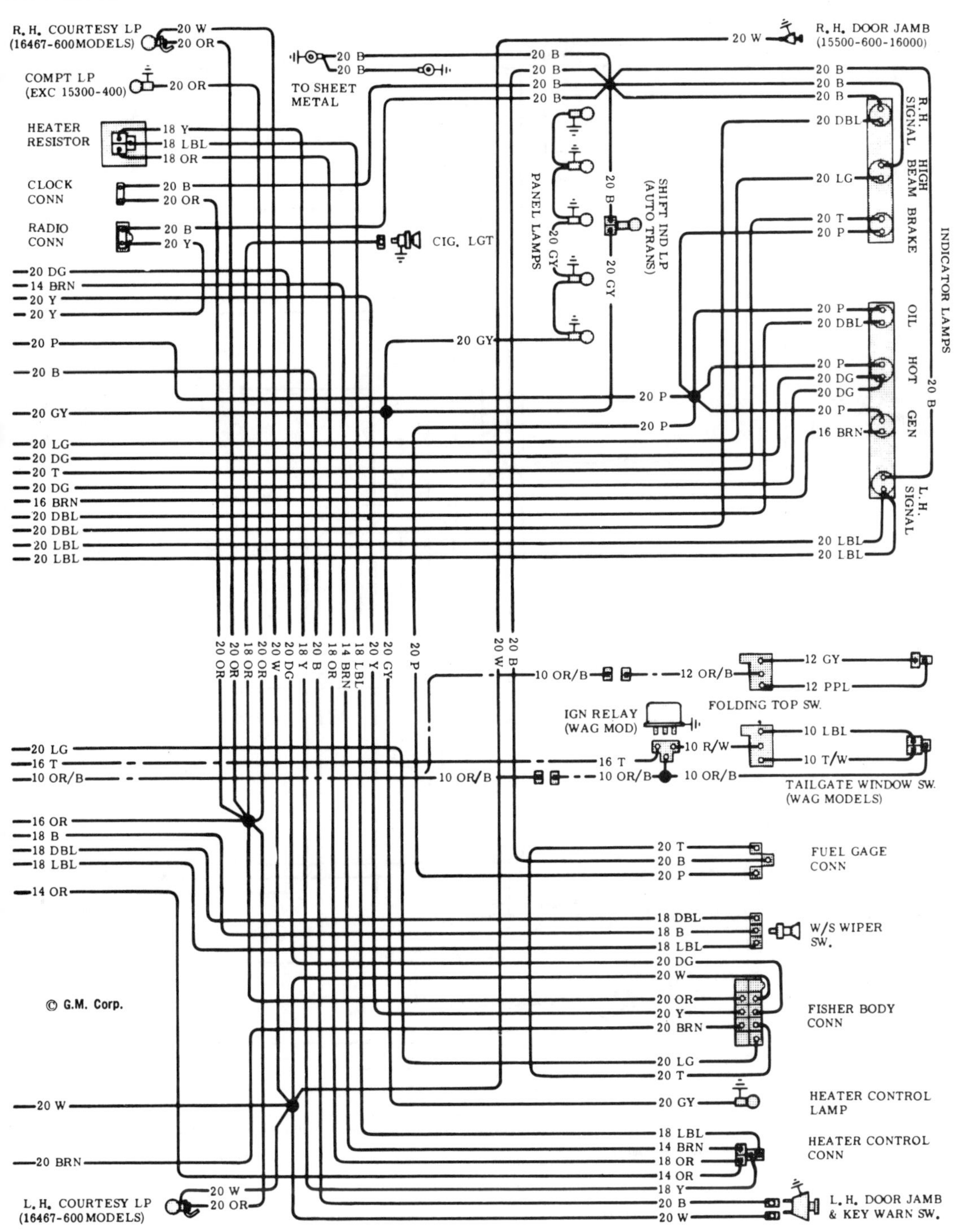

1970 center section

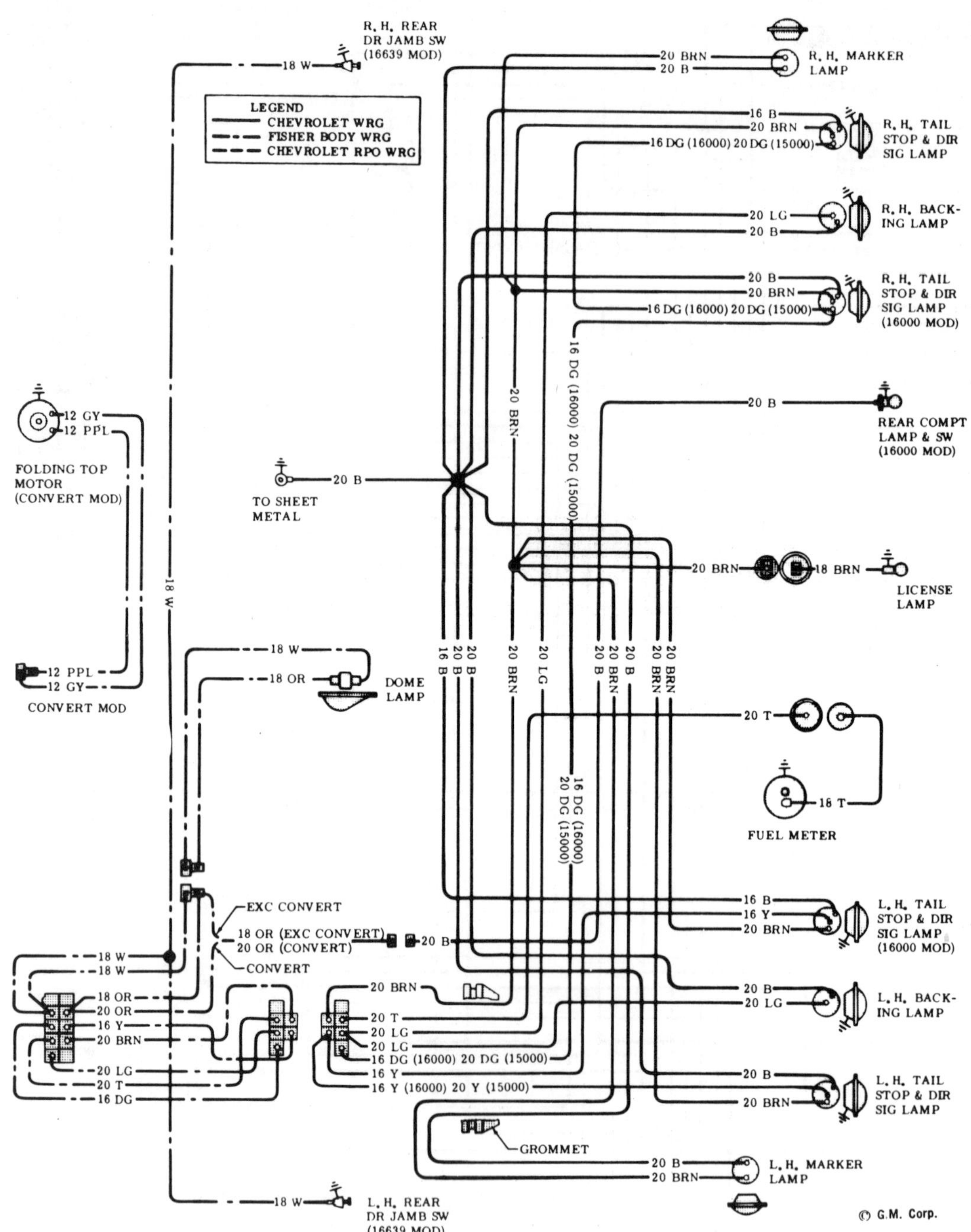

1970 rear section (except station wagon)

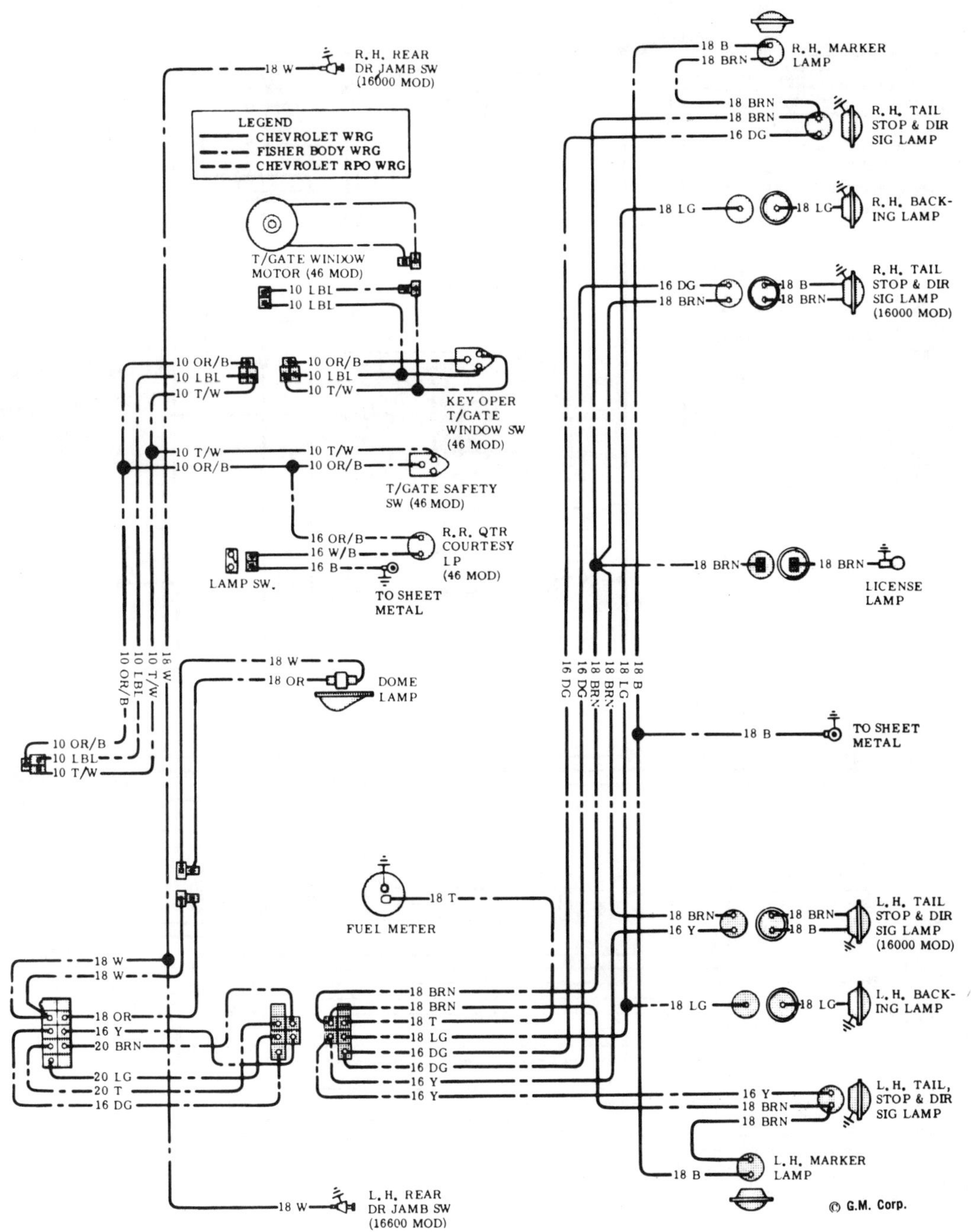

1970 rear section—station wagon

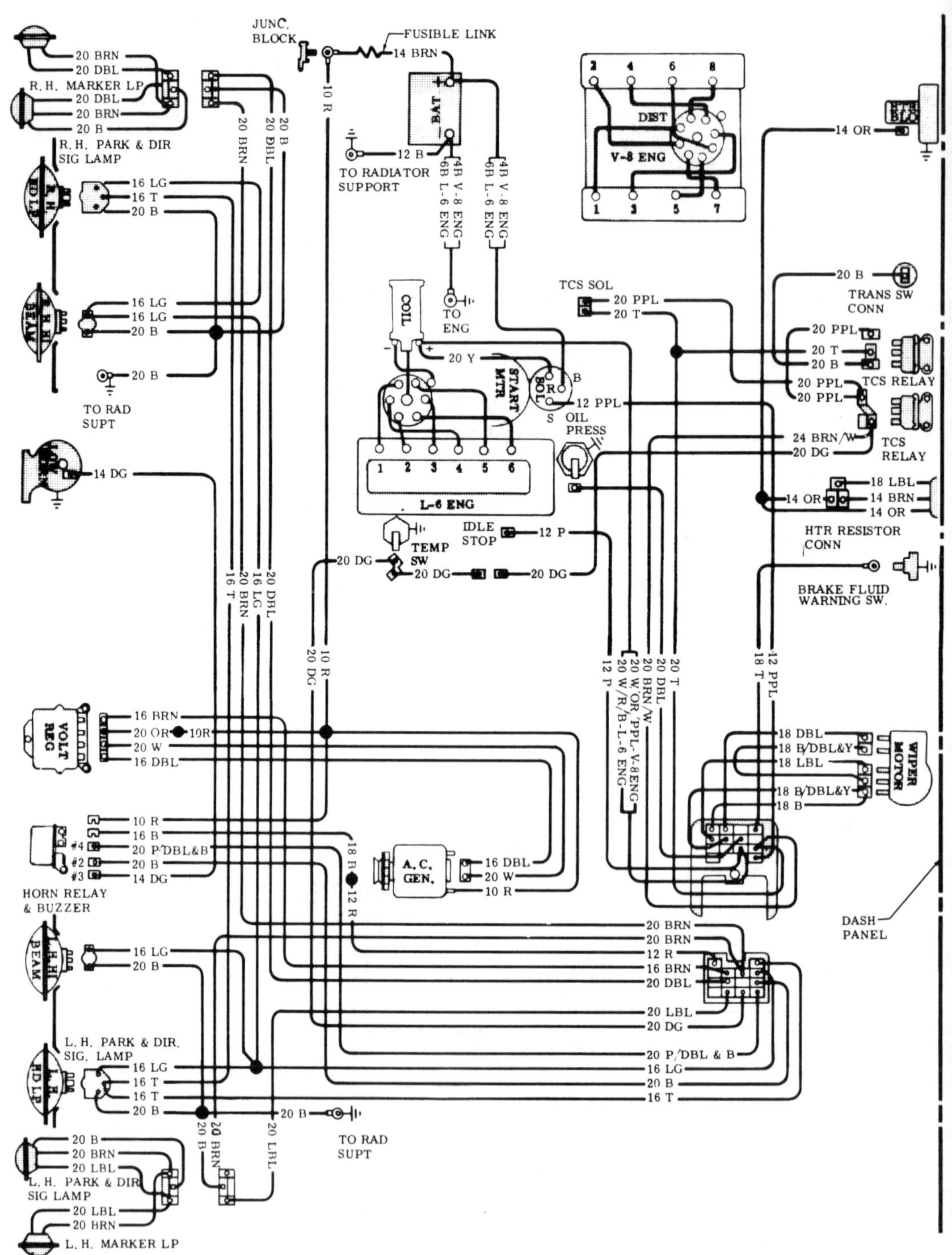

1971 front section

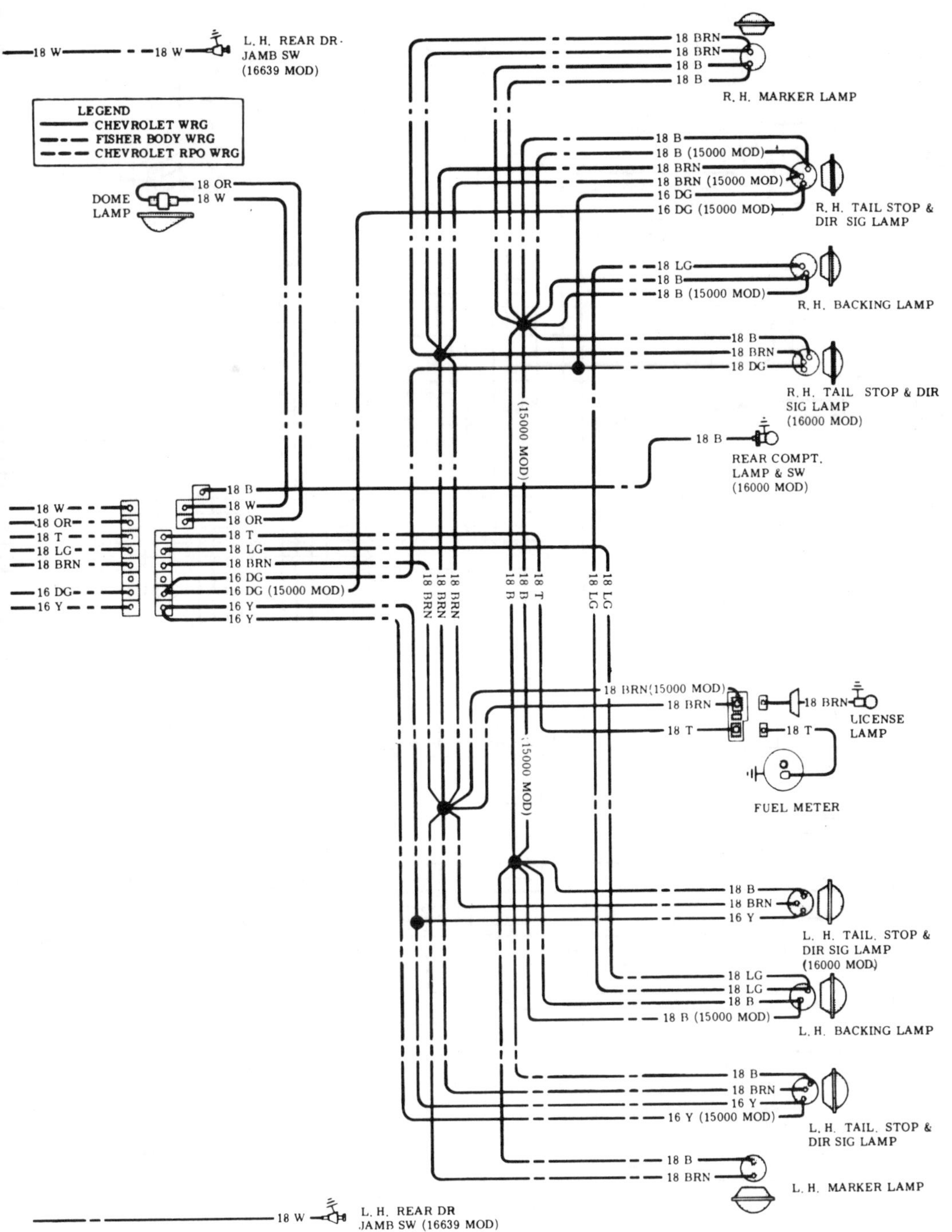

1971 rear section

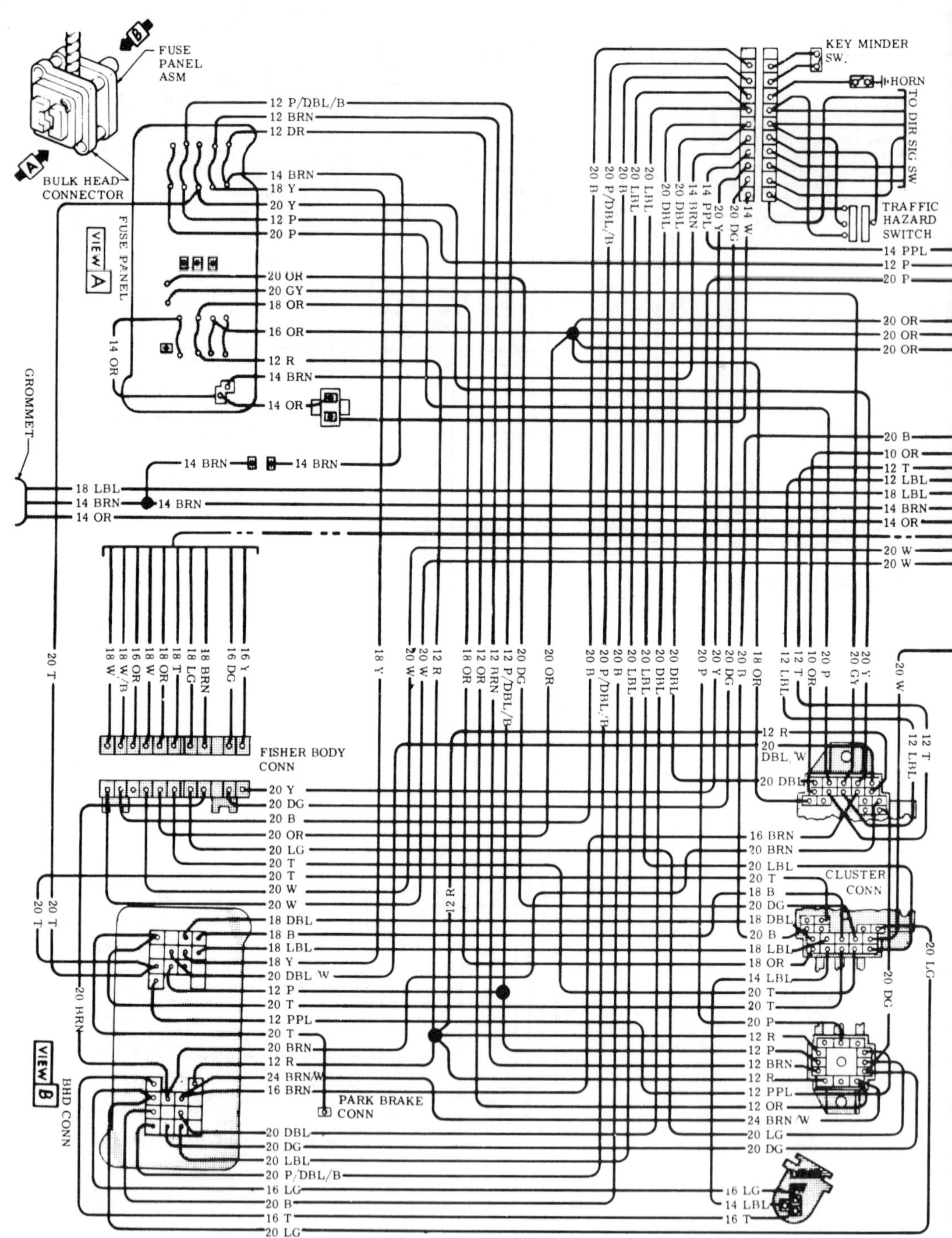

1971 center section

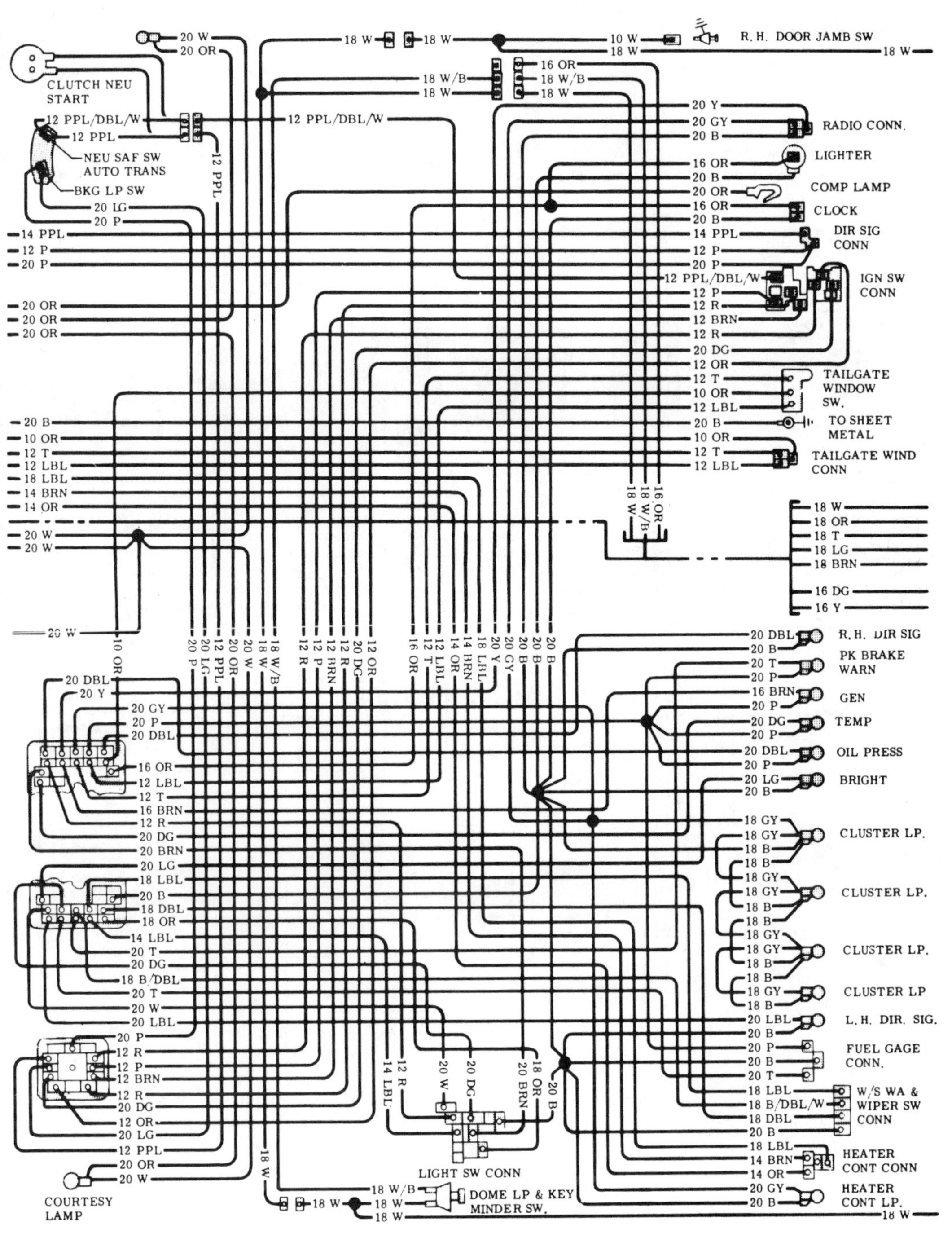

1971 center section

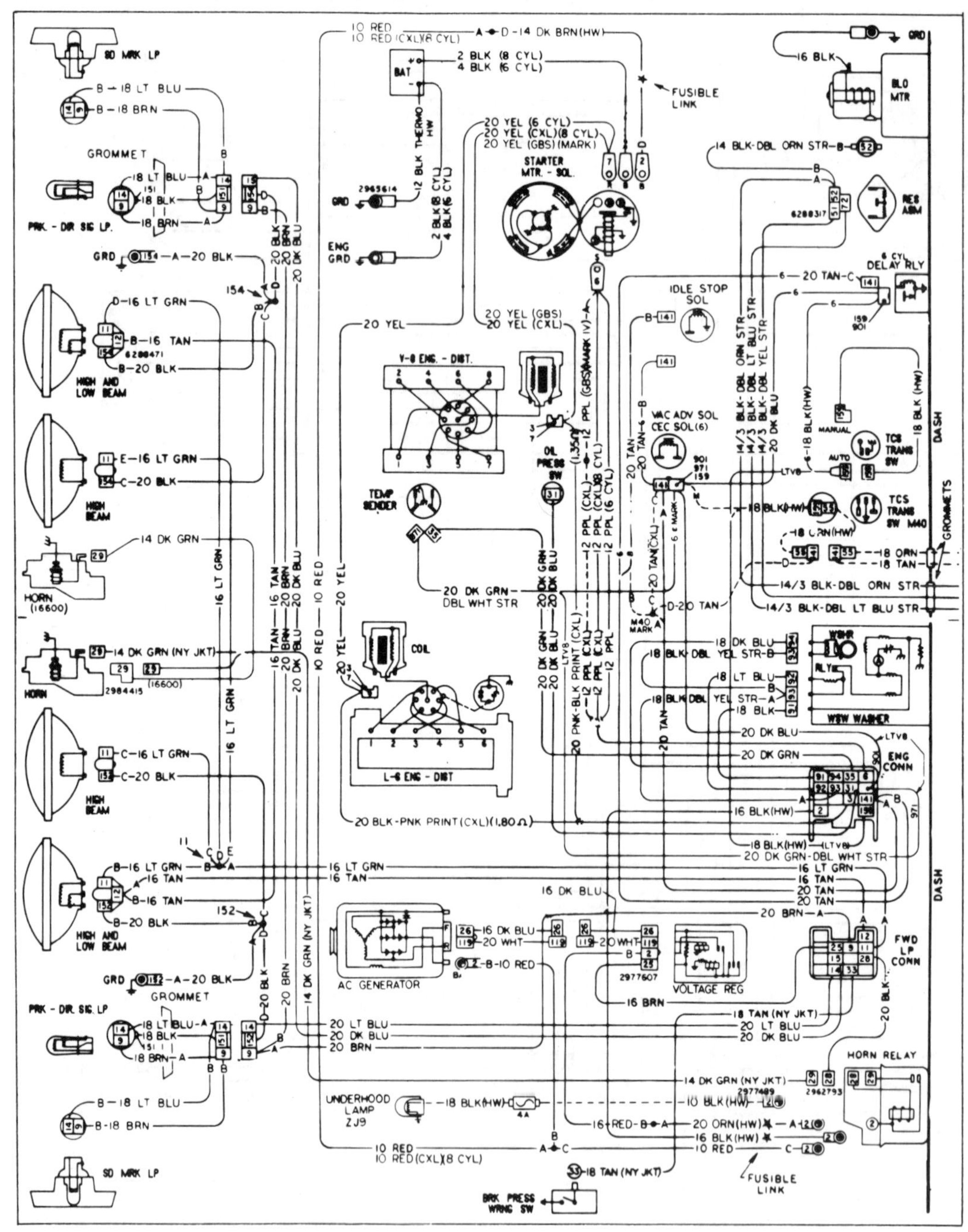

1972 front section

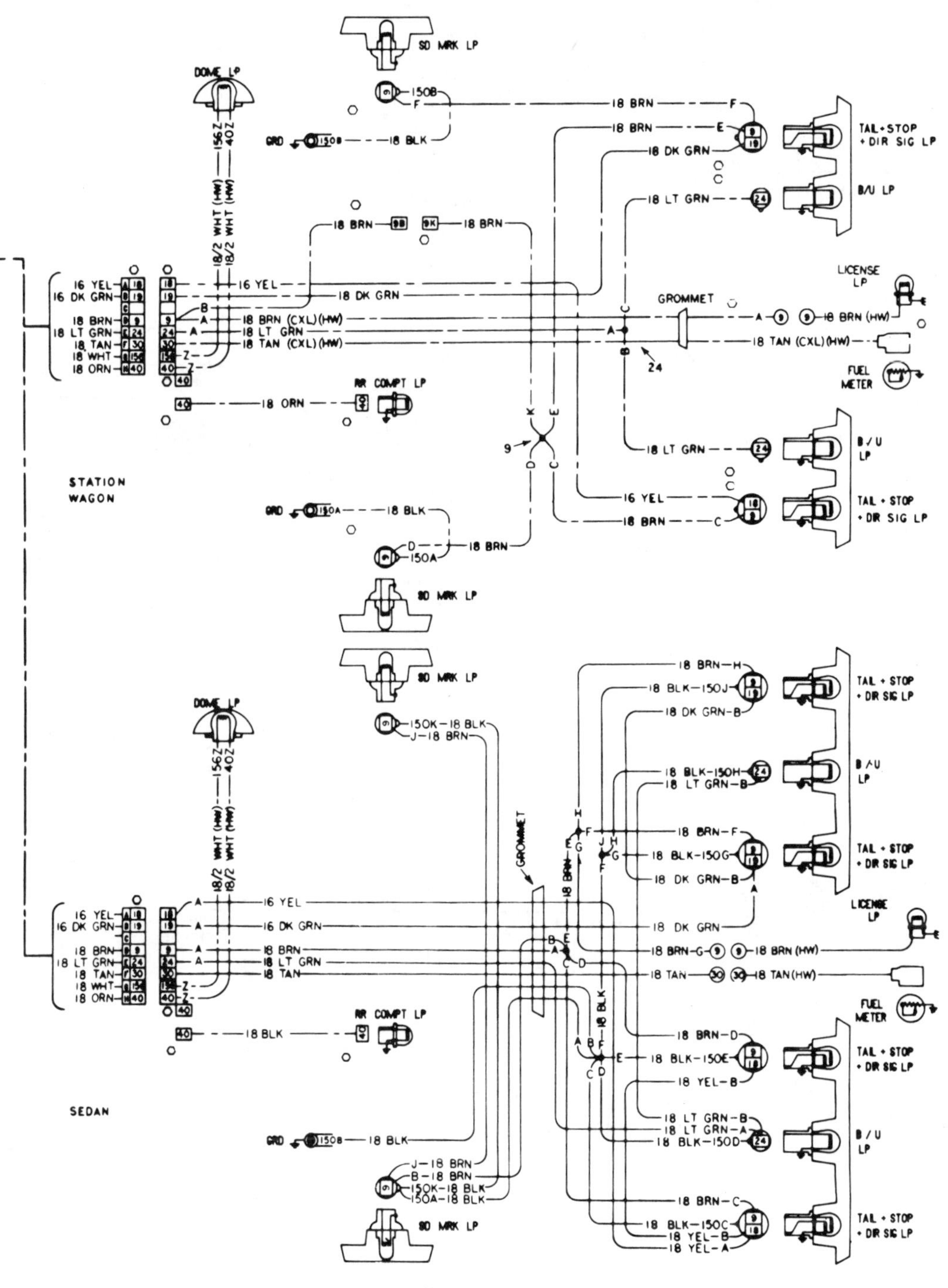

1972 rear section

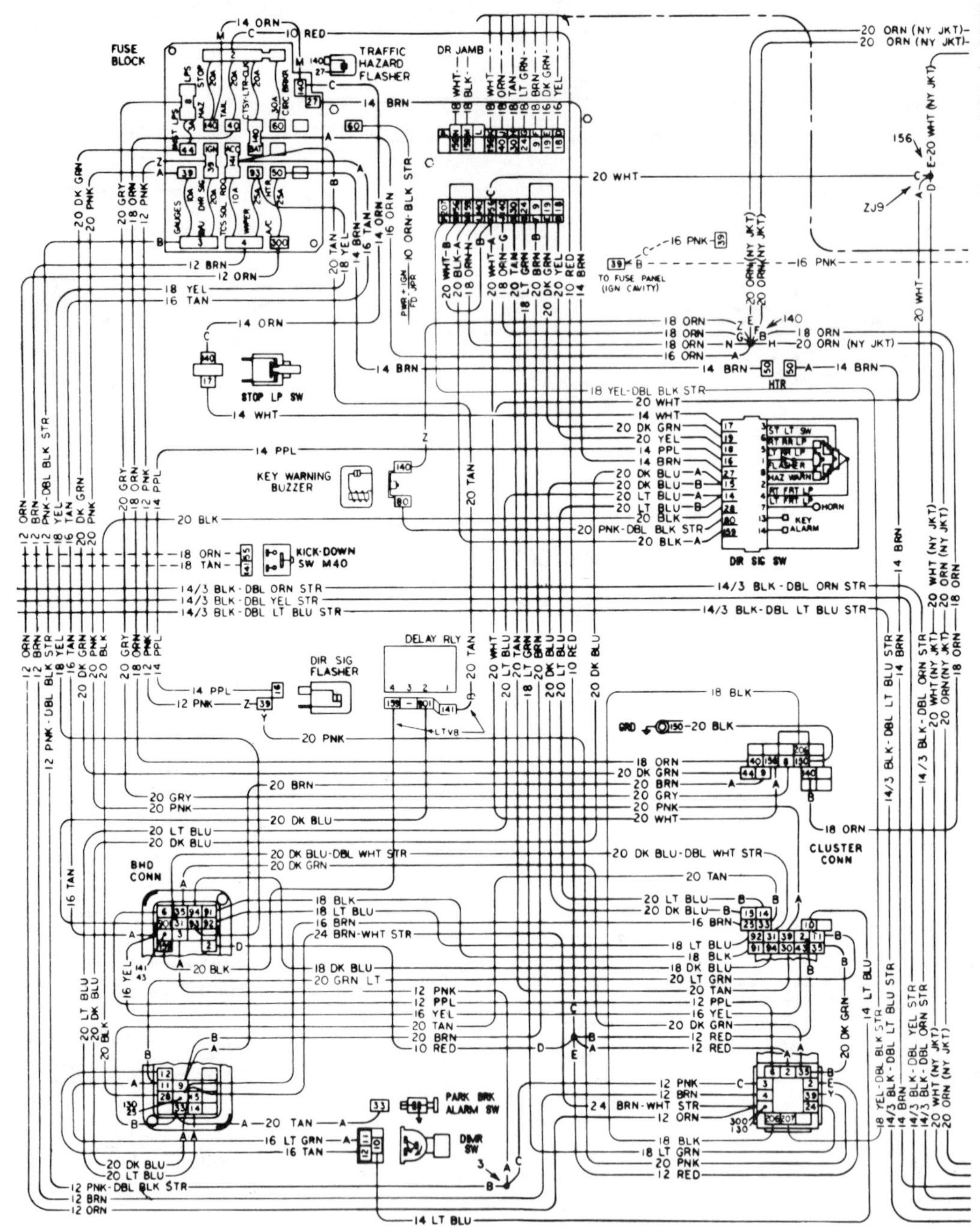

1972 center section

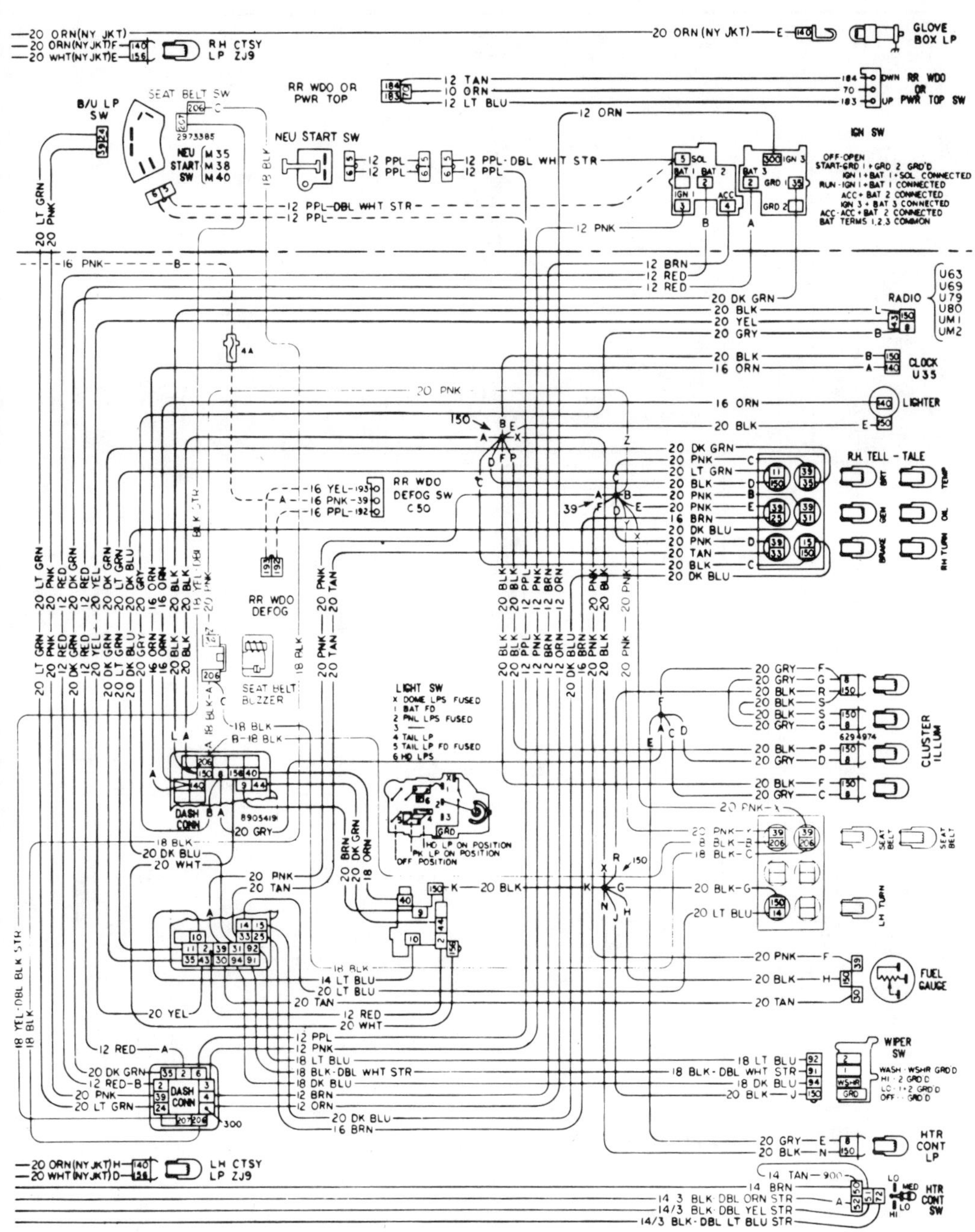

1972 center section

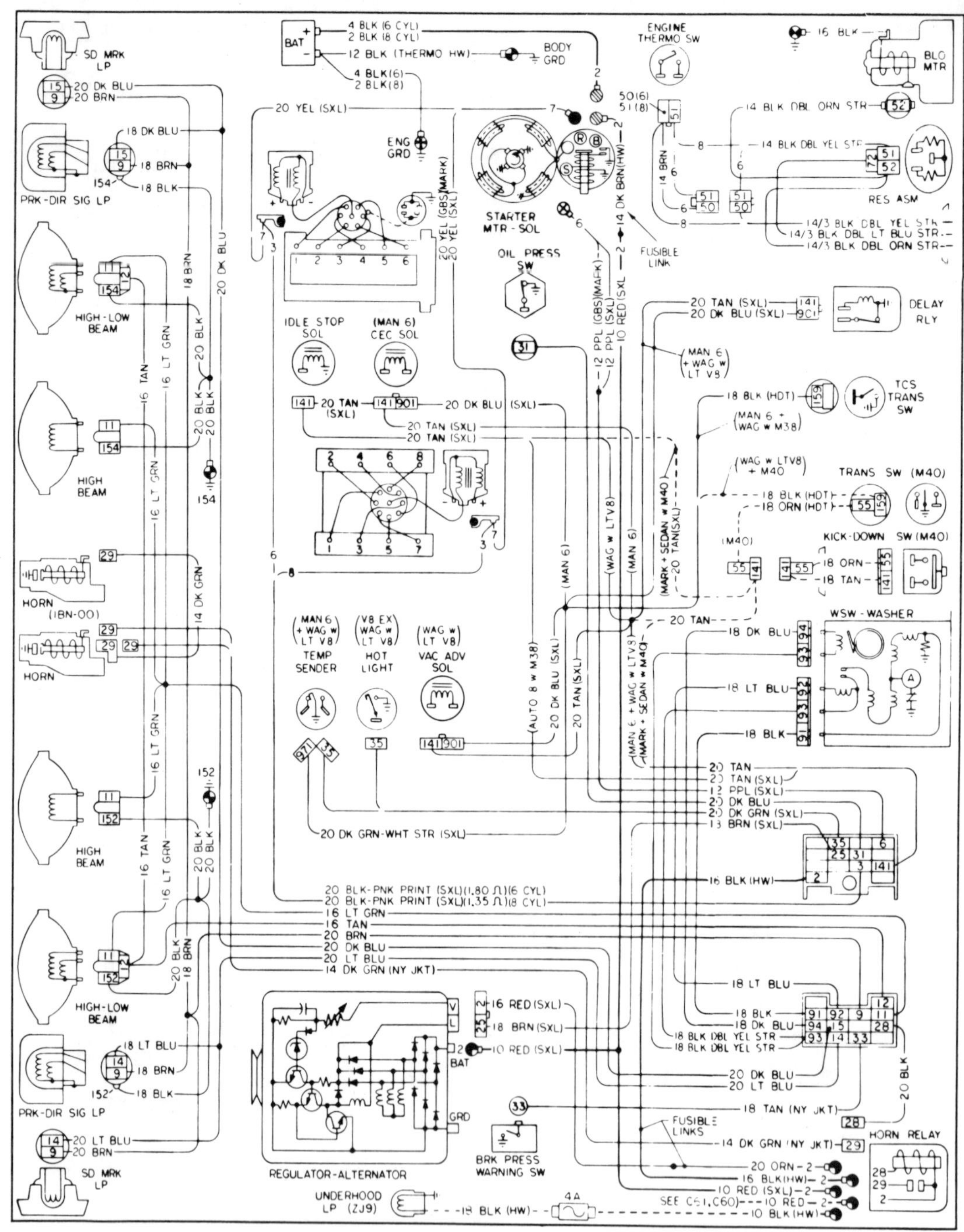

1973 front section

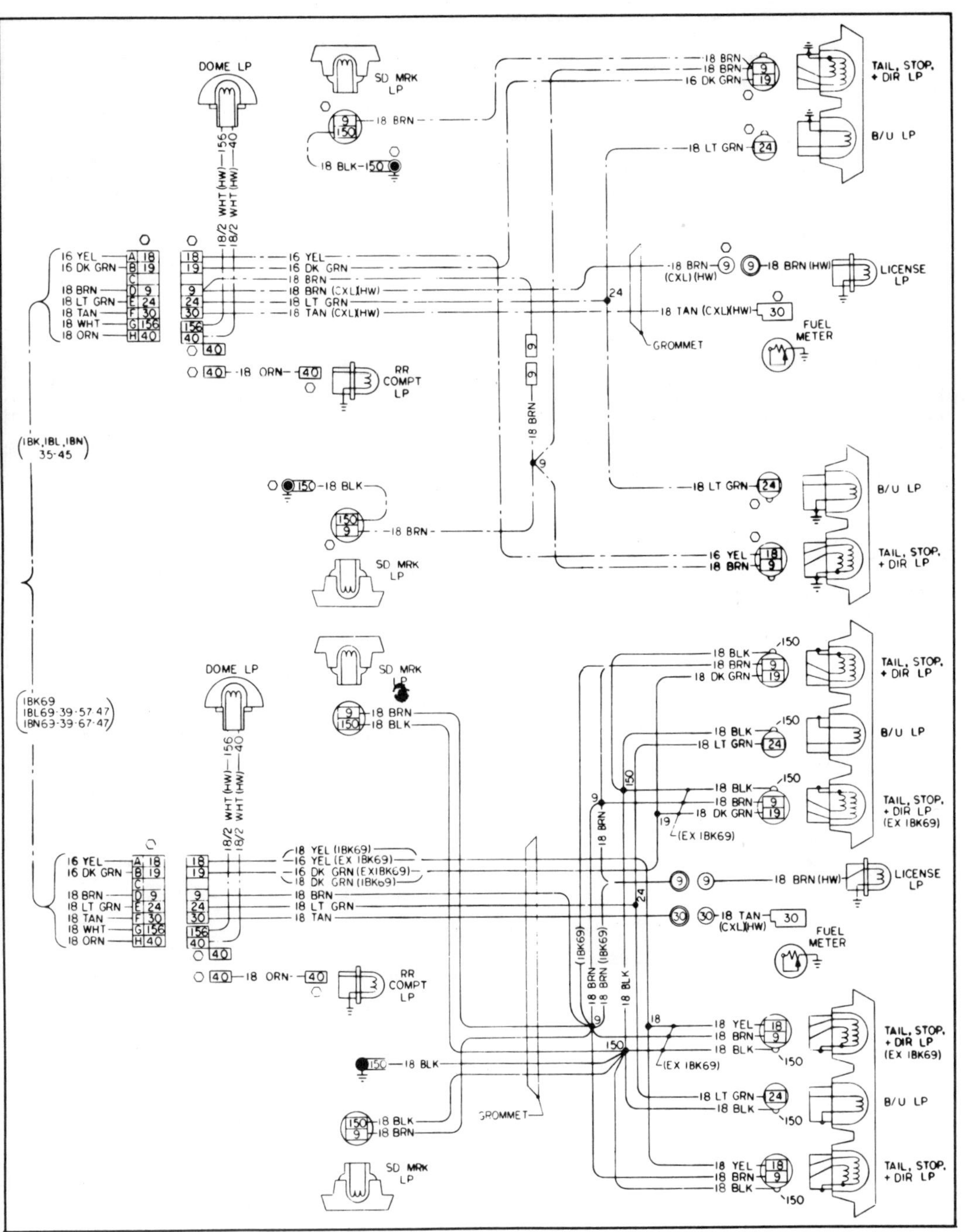

1973 rear section

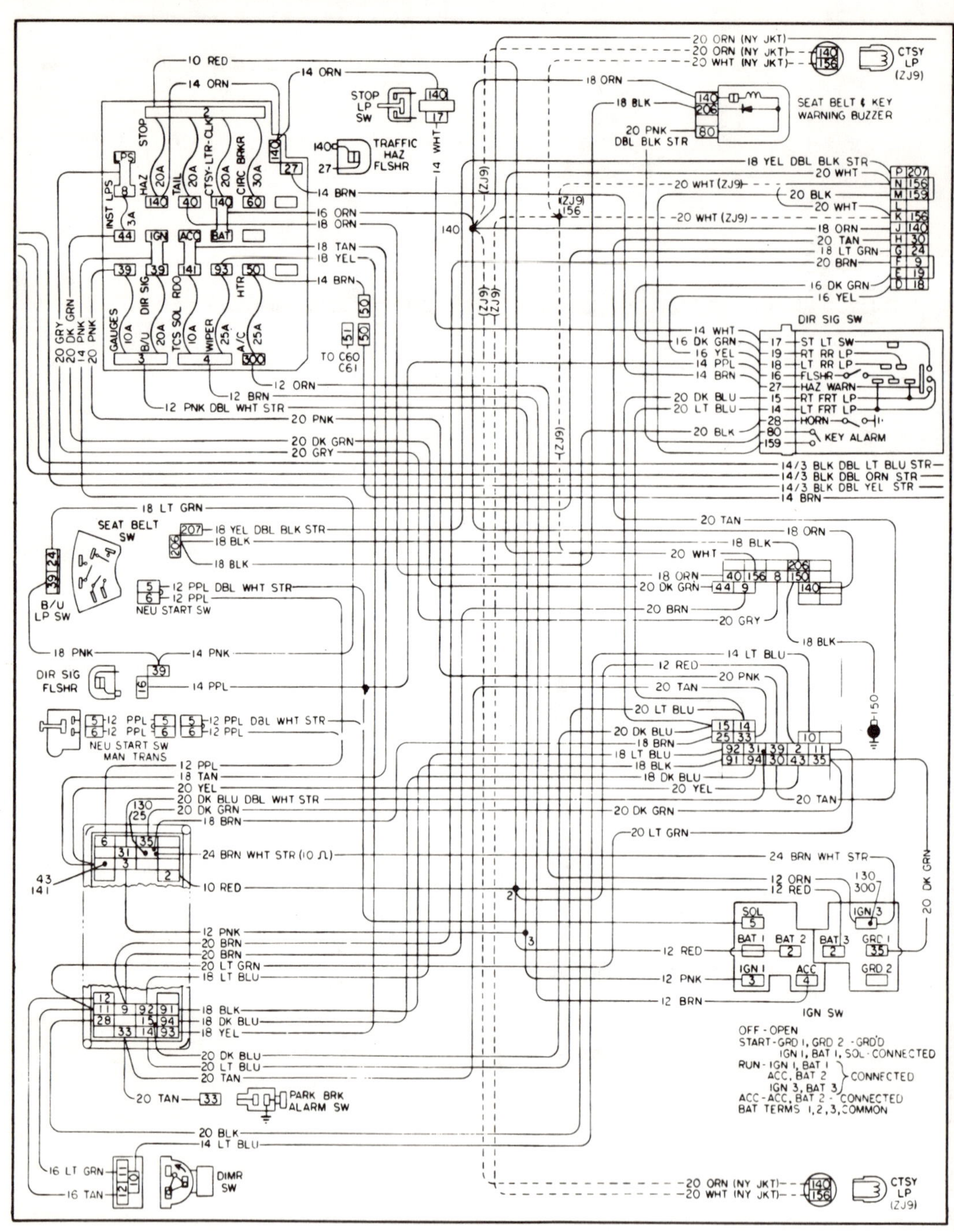

1973 center section

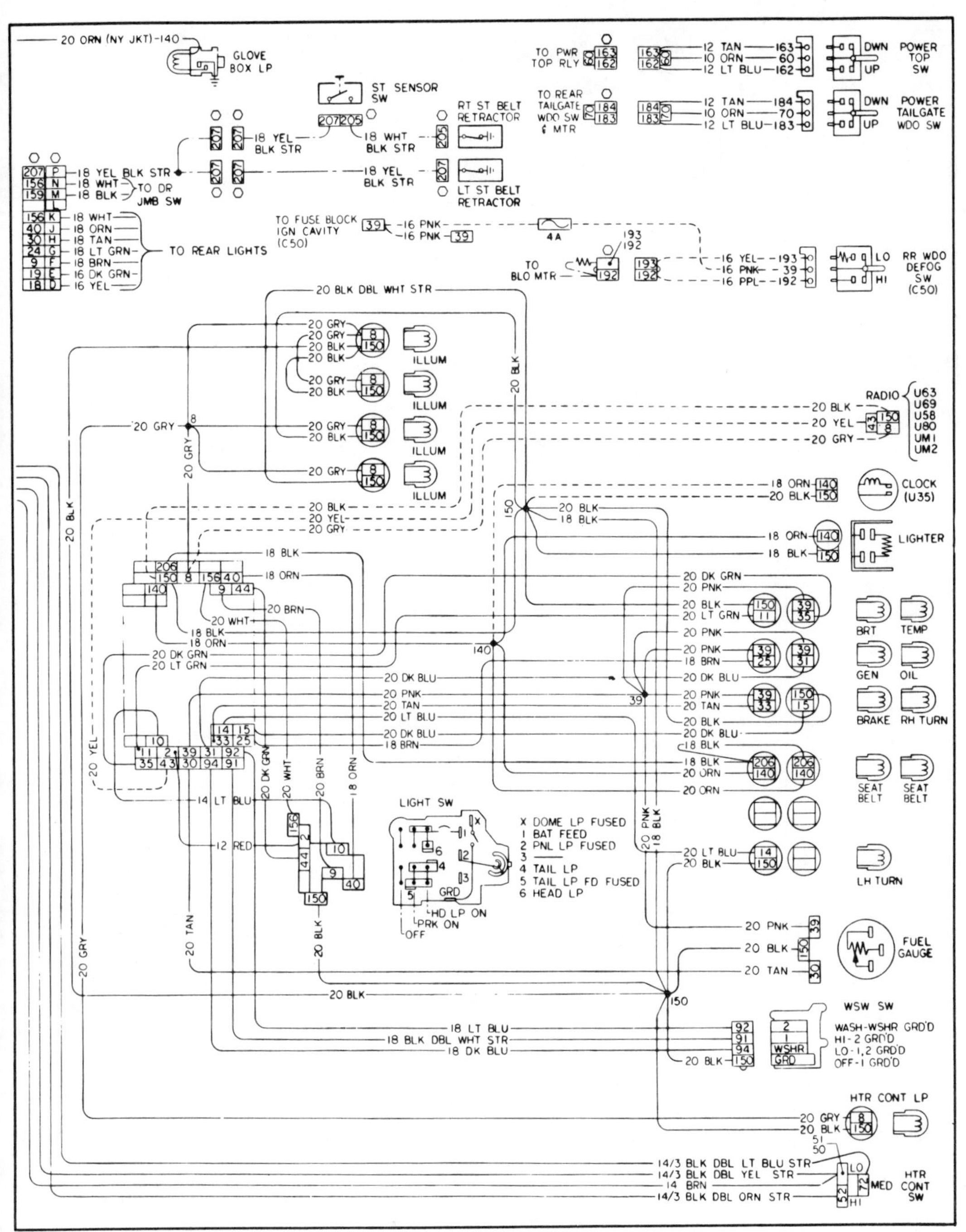

1973 center section

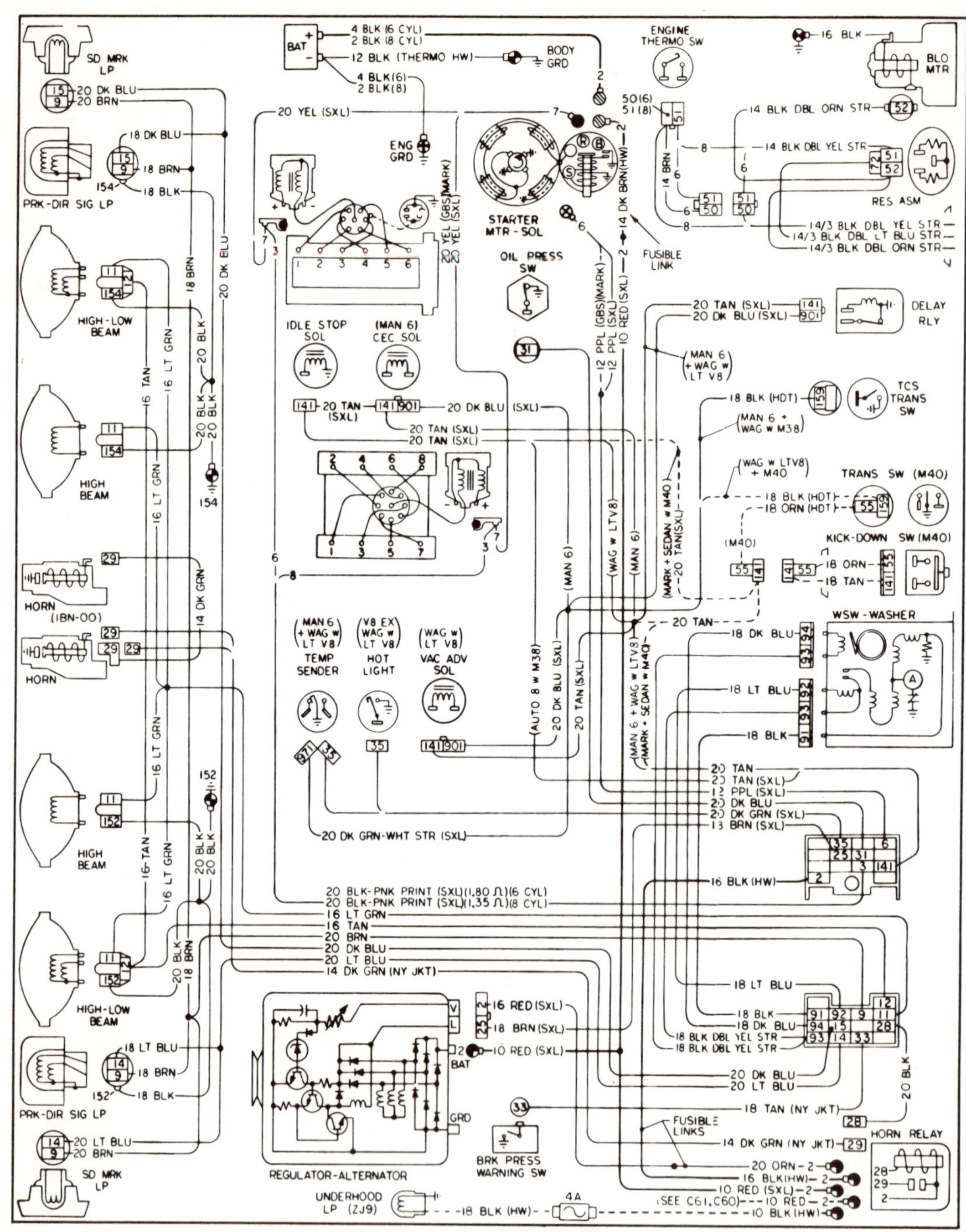

1974 front section

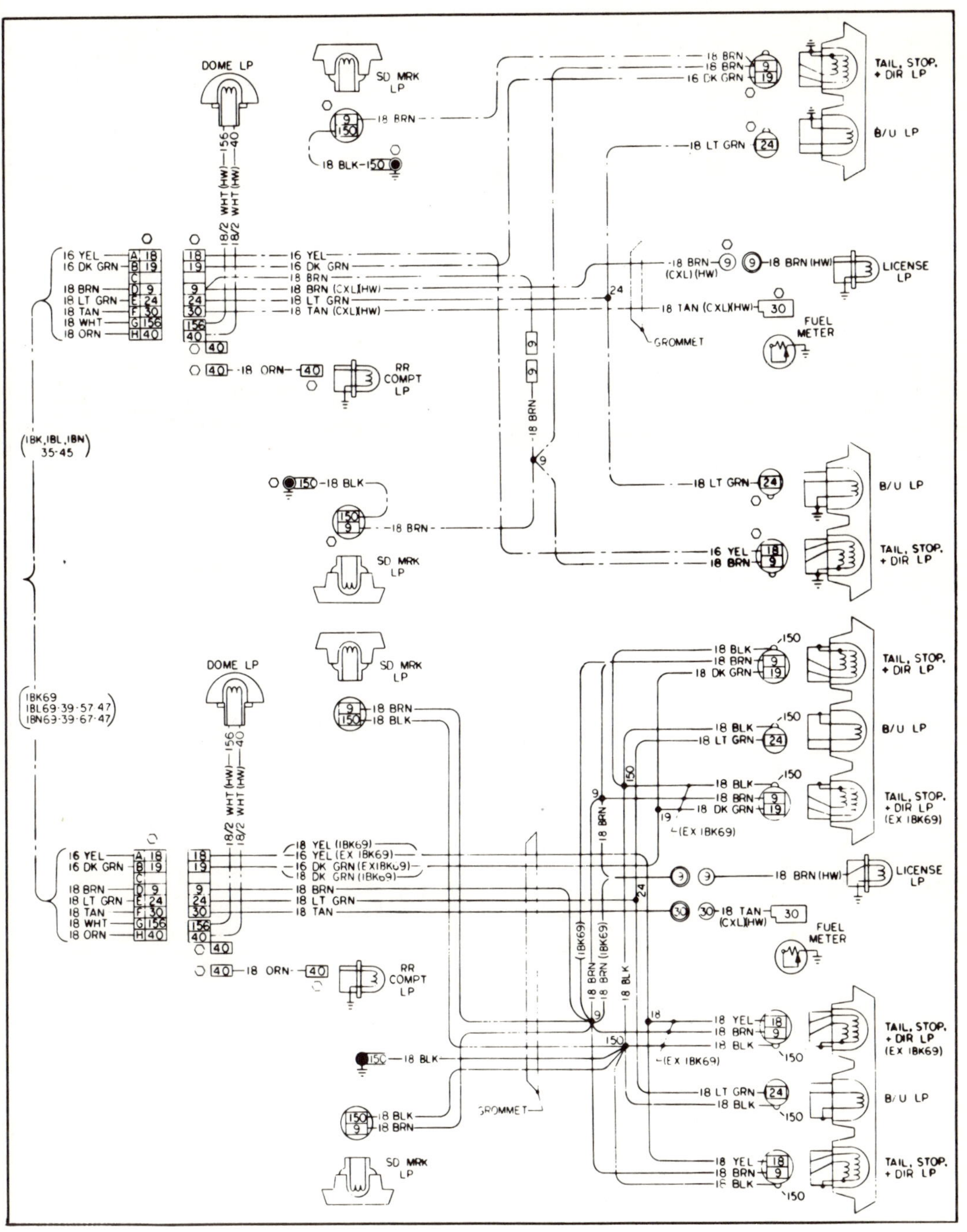

1974 rear section

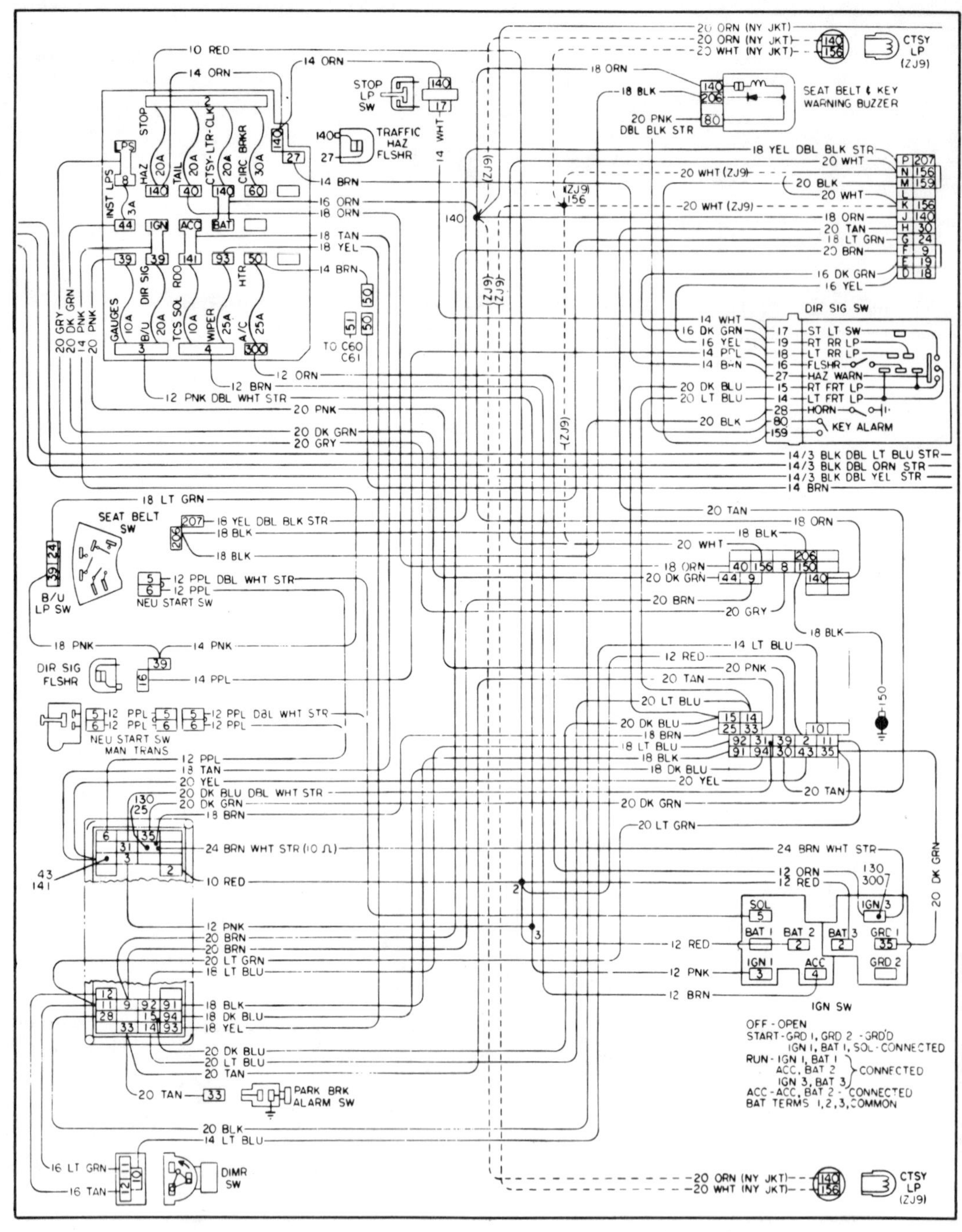

1974 center section

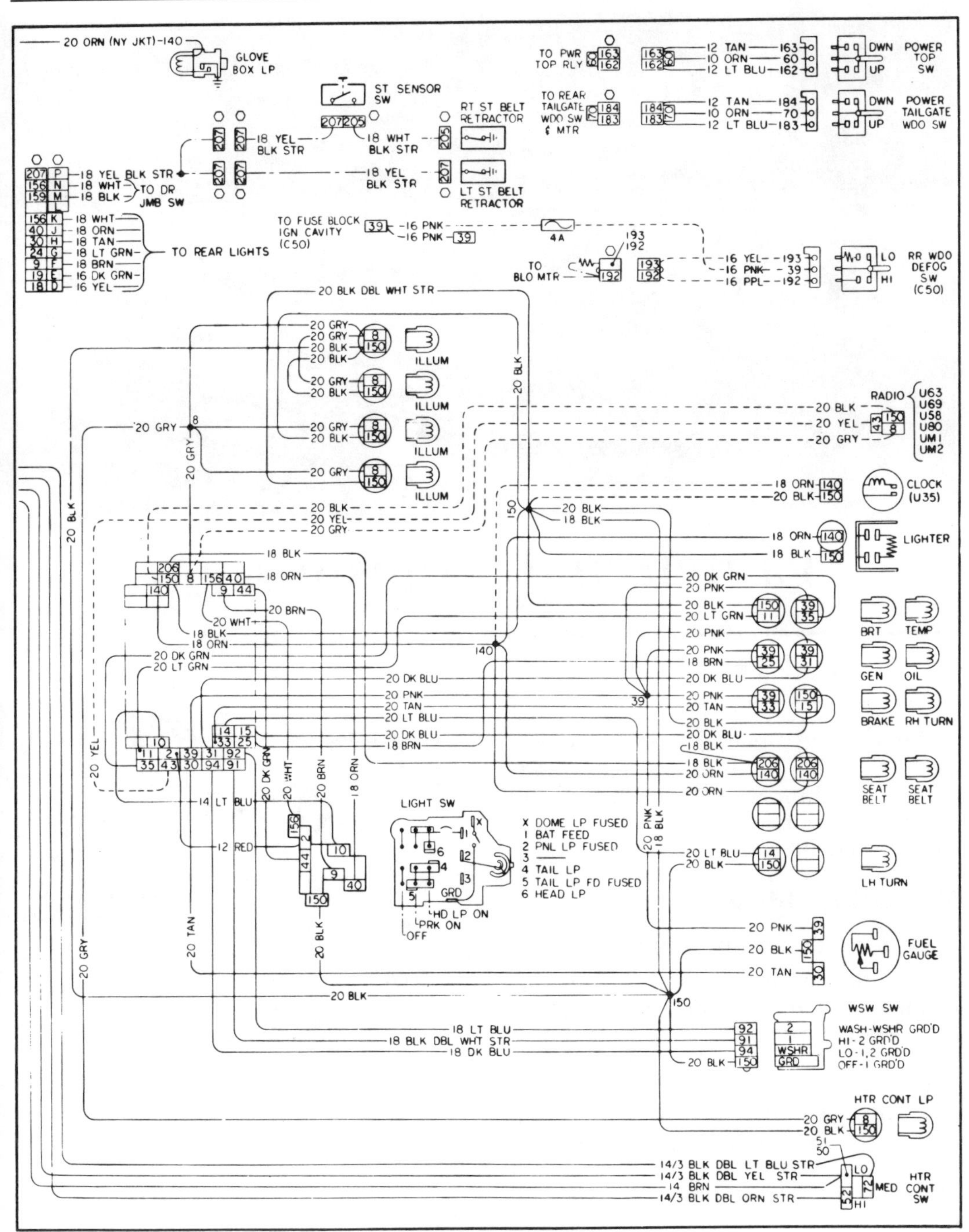

1974 center section

Chapter 6

Clutch and Transmission

Manual Transmission

Three-speed manual transmissions were available in full size Chevrolets from 1968 through 1973. A four-speed manual transmission was available only in 1968 and 1969.

Shift Linkage Adjustment

1968 THREE-SPEED COLUMN SHIFT

1. With transmission shifter rods disconnected at transmission levers, move both levers into neutral detents.
2. Move manual selector lever into neutral position.
3. Align first and reverse shifter tube lever with second and high shifter tube lever on the mast jacket. In some cases, a pin may be used to hold the levers in alignment.
   NOTE: *The key is engaged with the slot on the second and third shifter tube lever when selector lever is in the Neutral position.*
4. Loosen control rod clamp bolts. Install control rods on mast jacket shifter levers and secure with retaining clips.
5. Adjust length of first-reverse rod. Tighten clamp bolt.
6. Adjust length of second-third control rod. Tighten clamp bolt.

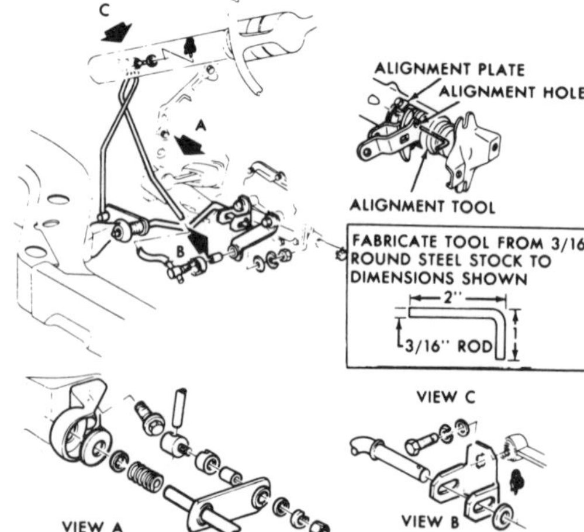

1968 column shift adjustment

7. Shift through all positions to check adjustment, and to insure positive and full gear engagement.

1969–73 THREE-SPEED COLUMN SHIFT

1. With transmission in Reverse, place ignition switch in Off position up to 1970, Lock for 1971–73.
2. Loosen shift rod locknuts.
3. Set transmission first-reverse lever in reverse position. Push up on first-reverse control rod to 1970, pull down for 1971–73 until column lever is in reverse detent position. Tighten first-reverse locknut.
4. Shift column and transmission

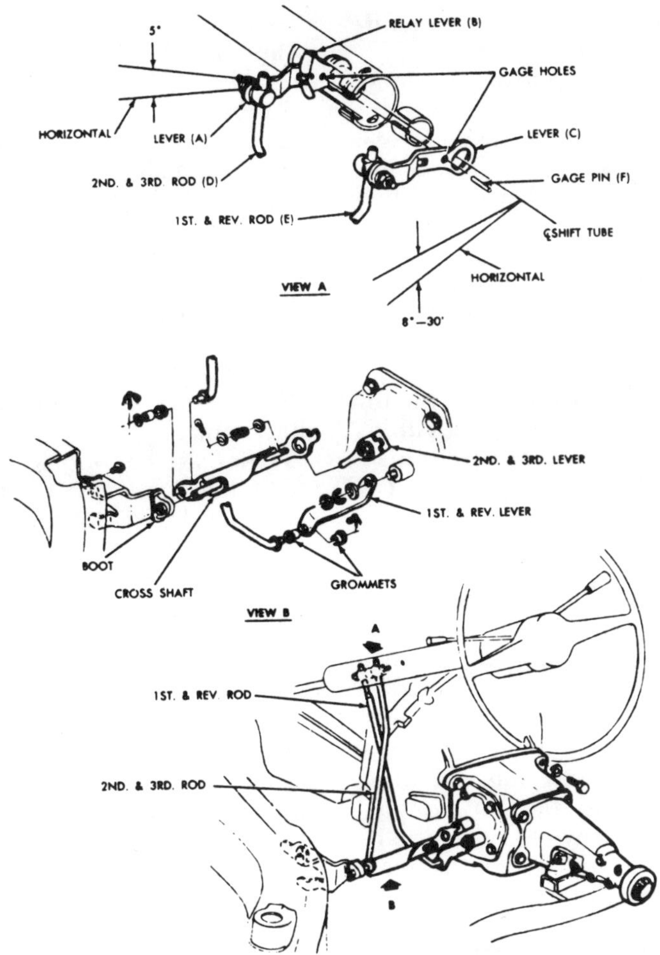

1969–73 column shift adjustment

levers to Neutral position. Insert a $^3/_{16}$ in. dia. rod into alignment holes in levers and alignment plate.

5. Tighten second-third locknut.

6. Remove alignment rod. Shift column lever to reverse. Turn key to Lock. Ignition switch must move freely to Lock position and it must not be possible to turn key to Lock when in any transmission position other than reverse. If this interlock binds, leave switch in Lock position and readjust first-reverse rod.

7. Check shifting.

FOUR-SPEED—1968–69

Since 1968, two makes of four-speed transmission have been used, Muncie and Saginaw. Linkage adjustments, however, are typical. Four-speeds were not available in the Chevrolet after 1969. A gauge $^1/_8$ in. thick by $^{41}/_{64}$ in. wide and 3

in. long should be used to locate and maintain neutral detent position of the shift lever while making linkage adjustments.

1968 Four Speed Floorshift

1. Loosen shift rod clamp nuts or remove clevis pins.

2. Set transmission shift levers in Neutral position.

3. Insert locating gauge, $^1/_8$ thick x $^{41}/_{64}$ wide x 3 in. long, into control lever bracket assembly.

4. Adjust length of shifting rods. Tighten clamp nuts or replace clevis pins.

5. Remove gauge. Check shifting operation.

1969 Four-Speed Floorshift

1. Place ignition switch in Lock position.

2. Loosen locknuts at swivels on shift rods and back drive control rod.

3. Set transmission shift levers in Neutral positions.

4. Shift lever into Neutral. Insert locating gauge, $1/8$ thick x $41/64$ wide x 3 in. long, into control lever bracket assembly.

5. Tighten shift rod locknuts and remove gauge.

6. Shift lever into Reverse, then pull down slightly on back drive rod to remove slack. Tighten back drive rod locknut.

7. Ignition switch must move freely to Lock position and it must not be possible to turn key to Lock when in any transmission position other than reverse. Readjust back drive rode, if necessary.

8. Check for proper shifting operation.

Transmission Removal and Installation

1. Raise the car and drain the transmission. Disconnect the speedometer cable and the control levers. Disconnect the driveshaft. Remove two bolts attaching the center bearing to the frame. Remove nuts and U-bolts retaining the rear universal joint bearing to the differential pinion drive flange. Move the driveshaft rearward to the left and under the rear axle housing to withdraw the front universal joint from the transmission output shaft. Remove the transmission rear mounting pad bolts and unbolt the support member from the frame.

2. On all models, remove the two top transmission-to-clutch housing capscrews, and insert guide pins to keep the weight of the transmission from falling on the clutch assembly.

3. Remove the lower transmission-to-clutch housing capscrews. Slide the transmission straight back on the guide pins until the input shaft of the transmission is free of the clutch.

4. Remove the transmission from under the car.

5. Install in reverse order of removal.

Clutch

TROUBLESHOOTING

There is no substitute for careful examination and experience when attempting a diagnosis. The following are some symptoms that may accompany clutch troubles.

1. Excessive noise.
2. Clutch chatter or grab.
3. Clutch slip.
4. Clutch drag or failure to release.
5. Pedal pulsation.
6. Low clutch facing life.
7. Gear lock-up or hard shifting.
8. Hard pedal.

Excessive Noise

There are five common sources of clutch noise:

1. Release bearing.
2. Clutch shaft pilot bearing.
3. Transmission pinion shaft bearing.
4. Transmitted engine noises.
5. Clutch linkage noises.

RELEASE BEARING

Release bearing noises vary with the degree of bearing failure. A dry or damaged bearing usually makes a shrill or scraping sound when depressing the clutch pedal to the point of release finger-to-bearing contact. This means that the noise should be audible at the lower end of clutch pedal free-play. Continued use of a car, with the release bearing in this condition, is damaging to the clutch release fingers.

The usual cause of release bearing failure is overwork—caused by riding the clutch. Other causes are not enough pedal free-play, lack of lubricant in the bearing, or clutch release fingers that are worn or out of true.

PILOT BEARING

Clutch shaft pilot bearing noises can be heard only when the bearing is in operation. This is at any time crankshaft speed is different from that of the clutch shaft, (clutch disengaged with transmission in gear).

This is a high-pitched squeal, caused by a dry bearing and requires replacement.

TRANSMISSION PINION SHAFT BEARING

A rough, or otherwise damaged, transmission pinion (input) shaft bearing noise can be heard only when the clutch is engaged, with the transmission in any shift position. The noise is usually quite noticeable with the gears in Neutral. This noise should diminish and completely disappear as the transmission pinion gear slows down and stops after clutch release. This noise is easily distinguished from release bearing noise because of the opposite conditions of encounter.

TRANSMITTED ENGINE NOISES

Assuming that the clutch pedal has the required amount of free-play, there should be no objectionable amount of engine noise transmitted to the passenger area via the clutch. Some engine noises are transmitted through the positive pressure of the clutch release bearing and fingers to the clutch housing. Here they are amplified by the shape of the clutch housing and heard in the passenger compartment in the guise of clutch or transmission trouble. Engine noise transmission can usually be modified through clutch pedal manipulation.

CLUTCH LINKAGE NOISE

Clutch linkage noise is usually a clicking or snapping sound that can be heard or felt in the pedal itself when moving it completely up or down. Locating the cause of trouble and correcting it is a matter of repositioning and lubrication. The trouble may be in the clutch assist spring, the retract spring, the release bearing lever, or even at the release bearing.

Clutch Chatter or Grab

The cause of clutch chatter or grab can usually be located within the clutch assembly. To correct the trouble the clutch must be removed. Symptoms resembling clutch trouble may be misleading and originate in other areas.

In order to isolate the cause of the problem, it is suggested that the following items be checked in this order.

1. Be sure that the clutch linkage is in adjustment and not binding. If necessary, lubricate, align, and adjust the linkage.

2. Check for worn or loose engine or transmission mounts. If necessary, tighten or replace mounts.

3. Check for wear, looseness, or misalignment of the universal joints. Check the attaching bolts on the clutch pressure plate, transmission, and clutch housing. Tighten, align, or replace as necessary.

4. Check the freedom of movement of the clutch release bearing on its sleeve. Free up or replace as necessary.

5. Check for oil or grease on the flywheel, friction disc, or pressure plate.

6. Make sure that the friction disc is true and that the disc hub is not binding on the splines of the transmission input shaft (clutch shaft).

7. Be sure that the disc or the pressure plate is not broken.

8. Examine the clutch pressure plate and cover plate assembly for cracks or heat discoloration.

Clutch Slip

Clutch slippage is usually most noticeable when pulling away, and during acceleration from a standing start. A severe, but positive, test for slipperage is to start the engine, set the parking brake and apply the service brakes; shift the transmission into High gear and release the clutch pedal while accelerating the engine. A clutch in good condition should hold and stall the engine. If the clutch slips, the cause may be one or more of the following:

1. Improper linkage adjustment (not enough free-play).

2. Broken or disconnected parts.

3. Clutch linkage or lever mechanism binding or broken, not allowing full pressure plate application.

4. Friction disc oil-saturated or excessively worn.

5. Pressure plate worn, springs weak from temper loss or failure (damaging heat will usually cause parts to appear blue).

Clutch Drag or Failure to Release

There are many reasons for clutch drag (spin) or failure to release. The following conditions, therefore, apply to unmodified versions of standard vehicles. Changing the driven plate mass (replacing the standard driven plate with a heavy-duty unit), changing transmission oil viscosity, etc., may influence clutch spin-time. Three seconds is a good, typical, spin-time for the standard transmission and clutch, driven under normal conditions, in average temperate zone climates.

The friction disc and some of the transmission gears spin briefly after clutch disengagement, so normal clutch action should not be confused with a dragging clutch.

Clutch drag, failure to release, or abnormal spin-time may be caused by one or more of the following:

1. Improper clutch linkage adjustment.

2. Clutch plate hub binding on the transmission input (pinion) shaft.

3. A warped or bent friction disc or pressure plate; or loose friction material on the driven disc.

4. The transmission input shaft may be binding or sticking in the pilot bearing.

5. Misalignment of transmission to the engine.

6. Transmission lubricant low or not heavy enough.

Pedal Pulsation

This condition can be felt by applying light foot pressure to the clutch pedal with the engine idling. It may be caused by any of the following:

1. Bent or uneven clutch release finger adjustment.

2. Excessive flywheel run-out due to bent wheel or crankshaft flange; or the flywheel may not be properly seated on the crankshaft flange.

3. Release bearing cocked on transmission bearing retainer.

4. Poor alignment of transmission with the engine.

Low Clutch Facing Life

This sort of complaint warrants a close study of the operator's driving habits. Poor clutch facing wear may be caused by any of the following:

1. Riding the clutch.

2. Drag strip type operation.

3. Continuous overloading, or the hauling of heavy trailers or other equipment.

4. Holding the car from drifting backward on a grade by slipping the clutch instead of using the brakes.

5. Improper pedal linkage adjustment (free-play and pedal height).

6. Rough surface on flywheel or pressure plate.

7. Presence of oil or water on clutch facing.

8. Weak pressure plate springs, causing clutch creep or slip.

Gear Lock Up or Hard Shifting

This trouble is so closely related to "Clutch Drag or Failure to Release" that diagnosis should be conducted in the same way as given under that heading. If, after checking the items listed and finding that the transmission still locks up or is hard to shift, the trouble probably lies in the transmission cover or shifter assembly, or in the transmission proper. In that case, transmission work is needed.

Hard Pedal

A stiff clutch pedal or a clutch release that requires abnormal pedal pressure may result from one or more of the following:

1. Dry and binding clutch linkage and levers.

2. Linkage out of alignment.

3. Improper (heavy) retracting spring.

4. Dry or binding release bearing sleeve or transmission bearing retainer.

5. Assist spring missing or improperly adjusted.

6. Wrong type clutch assembly (heavy-duty) being used.

Linkage Inspection

A clutch may have all the symptoms of going bad when the real trouble lies in the linkage. To avoid the unnecessary replacement of a clutch, make the following linkage checks:

a. Start the engine and depress the clutch pedal until it is about ½ in. from the floor mat and move the shift lever between First and Reverse (First and Second on a four-speed) several times. If this can be done smoothly without any grinding, the clutch is releasing fully. If the shifting is not smooth, the clutch is not releasing fully and adjustment is necessary.

b. Check the condition of the clutch pedal bushings for signs of sticking or excessive wear.

c. Check the throwout bearing fork for proper installation on the ball stud. The fork could possibly be pulled off the ball if not properly lubricated.

d. Check the cross-shaft levers for distortion or damage.

e. Check the car for loose or damaged motor mounts. Bad motor mounts can cause the engine to shift under acceleration and bind the clutch linkage at the cross-shaft. There must be some clearance between the cross-shaft and motor mount.

f. Check the throwout bearing clearance between the clutch spring fingers and the front bearing retainer on the transmission. If there is no clearance, the fork may be improperly installed on the ball stud or the clutch disc may be worn out.

SERVICE

Clutch Pedal Free-Travel

The pedal should travel 1 in. to $1\frac{1}{2}$ in. before the throw-out bearing engages the diaphragm spring.

This should be checked at the pedal by hand; $\frac{3}{4}$ in. true free-travel of the bearing will approximate 1 in. feel at the pedal.

The adjustment is made on the fork pushrod running from the lever and shaft assembly to the clutch fork. On some models, the adjustment is made at the fork end by changing the position of two jam nuts. On other models, the adjustment is made at the front end of the rod by turning an adjustable swivel. On this type, one turn of the swivel equals approximately $\frac{3}{16}$ in. at the pedal. The ad-

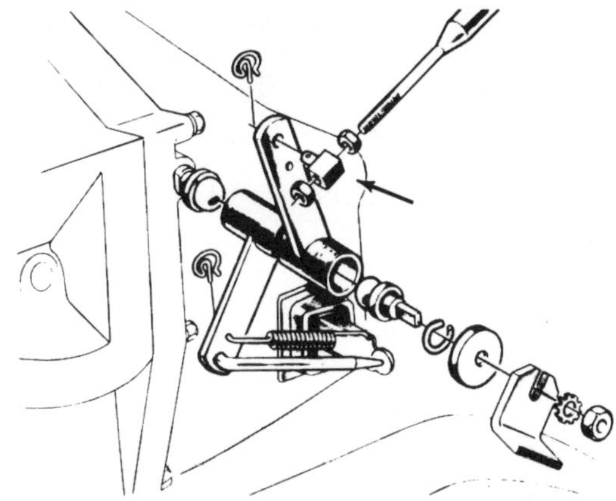

Clutch linkage—adjustment is made at arrow

justment can be made by holding the fork pushrod rearward to remove all lash, then adjusting the swivel to line up a conical point stamped on the swivel with a dimple stamped on the lever to which it attaches.

Removal and Installation

1. Support the engine and remove the transmission as described in "Removal and Installation."

2. Disconnect the clutch fork pushrod and spring.

3. Remove the flywheel housing.

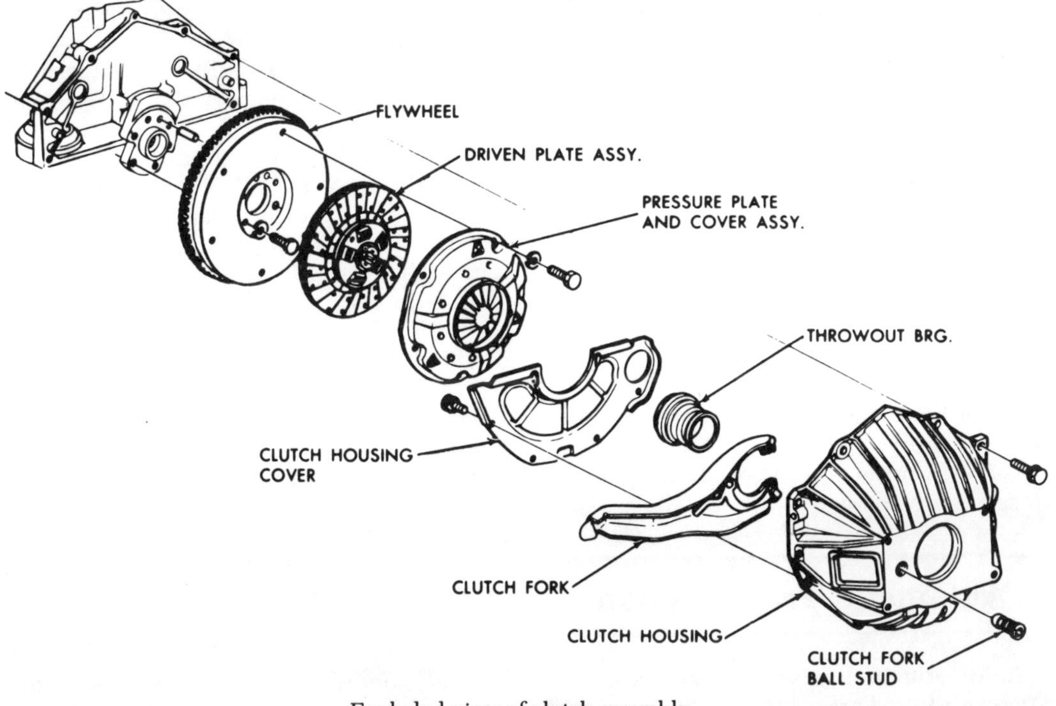

Exploded view of clutch assembly

4. Slide the clutch fork from the ball stud and remove the fork from the dust boot. The ball stud is threaded into the clutch housing and is easily replaced, if necessary.

5. Install a clutch pilot tool.

NOTE: *Look for the assembly markings "X" on the flywheel and the clutch cover (pressure plate assembly). If there are none, scribe marks to identify the position of the clutch cover relative to the flywheel.*

6. Loosen the clutch cover bolts evenly until the spring pressure is relieved, then remove the bolts and clutch assembly.

7. Before installing, clean the pressure plate and the flywheel face.

8. Position the disc and pressure plate assembly on the flywheel and install a pilot tool.

NOTE: *The disc on six-clyinder engines is installed with the springs facing the flywheel. On V8 engines, the grease slinger must face the transmission.*

9. Install the pressure plate assembly bolts. Make sure the mark on the cover is aligned with the mark on the flywheel. Tighten the bolts alternately and evenly to 35 ft lbs.

10. Remove the pilot tool.

11. Remove the release fork and lubricate the ball socket and the fork fingers at the throwout bearing with graphite or moly grease. Reinstall the release fork.

12. Lubricate the inside recess and the fork groove of the throwout bearing with a light coat of graphite or moly grease.

13. Install the clutch release fork and dust boot in the clutch housing and the throwout bearing on the fork, then install the flywheel housing. Tighten flywheel housing bolts to 30 ft lbs.

14. Connect the fork pushrod and spring.

15. Adjust the shift linkage as described later.

16. Adjust the clutch pedal free-play as described previously.

Automatic Transmission

Automatic transmissions used are the Powerglide, Turbo Hydra-Matic 200, Turbo Hydra-Matic 350, and Turbo Hydra-Matic 400. Powerglide is a two-speed planetary transmission and the three Turbos are three-speed transmissions.

Pan Removal and Installation
Fluid and Filter Change

The fluid should be changed with the transmission warm.

1. Raise and support the vehicle, preferably in a level attitude.

2. Place a large pan under the transmission pan. Remove all the front and side pan bolts. Loosen the rear bolts about four turns. Pry the pan loose and let it drain.

3. Remove the pan and gasket. Clean the pan throughly with solvent and air dry it. Be very careful not to get any lint from rags in the pan.

4. Remove the strainer to valve body screws, the strainer, and the gasket. Most 350 transmissions will have a throw-away filter instead of a strainer. On the 400 transmission, remove the filter retaining bolt, filter, and intake pipe O-ring.

5. If there is a strainer, clean it in solvent and air dry.

6. Install the new filter or cleaned strainer with a new gasket. Tighten the screws to 12 ft lbs (6–10 ft lbs on the 200). On the 400, install a new intake pipe O-ring and a new filter, tightening the retaining bolt to 10 ft lbs.

7. Install the pan with a new gasket. Tighten the bolts evenly to 12 ft lbs (8 for Powerglide).

8. Lower the car and add 5 pts (3 on Powerglide), of DEXRON® or DEXRON II® automatic transmission fluid through the dipstick tube. Start the engine in Park and let it idle. Do not race the engine. Shift into each shift lever position, shift back into Park, and check the fluid level on the dipstick. The level should be ¼ in. below ADD. Be very careful not to overfill. Recheck the level after the car has been driven long enough to thoroughly warm up the transmission. Add fluid as necessary. The level should then be at FULL.

Neutral Safety Switch Adjustment

1968–77

In all models the adjustment is made with the shift lever in Drive position. Loosen the switch mounting screws.

Align the slot in the contact support with the hole in the switch and insert a ³/₃₂ in. pin to hold the support in place.

On column shift models, place the contact support drive slot over the shifter tube drive tang and tighten the screws.

On floor shift models, the ash tray, trim plate assembly and indicator lens and housing must be removed from the console before proceeding as described in the first paragraph above. Clamp the control lever pawl against the contact point of the detent. Tighten the switch mounting screws, then remove the pin and reinstall all the console components which were removed.

Linkage Adjustments

COLUMN SHIFT

1. Make sure that the shift lever works freely in the mast jacket.

2. Check for proper linkage adjustment:

a. Pull the selector lever back and allow the lever to be positioned in Drive by the transmission detent.

NOTE: *Do not use the indicator pointer as a reference. The indicator pointed will be adjusted after the linkage.*

b. Release the lever. The lever should not go into Low range unless it is lifted.

c. Lift the shift lever and allow the lever to be positioned in Neutral by the transmission detent.

d. Release the lever. The lever should not go into Reverse unless it is lifted.

e. If the selector lever can move beyond the Neutral and Drive detents without being lifted, then the mechanical stops in the steering column are not coordinated with the transmission detents and adjustment is required.

3. To adjust, place the selector lever in Drive as determined by the transmission detent.

4. Loosen the adjustment clamp or swivel at the cross-shaft and position the selector lever in Drive.

5. With the selector lever in Drive and the transmission lever in Drive detent position, tighten the clamp or swivel bolt.

6. Repeat Step 2 above to check for proper adjustment.

7. If necessary, readjust the selector pointer to agree with the transmission detents.

8. Readjust the neutral safety switch if necessary.

9. When properly adjusted:

a. From Reverse to Drive position

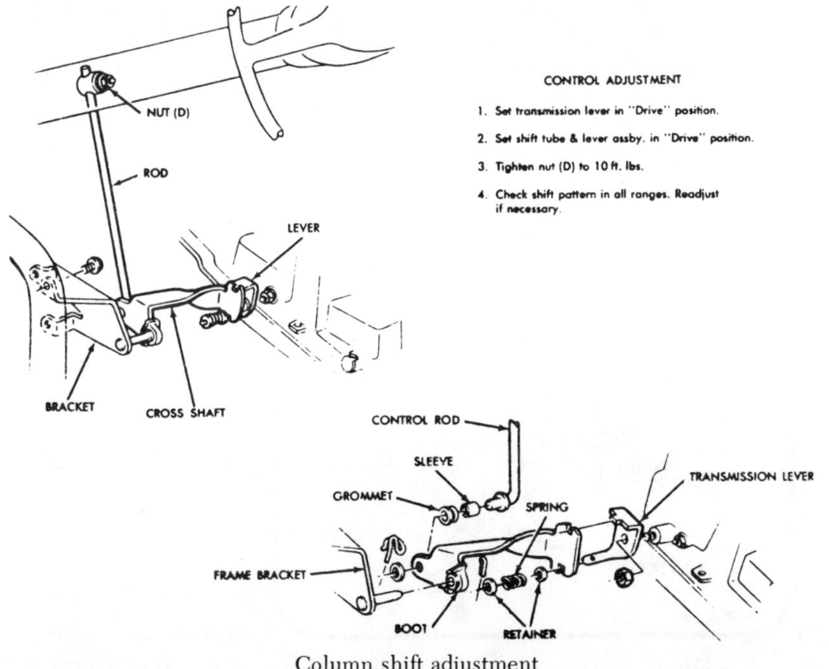

Column shift adjustment

travel, the transmission detent must be noted and related to the indicated position on the dial.

b. In Drive and Reverse positions, the selector lever must drop back into position freely when lifted.

1968–69 Floorshift

NOTE: *This procedure covers both Powerglide and Turbo Hydra-Matic transmissions.*

1. Shift the lever into Drive.

2. Remove the cable clip and disconnect the cable from the lever. Position the transmission lever in Drive.

3. Measure the distance from the rear face of the attaching bracket to the stud on the transmission bracket. If this distance is not 5.5 in., loosen the stud and adjust it.

4. Adjust the end of the cable and reinstall it on the stud.

5. Remove the console quadrant cover and disconnect the cable from the shift lever.

6. A 0.07 in. feeler gauge should fit between the pawl and the Drive detent of the detent plate. Adjust the detent plate, if necessary.

7. Measure the distance from the front of the shifter bracket to the center of the cable pivot pin. If this distance is not 6.25 in., loosen the bolt and move the lever as necessary.

8. Reinstall the quadrant cover.

Throttle Valve Adjustment

1968–73 6-Cylinder

Adjustment is made with the throttle pedal completely depressed and the bell-crank in wide open position.

Adjust the length of the linkage to obtain a $1/64$ in. to $1/16$ in. clearance between the lever on the firewall and its stop when the transmission lever is against its stop.

1968–72 V8 Powerglide

1. Remove the air cleaner and disconnect:

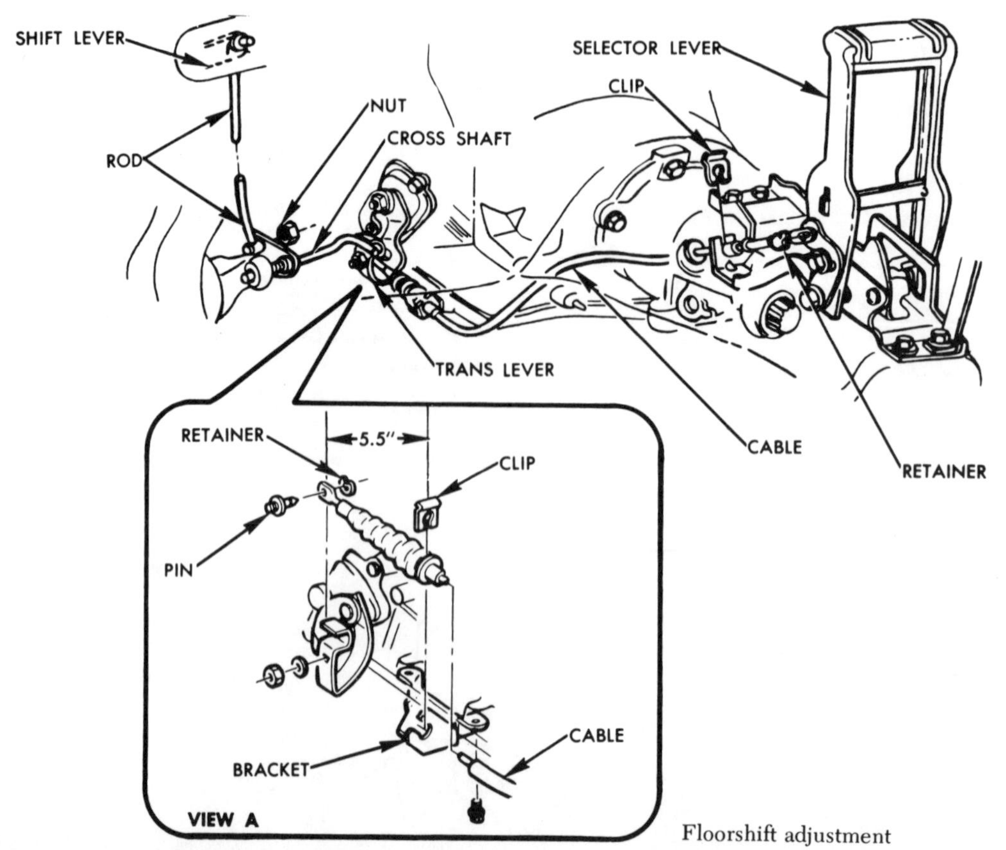

Floorshift adjustment

a. Accelerator linkage at the carburetor.

b. Accelerator return spring.

c. Throttle valve rod return spring.

2. Pull the throttle valve upper rod forward until the transmission is through detent and place the carburetor in wide open position. The carburetor must reach wide open position at the same time that the ball stud contacts the end of the slot in the upper throttle valve rod.

3. Adjust the swivel on the end of the upper throttle valve rod to obtain the setting described in Step 2 above. Allowable tolerance is approximately $^{1}/_{32}$ in.

4. Connect and adjust the carburetor linkage.

Detent Adjustment

1969–77 TURBO HYDRA-MATIC 200–350 (CABLE)

1. 1973–77 cable adjusts itself after pedal is floored. Disengage the snap lock on the detent cable.

2. Place the carburetor in wide open position (lever against the stop). On Quadrajet carburetors, disengage the secondary locknut before placing the lever in wide open position.

NOTE: *Detent cable must be through detent.*

3. Holding the carburetor in wide open position, push the snap lock on the detent cable downward until the top is flush with the cable.

1968–77 TURBO HYDRA-MATIC 400 (SWITCH)

The 1968–72 detent switch is located on the carburetor; 1973–77 is located over pedal.

1. Loosen the switch mounting bolt.

2. Holding the throttle in wide open position (choke fully open), depress the detent switch plunger until it bottoms in the switch. Move the switch toward the throttle lever paddle until there is a clearance of 0.23 ± 0.01 in. (1969–72 models), 0.20 in. (1968 models with 396 or 427 engine) or 0.05 in. (1968 models with 307 or 327 engine) between the face of the lever paddle and the depressed detent switch plunger.

3. Tighten the switch mounting bolts.

Chapter 7

Drive Train

Driveline

DRIVESHAFT AND U-JOINTS

The driveshaft is a long steel tube which transmits engine power from the transmission to the rear axle assembly. It is connected to, and revolves with, the transmission output shaft (remember, the transmission shaft is connected to and revolves with the engine crankshaft) whenever the transmission is put into gear. With the transmission in Neutral, the driveshaft does not move. Located at each end of the driveshaft is a flexible joint which rotates with the shaft. These flexible joints, known as U-joints (universal joints) perform an important function. The rear axle assembly moves with the car. It moves up and down with every bump or dip in the road. The driveshaft by itself is a rigid tube incapable of bending. When combined with the flexing capabilities of the U-joints, however, it can do so. A slip joint is coupled to the front of the driveshaft by a universal joint. This U-joint allows the yoke (slip joint) to move up or down with the car. The yoke is a cylinder containing splines which slides over and meshes with the splines on the transmission output shaft. When the rear axle moves up and down, the yoke slides back and forth a small amount on the transmission shaft. Therefore, it combines with the U-joints in allowing the driveshaft to move with the movements of the car. The rear universal joint is secured to a companion flange which is attached to, and revolves with, the rear axle drive pinion.

A U-joint consists of a cross piece (trunnion) and, on each of the four ends, a dust seal and a series of needle bearings that fit into a bearing cup. Each U-joint connects one yoke with another and the bearings allow the joints to revolve within each yoke.

Two basic universal joints are used. The Dana or Cleveland type uses snapring bearing cap retainers. The Saginaw uses injection molded plastic to retain the bearing caps. On the Saginaw type there is a snap-ring groove in the bearing housing inboard of the yoke to hold the bearings in place. Disassembly of the later model U-joint requires the joint to be pressed from the yoke. This results in damage to the bearing cups and destruction of the nylon rings. Replacement kits include new bearing cups and snap-rings to replace the original nylon rings. These replacement rings must go inboard of the yoke in contrast to outboard mounting of the other models. Previous service to the Saginaw U-joints can be recognized by

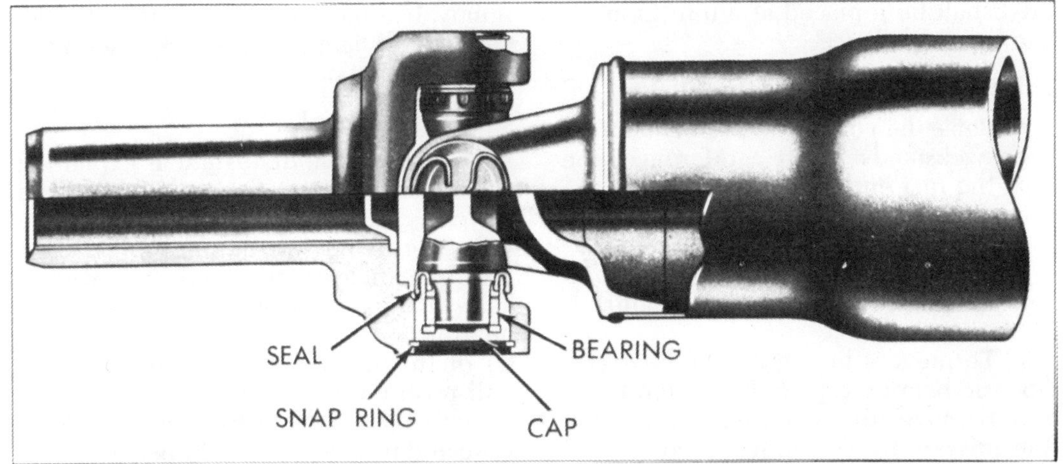

Cleveland type driveshaft

the presence of snap-rings inboard of the yoke.

Bad U-joints, requiring replacement, will produce a clunking sound when the car is put into gear. This is due to worn needle bearings or a scored trunnion end possibly caused by improper lubrication during assembly. Chevrolet U-joints require no periodic maintenance and therefore have no lubrication fittings. A clunking sound can also be produced by two other components. The Chevrolet three-speed automatic transmission has a rear seal that prevents the transmission from lubricating the front slip joint. All other transmissions allow a slight lubrication of this slip joint because they contain a different type of rear seal. If a driveline clunk should develop in a Chevrolet with a three-speed automatic, clean the slip joint and pack it with one tablespoon of chassis lube. A similar clunk can be the result of improper rear end gear lash but, due to its complexity, should be checked only after checking the more probable causes.

1971 and later station wagons and some other models are equipped with driveshafts which incorporate constant velocity U-joints. The driveshaft yokes on each end of the driveshaft contain two U-joints which are connected within the yoke by a centering ball. Factory installed U-joints do not have grooves for snap-rings and are retained in the yokes by injected plastic. This makes the joints non-repairable by conventional methods. Some aftermarket kits are available with screw-in bearing caps to repair this type of joint. It is recommended, however, that the

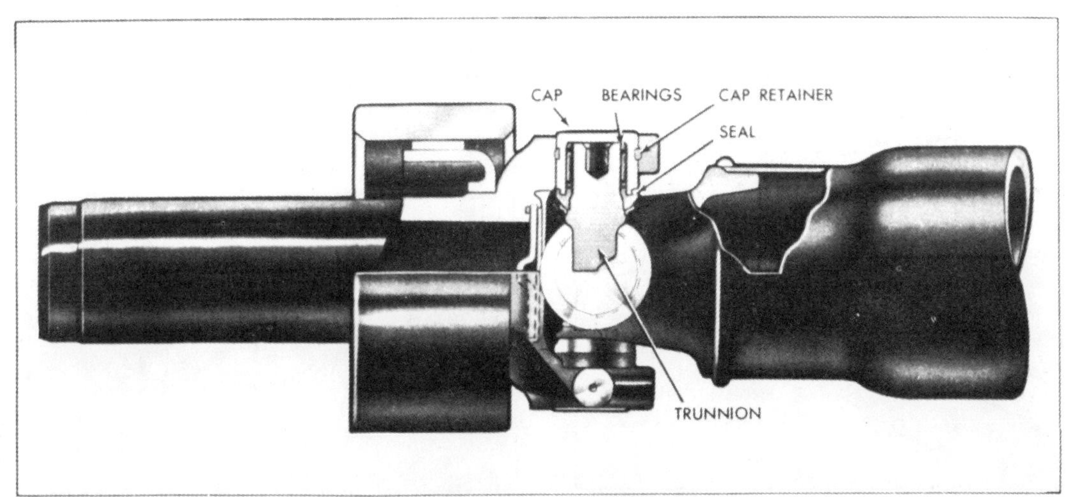

Saginaw type driveshaft

driveshaft be replaced as a unit to maintain correct balance.

Driveshaft Removal and Installation

1. Raise the vehicle and safely support it on jackstands. Paint a reference line from the rear end of the driveshaft to the companion flange so that they can be re-assembled in the same position.

2. Disconnect the rear universal joint by removing the U-bolts, flange bolts, or retaining straps.

3. To prevent loss of needle bearings, tape the bearing caps to the trunnion.

4. Remove the driveshaft from the transmission by sliding rearward.

NOTE: *Do not be alarmed by oil leakage at transmission output shaft. This oil is there to lubricate the splines of the front yoke.*

5. Check the yoke seal in the transmission case extension and replace it if necessary.

6. Position the driveshaft and insert the front yoke into the transmission so that the splines mesh with the splines of the transmission shaft.

7. Using reference marks made during removal, align the driveshaft with the companion flange and secure it with the U-bolts or retaining straps.

U-Joint Overhaul

1. Remove the driveshaft as explained above and remove the snap-rings from the ends of the bearing cup.

2. After removing the snap-rings, place the driveshaft on the floor and place a large diameter socket under one of the bearing cups. Using a hammer and a drift, tap on the bearing opposite this one. This will push the trunnion through the yoke enough to force the bearing cup out of the yoke and into the socket. Repeat this procedure for the other bearing cups. If a hammer doesn't loosen the cups, they will have to be pressed out.

NOTE: *A Saginaw design driveshaft secures its U-joints in a different manner than the conventional snap-rings of the Dana and Cleveland designs. Nylon material is injected through a small hole in the yoke and flows along a circular groove between the U-joint and the yoke thus creating a syn-*

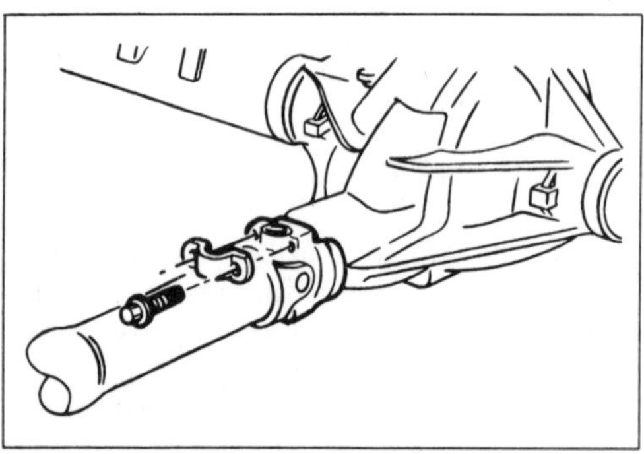

Strap-type driveshaft mounting

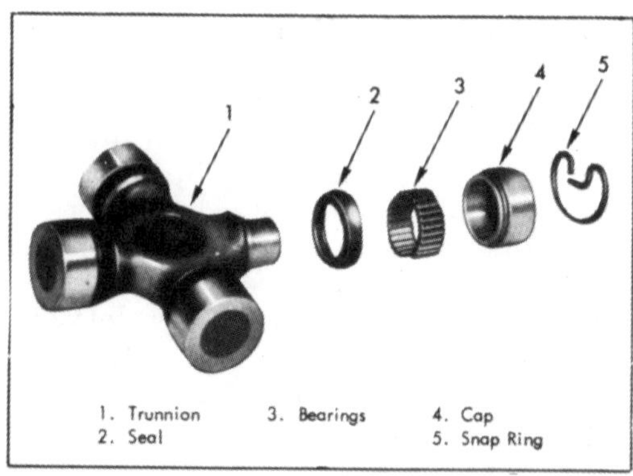

Cleveland universal joint

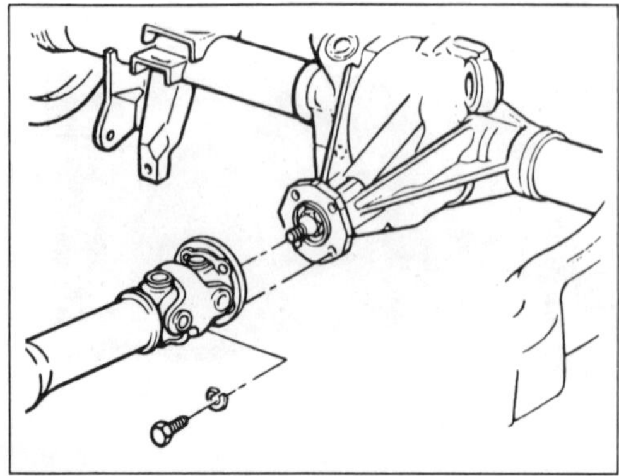

Flange-type driveshaft mounting

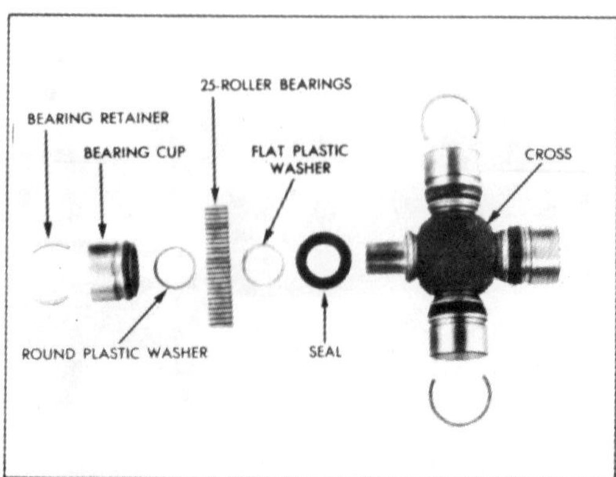

Saginaw universal joint

ethtic snap-ring. Disassembly of this Saginaw-type U-joint requires that the joint be pressed from the yoke. If a press is not available, it may be carefully hammered out using the same procedure (Step 2) as the Dana design although it may require more force to break the nylon ring. Either method, press or hammer, will damage the bearing cups and destroy the nylon rings. Replacement kits include new bearing cups and conventional metal snap-rings to replace the original nylon type rings.

3. Using solvent, thoroughly clean the entire U-joint assembly. Inspect for excessive wear in the yoke bores and on the four ends of the trunnion. The needle bearings should not be scored, broken, or loose in their cups. Bearing cups may suffer slight distortion during removal and should be replaced.

4. Pack the bearings with chassis lube (lithium base) and completely fill each trunnion end with the same lubricant.

5. Place new dust seals on trunnions with cavity of seal toward end of trunnion. Care must be taken to avoid distortion of the seal. A suitable size socket and a vise can be used to press on the seal.

6. Insert one bearing cup about ¼ of the way into the yoke and place the trunnion into yoke and bearing cup. Install another bearing cup and press both cups in and install the snap-rings. Snap-rings on the Dana and Cleveland shafts must go on the outside of the yoke while the Saginaw shaft requires that the rings go on the inside of the yoke. The gap in the Saginaw ring must face in toward the yoke. Once installed, the trunnion must move freely in yoke.

NOTE: *The Saginaw shaft uses two different size bearing cups at the differential end. The larger cups (the ones with the groove) fit into the driveshaft yoke.*

Rear Axle

AXLE SHAFT

Removal and Installation

Two types of axles are used on these models, the C and the non-C type. Axle shafts in the C type are retained by C-shaped locks, which fit grooves at the inner end of the shaft. Axle shafts in the non-C type are retained by the brake backing plate, which is bolted to the axle housing. Bearings in the C type axle consist of an outer race, bearing rollers, and a roller cage retained by snap-rings. The non-C type axle uses a unit roller bearing (inner race, rollers, and outer race), which is pressed onto the shaft up to a shoulder. When servicing C or non-C type axles, it is imperative to determine the axle type before attempting any service. Before attempting any service to the drive axle or axle shafts, remove the axle carrier cover and visually determine if the axle shafts are retained by C-shaped locks at the inner end, or by the brake backing plate at the outer end. If the shafts are *not* retained by C locks, proceed as follows.

NON-C TYPE

1. Remove the wheel, tire, and brake drum.

2. Remove the nuts which hold the retainer plate to the backing plate. Disconnect the brake line.

3. Remove the retainer and install the nuts fingertight to prevent the brake backing plate from being dislodged.

4. Pull out the axle shaft and bearing assembly, using a slide hammer.

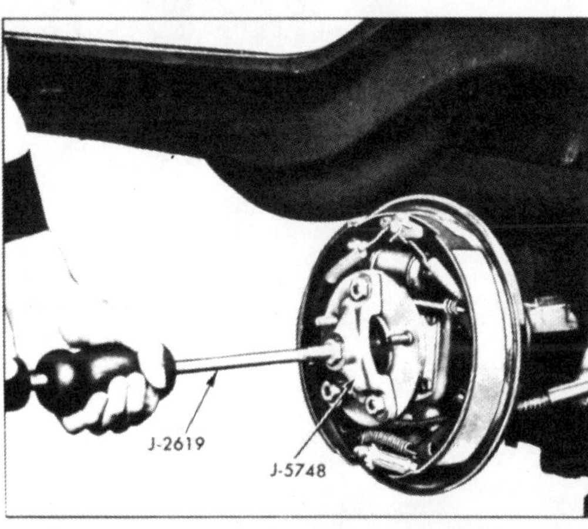

Removing axle shaft with slide hammer

5. Install the axle shaft into the housing. Turn it until the grooves mesh.

6. Install the retainer nuts.

7. Connect the brake line.

8. Install the brake drum, wheel, and tire.

9. Bleed the brakes.

C Type

1. Raise the vehicle and remove the wheels.

2. The differential cover has already been removed (see NOTE above). Remove the differential pinion shaft lockscrew and the differential pinion shaft.

3. Push the flanged end of the axle shaft toward the center of the vehicle and remove the C lock from the end of the shaft.

4. Remove the axle shaft from the housing, being careful not to damage the oil seal.

5. Install the axle into the housing.

6. Install the C lock to the shaft.

7. Install the differential pinion lockscrew.

8. Install the differential cover.

9. Install the wheels and lower the car to the ground.

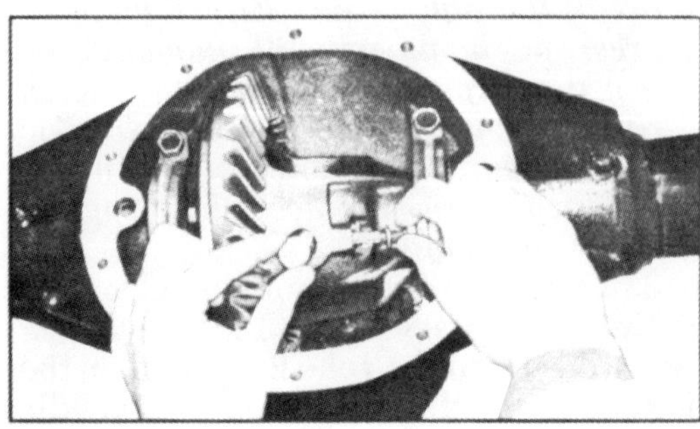

Removing pinion shaft on C-type axle

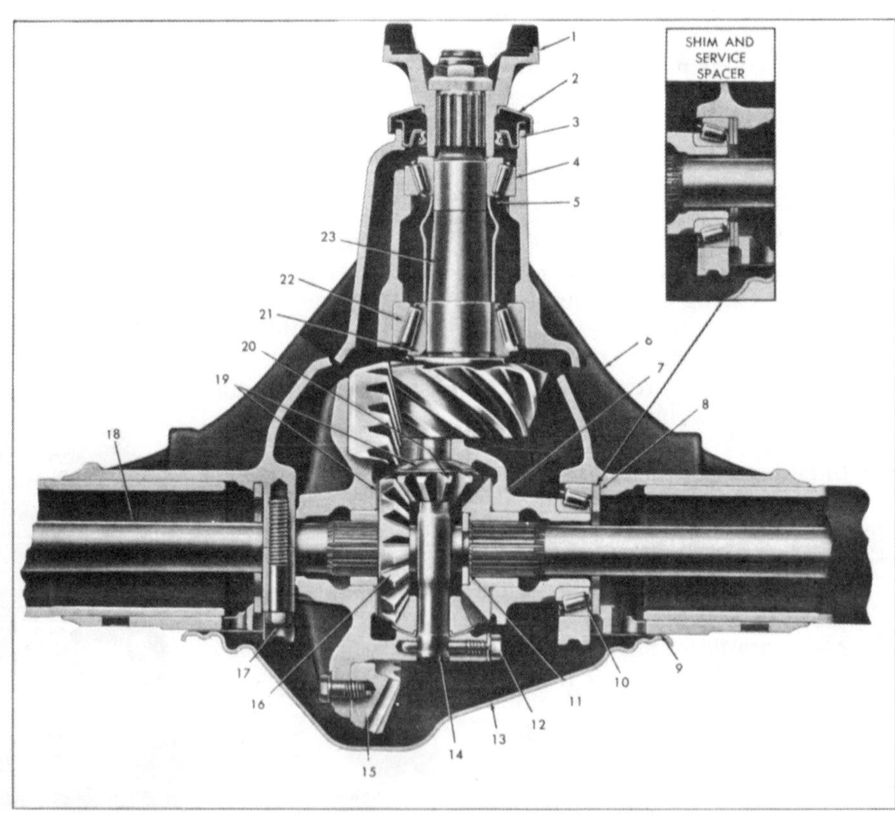

Rear axle cross-section

1. Companion flange	9. Gasket	17. Bearing cap
2. Deflector	10. Differential bearing	18. Axle shaft
3. Pinion oil seal	11. C-lock	19. Thrust washer
4. Pinion front bearing	12. Pinion shaft lockbolt	20. Differential pinion
5. Pinion bearing spacer	13. Cover	21. Shim
6. Differential carrier	14. Pinion shaft	22. Pinion rear bearing
7. Differential case	15. Ring gear	23. Drive pinion
8. Shim	16. Side gear	

Chapter 8

Suspension and Steering

Front Suspension

Front suspension is the conventional short-long control arm type. Springing is provided by coils located between the upper and lower control arms. A concentric shock absorber is mounted within each spring. The steering knuckle/spindle assembly pivots on an upper and lower ball joint. All models are equipped with an anti-roll bar, rubber mounted to the frame and connected to the frame by link bolts.

SHOCK ABSORBER

Removal and Installation

1. Remove the upper stem nut while holding the stem to keep it from turning.

2. Remove the two bolts holding the shock absorber to the lower control arm and pull the shock through the arm.

3. Extend the shock absorber and insert it up through the lower control arm. Make sure that the upper stem goes through the hole in the upper control arm frame bracket.

4. Install the grommet, retainer cup, and nut to the shock absorber upper stem.

5. Hold the shock absorber stem and tighten the upper nut to 8 ft lbs.

6. Install the lower control arm retaining bolts and tighten to 20 ft lbs.

SPRINGS

Removal and Installation

1968–70

1. Remove shock absorber upper stem retaining nut and grommet.

2. Support the car by the frame so that the control arms hang free. Remove the wheel assembly, shock absorber, stabilizer to lower control arm link, strut rod to

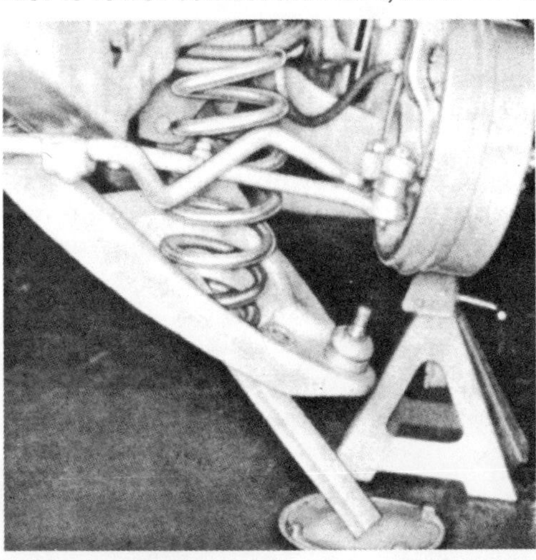

Coil spring removal

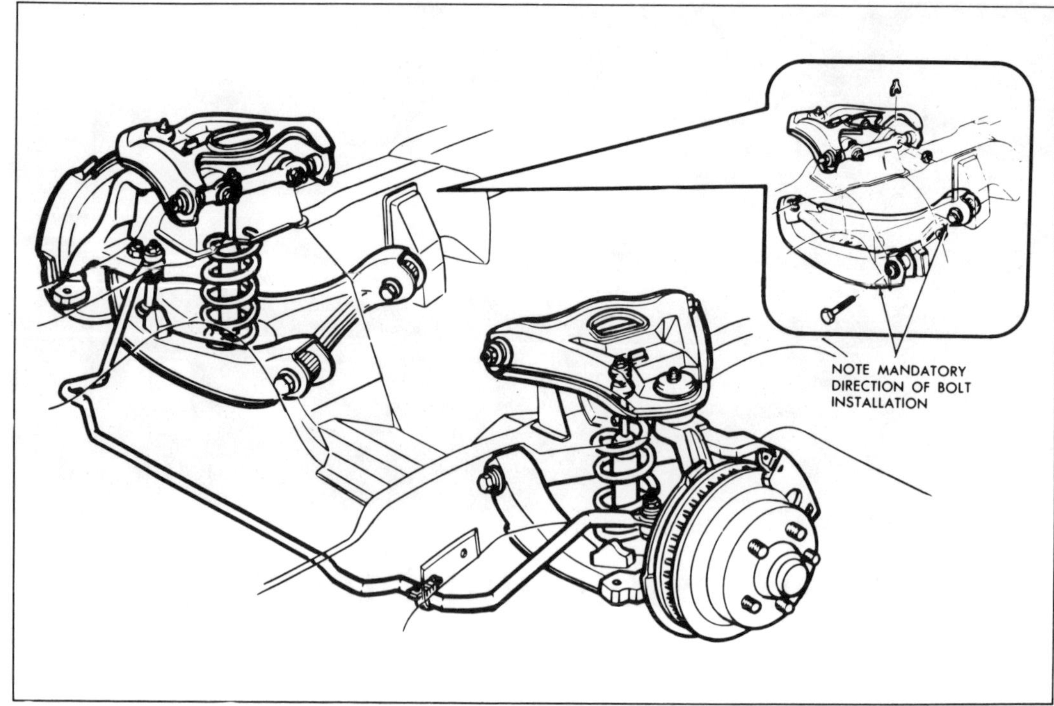

Front suspension

lower control arm attaching nuts, bolts and lockwashers, and the tie-rod end.

3. Scribe the position of the inner pivot camber adjusting cam bolt and then remove the nut, lock washer and outer cam.

4. Install a steel bar through the shock absorber mounting hole in the lower control arm so that the notch in the bar seats over the bottom spring coil and the bar extends inboard and under the inner bushing. Fit a 5 in. wood block between the bar and the lower arm inner support bushing.

5. With a floor jack, raise the end of the steel bar enough to remove tension from the inner pivot cam bolt. The bolt can then be removed.

6. Carefully lower the inner end of the control arm. Tension on the spring must be removed before the spring can be taken out of the car.

7. Remove the spring.

8. Install by reversing removal procedure.

1971 AND LATER

1. Raise car on hoist and remove nut, retainer and grommet from top of shock absorber. Support car so that control arms swing free.

2. Disconnect stabilizer bar from lower control arm and remove shock absorber.

3. Bolt spring remover tool (J-22944) to a suitable jack and place it under the lower control arm bushings so that the bushings seat in the grooves of the tool.

NOTE: *This tool is a cradle which, when fastened to a hydraulic jack, allows the lowering of the control arm and slow decompression of the spring. A similar tool can be fabricated in the shop. Always safety-chain the spring and control arm when using this method.*

4. Remove cross-shaft rear retaining nut and the two front retaining bolts.

5. Slowly release jack, swing control arm forward, then remove spring.

6. Install by reversing procedure above.

NOTE: *Chevrolet recommends this cradle spring removal tool for all models, beginning in 1971. Either of the other two methods may be used, depending on the availability of tools.*

BALL JOINT

Inspection

NOTE: *Before performing this inspection, make sure that the wheel bear-*

ings are adjusted correctly and that the A arm bushings are in good condition.

1. Jack the car up under the front lower control arm at the spring seat.

2. Raise the car until there is 1–2 in. of clearance under the wheel.

3. Insert a bar under the wheel and pry upward. If the wheel raises more than 1/8 in. the ball joints are worn. Determine if the upper or lower ball joint is worn by visual inspection while prying on the wheel.

NOTE: *Due to the distribution of forces on the suspension, the lower ball joint is usually the defective joint. Also, 1973 and later Chevrolets are equipped with wear indicators on the lower ball joint. As long as the wear indicator neck extends below the ball stud seat, replacement is unnecessary.*

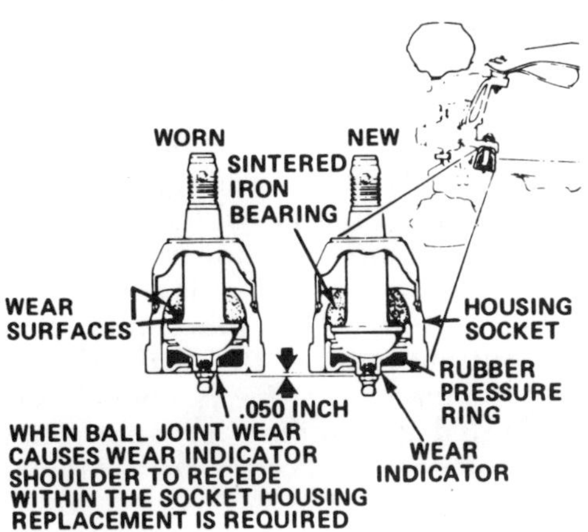

Ball joint wear indicator

Upper Ball Joint Removal and Installation

1. Raise the car on a hoist.

2. Remove the tire and wheel assembly.

3. Support the lower control arm with a jack.

4. Loosen the upper ball stud nut.

5. Install a ball joint remover tool and unseat the upper joint from the steering knuckle. Remove the upper stud nut and install a block of wood under the upper A-arm.

6. Chisel or grind off the ball joint mounting rivets.

7. Drill out the ball stud attaching holes to accept the service ball joint attaching bolts.

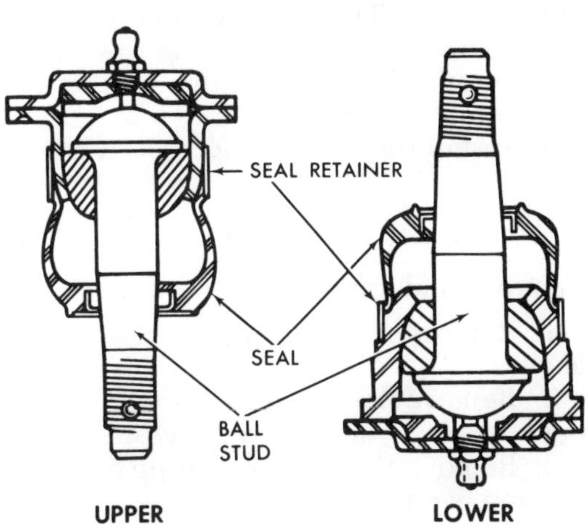

8. Install the ball joint with the nuts and bolts supplied with the new joint.

9. Install the lube fitting in the new joint.

10. Mate the upper control arm to the steering knuckle and install the ball stud through the knuckle boss.

11. Tighten the ball stud nut to 50 ft lbs plus whatever is necessary to align the cotter pin holes. Install the cotter pin.

12. Install the wheel and lower the vehicle.

Lower Ball Joint Removal and Installation

1. On pre-1971 models, raise the vehicle on a hoist and remove the wheel. On vehicles equipped with disc brakes, remove the caliper assembly.

2. Support the lower control arm with a jack.

3. Loosen the lower ball stud nut. Break the ball stud loose. Remove the ball stud nut.

4. Remove the ball stud from the steering knuckle.

5. The ball joint in 1968–70 models is attached with rivets which must be chiseled or ground off. Beginning with 1971 models, the ball joint is pressed in and must be pressed out.

6. Install the new ball joint, using the bolts supplied with the service ball joint (drill out the rivet holes to accommodate the mounting bolts) on 1968–70 models. The thick-headed bolt is installed on the forward side of the control arm. Press in the ball joint on 1971 and later models.

7. Install the ball stud in the steering knuckle boss. This may be done by raising the lower control arm with the jack.

8. Install the nut on the ball stud, tightening the 80–90 ft lbs.

9. Install the lube fitting.

LOWER CONTROL ARM

Removal and Installation

1. Remove the spring as described above.

2. Remove the ball stud from the steering knuckle as described above.

3. Remove the control arm pivot bolts and remove the control arm.

4. To install, reverse the above procedure.

UPPER CONTROL ARM

Removal and Installation

1. Raise the vehicle on a hoist.

2. Support the outer end of the lower control arm, with a jack.

3. Remove the wheel.

4. Separate the upper ball joint from the steering knuckle as described above under "Upper Ball Joint Removal and Installation."

5. Remove the control arm shaft to frame nuts.

NOTE: *Tape the shims together and identify them so that they can be installed in the positions from which they were removed.*

6. Remove the bolts which attach the control arm shaft to the frame and remove the control arm. Note the positions of the bolts.

7. Install in the reverse order of removal. Make sure that the shaft-to-frame bolts are installed in the same position they were in before removal and that the shims are in their original positions. Tighten the shaft-to-frame bolts to 85 ft lbs. The control arm shaft nuts are torqued to 60 ft lbs.

FRONT END ALIGNMENT

Caster and Camber

1968–70

On 1968–70 models, caster is adjusted by lengthening or shortening the struts at the frame crossmember. Camber is adjusted by loosening the lower control arm pivot bolt and rotating the eccentrics.

1971 AND LATER

Adjustment of caster and camber is carried out by adding or subtracting shims between the upper control arm shaft and the frame bracket. Camber is adjusted by adding or subtracting shims from both the front and rear of the shaft. Adding shims decreases positive camber. Caster is adjusted by adding or subtracting shims from one end of the shaft. Moving

Wheel Alignment Specifications

	CASTER		CAMBER			
Year	Range (deg)	Pref Setting (deg)	Range (deg)	Pref Setting (deg)	Toe-in (in.)	Steering Axis Inclin
'68–'69	¼P to 1¼P	¼P	¼N to ¾P	¼P	⅛ to ¼	7 to 8
'70	¼P to 1¼P	¼P	¼N to ¾P	¼P	⅛ to ¼	7 to 8
'71	1½N to ½N	1N	0 to 1P	½P	⅛ to ¼	9½ to 10½
'72	½P to 1½P	1P	0 to 1P	½P	³⁄₁₆ to ⁵⁄₁₆	9½ to 10½
'73	0 to 2P	1P	¼P to 1¾P①	1P	¹⁄₁₆N to ³⁄₁₆P	10½
'74	½–1½P	1P	½–1½P①	1P②	¹⁄₁₆ to ³⁄₁₆	9½
'75–'76	½P–2½P	1½P	½P–1½P①	1P②	¹⁄₁₆ to ³⁄₁₆	9⁷⁄₆₄
'77	2½P–3½P	3P	¼P–1¼P	¾P	¼P	9⁷⁄₆₄

① Left wheel given, right wheel is ¼N to 1¼P, preferred ½P
② Left wheel given, right wheel is ½P
N Negative   P Positive

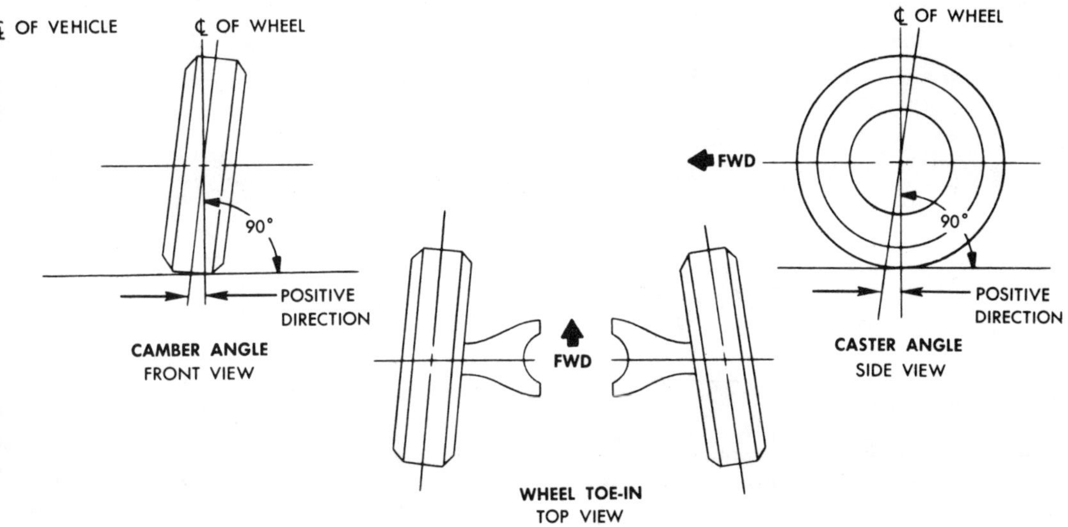

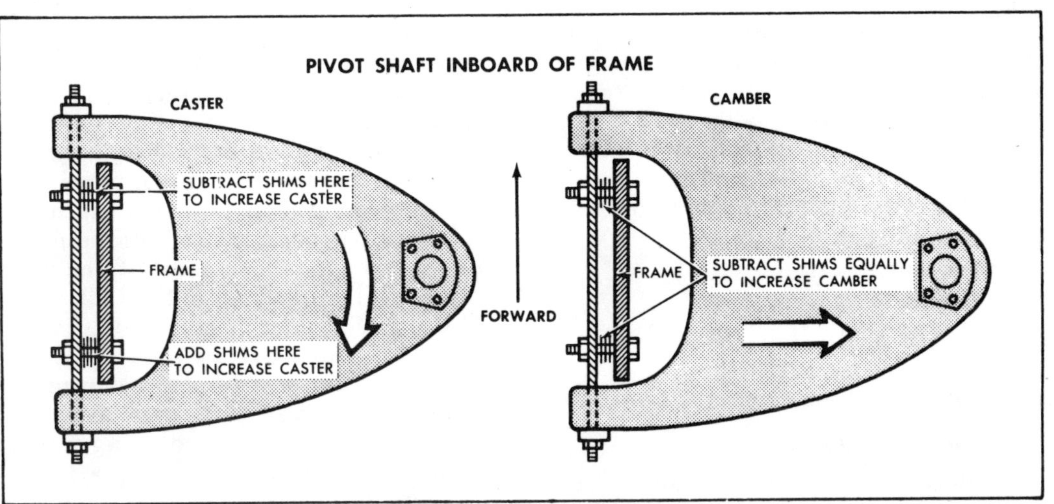

Caster and camber adjustment

one shim to the front bolt from the rear bolt will decrease positive caster. To adjust, loosen the shaft-to-frame nuts and add or subtract shims as necessary. Torque the nuts to 55 ft lbs when the adjustment is final. At least two bolt threads should be protruding from the shim pack. The difference between the front and rear shim pack should never exceed 2/5 in.

Toe-in

Toe-in is adjusted after the caster and camber adjustments are carried out. Adjust the toe-in by loosening the clamps on the tie-rod sleeves, and turning the sleeves an equal amount in the opposite direction, to maintain wheel spoke alignment while adjusting.

Rear Suspension

The Chevrolet uses a coil sprung Salisbury axle located by two trailing arms on each side, except the 1971–76 station wagon which has semi-elliptical leaf springs.

SHOCK ABSORBER

Removal and Installation

1. Jack the car to a convenient working height.
2. If the car is equipped with superlift shock absorbers, disconnect the air line.
3. Remove the two retaining bolts from the upper mounting bracket.

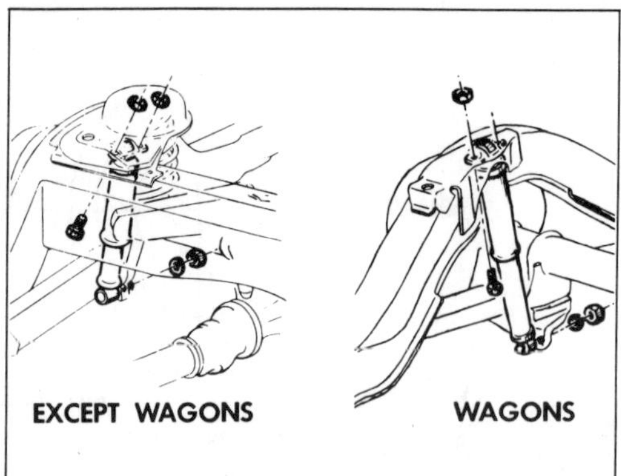

Shock absorber mounting

4. Hold the hex on the bottom stud and disconnect the lower mounting. Remove the shock absorber.

5. Install the top two bolts handtight.

6. Install the lower stud into the axle bracket and install the lockwasher and nut hand-tight.

7. Torque the upper bolts to 12 ft lbs.

8. While holding the hex stud, torque the nut to 65 ft lbs.

9. Attach the air line, if so equipped, and lower the car.

COIL TYPE REAR SPRINGS

ALL COUPES, SEDANS and 1977 WAGON

Removal and Installation

1. Raise rear of vehicle and place jackstands under frame. Support weight of vehicle at rear axle housing separately from above frame position.

2. Remove both rear wheels.

3. With car supported as in Step 1, and springs compressed by weight of vehicle:

a. Disconnect both rear shocks from anchor pin lower connection, then on '77 models, disconnect the brake hy-

draulic line at the junction block located on the axle housing.

b. Loosen the upper control arm(s) rear pivot bolt (do not remove the nut).

c. Loosen both left and right lower control arm rear attachment (do not disconnect from axle brackets).

d. Remove rear suspension tie rod from stud on axle tube.

4. Slightly loosen the nut on the bolt that retains the spring and seat to control arm at lower seat of both rear springs. When bolt has been backed off the maximum distance, all threads of the nut should still be engaged on the bolt.

CAUTION: *Under no condition should the nut, at this time, be removed from the bolt in the seat of either spring.*

5. Slowly lower the rear axle assembly, allowing the axle to swing down, carrying the springs out of the upper seat. This provides access for spring removal.

6. Remove the lower seat attaching parts from each spring, then remove springs from vehicle.

7. Position springs in upper seat and install lower seat parts on control arm. Install nut of spring retaining bolt finger-tight.

NOTE: *Omit lockwasher under the special high carbon bolt, so that sufficient threads will be available to start the nut. Lockwashers will be installed later.*

8. Alternately raise the axle slightly and retighten the nut on each spring lower seat bolt. Continue in until the weight is fully supported on the jack or lift. With spring now completely compressed to approximate curb position, completely position the springs in the lower seats by torquing the nut on the lower seat bolt.

9. Reconnect shock absorbers, torque

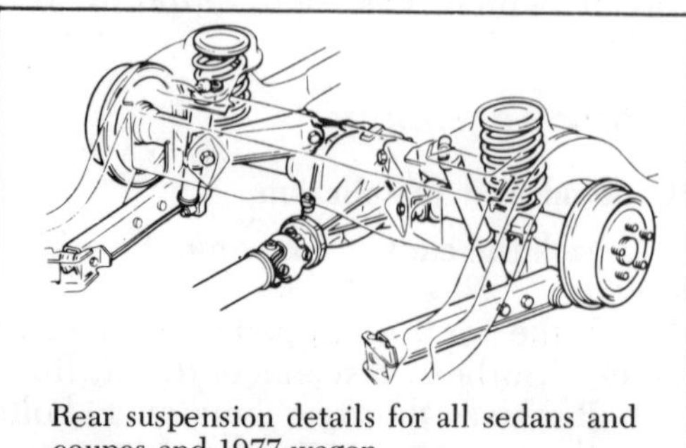

Rear suspension details for all sedans and coupes and 1977 wagon

rear attachment of upper and lower control arms, and reconnect the axle tie-rod.

10. While still jacked under axle, remove the nut from the lower seat bolt of one rear spring and install lockwasher and replace nut and tighten. Similarly install lockwasher at other spring.

11. On '77 models, connect the brake hydraulic line and bleed the brakes; then on all models, install the rear wheels and lower the car.

LEAF SPRING (1971–76 STATION WAGON)

Removal and Installation

1. Raise the vehicle on a hoist and place an adjustable jack under the axle.

2. Raise the axle until all tension is relieved from the spring.

3. Disconnect the shock absorber from the spring retainer plate.

4. Remove the upper shackle retaining bolt, then the front spring eye bolt.

5. Remove the spring/axle U-bolts, lower plate, spring pads, and spring.

6. Remove the shackle from the spring.

7. Before installing the spring, install the shackle on the rearward end.

8. Replace the upper cushion on the spring, then insert the front of the spring into the frame and attach the rear shackle, leaving the bolt loose.

9. Install the lower spring pad and retainer plate, tightening the U-bolt nuts to 40 ft lbs.

10. Tighten the rear shackle bolts to 80 ft lbs.

11. Tighten the front eye bolt to 115 ft lbs.

12. Attach the shock absorber to spring retainer plate, tightening to 65 ft lbs.

13. Remove the jack and lower the vehicle.

Steering

Manual steering gear on the Chevrolet is of the recirculating ball type. Relay-type steering linkage is used on all models, with a pitman arm connected to one end of a relay rod and a frame-mounted idler arm at the other end. Two tie-rods assemblies connect the relay rod to the

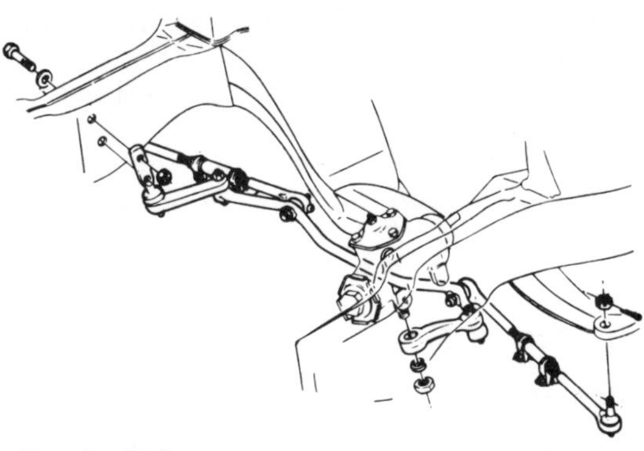

Steering linkage

steering arms. The tie-rod ends are threaded into sleeves to provide adjustment.

Chevrolet power steering is the integral-gear type. The only external hydraulic lines on this system are the pressure and return hoses to the pump.

TIE-ROD

Removal and Installation

1. Remove the cotter pins and nuts from the tie-rod end studs.

2. Tap on the steering arm near the tie-rod end (use another hammer as backing) and pull down on the tie-rod, if necessary, to free it.

3. Remove the inner stud in the same manner as the outer.

4. Loosen the clamp bolts and unscrew the ends if they are being replaced.

5. Lubricate the tie-rod end threads with chassis grease if they were removed. Install each end assembly an equal distance from the sleeve.

6. Ensure that the tie-rod end stud threads and nut are clean. Install new seals and install the studs into the steering arms and relay rod.

7. Install the stud nuts. Tighten the

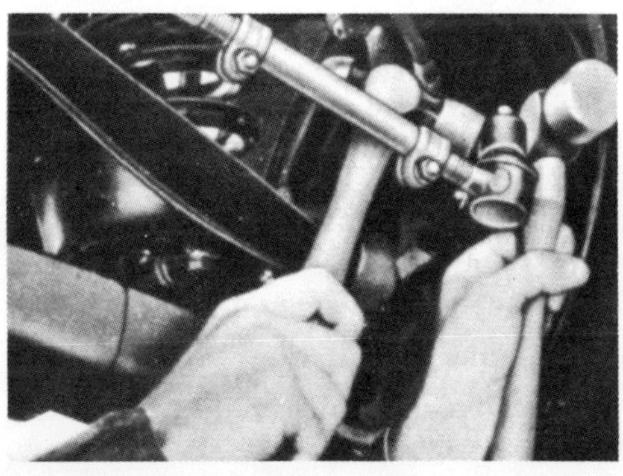

Freeing the tie-rod end

outer end nut to 35 ft lbs and the inner nut to 60 ft lbs.

8. Adjust the toe-in as described in the "Front End Alignment" section.

NOTE: *Before tightening the sleeve clamps, ensure that the clamps are positioned so that the adjusting sleeve slot is covered by the clamp.*

IDLER ARM

Removal and Installation

1. Remove the idler arm-to-frame nut, washer, and bolt.

2. Remove the cotter pin and nut from the idler arm-to-relay rod ball end stud.

3. Tap the relay rod firmly with a hammer, using another heavy hammer as backing on the opposite side of the relay rod to remove the relay rod from the idler arm.

4. Remove the idler arm.

5. To install the idler arm, install the seal on the idler arm stud; position the stud up through the frame, and install the lockwasher and nut. Tighten the nut to 45 ft lbs.

6. Position the relay rod on the idler arm. Ensure that the seal is on the stud. Install the nut and tighten to 40 ft lbs. Install a cotter pin.

RELAY ROD

Removal and Installation

1. Remove the inner tie-rod ends from the relay rod as outlined under "Tie-Rod Removal and Installation."

2. Remove the relay rod stud nut and cotter pin from the pitman arm. Free the relay rod from the pitman arm, moving the steering linkage if necessary. Repeat this operation to remove the relay rod from the idler arm and remove the relay rod from the car.

3. Install the relay rod on the idler arm. Tighten the nut to 40 ft lbs.

4. Raise the relay and install it on the pitman arm. Tighten the nut to 45 ft lbs.

5. Adjust the toe-in as described in the "Front End Alignment" section.

PITMAN ARM

Removal and Installation

1. Remove the pitman arm stud nut and cotter pin.

2. Tap the relay rod off the pitman arm, using another hammer as backing. Pull the relay rod off the pitman arm stud.

3. Remove the pitman arm nut and mark the arm-to-shaft relationship.

4. Remove the pitman arm using a puller.

5. Install the pitman arm on the shaft, aligning the previously made marks. Install the pitman shaft nut and tighten it to 180 ft lbs.

6. Install the relay rod on the pitman arm. Tighten the nut to 45 ft lbs and install a cotter pin.

POWER STEERING PUMP

Removal and Installation

1. Remove the hoses at the pump and tape the openings shut to prevent contamination. Position the disconnected lines in a raised position to prevent leakage.

2. Remove the pump belt.

3. Loosen the retaining bolts and any braces, and remove the pump.

4. Install the pump on the engine with the retaining bolts hand-tight.

5. Connect and tighten the hose fittings.

6. Refill the pump and bleed by turning the pulley counterclockwise (viewed from the front). Stop the bleeding when air bubbles no longer appear.

7. Install the pump belt on the pulley and adjust the tension.

STEERING WHEEL

Removal and Installation

CAUTION: *Disconnect the battery ground cable before removing the steering wheel. When installing a steering wheel, always make sure that the turn signal lever is in the neutral position.*

1968

1. Pry out the center cap and retainer.

2. Remove the three receiving cup screws and the cup, belleville spring, bushing, and pivot ring.

3. Remove the steering wheel nut and washer.

4. Mark the wheel-to-shaft relationship, and then remove the wheel with a puller.

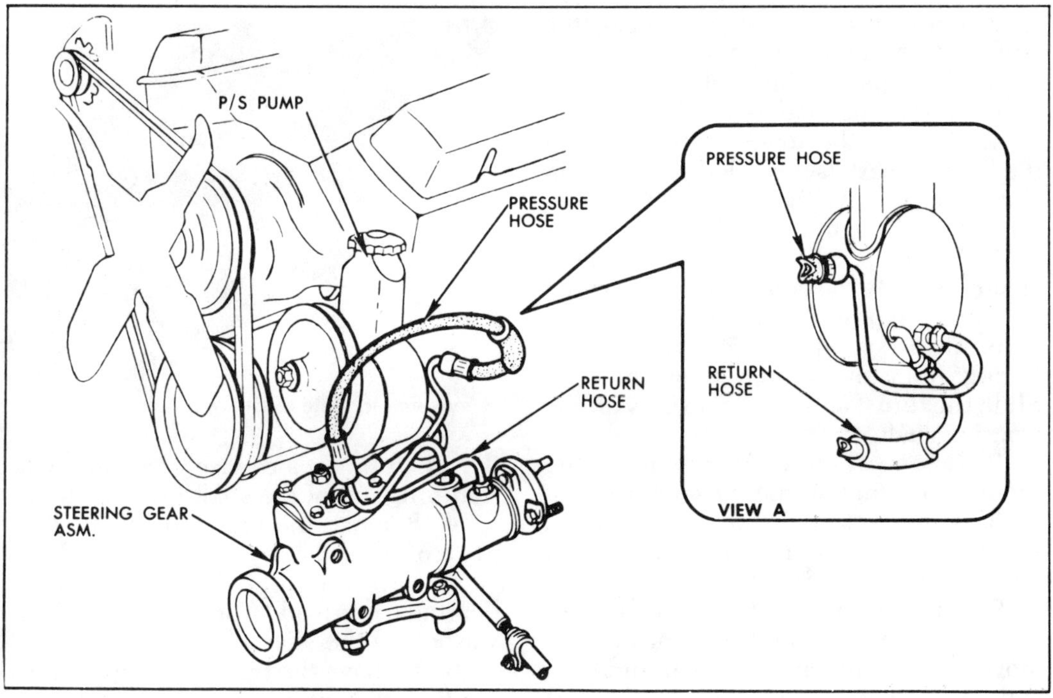

Typical power steering pump mounting

5. Install the wheel on the shaft, aligning the previously made marks. Tighten the nut to 35 ft lbs.

6. Install the belleville, spring (dished side up), pivot ring, bushing, and receiving cup. Install the center cap and reconnect the battery.

NOTE: *Removal of the 1970 padded steering wheel is similar to the above.*

1969 DELUXE WHEEL AND STANDARD WHEEL 1970 AND LATER

1. Remove the four trim retaining screws from behind the wheel.

2. Lift the trim off and pull the horn wires from the turn signal cancelling cam.

3. Remove the steering wheel nut.

4. Mark the wheel-to-shaft relationship, and then remove the wheel with a puller.

5. Install the wheel on the shaft, aligning the previously made marks. Tighten the nut to 30 ft lbs.

6. Insert the horn wires into the cancelling cam.

7. Install the center trim and reconnect the battery cable.

NOTE: *The 1968–69 simulated wood*

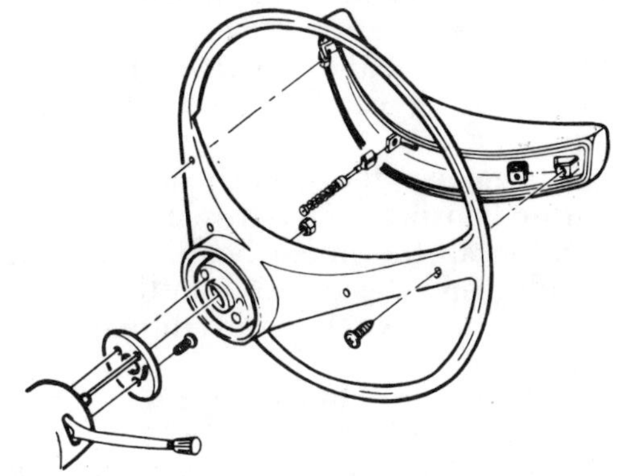

1969 deluxe steering wheel and 1970–76 standard wheel

wheel and the 1973 cushioned rim wheel do not require pulling for removal. Pry off the center cap and horn contact assembly. The wheel is held to the hub by phillips screws. Reverse the disassembly procedure to install the wheel.

TURN SIGNAL SWITCH

Removal and Installation

1968

1. Remove the steering wheel as outlined above.

2. On column-shift cars, remove the shift lever retaining pin and the lever.

3. Disconnect the column wiring harness from the chassis harness.

4. Remove the lower trim plate and the upper mast jacket clamp. On automatic cars, remove the indicator retaining screw and the pointer.

5. Remove the wiring harness clamps, sliding the components up on the column to expose the upper clamp.

6. Using snap-ring pliers, remove the C-ring from the upper steering shaft. Slide the thrust and wave washers off the steering shaft.

7. Loosen, but do not remove, the three turn signal mounting screws.

8. Turn the switch counterclockwise. Pull the switch out of the mast jacket and let it hang by its wiring.

9. Support the column, and then remove the upper mounting bracket. Remove the wiring harness cover and clip, and then reinstall the upper bracket hand-tight.

10. Remove the shift lever bowl from the mast jacket and disconnect it from the wiring harness.

11. Remove the switch retaining screws, being careful not to lose the springs.

12. Remove the switch and upper bearing housing from the switch cover.

13. Install the upper bearing housing assembly and the switch into the cover, working the switch wires through the cover.

14. Install the remaining components in a reverse order of removal.

NOTE: *The procedure for the tilt wheel is similar, with the exceptions that turn signal cover removal requires a slide hammer and special attachment and that the switch wiring connector must be cut.*

1969–76

1. Remove the steering wheel as previously outlined.

2. Loosen the three cover screws and lift the cover off the shaft (pry cover off in '76).

3. Position the special lockplate compressing tool (J-23131 1969–70 or J-23653 1971–75) on the end of the steering shaft and compress the lockplate by turning

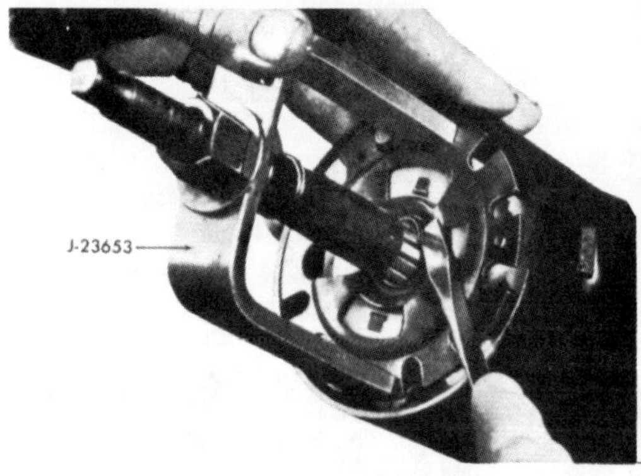

Removing lockplate retaining ring

the shaft nut clockwise. Pry the wire snap-ring out of the shaft groove.

4. Remove the tool and lift the lockplate off the shaft.

5. Slip the cancelling cam, upper bearing pre-load spring, and thrust washer off the shaft.

6. Remove the turn signal lever. Push the flasher knob in and unscrew it.

7. Pull the switch connector out of the mast jacket and tape the upper part to facilitate switch removal. On tilt wheels, place the turn signal and shifter housing in Low position and remove the harness cover.

8. Remove the three switch mounting screws. Remove the switch by pulling it straight up while guiding the wiring harness cover through the column.

9. Install the replacement switch by working the connector and cover down through the housing and under the bracket. On tilt models, the connector is worked down through the housing, under the bracket, and then the cover is installed on the harness.

10. Install the switch mounting screws and the connector on the mast jacket bracket. Install the column-to-dash trim plate.

11. Install the flasher knob and the turn signal lever.

12. With the turn signal lever in neutral and the flasher knob out, slide the thrust washer, upper bearing pre-load spring, and cancelling cam onto the shaft.

13. Position the lockplate on the shaft and press it down until a new snap-ring can be inserted in the shaft groove.

14. Install the cover and the steering wheel.

PITMAN SHAFT SEAL

Removal and Installation

The pitman shaft seal can be replaced without removing the steering gear from the vehicle as follows:

1. Place the steering wheel in center position.

2. Remove the bolts which secure the gear side housing, then remove the pitman shaft and side cover as a unit.

3. Remove the pitman shaft seal from the steering gear body.

4. Grease the new seal and drive it into place with a suitable socket.

5. Install the side cover and pitman shaft assembly, being careful not to damage the new seal and using a new cover gasket.

6. Install the side cover retaining bolts.

STEERING KNUCKLE

Removal and Installation

1. Raise the vehicle on a hoist.

2. Support the lower control arm with a jack.

3. Remove the wheel.

4. Remove the brake drum and backing plate or the caliper, disc and splash shield. Do not disconnect the brake hydraulic line and do not let the backing plate or caliper hang by the hydraulic line.

5. Remove the upper and lower ball studs from the steering knuckle as described in "Ball Joint Removal and Installation."

6. Install in the reverse order of removal, referring to "Ball Joint Removal and Installation" if necessary.

BLEEDING POWER STEERING SYSTEM

1. Fill the fluid reservoir.

2. Let the fluid stand undisturbed for two minutes, then crank the engine for about two seconds. Refill reservoir if necessary.

3. Repeat Steps 1 and 2 above until the fluid level remains constant after cranking the engine.

4. Raise the front of the car until the wheels are off the ground, then start the engine. Increase the engine speed to about 1,500 rpm.

5. Turn the wheels to the left and right, checking the fluid level and refilling if necessary.

IGNITION SWITCH

Removal and Installation

1969–76

The switch is located inside the channel section of the brake pedal support and is completely inaccessible without first lowering the steering column. The switch is actuated by a rod and rack assembly. A gear on the end of the lock cylinder engages the toothed upper end of the rod.

1. Remove or lower the steering column. If steering column is lowered, be sure to properly support it.

2. Put the switch in "Lock" position. With the cylinder removed, the rod is in "Lock" position when it is in the next to the uppermost detent.

3. Remove the two switch screws and remove the switch assembly.

4. Before installing, place the new switch in "Lock" position and make sure that the lock cylinder and actuating rod are in "Lock" position (second detent from the top).

5. Install the activating rod into the switch and assemble the switch on the column. Tighten the mounting screws. Use only the specified screws since overlength screws could impair the collapsibility of the column.

6. Reinstall the steering column.

LOCK CYLINDER
REMOVAL AND INSTALLATION

1. Remove steering wheel and directional signal switch.

2. Place lock cylinder in Lock position up to 1970, Run position starting 1971.

CAUTION: *Do not remove the ignition key buzzer*

3. Insert a small screwdriver into the turn signal housing slot. Keeping the screwdriver to the right-side of the slot, break the housing flash loose and depress the spring latch at the lower end of the lock cylinder. Remove the lock cylinder.

NOTE: *Considerable force may be necessary to break this casting flash, but be careful not to damage any other parts. When ordering a new lock cylin-*

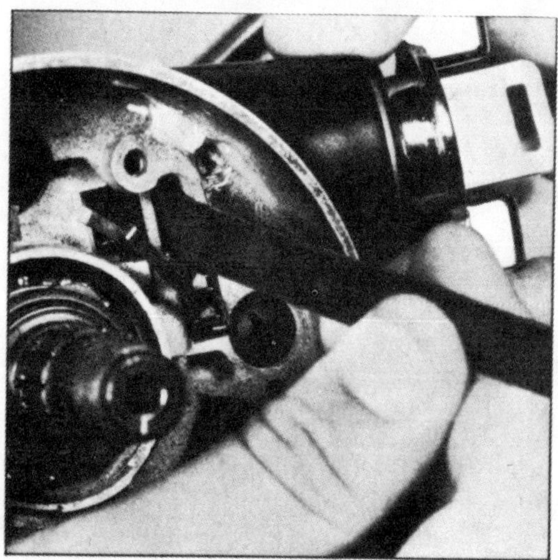

Removing lock cylinder

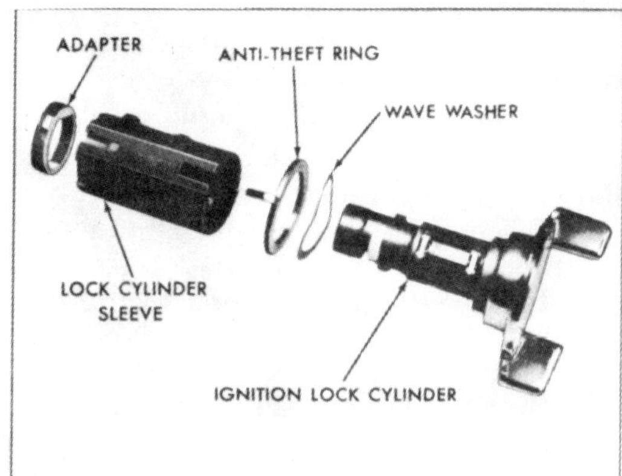

Exploded view of lock cylinder

der, specify a cylinder assembly. This will save assembling the cylinder, washer, sleeve and adapter.

4. To install, hold the lock cylinder sleeve and rotate the knob clockwise against the stop. Insert the cylinder into the housing, aligning the key and keyway. Hold a 0.070 in. drill between the lock bezel and housing. Rotate the cylinder counterclockwise, maintaining a light pressure until the drive section of the cylinder mates with the sector. Push in until the snap-ring pops into the grooves. Remove drill. Check cylinder operation.

CAUTION: *The drill prevents forcing the lock cylinder inward beyond its normal position. The buzzer switch and spring latch can hold the lock cylinder in too far. Complete disassembly of the upper bearing housing is necessary to release an improperly installed lock cylinder.*

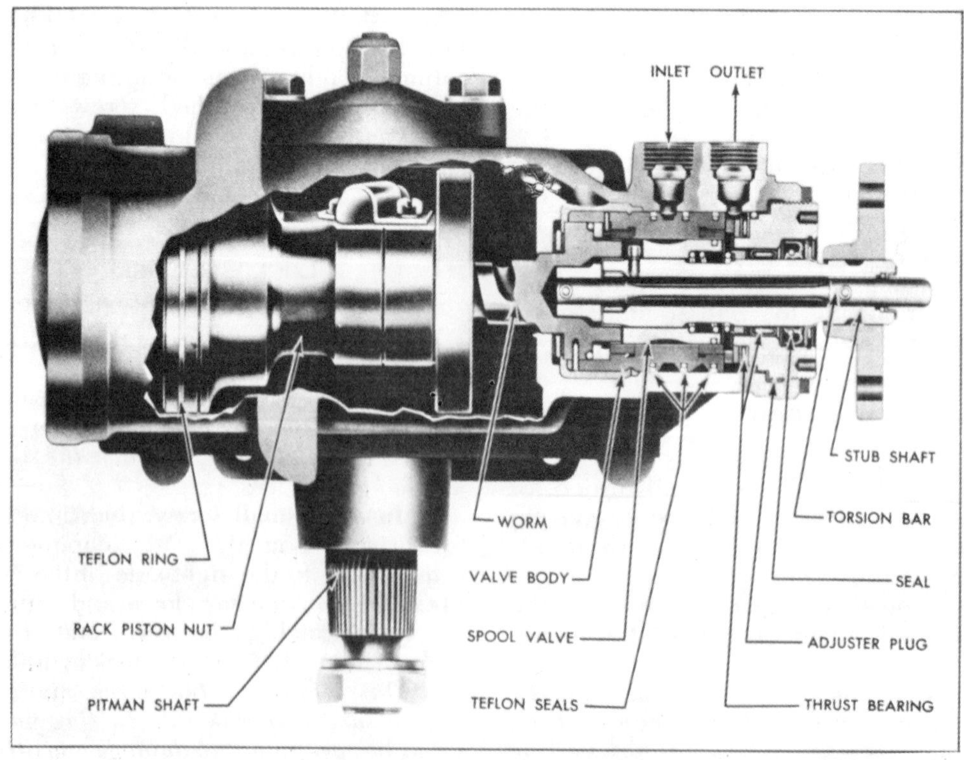

Power steering gearbox cross-section

Chapter 9

Brakes

Four wheel drum brakes were standard equipment from 1968 through 1970; front disc brakes being an option. The optional front disc brakes available in 1968 were a four-piston, fixed caliper design. The optional front disc brakes for 1969–70 and the standard disc brakes from 1971 through 1977 are a single-piston, sliding caliper type. The drum brakes used on the front and rear of 1968–70 models and the rear of all 1971–77 models are basically the same—a single pivot, two-piston wheel cylinder design. All brakes used on Chevrolets, whether drum or disc, are self-adjusting.

Hydraulic System

MASTER CYLINDER

Removal and Installation

NOTE: *Clean any master cylinder parts in alcohol or brake fluid. Never use mineral-based cleaning solvents such as gasoline, kerosene, carbon-tetrachloride, acetone, or paint thinner as these will destroy rubber parts.*

1. Using a clean cloth, wipe the master cylinder and its lines to remove excess dirt and then place cloths under the unit to absorb spilled fluid.

2. Remove the hydraulic lines from the master cylinder and plug the outlets to prevent the entrance of foreign material.

3. Disconnect the brake pushrod from the brake pedal.

4. Remove the two attaching nuts and remove the master cylinder from the fire wall or the brake booster.

5. Connect the pushrod to the brake pedal with the pin and retainer.

6. Connect the brake lines and fill the master cylinder reservoirs to the proper levels.

7. Bleed the brake system as outlined in this Section.

8. If necessary, adjust the brake pedal free-play.

Overhaul

In most years, there are two sources for master cylinders, Delco-Moraine and Bendix. The Bendix unit can readily be identified by the secondary stop bolt on the bottom, which is not present on the Delco-Moraine unit. Master cylinders should only be replaced with cylinders bearing the same code letters. The identification code is stamped on the end of the master cylinder. Secondary pistons are also coded by rings or grooves on the shank or center section of the piston, and should only be replaced with pistons having the same code. The primary pis-

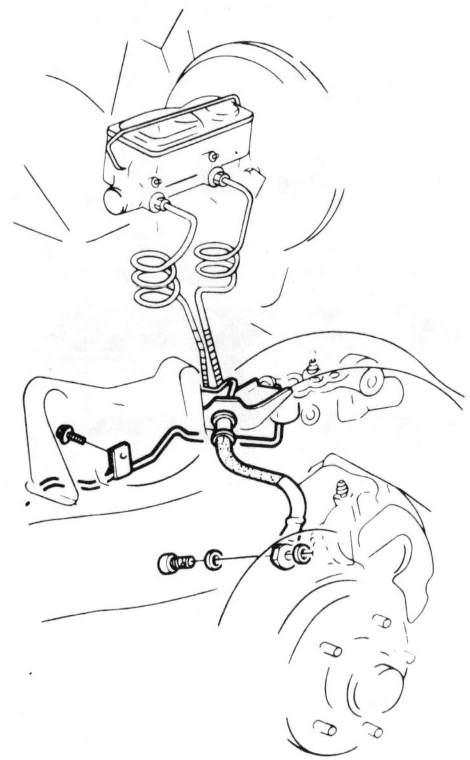

Master cylinder mounting

tons also are of two types. One has a deep socket for the pushrod and the other has a very shallow socket. Be sure to replace pistons with identical parts. Failure to do this could result in a malfunction of the master cylinder.

1. Remove the secondary piston stop screw (if equipped) which is located at the bottom of the master cylinder front reservoir.

2. Position the master cylinder in a vise covering the jaws with cloth to prevent damage. (Do not tighten the vise too tightly.)

3. Remove the lockring from the inside of the piston bore. Once this is done, the primary piston assembly may be removed.

4. The secondary piston, piston spring, and the retainer may be removed by blowing compressed air through the stop screw hole. If compressed air is not available, the piston may be removed with a small piece of wire. Bend the wire ¼ in. from the end into a right angle. Hook this end to the edge of the secondary piston and pull it from the bore. The brass insert should not be removed unless it is being replaced.

5. Inspect the piston bore for corrosion or other obstructions. Make certain that the outer ports are clean and the fluid reservoirs are free of foreign matter. Check the by-pass and the compensating ports to see if they are clogged.

6. Remove the primary seal, seal protector, and secondary seals from the secondary piston.

Clean all parts in denatured alcohol or brake fluid. Use a soft brush to clean metal parts and compressed air to dry all parts. If corrosion is found inside the housing, either a crocus cloth or fine emery paper can be used to remove these deposits. Remember to wash all parts after this cleaning. Be sure to keep the parts clean until assembly. If there is any doubt of cleanliness, wash the part again. All rubber parts should be clean and free of fluid. Check each rubber part for cuts, nicks, or other damage. If there is any doubt as to the condition of any rubber part, it is best to replace it.

NOTE: *Since there are differences between master cylinders, it is important that the assemblies are identified correctly. There is a two-letter metal stamp located at the end of the master cylinder. The stamp indicates the displacement capabilities of the particular master cylinder. If the master cylinder is replaced, it must be replaced with a cylinder with the same markings.*

7. Install the new secondary piston assembly.

NOTE: *The seal which is nearest the flat end has its lips facing toward the*

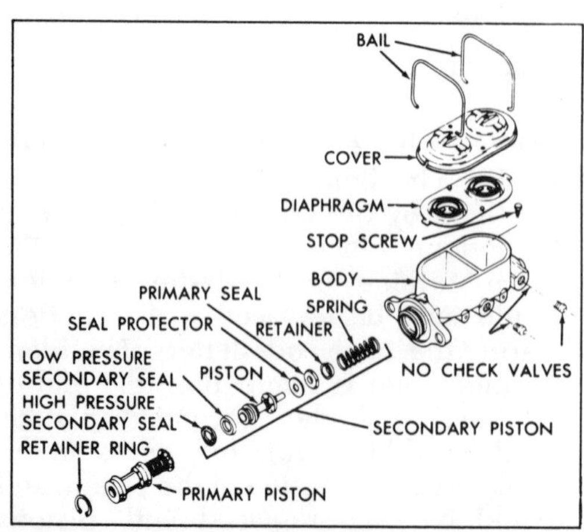

Exploded view of master cylinder

flat end. On Delco units, the seal in the second groove has its lips facing toward the compensating holes of the secondary piston. On Bendix units, the seal is an O-ring.

8. Install the new primary seal and seal protector over the end of the secondary piston opposite the secondary seals. It should be positioned so that the flat side of the seal seats against the flange of the piston with the compensating holes.

9. Install the complete primary piston assembly included in every repair kit.

10. Coat the master cylinder bore and the primary and secondary seals with brake fluid. Position the secondary seal spring retainer into the secondary piston spring.

11. Place the retainer and spring over the end of the secondary piston so that the retainer is placed inside the lips of the primary seal.

12. Seat the secondary piston. It may be necessary to manipulate the piston to get it to seat.

13. Position the master cylinder with the open end up and coat the primary and secondary seals on the primary piston with brake fluid. Push the primary piston into the bore of the master cylinder. Hold the piston and position the lockring.

14. Still holding the piston down, install and tighten the stop screw to a torque of 25 to 40 in. lbs.

15. Install the reservoir cover and also the cover on the master cylinder and its retaining clip.

16. Bleed the system. (See "Bleeding the Brakes.")

BLEEDING THE BRAKES

The brake system must be bled when any brake line is disconnected or there is air in the system.

NOTE: *Never bleed a wheel cylinder when a drum is removed.*

Manual Bleeding

1. Clean the master cylinder of excess dirt and remove the cylinder cover and the diaphragm.

2. Fill the master cylinder to the proper level and replace the cover.

3. Install the bleeder hose and recovery bottle to the bleeder valve.

NOTE: *When bleeding the system, the combination valve must be open. Also,*

if the master cylinder is equipped with bleeder valves, these must be bled first. Proceed with the wheel nearest the master cylinder, then the next nearest, and so forth.

4. Make certain that the recovery bottle has enough fluid to cover the end of the recovery hose.

CAUTION: *Check the fluid level in the reservoir during the bleeding procedure. Do not drain all the fluid.*

5. Open the bleeder valve after an assistant has pumped the brake pedal and is applying constant pressure to the pedal. As the brake pedal approaches the floorboard, close the valve and allow the pedal to return to the rest position. Repeat this procedure until a solid stream of fluid, with no air bubbles, comes from the valve. Lock the valve tightly but do not overtighten it. Use the same procedure for the other cylinders.

6. Remove all the bleeding equipment and fill the master cylinder to the proper level. Replace the diaphragm and cover making sure that they are positioned correctly and securely.

Front Disc Brakes

DISC BRAKE PADS

Removal and Installation

1968

1. Siphon off ²/₃ of the brake fluid from the master cylinder.

NOTE: *The insertion of the thicker replacement pads will push the caliper pistons back into their bores and will cause a full master cylinder to overflow.*

2. Jack the car up and support it with jackstands. Remove the wheel(s).

3. Extract and discard the pad retaining pin cotter key.

4. Remove the retaining pin and remove the brake pads.

5. Force the caliper pistons into their bores with a putty knife and install the replacement pads.

6. Install the retaining pin and insert a new cotter key.

7. Refill the master cylinder and bleed the system if necessary.

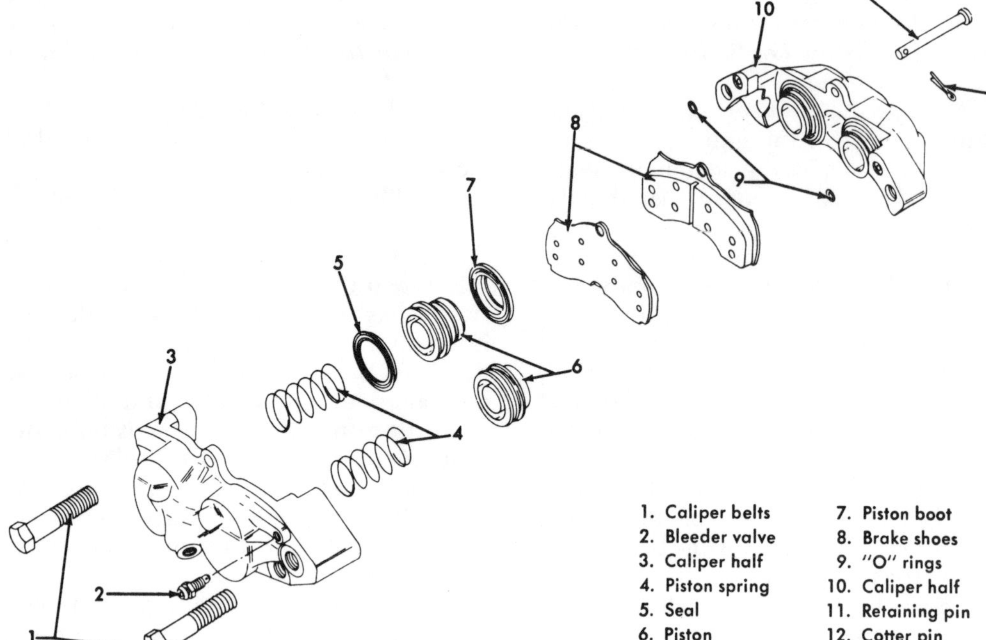

1. Caliper belts
2. Bleeder valve
3. Caliper half
4. Piston spring
5. Seal
6. Piston
7. Piston boot
8. Brake shoes
9. "O" rings
10. Caliper half
11. Retaining pin
12. Cotter pin

Exploded view of four-piston brake caliper

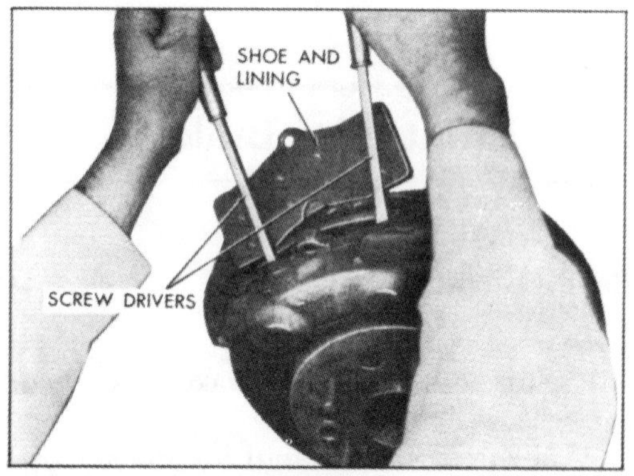

Installing pads in four-piston caliper

1969–77

1. Siphon off ⅔ of the brake fluid from the master cylinder.

NOTE: *The insertion of the thicker replacement pads will push the caliper piston back into its bore and will cause a full master cylinder to overflow.*

2. Jack the car up and support it with jackstands. Remove the wheel(s).

3. Install a C-clamp on the caliper so that the solid side of the clamp rests against the back of the caliper and the screw end rests against the metal part of the outboard pads.

4. Tighten the clamp until the caliper moves enough to bottom the piston in its bore. Remove the clamp.

5. Remove the two allen head caliper mounting bolts enough to allow the caliper to be pulled off the disc.

6. Remove the inboard pad and dislodge the outboard pad. Place the caliper where it won't be supported by the brake hose.

7. Remove the pad support spring clip from the piston.

8. Remove the two bolt ear sleeves and the four rubber bushings from the ears.

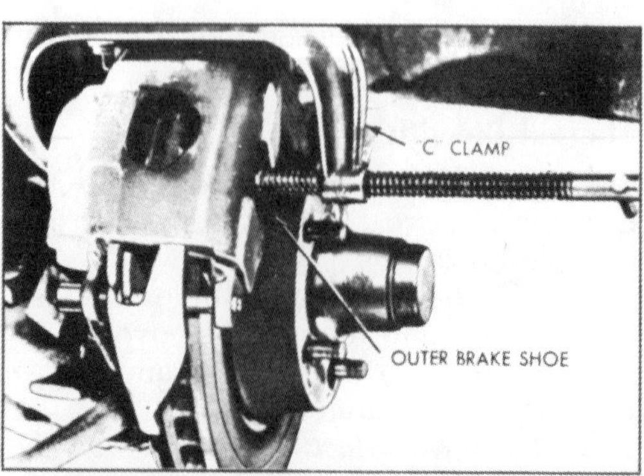

C-clamp positioning for pad removal

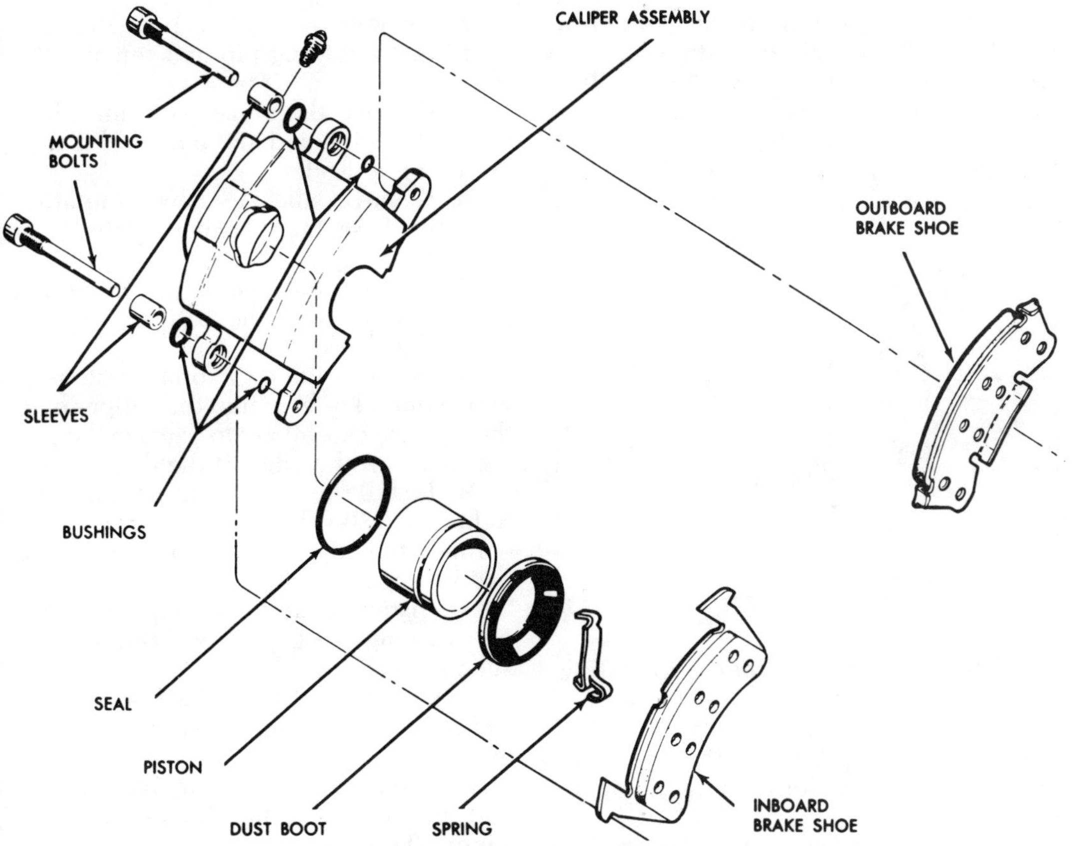

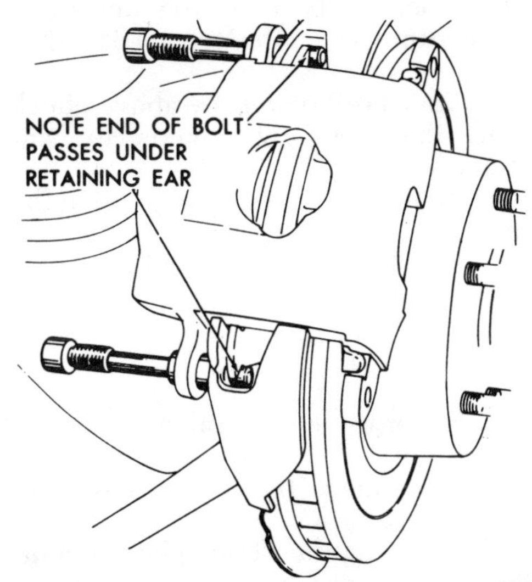

Exploded view of single-piston caliper

Caliper removal and installation

9. Brake pads should be replaced when they are worn to within $1/32$ in. of the rivet heads.

10. Check the inside of the caliper for leakage and the condition of the piston dust boot.

11. Lubricate the two new sleeves and four bushings with a silicone spray.

12. Install the bushings in each caliper ear. Install the two sleeves in the two inboard ears.

NOTE: *On models with wear sensors (this is a little clip attached to the pad which contacts the rotor when the pad wears down) on the inside pad, make sure you install the pad so the wear sensor points toward the rear of the caliper.*

13. Install the pad support spring clip and the pad into the center of the piston. Push the pad down until it is flat against the caliper.

14. Place the outboard pad in the caliper with its top ears over the caliper ears and the bottom tab engaged in the caliper cutout.

15. After both pads are installed, lift the caliper and place the bottom edge of the outboard pad on the outer edge of the disc to make sure that there is no clear-

ance between the tab on the bottom of the shoe and the caliper abutment.

16. Place the caliper over the disc, lining up the hole in the caliper ear with the hole in the mounting bracket. Don't kink the brake hose.

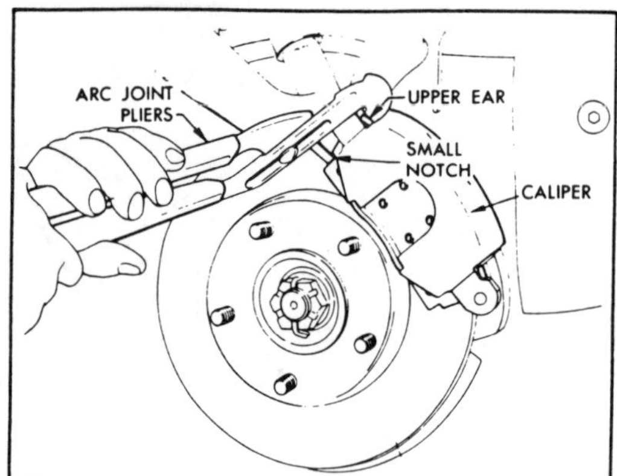

Installing pads in single-piston caliper

17. Start the caliper-to-mounting bracket bolts through the sleeves into the inboard caliper ears and through the mounting bracket. Be sure that the ends of the bolts pass under the retaining ears of the inboard shoe.

18. Push the mounting bolts through to engage the holes in the outboard shoes and the outboard caliper ears and then thread them into the mounting bracket.

19. Torque the mounting bolts to 35 ft lbs. Pump the brake pedal to seat the pads against the rotors.

20. With a pair of channel lock pliers placed on the caliper housing notch, bend the upper caliper ears until no clearance exists between the shoe and the caliper housing.

21. Install the wheels, lower the car, and refill the master cylinder. Pump the brake pedal to make sure that it is firm. If it isn't, bleed the brakes.

DISC BRAKE CALIPERS

Removal and Installation

1968

1. Raise the front of the car and place it on jackstands.

2. Remove the tire and wheel assembly on the side where the caliper is being removed.

3. Disconnect the brake hose at the support bracket. Tape the end of the line to prevent contamination.

4. Remove the cotter pin from the brake pad retaining pin and remove the pin.

5. Remove the brake pads and identify them as inboard and outboard if they are being reused.

6. Remove the U-shaped retainer from the hose fitting and pull the hose from the bracket.

7. Remove the two caliper retaining bolts, and remove the caliper from its mounting bracket.

8. While holding the brake pistons in with a putty knife, mount the caliper over the disc. Be careful not to damage the piston boots on the edge of the disc.

9. Install the two mounting bolts and tighten to 130 ft lbs.

10. Install the brake pads (see brake pad installation).

11. Install the brake hose into the caliper, passing the female end through the support bracket.

12. Ensure that the tube line is clear and connect the brake line nut to the caliper.

13. Install the hose fitting into the support bracket and install the U-shaped retainer. Turn the steering wheel from side-to-side to make sure that the hose doesn't interfere with the tire. If it does, turn the hose end one or two points in the bracket until the interference is eliminated.

14. After performing the above check, install the steel tube connector and tighten it.

15. Bleed the brakes as outlined in this chapter.

16. Install the wheel(s) and lower the car.

1969–77

1. Perform the removal steps for pad replacement.

2. Disconnect the brake hose and plug the line.

3. Remove the U-shaped retainer from the fitting.

4. Pull the hose from the frame bracket and remove the caliper with the hose attached.

5. Clean the outside of the caliper with denatured alcohol.

6. Remove the brake hose and discard the copper gasket.

7. Remove the brake fluid from the caliper.

8. Place clean rags inside the caliper opening to catch the piston when it is released.

9. Apply compressed air to the caliper fluid inlet hole and force the piston out of its bore. Do not blow the piston out, but use just enough pressure to ease it out.

10. Use a screwdriver to pry the boot out of the caliper. Avoid scratching the bore.

11. Remove the piston seal from its groove in the caliper bore. *Do not use a metal tool of any type for this operation.*

12. Blow out all passages in the caliper and bleeder valve. Clean the piston and piston bore with fresh brake fluid.

13. Examine the piston for scoring, scratches, or corrosion. If any of these conditions exist the piston must be replaced, as it is plated and cannot be refinished.

14. Examine the bore for the same defects. Light rough spots may be removed by rotating crocus cloth, using finger pressure, in the bore. Do not polish with an in and out motion or use any other abrasive.

15. Lubricate the piston bore and the new rubber parts with fresh brake fluid. Position the seal in the piston bore groove.

16. Lubricate the piston with brake fluid and assemble the boot into the piston groove so that the fold faces the open end of the piston.

17. Insert the piston into the bore, taking care not to unseat the seal.

18. Force the piston to the bottom of the bore. (This will require a force of 50–100 lbs). Seat the boot lip around the caliper counterbore. Proper seating of the boot is very important for sealing out contaminants.

19. Install the brake hose into the caliper using a new copper gasket.

20. Lubricate the new sleeves and rubber bushings. Install the bushings in the caliper ears. Install the sleeves so that the end toward the disc pad is flush with the machined surface.

NOTE: *Lubrication of the sleeves and bushings is essential to ensure the proper operation of the sliding caliper design.*

21. Install the shoe support spring in the piston.

22. Install the disc pads in the caliper and remount the caliper on the hub (see Disc Pad Replacement).

23. Reconnect the brake hose to the steel brake line. Install the retainer clip. Bleed the brakes (see Brake Bleeding).

24. Replace the wheels, check the brake fluid level, check the brake pedal travel, and road test the vehicle.

BRAKE DISC

Removal and Installation

1. Raise the car, support it with jackstands, and remove the wheel and tire assembly.

2. Remove the brake caliper as previously outlined.

3. Drill out the five rivets holding the disc to the hub.

4. Remove the brake disc.

5. Remove the rivet stubs from the hub.

6. Install the disc on the hub, aligning the lug bolts with the holes in the disc.

7. Install the brake caliper and shoes as previously outlined.

8. Bleed the brakes, install the wheel, and lower the car.

Checking

1. Tighten the spindle nut to remove all wheel bearing play.

2. Install a dial indicator on the caliper so that its feeler will contact the disc about one in. below its outer edge.

3. Turn the disc and observe the runout reading. If the reading exceeds 0.002 in., the disc should be replaced.

4. Minimum thickness dimensions are cast into the caliper for reference.

WHEEL BEARINGS

Properly adjusted bearings have a slightly loose feeling. Wheel bearings must never be preloaded. Preloading will damage bearings and eventually spindles. If bearings are too loose, they should be cleaned and inspected and then adjusted. Hold the tire at the top and bottom and move the wheel in and out of the spindle. If the movement is greater than 0.008 in. (0.005 in. 1974–76), the bearings are too loose.

Adjustment

1. Raise and support the car by the lower control arm.

2. Remove the hub cap, then remove the dust cap from the hub.

3. Remove the cotter pin and spindle nut.

4. Spin the wheel forward by hand and adjust the bearings as shown in the illustration.

5. Back off on the nut until it is just loose, then tighten it finger-tight.

6. Loosen the nut until either hole in the spindle lines up with a slot in the nut and then insert the cotter pin. This may appear to be too loose but it is the correct adjustment. The spindle nut should not even be finger-tight.

7. Proper adjustment creates 0.001–0.008 in. (0.001–0.005 in. 1974–77) of end-play.

Removal and Installation

1. Remove the wheel and tire assembly, and the brake drum or brake caliper.

2. Remove the hub and disc as an assembly. Remove the caliper mounting

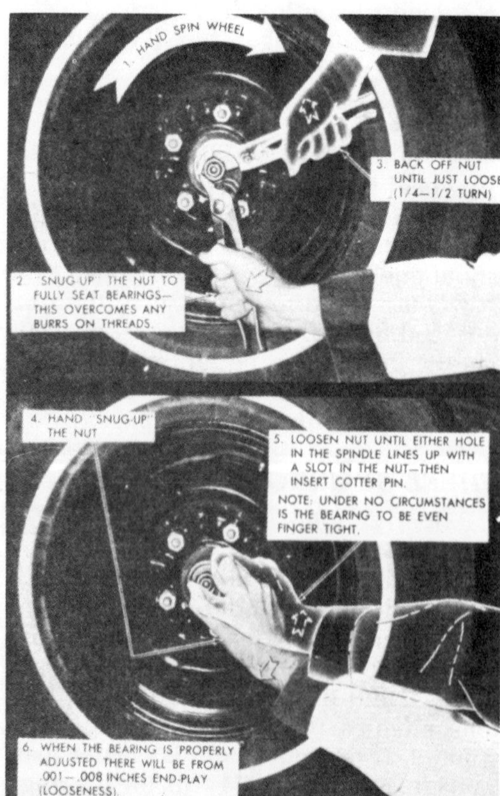

Adjusting wheel bearing

bolts and insert a block between the brake pads as the caliper is removed. Remove the caliper and wire it out of the way.

3. Pry out the grease cap, cotter pin, spindle nut, and washer, then remove the hub. Do not drop the wheel bearings.

4. Remove the outer roller bearing assembly from the hub. The inner bearing assembly will remain in the hub and may be removed after prying out the inner seal. Discard the seal.

5. Clean all parts in solvent (air dry) and check for excessive wear or damage.

6. Using a hammer and drift, remove the bearing cups from the hub. When installing new cups, make sure that they are not cocked and that they are fully seated against the hub shoulder.

7. Using a high melting-point bearing lubricant, pack both inner and outer bearings.

8. Place the inner bearing in the hub and install a new inner seal, making sure that the seal flange faces the bearing cup.

9. Carefully install the wheel hub over the spindle.

10. Using your hands, firmly press the outer bearing into the hub. Install the spindle washer and nut, and adjust as instructed above.

Packing

Clean the wheel bearings thoroughly with solvent and check their condition before installation.

CAUTION: *Do not blow the bearing dry with compressed air as this would allow the bearing to turn without lubrication.*

Apply a sizable daub of lubricant to the palm of one hand. Using your other hand, work the bearing into the lubricant so that the grease is pushed through the rollers and out the other side. Keep rotating the bearing while continuing to push the lubricant through it.

Front Drum Brakes

BRAKE DRUMS

Removal and Installation

Drums on all models can be removed by raising the vehicle, removing the wheel lugs and the tire, and pulling the drum from the brake assembly. If the brake drums have been scored from worn linings, the brake adjuster must be backed off so that the brake shoes will retract from the drum.

The adjuster can be backed off by inserting a brake adjusting tool through the access hole provided. In some cases the access hole is provided in the brake drum. A metal cover plate is over the hole. This may be removed by using a hammer and chisel.

NOTE: *Make sure that all metal particles are removed from the brake drum before reassembly.*

To install, reverse the removal procedure.

Inspection

LINING

Remove the drum and inspect the lining thickness on both brake shoes. A brake lining should be replaced if it is less than ⅛ in. thick at the lowest point on the brake shoe.

NOTE: *Brake shoes should always be replaced in axle sets.*

DRUM

When a drum is removed, it should be inspected for cracks, scores, or other imperfections. These must be corrected before the drum is replaced.

CAUTION: *If the drum is found to be cracked, replace it. Do not attempt to service a cracked drum.*

Minor drum score marks can be removed with fine emery cloth. Heavy score marks must be removed by "cutting the drum." This is removing metal from the entire inner surface of the drum in order to level the surface. Automotive machine shops and some large parts stores are equipped to perform this operation.

If the drum is not scored, it should be polished with fine emery cloth before replacement. If the drum is resurfaced, it should not be enlarged past 0.060 in. of the original diameter.

It is advisable, while the drums are off, to check them for out-of-round. An inside micrometer is necessary for an exact measurement, therefore unless this tool is available, the drums should be taken to a machine shop to be checked. Any drum which is more than 0.006 in. out-of-round will result in an inaccurate brake adjustment and other problems, and should be refinished or replaced.

NOTE: *If the micrometer is available, make all measurements at right angles to each other and at the open and closed edges of the drum machined surface.*

Check the drum with a micrometer in the following manner:

1. Position the drum on a level surface.

2. Insert the micrometer with its adapter bars if necessary.

3. Obtain a reading on the micrometer at the point of maximum contact. Record this.

4. Rotate the micrometer 45° and take a similar reading. The two readings must not vary more than 0.006 in.

BRAKE SHOES

Removal and Installation

1. Jack up and securely support the vehicle.

2. Remove the check nuts from the end of the parking brake equalizer bracket and remove all tension on the brake cable (rear brakes only).

3. Remove the brake drums.

CAUTION: *The brake pedal must not be depressed while the drums are removed.*

4. Using a brake tool, remove the shoe springs from their holder.

5. Remove the self-adjuster actuator spring.

6. Remove the spring from the secondary shoe by pulling it from the anchor pin.

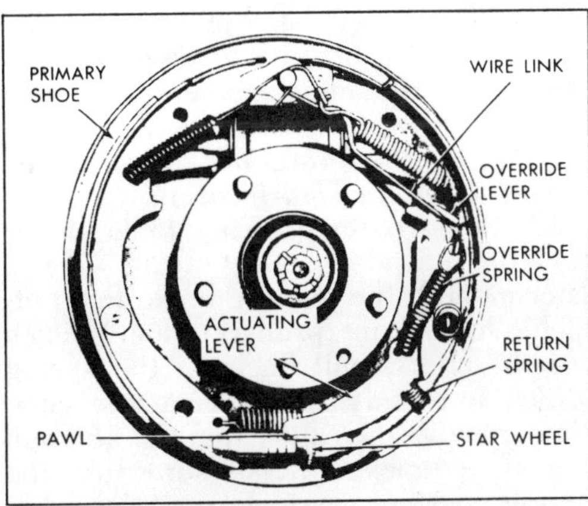

Drum brake components—left front shown

Hold-down spring and anchor pin removal

7. Remove the hold-down pins. These are the brackets which run through the backing plate. They can be removed with a pair of pliers. Reach around the rear of the backing plate and hold the back of the pin. Turn the top of the pine retainer 45° with the pliers. This will align the elongated tang with the slot in the retainer. Be careful, as the pin is spring-loaded and may fly off when released. Use the same procedure for the other pin assembly.

8. Remove the adjuster actuating lever assembly by removing the hold-down pin which is attached to the secondary brake shoe.

NOTE: *Since the actuator, pivot, and override spring are considered an assembly it is not recommended that they be disassembled.*

9. Remove the shoes from the backing plate. Make sure that you have a secure grip on the assembly as the bottom spring will still exert pressure on the shoes. Slowly let the tops of the shoes come together and the tension will decrease and the adjuster and spring may be removed.

NOTE: *If the linings are to be reused, mark them for identification.*

10. Remove the parking brake lever from the secondary shoe. On all 1977 and later models, the parking brake lever attaches to the front (primary) shoe. Using a pair of pliers, pull back on the spring which surrounds the cable. At the same time, remove the cable from the notch in the shoe bracket. Make sure that the spring does not snap back or injury may result.

11. Use compressed air or a cloth to remove dirt from the brake drum. Check the drums for scoring and cracks. Have the drums checked for out-of-round and service the drums as necessary.

12. Check the wheel cylinders by carefully pulling the lower edges of the wheel cylinder boots away from the cylinders. If there is excessive leakage, the inside of the cylinder will be moist with fluid. If there is any leakage at all, a cylinder overhaul is in order. DO NOT delay, as a brake failure could result.

NOTE: *A small amount of fluid will be present to act as a lubricant for the wheel cylinder pistons.*

13. Check the flange plate, which is located around the axle, for leakage of differential lubricant. This condition cannot be overlooked as the lubricant will be absorbed into the brake linings and brake failure will result. Replace the seals as necessary. (See "Axle Removal.")

NOTE: *If new linings are being installed, check them against the old units for length and type.*

14. Check the new linings for imperfections.

CAUTION: *It is important to keep your hands free of dirt and grease when handling the brake shoes. Foreign matter will be absorbed into the linings and result in unpredictable braking.*

15. Lightly lubricate the parking brake cable and the end of the parking brake lever where it enters the shoe.

16. Install the parking brake lever into the secondary shoe with the attaching bolt, spring washer, lockwasher, and nut. It is important that the lever move freely before the shoe is attached. Move the assembly and check for proper action.

17. Lubricate the adjusting screw and make sure that it works freely. Sometimes the adjusting screw will not move due to lack of lubricant or dirt contamination and the brakes will not adjust. In this case, the adjuster should be disassembled, thoroughly cleaned, and lubricated before installation.

18. Connect the brake shoe spring to the bottom portion of both shoes. Make certain that the brake linings are installed in the correct manner, the primary and secondary shoe in the correct position. If you are not sure remove the other brake drum and check it.

19. Install the adjusting mechanism below the spring and separate the top of the shoes.

NOTE: *Make the following checks before installation:*

a. Be certain that the right-hand thread adjusting screw is on the left-hand side of the vehicle and the left-hand screw is on the right-hand side of the vehicle.

b. Make sure that the star adjuster is aligned with the hole in the flange plate.

c. The adjuster should be installed with the starwheel nearest the secondary shoe and the tension spring away from the adjusting mechanism.

d. If the original linings are being reused, position the linings in relation to the scribe marks which were made during disassembly.

20. Install the parking brake and adjust to the correct tension.

21. Position the primary shoe (the shoe with the short lining) first. Secure it with the hold-down pin and with its spring by pushing the pin through the back of the backing plate and, while holding it with one hand, install the spring and the retainer using a pair of needlenose pliers.

22. Install the parking brake strut and the strut spring by pulling back the spring with pliers and engaging the end of the cable onto the brake strut and then releasing the spring.

23. Place the small metal guide plate over the anchor pin and position the self-adjuster wire cable eye.

CAUTION: *The wire should not be positioned with the conventional brake installation tool or damage will result. It should be positioned on the actuator assembly first and then placed over the anchor pin stud by hand with the adjuster assembly in full downward position.*

24. Install the actuator return spring. DO NOT pry the actuator lever to install the return spring. Position it using the end of a screwdriver or another suitable tool.

NOTE: *If the return springs are bent or in any way distorted, they should be replaced.*

25. Using the brake installation tool, place the brake return springs in position. Install the primary spring first over the anchor pin and then place the spring from the secondary shoe over the wire link end.

26. Pull the brake shoes away from the backing plate and apply a *thin* coat of grease to the brake shoe contact points.

CAUTION: *Only a small amount is necessary. Keep the lubricant away from the brake facings.*

27. Once the complete assembly has been installed, check the operation of the self-adjuster mechanism by moving the actuating line by hand.

28. Adjust the brakes.

a. Turn the star adjuster until the drum slides over the brake shoes with only a slight drag. Remove the drum.

b. Turn the adjuster back one complete turn.

c. Install the drum and wheel and lower the vehicle.

NOTE: *If the adjusting hole in the drum has been punched out, make certain that the insert has been removed from the inside of the drum. Install a rubber hole cover to keep dirt out of the brake assembly. Also, be sure that the drums are installed in the same position as they were when removed— with the locating tang in line with the location hole in the axle shaft flange.*

d. Make the final adjustment by backing the vehicle and pumping the brakes until the self-adjusting mechanisms adjust to the proper level and the brake pedal reaches satisfactory height.

NOTE: *Some drivers use a shift into the Drive position to slow the vehicle when backing slowly instead of the brakes. This will not operate the adjusting mechanisms.*

29. Adjust the parking brake (See "Parking Brake Adjustment.")

30. Make tests of the braking action and the parking brake.

BRAKE BACKING PLATE

Removal and Installation

1. Remove the complete brake mechanisms as outlined in "Brake Removal and Installation."

2. Remove the rear axles as outlined in "Rear Axle Shaft Removal."

3. Remove the attaching bolts and pull off the backing plate.

4. To install, reverse the removal procedure.

WHEEL CYLINDERS

Removal

1. Jack and support the axle.
2. Remove the wheel and tire.
3. Back off the brake adjustment and remove the drum.
4. Disconnect and plug the brake line.
5. Remove the brake shoe pull-back springs.
6. Remove the screws securing the wheel cylinder to the backing plate.
7. Disengage the wheel cylinder pushrods from the brake shoes and remove the wheel cylinder.
8. Installation is the reverse of removal. Adjust the brakes and bleed the system.

Overhaul

As is the case with master cylinders, overhaul kits for wheel cylinders are readily available. When rebuilding and installing wheel cylinders, avoid getting any contaminants into the system. Always install clean, new high-quality brake fluid. If dirty or improper fluid has been used, it will be necessary to drain the entire system, flush the system with proper brake fluid, replace all rubber components, refill, and bleed the system.

1. Remove the rubber boots from the cylinder ends with pliers. Discard the boots.
2. Remove and discard the pistons and cups.
3. Wash the cylinder and metal parts in denatured alcohol or clean brake fluid.

CAUTION: *Never use a mineral-based solvent such as gasoline, kerosene, or paint thinner for cleaning purposes. These solvents will swell rubber components and quickly deteriorate them.*

4. Allow the parts to air dry or use compressed air. Do not use rags for cleaning since lint will remain in the cylinder bore.
5. Inspect the piston and replace it if it shows scratches.
6. Lubricate the cylinder bore and counterbore with clean brake fluid.
7. Install the rubber cups (flat side out) and then the pistons (flat side in).
8. Insert new boots into the counterbores by hand. Do not lubricate the boots.

WHEEL BEARINGS

Removal and Installation

1. Jack and support the front of the car.
2. Remove the wheel and tire.
3. Remove the dust cap from the end of the hub and remove the cotter pin.
4. Remove the hub and drum.
5. Remove the outer bearing from the hub. The inner bearing will remain in the hub and can be removed by prying out the inner grease seal.
6. Wash all parts in solvent.
7. Pack the inner and outer bearings with grease. See the "Front Disc Brakes—Wheel Bearings" Section for the packing procedure.
8. Place the inner hub bearing in the hub and install a new seal assembly, tapping it into place.
9. Install the hub on the spindle and install the outer bearing, pressing it firmly into position.
10. Adjust the wheel bearings.
11. Reinstall the dust cap, wheel and tire and lower the car.

Adjustment

1. Tighten the adjusting nut to 15 ft lbs while rotating the hub in both directions.
2. Back the nut off 1 flat ($1/16$ turn) and insert a new cotter pin. If the nut and spindle hole do not align, back the nut off slightly until they do align.
3. This adjustment provides for 0.000–0.007 in. (1968) or 0.000–0.008 in. (1969–70) end-play.

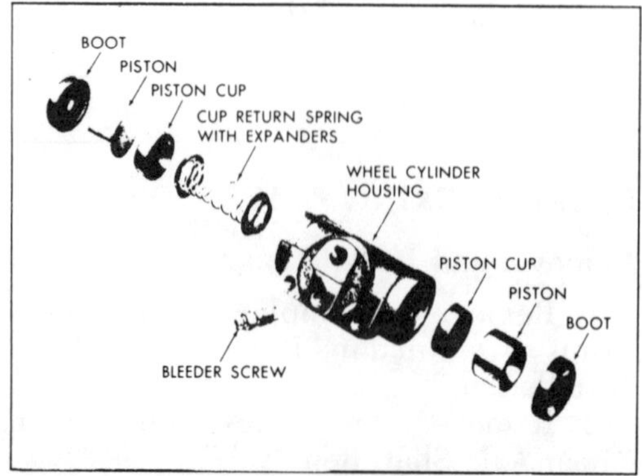

Exploded view of wheel cylinder

Rear Drum Brakes

BRAKE DRUMS

Removal and Installation

Rear brakes are basically the same type as those used on the front. See the "Front Drum Brakes" Section for drum removal and inspection procedures.

Brake Shoes

See the procedures under "Front Drum Brakes." Brake shoes should be replaced when lining thickness is $1/16$ in. (bonded) or $3/16$ in. (riveted).

Wheel Cylinders

Removal and installation procedures, as well as overhaul procedures are the same as for the front wheel cylinders.

Parking Brake

Cable Removal and Installation

1968–70

There are three parking brake cables: the front cable runs between the pedal assembly and the looped center cable; the center cable is a large loop, each end connected to the short rear cables and the center (forward) attached to the front cable with the equalizer; the rear cables are attached to brake shoe actuating levers.

To remove any of the cables, first release the brake pedal and loosen the equalizer adjusting nuts. The front cable slips into a clevis at the pedal lever and is connected to the equalizer by means of a threaded rod. The outer cable has locking fingers which secure it in a hole in the firewall.

The center cable is removed by disconnecting the equalizer, disconnecting each end from the rear cables and by removing it from the frame guides and hook. The rear cables are removed by disconnecting the forward end from the center cable, removing the retainers at the frame and by removing the rear end from the brake actuating levers. The brake drum and shoes must be removed to disconnect the rear cable from the actuating lever. Adjust the parking brake after replacing any of the cables.

1971–77

The parking brake cable design is essentially the same as that used in 1968–70 models with a forward, center and two rear cables. The front outer cable, how-

Brake Specifications

| | | MASTER CYLINDER | | WHEEL CYLINDER | | | BRAKE DISC OR DRUM DIAMETER | | |
| | | | | Front | | | Front | | |
Year	Model	Disc	Drum	Disc	Drum	Rear	Disc	Drum	Rear
'68	All	1.0	1.0①	$2^{15}\!/_{16}$	$1^{3}\!/_{16}$	1.00	11.75	11.0	11.0
'69–'70	All	$1\frac{1}{8}$	1.0	$2^{15}\!/_{16}$	$1^{3}\!/_{16}$	1.00	11.75	11.0	11.0
'71–'76	Exc. Sta. Wag.	$1\frac{1}{8}$	——	$2^{15}\!/_{16}$	——	$^{15}\!/_{16}$	11.86	——	11.0
	Sta. Wag.	$1\frac{1}{8}$	——	$2^{15}\!/_{16}$	——	1.00	11.86	——	12.0
'77	Exc. Sta. Wag.	$1\frac{1}{8}$	——	——	——	$\frac{7}{8}$	11.00	——	9.50
	Sta. Wag. and Police	$1\frac{1}{8}$	——	——	——	$^{15}\!/_{16}$	11.86	——	11.00

① Metallic linings—$7/8$ in.
—— Not applicable

ever, is clipped to the pedal bracket. When replacing the front cable, tie a rope onto the top of the old cable and pull it through the cable route so that it may be used to pull the new cable into place. Remove the rear screws holding the inner fender panel to the fender to get at the cable grommet in the firewall.

Cable Adjustment

1968–76

1. Jack up rear of car and support with both rear wheels off floor.

2. Apply parking brake two notches from fully released position.

3. Loosen the equalizer front jam nut, then tighten rear nut until a light to moderate drag is felt when rear wheels are rotated.

4. Tighten jam nuts.

5. Fully release parking brake and rotate rear wheels—no drag should be felt.

1977

1. Jack up the rear of the car and safely support it.

2. Apply the parking brake not notch from full release.

3. The adjusting nut should be tightened to a point where you can just turn the left rear wheel backward using both hands and is locked when you try to turn it forward.

4. Release the parking brake, the wheel should rotate without any drag. If it drags, reapply the brake one notch and loosen the adjusting nut.

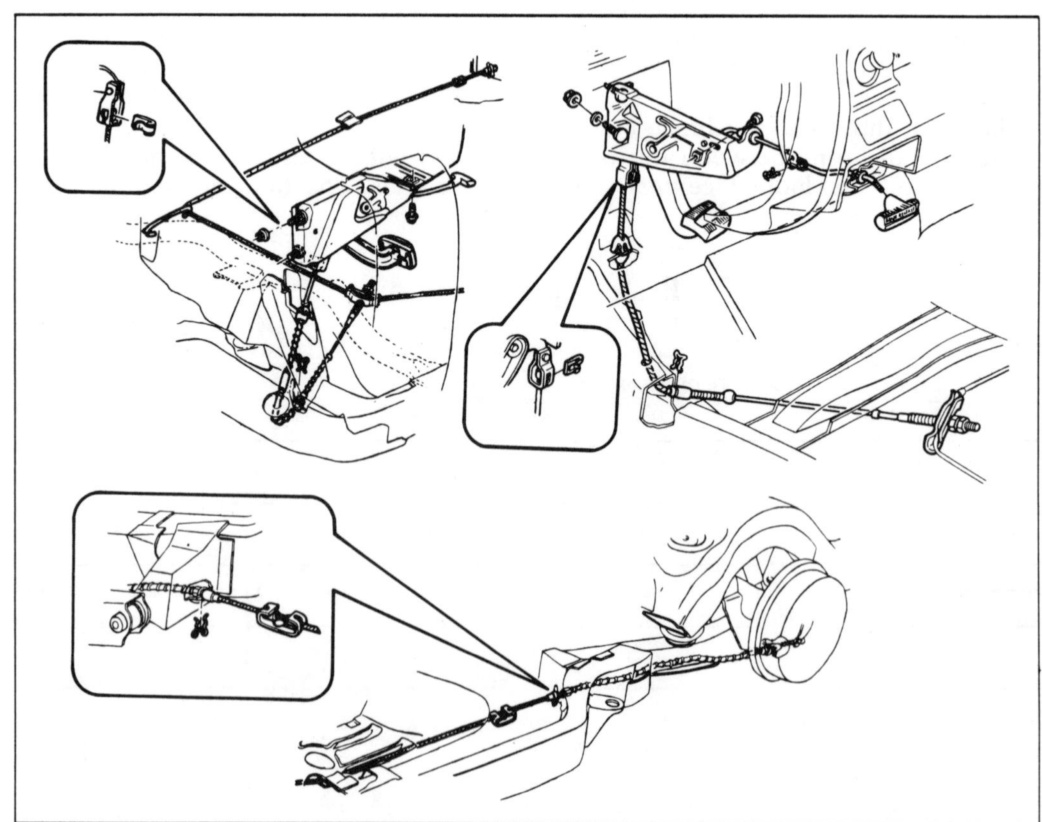

1968–76 parking brake cable routing

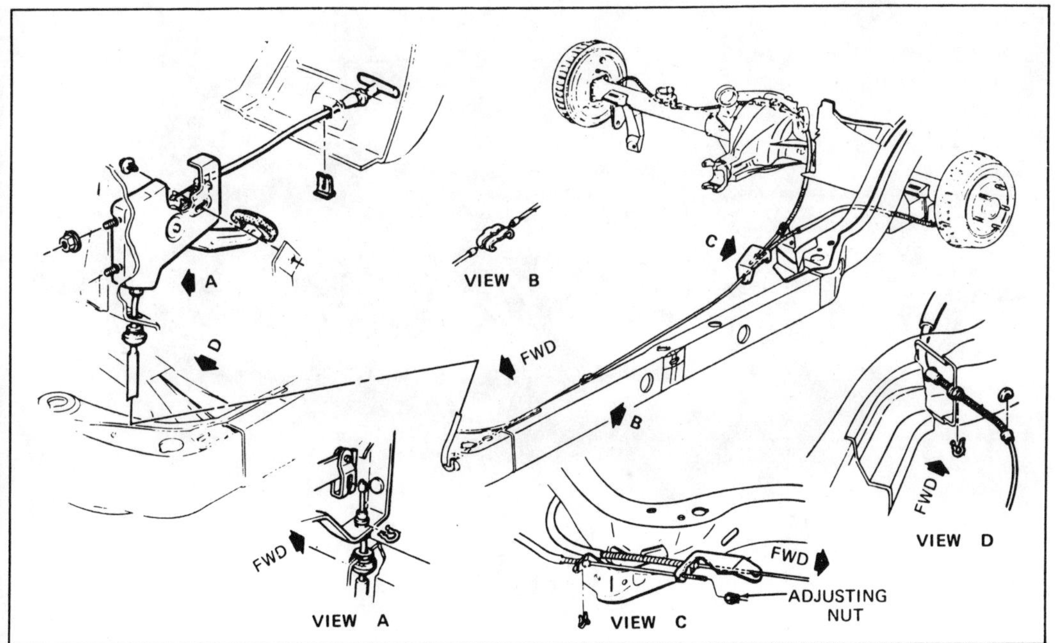

1977 parking brake cable routing

Chapter 10

Body

Doors

Adjustment

FRONT

Door adjustment is provided by the use of floating anchor plates in the door and body hinge pillar. Remove the door lock striker and let the door hang freely on its hinges before adjusting. It may be necessary to loosen the front fender for access to the hinge bolts.

NOTE: *Loosening the hinge retaining bolts will require a universal socket setup, a 1/2 in. distributor wrench, or a special hinge wrench (commercially-available).*

Adjustment at the body hinge pillars: up-and-down, and backward-and-forward.

NOTE: *If the door is adjusted to the rear, the door jamb switch will have to be replaced. This switch has an adjusting sleeve with collapsible ridges. After initial adjustment (when the door is first closed) there is further inward adjustment available but no outward adjustment.*

Adjustment at the door hinge pillars: in-and-out.

REAR

The door side hinge retaining screws may be adjusted for an in-and-out, and up-and-down motion. The body side hinge retaining screws may be adjusted for an up-and-down, and forward-and-backward motion.

Removal and Installation

FRONT

Front doors may be removed from the car with or without the hinges attached. Removal will be much easier if only the door is removed, as the body side hinge bolts are more difficult to reach.

1. Scribe the relationship of the hinge and the door before loosening any bolts. This will ease installation.

2. If the car is equipped with power windows, mirror, or door locks, remove the trim pad and separate the inner panel water deflector enough to disconnect the harness assembly(ies) and remove them from the door.

3. Have an assistant hold the door in the open position and remove the upper and lower hinge-to-door bolts.

4. Install the door(s) using a reverse of the removal procedure. Adjust the door(s) as previously outlined. Apply body sealer to the hinge mating surfaces.

REAR

Rear doors may be removed from the car with or without the hinges attached.

1. Scribe the relationship of the hinge and the door before loosening any bolts. This will ease installation.

2. If the car is equipped with power windows or door locks, remove the door trim and inner panel water deflector. Disconnect the wire harness connector from the window motor and/or the lock solenoid. Remove the electric conduit from the door, and then remove the wire harness through the conduit access hole.

3. Have an assistant hold the door in the open position and remove the upper and lower hinge retaining bolts. Remove the door.

4. Install the door using the previously made scribe marks to properly locate the door. Coat the mating surface of the hinge with body sealer prior to installation.

DOOR PANELS

Removal and Installation

All models have one piece door panels. The panel hangs over the inner door panel, and is held by clips or pins along the sides. The bottom of the panel is fastened to the inner door panel with screws.

1. Remove the window crank handles. These are held by spring clips, which must be expanded to allow the handle to be pulled off. A special tool for this operation is readily available from several tool companies. The factory tool is shown in the figure.

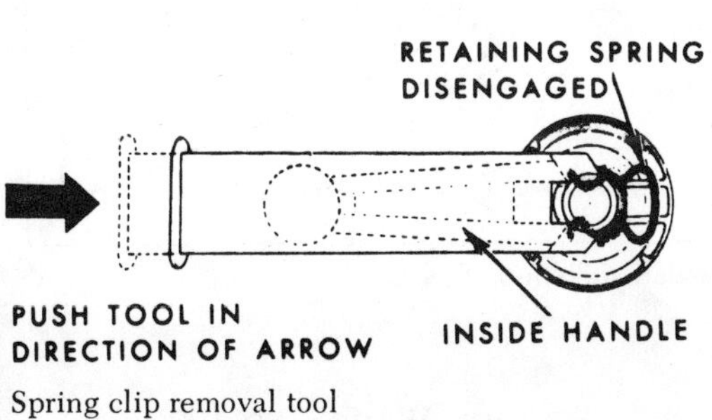

Spring clip removal tool

2. Remove the inside door handles and arm rests, if so equipped.

3. Remove the inside door lock knob.

4. On models with door pull handles, remove the screws inserted through the handle into the inner door panel.

5. On cars with remote control mirrors, remove the control escutcheon and disengage the control cable from the escutcheon.

6. Remove all the retaining screws from the door panel.

7. Starting at a lower corner, insert a putty knife (or other flat tool) and pry the panel out to disengage the retaining clips or pins from their plastic cups in the inner door panel.

8. Lift the door panel upward and slide it slightly to the rear to disengage it from the inner panel. If the car is equipped with electric controls in the door, disconnect the wiring harnesses. Remove the panel from the door.

9. Reverse the above procedure to install the door panel.

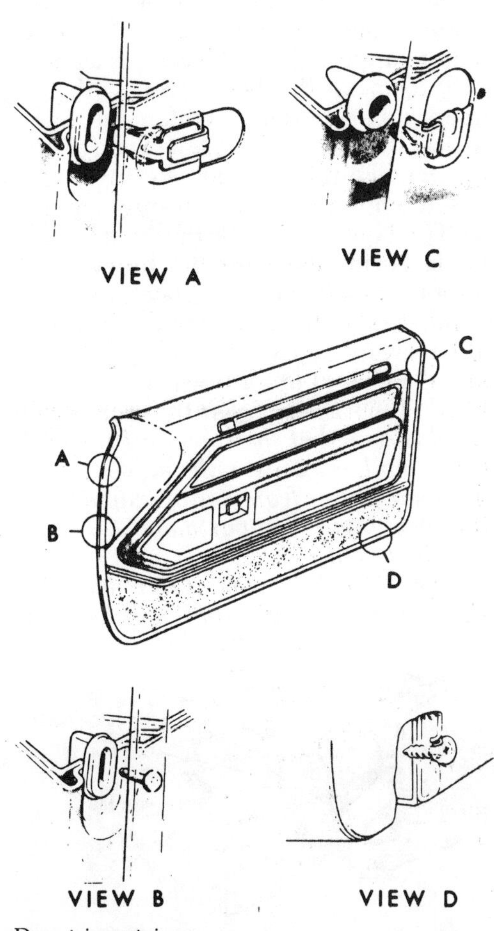

Door trim retainers

Hood

Alignment

Hood hinges on all models have slotted retaining bolt holes which allow adjusting the hinge-to-hood relationship. The hood-mounted end of the hinge is slotted for forward-and-backward motion. The body-mounted end of the hinge is slotted for an up-and-down motion.

1. Scribe the beginning position of the hinge in relation to the body. This will give you an idea of how much the hinges are being moved.

2. Loosen the necessary hinge retaining bolts and change the hinge positioning for correct hood alignment.

3. Tighten the bolts and close the hood to check the adjustment. The hood-to-fender and hood-to-cowl clearances should be within the tolerances shown in the figures.

4. Remove the rubber bumpers from the adjustable screws at either end of the radiator support. Turn the screws as necessary to make the hood even with the fenders when closed. Tighten the locknut after the final adjustment. The rubber bumpers should just be slightly compressed when the hood is firmly closed.

5. The hood latch adjustment, if necessary, is performed after the hinges and bumpers are adjusted. The latch plate on the hood is slotted to provide forward-and-backward adjustment. The lock bolt may be adjusted up-or-down.

CAUTION: *Ensure that the rear of the hood is sealed at the cowl on 1971 and later models. This will prevent underhood fumes from being pulled into the passenger compartment through the cowl vent.*

NOTE: *On 1972 and later models, there is an adjustable bolt and locknut on either end of the upper cowl surface. These bolts must be adjusted so that the bolt head protrudes into the inner hood panel. The bolts prevent the hood from sliding back into the windshield during a front end collision.*

Fuel Tank

Removal and Installation

COUPES AND SEDANS

1. Siphon the fuel from the tank, as there is no drain plug.

2. Disconnect the fuel gauge sending unit wire from the rear wiring harness connector. On sedans, push the grommet out and work the gauge wire through the trunk floor hole.

3. Raise the car to a convenient working height.

4. Remove the fuel gauge ground wire screw from the underbody.

5. Disconnect the fuel line at the sending unit pickup line.

6. Remove the vent hose (hoses for evaporative control on 1970 and later models).

7. Remove the strap retaining bolts, lower the support straps, and carefully drop the tank out of the car.

8. Reverse the removal steps to install the fuel tank.

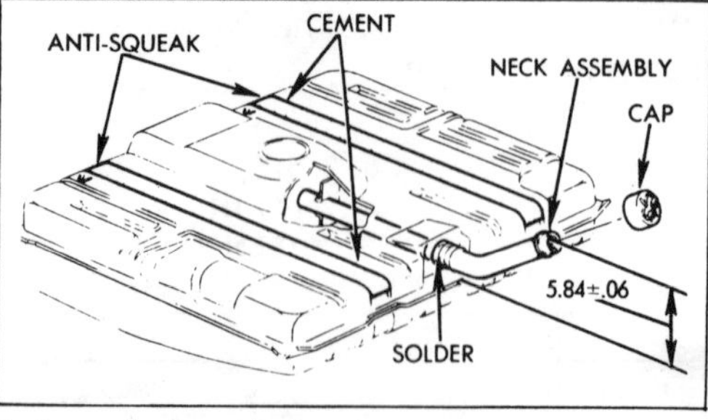

Sedan and coupe fuel tank

STATION WAGON TO 1976

1. Siphon the fuel from the tank.

2. Jack the car up, and place the rear on stands.

3. Lower the rear axle into the full re-

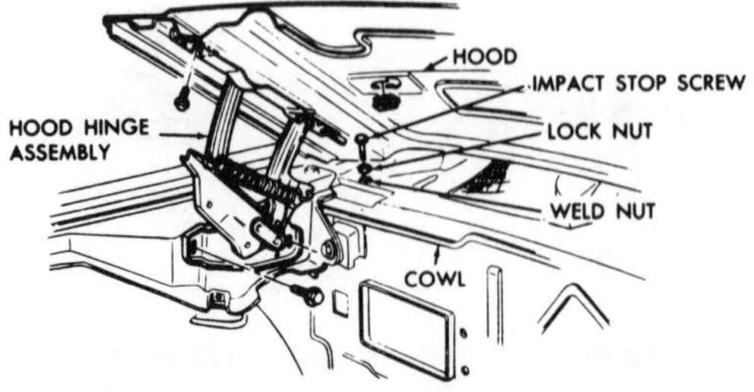

Impact hood-stop bolts

bound position, and remove the left rear wheel assembly.

NOTE: *It may be necessary to disconnect the bottom of the left shock absorber for working room.*

4. Disconnect the fuel gauge sending unit wire at the rear wiring harness.

5. Remove the fuel tank front shield.

6. Remove the fuel gauge ground wire from the rear quarter panel.

7. Remove the fuel line and wires from the gauge sending unit.

8. Remove the strap retaining bolts and lower the tank carefully.

9. Reverse the removal procedure to install the tank.

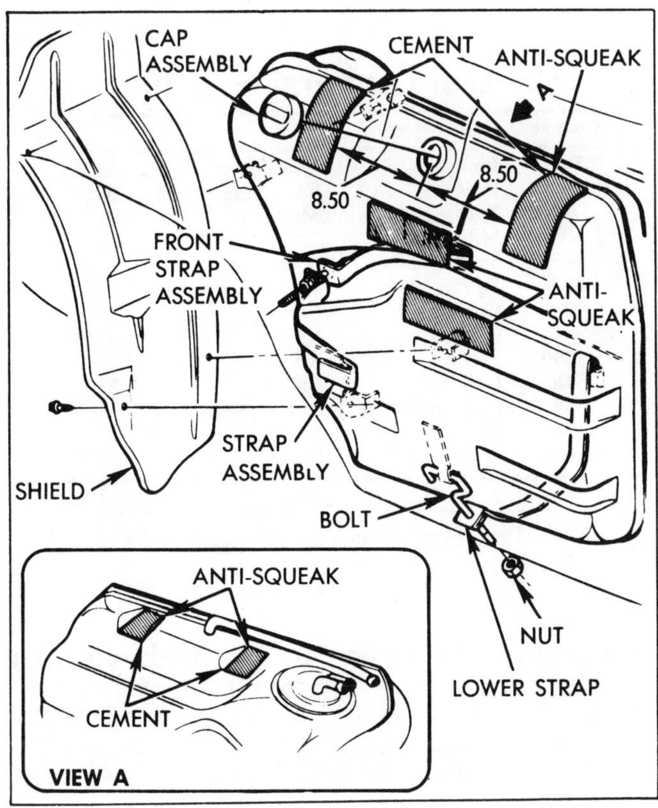

Station wagon fuel tank

General Conversion Table

Multiply by	To convert	To	
2.54	Inches	Centimeters	.3937
30.48	Feet	Centimeters	.0328
.914	Yards	Meters	1.094
1.609	Miles	Kilometers	.621
.645	Square inches	Square cm.	.155
.836	Square yards	Square meters	1.196
16.39	Cubic inches	Cubic cm.	.061
28.3	Cubic feet	Liters	.0353
.4536	Pounds	Kilograms	2.2045
4.546	Gallons	Liters	.22
.068	Lbs./sq. in. (psi)	Atmospheres	14.7
.138	Foot pounds	Kg. m.	7.23
1.014	H.P. (DIN)	H.P. (SAE)	.9861
——	To obtain	From	Multiply by

Note: 1 cm. equals 10 mm.; 1 mm. equals .0394″.

Conversion—Common Fractions to Decimals and Millimeters

INCHES			INCHES			INCHES		
Common Fractions	Decimal Fractions	Millimeters (approx.)	Common Fractions	Decimal Fractions	Millimeters (approx.)	Common Fractions	Decimal Fractions	Millimeters (approx.)
1/128	.008	0.20	11/32	.344	8.73	43/64	.672	17.07
1/64	.016	0.40	23/64	.359	9.13	11/16	.688	17.46
1/32	.031	0.79	3/8	.375	9.53	45/64	.703	17.86
3/64	.047	1.19	25/64	.391	9.92	23/32	.719	18.26
1/16	.063	1.59	13/32	.406	10.32	47/64	.734	18.65
5/64	.078	1.98	27/64	.422	10.72	3/4	.750	19.05
3/32	.094	2.38	7/16	.438	11.11	49/64	.766	19.45
7/64	.109	2.78	29/64	.453	11.51	25/32	.781	19.84
1/8	.125	3.18	15/32	.469	11.91	51/64	.797	20.24
9/64	.141	3.57	31/64	.484	12.30	13/16	.813	20.64
5/32	.156	3.97	1/2	.500	12.70	53/64	.828	21.03
11/64	.172	4.37	33/64	.516	13.10	27/32	.844	21.43
3/16	.188	4.76	17/32	.531	13.49	55/64	.859	21.83
13/64	.203	5.16	35/64	.547	13.89	7/8	.875	22.23
7/32	.219	5.56	9/16	.563	14.29	57/64	.891	22.62
15/64	.234	5.95	37/64	.578	14.68	29/32	.906	23.02
1/4	.250	6.35	19/32	.594	15.08	59/64	.922	23.42
17/64	.266	6.75	39/64	.609	15.48	15/16	.938	23.81
9/32	.281	7.14	5/8	.625	15.88	61/64	.953	24.21
19/64	.297	7.54	41/64	.641	16.27	31/32	.969	24.61
5/16	.313	7.94	21/32	.656	16.67	63/64	.984	25.00
21/64	.328	8.33						

Conversion—Millimeters to Decimal Inches

mm	inches	mm	inches	mm	inches	mm	inches	mm	inches
1	.039 370	31	1.220 470	61	2.401 570	91	3.582 670	210	8.267 700
2	.078 740	32	1.259 840	62	2.440 940	92	3.622 040	220	8.661 400
3	.118 110	33	1.299 210	63	2.480 310	93	3.661 410	230	9.055 100
4	.157 480	34	1.338 580	64	2.519 680	94	3.700 780	240	9.448 800
5	.196 850	35	1.377 949	65	2.559 050	95	3.740 150	250	9.842 500
6	.236 220	36	1.417 319	66	2.598 420	96	3.779 520	260	10.236 200
7	.275 590	37	1.456 689	67	2.637 790	97	3.818 890	270	10.629 900
8	.314 960	38	1.496 050	68	2.677 160	98	3.858 260	280	11.032 600
9	.354 330	39	1.535 430	69	2.716 530	99	3.897 630	290	11.417 300
10	.393 700	40	1.574 800	70	2.755 900	100	3.937 000	300	11.811 000
11	.433 070	41	1.614 170	71	2.795 270	105	4.133 848	310	12.204 700
12	.472 440	42	1.653 540	72	2.834 640	110	4.330 700	320	12.598 400
13	.511 810	43	1.692 910	73	2.874 010	115	4.527 550	330	12.992 100
14	.551 180	44	1.732 280	74	2.913 380	120	4.724 400	340	13.385 800
15	.590 550	45	1.771 650	75	2.952 750	125	4.921 250	350	13.779 500
16	.629 920	46	1.811 020	76	2.992 120	130	5.118 100	360	14.173 200
17	.669 290	47	1.850 390	77	3.031 490	135	5.314 950	370	14.566 900
18	.708 660	48	1.889 760	78	3.070 860	140	5.511 800	380	14.960 600
19	.748 030	49	1.929 130	79	3.110 230	145	5.708 650	390	15.354 300
20	.787 400	50	1.968 500	80	3.149 600	150	5.905 500	400	15.748 000
21	.826 770	51	2.007 870	81	3.188 970	155	6.102 350	500	19.685 000
22	.866 140	52	2.047 240	82	3.228 340	160	6.299 200	600	23.622 000
23	.905 510	53	2.086 610	83	3.267 710	165	6.496 050	700	27.559 000
24	.944 880	54	2.125 980	84	3.307 080	170	6.692 900	800	31.496 000
25	.984 250	55	2.165 350	85	3.346 450	175	6.889 750	900	35.433 000
26	1.023 620	56	2.204 720	86	3.385 820	180	7.086 600	1000	39.370 000
27	1.062 990	57	2.244 090	87	3.425 190	185	7.283 450	2000	78.740 000
28	1.102 360	58	2.283 460	88	3.464 560	190	7.480 300	3000	118.110 000
29	1.141 730	59	2.322 830	89	3.503 903	195	7.677 150	4000	157.480 000
30	1.181 100	60	2.362 200	90	3.543 300	200	7.874 000	5000	196.850 000

To change decimal millimeters to decimal inches, position the decimal point where desired on either side of the millimeter measurement shown and reset the inches decimal by the same number of digits in the same direction. For example, to convert .001 mm into decimal inches, reset the decimal behind the 1 mm (shown on the chart) to .001; change the decimal inch equivalent (.039″ shown to .000039″).

Tap Drill Sizes

National Fine or S.A.E.				National Coarse or U.S.S.		
Screw & Tap Size	Threads Per Inch	Use Drill Number		Screw & Tap Size	Threads Per Inch	Use Drill Number
No. 5	44	37		No. 5	40	39
No. 6	40	33		No. 6	32	36
No. 8	36	29		No. 8	32	29
No. 10	32	21		No. 10	24	25
No. 12	28	15		No. 12	24	17
$\frac{1}{4}$	28	3		$\frac{1}{4}$	20	8
$\frac{5}{16}$	24	1		$\frac{5}{16}$	18	F
$\frac{3}{8}$	24	Q		$\frac{3}{8}$	16	$\frac{5}{16}$
$\frac{7}{16}$	20	W		$\frac{7}{16}$	14	U
$\frac{1}{2}$	20	$\frac{29}{64}$		$\frac{1}{2}$	13	$\frac{27}{64}$
$\frac{9}{16}$	18	$\frac{33}{64}$		$\frac{9}{16}$	12	$\frac{31}{64}$
$\frac{5}{8}$	18	$\frac{37}{64}$		$\frac{5}{8}$	11	$\frac{17}{32}$
$\frac{3}{4}$	16	$\frac{11}{16}$		$\frac{3}{4}$	10	$\frac{21}{32}$
$\frac{7}{8}$	14	$\frac{13}{16}$		$\frac{7}{8}$	9	$\frac{49}{64}$
				1	8	$\frac{7}{8}$
$1\frac{1}{8}$	12	$1\frac{3}{64}$		$1\frac{1}{8}$	7	$\frac{63}{64}$
$1\frac{1}{4}$	12	$1\frac{11}{64}$		$1\frac{1}{4}$	7	$1\frac{7}{64}$
$1\frac{1}{2}$	12	$1\frac{27}{64}$		$1\frac{1}{2}$	6	$1\frac{11}{32}$

Decimal Equivalent Size of the Number Drills

Drill No.	Decimal Equivalent	Drill No.	Decimal Equivalent	Drill No.	Decimal Equivalent
80	.0135	53	.0595	26	.1470
79	.0145	52	.0635	25	.1495
78	.0160	51	.0670	24	.1520
77	.0180	50	.0700	23	.1540
76	.0200	49	.0730	22	.1570
75	.0210	48	.0760	21	.1590
74	.0225	47	.0785	20	.1610
73	.0240	46	.0810	19	.1660
72	.0250	45	.0820	18	.1695
71	.0260	44	.0860	17	.1730
70	.0280	43	.0890	16	.1770
69	.0292	42	.0935	15	.1800
68	.0310	41	.0960	14	.1820
67	.0320	40	.0980	13	.1850
66	.0330	39	.0995	12	.1890
65	.0350	38	.1015	11	.1910
64	.0360	37	.1040	10	.1935
63	.0370	36	.1065	9	.1960
62	.0380	35	.1100	8	.1990
61	.0390	34	.1110	7	.2010
60	.0400	33	.1130	6	.2040
59	.0410	32	.1160	5	.2055
58	.0420	31	.1200	4	.2090
57	.0430	30	.1285	3	.2130
56	.0465	29	.1360	2	.2210
55	.0520	28	.1405	1	.2280
54	.0550	27	.1440		

Decimal Equivalent Size of the Letter Drills

Letter Drill	Decimal Equivalent	Letter Drill	Decimal Equivalent	Letter Drill	Decimal Equivalent
A	.234	J	.277	S	.348
B	.238	K	.281	T	.358
C	.242	L	.290	U	.368
D	.246	M	.295	V	.377
E	.250	N	.302	W	.386
F	.257	O	.316	X	.397
G	.261	P	.323	Y	.404
H	.266	Q	.332	Z	.413
I	.272	R	.339		

ANTI-FREEZE INFORMATION

Freezing and Boiling Points of Solutions
According to Percentage of Alcohol or Ethylene Glycol

Freezing Point of Solution	Alcohol Volume %	Alcohol Solution Boils at	Ethylene Glycol Volume %	Ethylene Glycol Solution Boils at
20°F.	12	196°F.	16	216°F.
10°F.	20	189°F.	25	218°F.
0°F.	27	184°F.	33	220°F.
−10°F.	32	181°F.	39	222°F.
−20°F.	38	178°F.	44	224°F.
−30°F.	42	176°F.	48	225°F.

Note: above boiling points are at sea level. For every 1,000 feet of altitude, boiling points are approximately 2°F. lower than those shown. For every pound of pressure exerted by the pressure cap, the boiling points are approximately 3°F. higher than those shown.

ANTI-FREEZE CHART

Temperatures Shown in Degrees Fahrenheit
+32 is Freezing

Quarts of **ETHYLENE GLYCOL** Needed for Protection to Temperatures Shown Below

Cooling System Capacity Quarts	1	2	3	4	5	6	7	8	9	10	11	12	13	14
10	+24°	+16°	+ 4°	−12°	−34°	−62°								
11	+25	+18	+ 8	− 6	−23	−47								
12	+26	+19	+10	0	−15	−34	−57°							
13	+27	+21	+13	+ 3	− 9	−25	−45							
14			+15	+ 6	− 5	−18	−34							
15			+16	+ 8	0	−12	−26							
16			+17	+10	+ 2	− 8	−19	−34	−52°					
17			+18	+12	+ 5	− 4	−14	−27	−42					
18			+19	+14	+ 7	0	−10	−21	−34	−50°				
19			+20	+15	+ 9	+ 2	− 7	−16	−28	−42				
20				+16	+10	+ 4	− 3	−12	−22	−34	−48°			
21				+17	+12	+ 6	0	− 9	−17	−28	−41			
22				+18	+13	+ 8	+ 2	− 6	−14	−23	−34	−47°		
23				+19	+14	+ 9	+ 4	− 3	−10	−19	−29	−40		
24				+19	+15	+10	+ 5	0	− 8	−15	−23	−34	−46°	
25				+20	+16	+12	+ 7	+ 1	− 5	−12	−20	−29	−40	−50°
26					+17	+13	+ 8	+ 3	− 3	− 9	−16	−25	−34	−44
27					+18	+14	+ 9	+ 5	− 1	− 7	−13	−21	−29	−39
28					+18	+15	+10	+ 6	+ 1	− 5	−11	−18	−25	−34
29					+19	+16	+12	+ 7	+ 2	− 3	− 8	−15	−22	−29
30					+20	+17	+13	+ 8	+ 4	− 1	− 6	−12	−18	−25

For capacities over 30 quarts divide true capacity by 3. Find quarts Anti-Freeze for the 1/3 and multiply by 3 for quarts to add.

For capacities under 10 quarts multiply true capacity by 3. Find quarts Anti-Freeze for the tripled volume and divide by 3 for quarts to add.

To Increase the Freezing Protection of Anti-Freeze Solutions Already Installed

Number of Quarts of **ETHYLENE GLYCOL** Anti-Freeze Required to Increase Protection

Cooling System Capacity Quarts	From +20°F. to					From +10°F. to					From 0°F. to			
	0°	−10°	−20°	−30°	−40°	0°	−10°	−20°	−30°	−40°	−10°	−20°	−30°	−40°
10	1¾	2¼	3	3½	3¾	¾	1½	2¼	2¾	3¼	¾	1½	2	2½
12	2	2¾	3½	4	4½	1	1¾	2½	3¼	3¾	1	1¾	2½	3¼
14	2¼	3¼	4	4¾	5½	1¼	2	3	3¾	4½	1	2	3	3½
16	2½	3½	4½	5¼	6	1¼	2½	3½	4¼	5¼	1¼	2¼	3¼	4
18	3	4	5	6	7	1½	2¾	4	5	5¾	1½	2½	3¾	4¾
20	3¼	4½	5¾	6¾	7½	1¾	3	4¼	5½	6½	1½	2¾	4¼	5¼
22	3½	5	6¼	7¼	8¼	1¾	3¼	4¾	6	7¼	1¾	3¼	4½	5½
24	4	5½	7	8	9	2	3½	5	6½	7½	1¾	3½	5	6
26	4¼	6	7½	8¾	10	2	4	5½	7	8¼	2	3¾	5½	6¾
28	4½	6¼	8	9½	10½	2¼	4¼	6	7½	9	2	4	5¾	7¼
30	5	6¾	8½	10	11½	2½	4½	6½	8	9½	2¼	4¼	6¼	7¾

Test radiator solution with proper hydrometer. Determine from the table the number of quarts of solution to be drawn off from a full cooling system and replace with undiluted anti-freeze, to give the desired increased protection. For example, to increase protection of a 22-quart cooling system containing Ethylene Glycol (permanent type) anti-freeze, from +20°F. to −20°F. will require the replacement of 6¼ quarts of solution with undiluted anti-freeze.